ABLETON LIVE™ 4
P O W E R !

Chad Carrier and Dave Hill Jr.

*Yo Hal !!
Cheers to you! All my best
and happy looping !
Dave Hill Jr.*

THOMSON
—————— ✦ ——————
™
COURSE TECHNOLOGY
Professional ■ Trade ■ Reference

ABLETON LIVE™ 4
P O W E R !

SVP, Thomson Course Technology PTR: Andy Shafran
Publisher: Stacy L. Hiquet
Senior Marketing Manager: Sarah O'Donnell
Marketing Manager: Heather Hurley
Manager of Editorial Services: Heather Talbot
Senior Editor and Acquisitions Editor: Mark Garvey
Associate Marketing Manager: Kristin Eisenzopf
Marketing Coordinator: Jordan Casey
Project Editor: Scott Harris/Argosy Publishing
Technical Reviewer: James Leighton, Shawn Balm
PTR Editorial Services Coordinator: Elizabeth Furbish
Copy Editor: D. A. de la Mora
Interior Layout Tech: Eric Rosenbloom
Cover Designer: Mike Tanamachi
Indexer: Nancy Fulton
Proofreader: Jan Cocker

Ableton is a trademark of Ableton AG. All other trademarks are the property of their respective owners.

Important: Thomson Course Technology PTR cannot provide software support. Please contact the appropriate software manufacturer's technical support line or Web site for assistance.

Thomson Course Technology PTR and the authors have attempted throughout this book to distinguish proprietary trademarks from descriptive terms by following the capitalization style used by the manufacturer.

Information contained in this book has been obtained by Thomson Course Technology PTR from sources believed to be reliable. However, because of the possibility of human or mechanical error by our sources, Thomson Course Technology PTR, or others, the Publisher does not guarantee the accuracy, adequacy, or completeness of any information and is not responsible for any errors or omissions or the results obtained from use of such information. Readers should be particularly aware of the fact that the Internet is an ever-changing entity. Some facts may have changed since this book went to press.

Educational facilities, companies, and organizations interested in multiple copies or licensing of this book should contact the publisher for quantity discount information. Training manuals, CD-ROMs, and portions of this book are also available individually or can be tailored for specific needs.

ISBN: 1-59200-531-4

Library of Congress Catalog Card Number: 2004109684

Printed in the United States of America

04 05 06 07 08 BH 10 9 8 7 6 5 4 3 2 1

THOMSON

COURSE TECHNOLOGY

Professional ■ Trade ■ Reference

Thomson Course Technology PTR, a division of Thomson Course Technology
25 Thomson Place
Boston, MA 02210
http://www.courseptr.com

Acknowledgments

Chad Carrier

Needless to say, I would not be where I am today without Live, both artistically and professionally. The program itself, and the fantastic people behind it, have opened doors for me that would have normally been impossible. I'd like to thank Gerhard Behles, Robert Henke, Dave Hill Jr., Shawn Balm, Ulf Kaiser, Jan Bohl, Rutger de Groot, and Martin Froelich of Ableton AG for being so helpful and starting the momentum that has propelled my career forward. I'd also like to thank Mark Garvey of Course Technology for being such a terrific editor. Though I was a first-time writer, he made the book-writing process absolutely painless for me. Thanks also to Scott Harris, who meticulously managed the book's production. James Leighton and Shawn Balm provided their technical editing efforts and they caught many things I'd missed—many thanks to you both. Finally, my deepest appreciation goes out to my friends at M-Audio Tech Support who have kept my brain sharp by asking me crazy questions all day about Live—you guys really forced me to think.

On a personal note, I'd like to thank my grandmother, Helen, for taking care of me while I worked evening after evening on this book. Without her, I would have been too overwhelmed with the tasks of everyday life to get it all done. I'd also like to thank my parents, Jan and Mike, for their assistance and support with my decision to move—it proved to be the right choice!

Most of all, I'd like to thank you, the reader, for choosing this book in your quest for Live knowledge. Dave and I have strived to make it as easy to comprehend as possible while keeping the tone interesting and inspiring. We have filled its pages with nearly every morsel of information we could muster, yet we still think of new uses every day. I hope that our work takes the confusion out of Live and gives you the confidence and knowledge to create anything you wish.

Dave Hill Jr.

Congratulations on your purchase of Ableton Live 4.0 and *Ableton Live 4 Power!* You have taken a brave and intelligent step toward the future of music—electronic and otherwise—by choosing to make music with Live. It is my sincere hope that this book lives up to the innovation and quality of its subject. Ableton Live is an incredibly powerful application that I have come to know intimately and rely upon daily. I put my all into *Ableton Live 2*

❀ ❀ ❀

Power!, but working for Ableton has kept me too busy to write a third-party book. Luckily for us all, my friend Chad Carrier of M-Audio fame has refreshed my text as well as added his own take on this magical application. Thank you, Chad, for being so smart and thorough! This project could not have happened without you.

This book was also made possible by the vision and perseverance of Thomson Course Technology PTR acquisitions man, Kevin Harreld, and his successor, Todd Jensen, along with the best first editor I could have asked for, Mark Garvey. Thank you, gentlemen, for making this project happen in the right way. I must also credit the incredible innovation of Ableton and its leaders, Gerhard Behles (CEO), Robert Henke (incredible musician behind Monolake and Ableton Live conceptualist), Bernd Roggendorf, and CFO Jan Bohl for giving me such brilliant subject matter. Watching the development and planning of Live 4.0 was an amazing experience. These guys are changing the way music is made for thousands of people which is just remarkable to me.

Personally, I must also thank my darling wife-to-be, Amber Vitti, for her infinite support, encouragement, love, and loop tolerance; Mr. James Rotondi, my first editor, best friend, and co-conspirator in my band Jettatura; Bob Green (a.k.a. The Grassy Knoll), who taught me how to finish what I start; and Bill and Nicky Walters, Steven Cope, and Clinton Mainland, for being there. My eternal thanks and love goes to Michael Shrieve, who taught me to embrace the future and to always be making music.

Finally, I want to send great thanks and love to my parents, Jean and Dave Sr., new family Brian Hard and Joanne Bradley, and to my dear sister for putting up with all the noise and for loving me always.

Thanks for listening and have a lot of fun with Live.

About the Authors

Chad Carrier

I've always had an affinity for music, even since early childhood, but I didn't learn to play an instrument until junior high. Before picking up the drums, my primary focus was computers. For years, the thought of using a computer to create music didn't even cross my mind—I was too immersed in the world of computer graphics and programming. Even through high school, as I progressed through marching and jazz bands, my musical knowledge didn't spill over into my computer endeavors.

Near the end of my junior year in high school, a friend laid a CD on me that changed my life: *Techno Mancer*. It was a collection of tracks from a Belgian record company, and it was also my first exposure to electronic dance music. It took everything I loved about rhythm and fused it with computer-whiz genius. I had finally found the perfect combination of music and computers. What I really loved was the sound—most of the drums were synthesized or sampled which gave them a unique sonic texture. They were sounds I'd never achieve with a regular drum set.

Shortly thereafter, I sold my acoustic drums to purchase a set of electronic drums. Then came the sampler and the analog synths. Piece by piece, I began to amass a full MIDI production studio in the living room of my apartment. There I spent countless nights toiling away at my machines, digging into their depths and honing my technical skills. When it came time to gig, I'd move my entire studio to the venue, as I had no other means of performing the compositions. Oh, to have had Live in those days!

I moved to California to get into the music biz. For a while, I was an assistant engineer at a Hollywood studio. I quickly found, however, that the studio scene was not for me—it lacked the collective, creative atmosphere I assumed it would have. Because of my technical background, I got a job at M-Audio in their Technical Support department. As support representatives, we all needed to be familiar with all of the products, which included a small program called Live. After only a few months, version 3 came out and Live started receiving some serious recognition.

During the 2004 Winter NAMM show in Anaheim, I had the great fortune of meeting the Ableton Team, which included CEO Gerhard Behles and conceptualist Robert Henke, who I knew from his musical project, Monolake. I also met Dave Hill Jr., who had just been hired by Ableton and was the author of *Ableton Live 2 Power!* After watching me show off my knowledge of Live at the M-Audio booth over the four days of the show, Dave asked if I'd be willing to update his book for version 3.0. Of course I agreed.

By the time we started gearing up for the Live 3.0 update, Live 4.0 was starting to peek over the horizon. We discussed all the new features Ableton had in store, and decided that updating the book to version 4.0 would be in the best interest for everyone, especially the readers. The work on this book began the moment the Live 4.0 beta was released and did not stop for a day. Every moment I played with Live 4.0, I found out a new trick or feature. Even now, after the book has been written, I'm still devising new ways to work in Live. You will, too, as you become familiar with this amazing musical tool.

Dave Hill Jr.

While I am first and foremost a drummer, I started toying with samplers at age 16, when I bought producer, composer, and guitarist extraordinaire David Torn's old Emax sampler. You could say my first few lessons in sampling were days spent sifting through Torn's spine-tinglingly cool sample patches, scratching my head, and then trying to create comparable sounds. Since that time, I have become fascinated with drum machines, synthesizers, effects, and the recording process. Through working with a number of inspiring people—most notably Michael Shrieve, ex-Santana drummer; Brad Houser of Edie Brickell; Critters Buggin' James Rotondi, former sideman with Air and Mr. Bungle; and Bob Green, a.k.a. The Grassy Knoll—I began to write music. Nearly a decade after purchasing my first sampler, I discovered the joys of working with audio inside computers, recombining my own drum recordings, and producing several different musical projects. I now live in New York where I produce music for my two projects, Jettatura (Jettatura.com) and Brainboxing (brainboxing.net)—best uncovered at www.sixtyonesixtyeight.com—and now work full-time for Ableton as Public Media and Artist Relations Manager.

Contents at a Glance

TABLE OF } Contents

Introduction

Ableton Live 4 Power! is the world's first comprehensive guide to making music with Ableton's revolutionary live performance and studio software, Live 4.0. Written for all Live users, from digital audio beginners to seasoned pros, this book explores each fundamental feature within Live and provides power-user tips and insider tricks for integrating Live into your home or professional studio. But Live's in-studio capabilities are just the beginning. Every last feature, button, fader, instrument, and effect in Live 4.0 was also designed with the Live performer in mind. *Ableton Live 4 Power!* is a book written for musicians by musicians who use and discuss the software on a daily basis. Whether you use Live for producing, composing, DJing, or film and television, *Ableton Live 4 Power!* will help you to put the fun back into making music with computers.

What You'll Find in This Book:

* Step-by-step instructions for creating, producing, and mixing music in Live.
* Definitions of key digital audio concepts such as: What is a sample? What is a loop? and How do my loops and samples become music?
* Music-making ideas and tips.
* Full explanation of Live's Devices and how to use third-party plug-ins in Live.
* Audio-interface and MIDI-controller tips and recommendations.
* Simple yet complete explanation of MIDI and its many uses in Live.
* Recommendations for choosing and using an audio editor for optimizing your loops and samples.
* In-depth guide to editing, recording, performing, and paint 'n' play composing with Ableton Live.
* Expert tips, tricks, and interview excerpts with world-famous Live power users and performers.
* Specialized hardware considerations to help musicians feel at home performing with Live.

- How Live will reinvent your own music and attitude about making music with a computer.
- How ReWire makes Live the hub of your software studio.
- Carefully edited and labeled screenshots that give you a first-person view of how experts work in Live.
- Solid web resources throughout the book that will link you to Live-related topics.
- Companion Web site with templates, updates, and free loops.

Who This Book Is For

This book is for anyone who wants to make music using the power of their computers. Ableton Live 4.0 sews the seams that exist between digital audio, MIDI files, live performance, software synchronization, musicality, and fun on a Mac or PC. If you've heard of Live's "magical" audio and loop dexterity, let this book be your guide to unlocking that power; or, if you have already discovered Live and want to take your performing and composing skills to the next level, *Ableton Live 4 Power!* is written for you.

How This Book Is Organized

Ableton Live 4 Power! is divided into fourteen chapters and two appendices. Each chapter contains targeted direction and thoughtful notes about every aspect of Live. The chapters can be read sequentially or used as a reference. This book is not intended to replicate the Ableton Live User Manual, but will instead serve as an informed supplement to transforming your PC or Mac into a musical instrument, audio workstation, or recording studio.

- **Chapter 1, "Live 4.0"** — We will begin with a brief introduction to Live, the concept behind its development, and a basic overview of how you might use Live both on stage and in the studio.
- **Chapter 2, "Back to School"** — If you're brand-new to the realm of MIDI and digital audio, this chapter's for you. MIDI messages, controllers, sample rate, bit depth, digital glitches and peaks—it's all here. Chapter 4 will also discuss how Live handles (renders and records) digital audio, what makes a sample a sample, and a loop a loop.
- **Chapter 3, "Getting Live Up and Running"** — To get you up and running, this chapter will provide key PC- and Mac-related recommendations for MIDI

hardware, choosing an audio interface, installing and running Live, and basic MIDI setup.

❋ **Chapter 4, "Live Interface Basics"**—This chapter will take you through Live's two main interfaces, Session and Arrangement; point out key controls; talk about how to get help; and instruct you on how to set up your first song. "Live Interface Basics" will also teach you about Live's Control (transport) bar, song settings, customization, and general maneuvering in Live. Though the chapter is an overview of Live, experts may still pick up tricks in this chapter.

❋ **Chapter 5, "Making Music In Live"**—Live is used by many different types of people for several different applications. "Making Music In Live" outlines the four most common ways to make music with Live, unveils key working methods for each group, introduces common sections of the Clip View, and dives deep into the Live composition process. Whether you are a DJ, producer, film/television composer, or live musician, this chapter is packed with intermediate level tips and will warm you up for what is to come.

❋ **Chapter 6, "The Audio Clip"**—Clips are the building blocks in Live. Every musical idea takes the form of a Clip. This chapter will delve into the world of Audio Clips, covering topics such as Warp Markers, Warp Modes, Clip Envelopes, and audio recording. Everyone should learn this chapter inside and out to get the most from Live.

❋ **Chapter 7, "The MIDI Clip"**—The new MIDI features of Live will be discussed at length in this chapter. You'll learn about overdub recording, quantizing, editing a performance, importing and exporting files, as well as MIDI control envelopes. This stuff is new information for everybody.

❋ **Chapter 8, "Using Effects and Instruments"**—Here we will explore the Track View and methods of using effects and virtual instruments within our projects. We'll also explain Live's signal routing possibilities and plug-in automation functions.

❋ **Chapter 9, "Live's Audio Effects"**—This chapter is the definitive reference for all of Live's built-in audio effects. Here, every dial and button is explained in detail and tips are provided for tweaking your effects into oblivion.

❋ **Chapter 10, "Live's MIDI Effects"**—Another reference chapter for Live's new MIDI effects. Here's where to find out how the power of these simple tools can be harnessed in your songs.

❋ **Chapter 11, "Live's Instruments"**—Live includes two virtual instruments: Simpler and Impulse. This chapter takes each instrument apart, explains its workings, and gives you some great tips along the way. If you're coming from the world of hardware synthesizers, you'll love seeing and hearing what your computer can do now!

❄ **Chapter 12, "ReWire"** — ReWire is the key to linking Live with other powerful applications. The good news is you already own it (once you own Live). Now make it swing. Both ReWire master and ReWire slave will be covered.

❄ **Chapter 13, "Playing Live . . . Live"** — Now that you're familiar with how music is made in Live, it's time to start playing. Learn how to set up your system for various types of gigs, methods for MIDI control, as well as some of the most detailed tips for importing and looping audio.

❄ **Chapter 14, "Live 4 Power"** — Chapter 14 is pure fun. This chapter is loaded with all sorts of juicy information including more Warp Marker trickery, methods for destroying beats, creating templates, editing samples, and the amazing new Follow Actions. Keep some water handy in case your head catches on fire.

Keeping the Book's Content Current

We have remained in close contact with Ableton throughout the writing of this book (Dave actually works for Ableton) to ensure that each instruction, recommendation, and tip works with the most recent version of Live — 4.0.4 at the time of this writing. What's more, Ableton reviewed and signed off on each chapter during the summer and fall of 2004; however, occasionally ghosts infiltrate the machine. If you should find any errors or have suggestions for future editions, please contact us via the Course Technology Web site:

www.courseptr.com

At this site, you can also find updates, corrections, and other information related to the content of the book. You should also regularly visit the Ableton Web site (www.ableton.com) for software updates and helpful advice found in Ableton's "user forum."

1 } Live 4.0

Every so often, a new piece of technology or software application makes an indelible mark on the way things are done. Be it the arrival of the electric guitar, a new kind of synthesizer, or the invention of digital audio recording—the impact on musicians and the artistic world can be both major and long lasting. Once conceived, technology can take on a life of its own, inspire a range of other complementary technologies, or even spawn a whole new school of thought. Ableton's Live has instigated a revolution in the audio software world by transforming computers into playable musical instruments, real-time remix stations, and the world's most dexterous audio environment. Live is the culmination of the studio software development of the mid-to-late 90s and the infusion of DJ and electronic music-making instincts. Live is also a labor of love born out of the desire of a few software-savvy musicians who wanted to take their elaborate computer-based recording studio on the road.

Like any new idea, the possible uses for Live are only beginning to emerge. From the laptop blip-hop stylings of musicians such as Kid606, Monolake, and Akufen, to jazz stylings of George Benson and David Garfield, Live's user base is made up of professionals who demand the most from their tools. Add film scoring and television music to Live's current resume of qualifications, such as Rick Marvin (*U-571* and HBO's *Six Feet Under*), or Klaus Badelt (*Mission Impossible 2*, *Pearl Harbor*, *Hannibal*, and *Pirates of the Caribbean*), and Ableton's endorsement list just continues to grow. Recently, former Nine Inch Nails keyboardist and television music composer Charlie Clouser said this of Live: "With Nine Inch Nails, it took us two years to finish a record. Today, I finish cues in seven minutes. Without Ableton, it simply couldn't happen. Within eight seconds of downloading the demo, I knew I

❋ ❋ ❋

had to have it—at any price." The ease and skill with which Live can handle audio is a natural for film and TV work.

With its expanded recording and MIDI functionality, Live is a full-blown music production environment suitable for any artistic style. You'll find all the features you'd expect from other digital audio workstations, such as multi-track audio and MIDI recording, non-linear editing, quantization, pitch shifting, and more. Live's advantage is that all these common features are implemented within its unique sequencing interface.

Live is also a digital DJ performance tool and has begun to replace MP3-based DJ units, CD spinners, and turntables. It is also becoming increasingly common to see laptop performing artists employing computers as their primary sound source or record collection. This makes perfect sense when you stop to think that—for the last couple of years—synthesizers, samplers, and their sounds have been purchased en masse via Web download or e-mail, instead of as a separate hardware component or sound module. In the next couple of years, more and more musicians, bands, and solo artists will be using Live's technology to realize their artistic vision from the comfort of their own laptop.

What Is Live?

In January 2000, Berlin-based Ableton knocked the audio software world on its ear by releasing Live 1.0. Since its inception, Live has evolved into a real-time music production system allowing users to integrate samples, MIDI, effects, and live audio data quickly and musically enough for a live performance.

Similar to modern software MIDI-sequencers or production suites, Live (Figure 1.1) allows you to create and modify musical elements, such as guitar riffs, bass lines, and piano parts, which can be arranged and played from a large, customizable grid. The grid can be thought of as both a music organizer and sonic palette. Once these elements have been placed into a cell on the grid, you may designate MIDI or computer keyboard triggering options for these pieces, alter their playback parameters, add effects, and more. After enough cells for the song are filled, it is time for "the take" or live performance.

This grid/sonic palette makes up the improvisational sequencer component of Live, and can be used to trigger groups of musical elements, like sections

Figure 1.1
Here is a quick peek at the
Session View grid in Live 4.0.
The rows make up musical sections called scenes, while the
columns function as virtual
mixer channels.

of a song. For instance, during a live performance, you might want to
progress from the verse to the chorus back to the verse—something you'd
never done in practice. You can do so by triggering a specified row in Live's
grid matrix, that in turn directs Live to play the second group of elements
(the chorus) and ceases play of verse parts. To go back you would merely
click on the preceding row. The song arrangement is under full real-time control. This makes it easy to jump around through various sub-sections of the
song, break down important song sections, and come up with new possibilities. In addition, any individual piece contained within a grid cell can be
played independently in similar fashion to an "old school" phrase sampler
(like Roland's Dr. Sample). It is quite possible to make new parts and original ideas by playing these parts as one-shot samples or to overdub a previously made arrangement. Keep in mind that these pieces can be tweaked to
oblivion, much like the sounds in a hardware sampler or synthesizer, only
more flexibly with Live.

The true power housed within Live 4.0 is the software's ability to play, or
play with, sound. Live can be played in a "jam" situation or simply used as a
creative tool for building a song in layers. Live 4.0 specializes in stretching
audio alongside MIDI to any desired tempo or pitch. What's more, Live can
bend audio within itself so that a sound may start at one tempo or pitch and
end up in an entirely different place (all within the same performance). The

3
❊ ❊ ❊

editing possibilities are nearly infinite. Ableton has made recording and editing the performance a main function of Live, so that a single software application turns your laptop (or desktop) PC/Mac into a live performance system, a multi-track audio and MIDI recording studio, a powerful loop and song editor, and a full-blown remix factory. Live enables you to map the cells of your grid-palette (full of musical parts) to a MIDI controller or computer keyboard. In essence, you can record a live improvisation or band performance for later editing, further arranging, overdubs, and added automation. If the final mix isn't to your liking, you can always take another pass. To get an idea of what we're talking about, look at Figure 1.2, which features a screenshot of Live's Arrangement View.

Musically speaking, Live 4.0 is a one-two punch whose focus is spread equally between live performance and recording/editing, all in one application. As you learn how to play (jam) in Live, you will also be gradually setting up your song's arrangement and learning new tactics to apply to your live performance. In other words, Live is quite unlike any other software application currently on the market and fills a certain void that has been overlooked by the majority of developers—the needs of the performing and recording musician.

Figure 1.2

If you are familiar with desktop audio, Live's Arrangement View may remind you of many different programs. However, Live's feature set is sure to raise a few standards for many years to come.

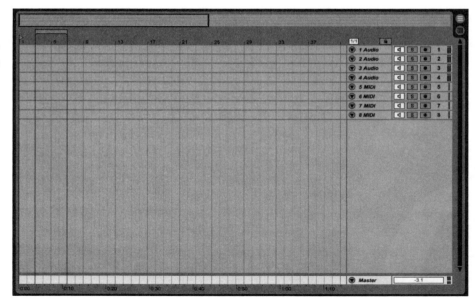

Why Was Live Developed?

One of the greatest advantages for musicians employing Live 4.0 is that it is a program written for musicians by musicians. They actually use the very software they create. Initially, Robert Henke and Gerhard Behles (paired in the Berlin-based electronica group Monolake) were looking for a better way to create their own music through the use of a computer. Both were experienced sound designers and had spent time working for Native Instruments, one of the industry's chief authorities on virtual or "soft" synthesizers and sound design software. At the time, the industry lacked a user-friendly software application conducive to creating music as a musician would: intuitively and spontaneously. There were plenty of "loop-friendly" applications, and more than a couple live jamming programs, but most audio software was built for studio use and lacked the interface necessary to create music the way a musician does: live.

Since the drawing board days of development, Behles, Henke, and the Ableton team honed Live's interface and functionality with the performing artist in mind. While complex, build-your-own software suites such as Native Instruments' Reaktor and Cycling '74's MAX/MSP are powerful sound-generators, they often prove too complex for the performing musician who may be contending with any number of distractions—including lighting, sound system woes, fog, etc. Live, on the other hand, was developed (and has been continually improved) to be the best possible live recording and performance system available on a computer. It contains professional-grade audio tools and software compliance such as VST and Audio Units effect plug-ins and instruments, plus ReWire software-studio synchronization. These tools will be discussed in greater detail as we progress. For now, recognize Ableton's commitment to the performing artist and to the end user. Don't just take our word for it; jump on out to Ableton's closely monitored user forum at www.ableton.com, where you can anonymously enter your own wish list of ideas for future development of Live. Don't be too surprised if Ableton CEO Gerhard Behles, Conceptualist Robert Henke, or any of the other Ableton developers chime in to discuss how your idea might better the world of Live.

The World of Live

Over the last several years, the idea of music creation and live performance on a PC or Mac has become increasingly attractive. With the increase in processing power and audio storage capacities, even relatively inexpensive computers have become powerful audio editing and recording studios. Producers using audio software have enjoyed exponential improvements in performance and the number and types of tasks performable by a computer. Also, the customization and potential for add-on software/hardware as new technology emerges has made it less intimidating to jump into the fray. For less than $2000 (US), you can acquire a decent laptop, a sound card, and Live 4.0, the most powerful and flexible live performance software on the planet. For just a bit more, it is quite possible that your bedroom studio could compete with the pros, not to mention the fact that an investment in an Ableton Live performance rig is cheaper and easier to maintain than a stack of hardware samplers, rack-mounted sound modules, outboard mixers, and, well, you get the point.

How Does It Work?

Live allows you to sort your music into easy-to-define sections, called scenes, while maintaining all the flexible effects and routing options made possible only via PC- or Mac-based software. These scenes, that spread horizontally across the screen, look like the rows of a spreadsheet or graph. The columns that are formed correspond with mixer channels. Within each column, only one sound—be it a MIDI sequence or audio sample—can play at a time. So to play through your track, you can literally run down the rows, letting each row represent a musical section. Live also enables you to trigger sequences, loops, and samples; tweak effects; and change mix settings from a MIDI controller, MIDI keyboard, or computer keyboard. You can preview any audio loop in real-time at any tempo from within your project. You can even record new pieces into your song without ever stopping playback. Enhancements in Live empower users to handle different kinds of musical parts specific to their content. For example, a drum beat can be handled differently than a synthesizer or vocal take. A drum loop typically contains several short sounds, such as hi-hat, snare, and kick drum hits, while a synthesizer or vocal part will most often sustain or consist of longer sounds. Since Live analyzes the audio's contents, it is necessary for Live to "look" at each loop in a different way to achieve the best results.

You may also turn off Live's time-correcting Warp feature to make your loops behave more like standard multi-track recording software. Live also encourages plenty of manipulation in terms of feel, tempo, and pitch; but how Live really works is up to you. Never before has software been so dependent upon its owner's proficiency, and never before has software been so intuitive and musical after a few basic principles are understood. Live works with your audio loops, MIDI sequences, hardware synthesizers, recorded material, and other software applications to make music. You can create new music from scratch, or build a "remix" from previously recorded material. When it comes to making music in Live, the creative possibilities are limitless.

What Sets Live Apart

If you are an audio software enthusiast, you've certainly heard of powerful digital multi-track studio applications such as Digidesign's Pro Tools, Emagic's Logic Audio, MOTU's Digital Performer, Cakewalk's Sonar, and Steinberg's Cubase (and Nuendo). These programs, and their hardware counterparts, are often referred to as DAWs, or Digital Audio Workstations. Their main task is to ensure that music is recorded and played back properly in a studio situation. Other, more loop-oriented, products such as Propellerhead's Reason, Arturia's Storm, Sonic Foundry's Acid Pro, Cakewalk's Project5, or Sonic Syndicate's Orion Pro are also touted in the media for their originality and have become popular along with the self-contained studio paradigm. Each of these programs allows for using the computer as a stand-alone music composition center and loop factory. Like the aforementioned products, Live can operate by itself, record multiple audio and MIDI sources, integrate loops, and handle other basic studio functions. But Live also introduces the idea of performing with software and editing your improvisation afterwards, and automating has never had a better platform.

To fully understand why Live is such an innovative program, it helps to take a look at 4.0's feature-set.

❋ First of all, Live works on both Mac (OS 9.2, 10.1.5 and up) and PC (Windows 98, ME, 2000, XP) platforms and takes advantage of all current industry standards such as ASIO drivers, VST and Audio Units effect plug-ins and instruments, and ReWire synchronization technology.

❋ Live is among the first programs for the Mac that allow loops to be previewed at the project tempo independently from pitch. Other programs have tried, but none have succeeded in bringing the Mac this kind of efficiency. As for PCs, Acid Pro and Sonar do a nice job of time stretching, and as long as you have Rex files, ReCycle can also help out too. But Ableton could definitely make a case that Live "sounds" better, provides more types of stretching algorithms, and can recalibrate tempos in an instant, which is important if you consider that some time-stretching may need to be done in front of an audience.

❋ In addition to generating MIDI Time Code and MIDI Beat Clock, Live can also be synched to another program's MIDI clock.

❋ As mentioned above, MIDI-note information can be used to trigger sounds or MIDI-controller info for knobs and sliders. Even your laptop computer keyboard can trigger parts. Better still, all MIDI-controller and keyboard triggering information can be assigned while Live is in playback mode, so the music doesn't have to stop.

❋ In terms of routing, Live is constrained only by the limitations of your sound card and MIDI interfaces. And as we've alluded to, ReWire-compatible software applications (such as Reason, MAX/MSP, FL Studio, and ReBirth) can be directed through Live's mixer in a variety of ways. Live's output may also be ReWired to another program's inputs. You can record audio from an outside source straight into Live or render (record) Live's own output to a fresh track (for later use) while you play.

❋ Another distinguishing feature of Live is the DJ-style crossfader built right into the performance mixer. Just like the DJ mixer pictured in Figure 1.3, you can assign mixer channels to A, B, or both channels and mix between the two with a MIDI- or mouse-controllable crossfader. This subtle tool enables gradual song and loop transitions, along with more flexible performance options, not to mention DJ-style fader-flipping and cross jags.

Figure 1.3

DJ mixers have evolved over the years to the point at which software counterparts can barely keep up. Live can be set up to function as a DJ system that will blow the doors off what a standard mixer can do, as you'll see in Chapter 14.

❋ ❋ ❋

❊ And while all of these elements make Live sound attractive, Ableton's not-so-secret weapon, the "Warp Engine," is the feature that has caused many a jaw to drop. Aside from being able to quickly quantize an audio loop's start and end points at the current project tempo, Live uses what's called "elastic audio" to wrestle WAV (or AIFF) files into submission. How is this done? Live has the ability to elasticize audio to any degree the composer would like. We will dive into this in great detail in subsequent chapters, but for now, be aware that Live makes a living out of dividing samples into sections, much in the way Propellerhead's ReCycle would. The difference with Live is that you are able to move slices (called warp markers), thereby stretching (or compressing) the loop's contents. This may seem minor, but consider for a moment that in Live, any sound within a given sample can be played at any time within itself.

Confused? Here is an example: Live can speed up a 25-second sample so that it will play in 5 seconds or vice versa (slowing down the 5-second sample to take up more time). Taking it a step further, you could chop up this sample and resize select portions of the sound, thereby causing the first half of the sample to play faster than the last, for example. Amazingly enough, Live can do this with just a couple of mouse clicks, while you monitor the results. More common examples include matching up bass and drum loops, using select portions of a long performance, correcting sloppy takes, fixing near perfect ones, humanizing a drum machine part, the list goes on. For more on the power of elastic audio, see the section on Clip View in Chapter 5, "Making Music in Live." You can also truncate the loop's end points, move the loop reference (starting point) anywhere you like, and fine tune the pitch in either half-step or cent increments.

❊ The elastic audio concept has now been expanded in Live 4.0 to the "elastic song." Global groove and swing templates allow us to apply subtle shuffle feels to all MIDI and audio parts in a project—all in real-time. Have you ever wondered what Kraftwerk's "Trans Europe Express" would sound like swinging? You can now find out within seconds. This will be extremely helpful for DJs who want to mix from a track with a straight feel to one with a triplet swing feel. The straight song can be gradually swung until it matches the second track without ever stopping the beat!

❊ While previous versions of Live were limited to manipulating samples and loops, Live 4.0 now lets us treat MIDI sequences with the same flexibility and control of their audio brothers. MIDI parts can be recorded, quantized, and edited on the fly (just like audio), plus MIDI overdub recording allows you to build musical elements, such as drum parts, in layers. Live 4.0 now hosts VST and Audio Units virtual instruments, commonly referred to as "soft synths," and can also drive external MIDI hardware such as samplers, synthesizers, or even light and video installations. The new MIDI effects work just like their audio counterparts allowing transposition, volume scaling, and more—all in real-time. In fact, the new MIDI features are so robust, Live is no longer a "loop tool" but a state-of-the-art production solution.

Because Live's design has been engineered for live performance, Ableton has created a powerful studio ally, almost by accident. Producers are already beginning to see the advantage of mocking up song sections in pre-production, remixing stale arrangements, or auditioning fresh material by using Live. Placing television and movie cues is a natural fit for Live. Let's face it, even the best-equipped recording studio would be doing itself a disservice by not integrating at least one computer running Live to handle some of these tasks. While most applications are focused on a specific task, such as sound design or the recording process, Ableton has zeroed in on the concept of making music, while still catering to the studio all the way.

Possible Applications

Before we jump in and start making music with Live, let's consider for a moment why this software was developed. Perhaps you have been lucky enough to spend some time in a recording studio using analog tape, or a digital medium (such as ADAT or Pro Tools). If not, you have most likely seen pictures of a decent-sized studio, and can imagine a fairly large mixer console (desk), accompanied by several pairs of different-sized speaker monitors, power amplifiers, racks of outboard effects, and the inevitable patch bay full of cables. Now imagine the last concert you attended. You may have seen a band complete with a cocky lead guitarist sporting shiny effects pedals; a keyboardist with bigger and shinier effects gear; or even a DJ with two-plus turntables, DJ mixer, and crate upon crate of back-breaking vinyl. Can you see where I'm going with this? Live eliminates the messy patch bay, the nightly set-up and teardown of elaborate effects and amplifiers, and the need to carry your vinyl. Live can even save your entire performance for later editing. To say Live is a replacement for tried-and-true analog studios (or a substitute for your obnoxious guitar player) is to miss the point entirely. What is certain is that Live cannot only survive in today's music-making environment, but thrive. What's more, Live is only beginning to realize its full potential.

Artists such as ex-Nine Inch Nails producer Charlie Clouser are using Live daily for scoring television and film music. Super-drummer Pat Mastelotto, pictured in Figure 1.4 (King Crimson, Sugarcubes, XTC), has taken to using Live both onstage and in the studio for creating music in ways he had only dreamed of previously. Even Sasha uses Live in his CD *Involver*. Electronic music is a natural beneficiary of a program such as Live, as sample- or loop-based dance music has proven to drive the audio software world in some fascinating ways. Thankfully, Live offers this power and wealth of tools to all musicians, not just DJs and remixers, allowing them to develop their music with the same free-form approach.

Here are some other possible Live scenarios:

❋ **Stage**—If your band plays with a sequencer and your drummer is used to playing with a click track, you could easily incorporate live loops into your music. Some bands use phrase samplers to add in a layer of percussion, noise or effects loops, or even backup vocals.

❋ **Studio**—We have already mentioned why Ableton Live would be a perfect addition to any studio. It can function as a high-power drum machine, a flexible loop remixer, or versatile musical sketchpad. While some may use Live as their only studio application, bigger Pro Tools studios may simply enjoy Live for its ability to take bits of a project and let artists, producers, and engineers hear some different arrangements quickly and easily.

❋ **Bedroom**—With a nice audio interface and a decent computer running Live, platinum hits can be fashioned while you're still in your shorts. If professional studios can benefit from the power of Live, a solo musician can reap the rewards ten times over. Recording a simple guitar and vocal demo or producing a full-blown masterpiece are all within the scope of Live's capabilities.

❋ **Club**—The Laptop DJ trend has been building steam for several years now. The benefits included less wear and tear on your vinyl, lightweight transport, the many possible software tricks for enhancing the sound, and more. To be fair, there are a few compromises to recognize, such as the time it takes to digitize vinyl and the look and feel of the performance. While paradigm shifts are always tricky, one thing is for sure: my vinyl weighs a ton.

Figure 1.4

Pat Mastelotto incorporates a laptop running Ableton Live and Propellerhead's Reason by triggering the software to produce sound via electronic drum pads. This is but one imaginative way to use Live.

Goals of This Book

Like Live 4.0, *Ableton Live 4.0 Power!* was written by musicians—two drummers, in fact—but don't let that scare you. We've spent plenty of time performing with Live and have been recording and remixing in Live since it was first released. Live is built to be musical and this book will aspire to be the same. It is our hope that you have many long hours of enjoyment using Live while creating some interesting new music. Though this book is designed to be a "power user" book, don't be deterred if you are new to Live, new to music, or new to computer-based production. This book will serve as a basic guide to interfacing with Live 4.0 and an advanced tips and tricks collection for taking advantage of Ableton's industry-rocking technology.

Many sections in this book are not specific to Live 4.0, but are included as a reference for novice and intermediate digital audio studio owners. Topics such as wave editing, loop making, and sample manipulation are broken down so that you won't have to seek out this information somewhere else. General audio computing tips, such as configuring your PC for audio, will help you make the most of any audio application you currently use and will only bolster your basic working knowledge of computer-based (digital) audio as musicians should understand it.

If you are already familiar with Live, this book should feel like a souped up reference manual with some powerful tips and musical ideas for you to incorporate into your Live vocabulary. This book should help you optimize Live's settings for speed and sound, which should translate into maximum musical output. *Ableton Live 4.0 Power!* covers some sticky but rewarding topics, such as Live 4.0's new MIDI implementation, editing Live's mix automation, and using virtual EQs and compressors for professional audio results.

For downloadable starter loops and demos, visit this book's Web site at www.courseptr.com.

2 Back to School

As a child, "back to school" was one of the most dreaded statements I could possibly hear. It signaled the time of the year when the carefree summer was over. No more fun—time to work. The first couple of days back were always torturous. I could see the beautiful day rolling by outside while I was forced to listen to the dribble of my new history teacher. Some of my friends were in other classes on different schedules, meaning we were not able to eat lunch together or fool around anymore. It was horrible.

As you read the title of this chapter, the same feelings of dread may begin to crop up inside you. Some of you may even be suffering from flashbacks of studying endless pages of technical jargon for chemistry finals right now. Fear not! This book is not a boring compendium of scientific babble. We will keep the mood lively, fun, and interesting; yet in order to be a skilled Live user, you need to understand a few basic concepts. Knowing these concepts will improve your creativity with Live, help you develop your own working methods, and give you a true appreciation for everything this extraordinary software can do.

If you've used computers for music before, you may already be familiar with these subjects. But we still encourage you to read these brief sections, even if it's only to reinforce what you already know. Those new to the world of computer music production and Live should study these next sections very closely.

While a lot of technical information, including computer number theory, is about to be dumped on you, you will not be expected to know or remember specific details from this text or perform tedious number crunching. The most important thing you should walk away with after reading this chapter is an understanding of the concepts—insight into what's happening "under the hood" of your computer. For example, you may not be able to solve

453×78.34 off the top of your head, but you still understand the concept of multiplication. That's the level we're shooting for here.

MIDI Primer

If you've read the first chapter, you've no doubt stumbled across the term MIDI a few times. In fact, if you've been even slightly involved in music electronics over the last two decades, you've probably had to deal with MIDI at some point along the way. Live is no exception. While MIDI was used only as a means of remote control in the previous versions of Live, Live 4.0 introduces MIDI as a core element of music and sound creation. This opens up a whole new set of doors for Live users by offering an expanded creative pallet to work from. We know that sounds exciting, but you may still be wondering what MIDI really is. To answer that, here is a brief history of MIDI development.

Why Was MIDI developed?

During the dawn of musical electronics in the 60s and 70s, there were no rules or standards for building instruments. Back then, the workings of every electronic instrument created were determined solely by the manufacturer. Some devices had traditional keyboards; others used resistive strips for playing tones. Heck, one of the first electronic instruments, the Theremin (Figure 2.1), was played without even touching it! Indeed, many companies had wonderful and unique products, but there was no interconnectivity between them. If a musician wanted to layer the sounds of two separate synthesizers, like a MiniMoog and a Prophet, or drive a synth with a sequencer, it required enlisting the services of a borderline mad scientist to create a unique, one of a kind connection interface. These interfaces were usually hand made, fragile, expensive, and extremely temperamental.

As the technology of electronic instruments continued to grow into the 80s, digital circuitry began to find its way into these devices. With that, a solution for a standardized interconnectivity protocol was realized and Musical Instrument Digital Interface (MIDI) was born. Nearly every synth manufacturer from then up to the present has included MIDI protocol and connections on their hardware. This allows information to be passed back and forth between instruments, regardless of type, model, or manufacturer. Keyboards can be connected together and connected to sequencers, which can be connected to more sound modules and drum machines. The possibilities are endless.

Figure 2.1

Here is Craig Perkins, author of the *Ableton Live 4 CSi Master* CD-ROM, playing his Theremin. You've probably been propelled through the stars in some of your favorite old sci-fi flicks by sounds from this esoteric instrument.

Remote Control

We all have probably used a TV set with a remote control (another gift of 80s technology) at some point in our lives. Many of these remote controls can actually perform functions not possible with the physical controls mounted on the TV set. For example, the only way I can control brightness, contrast, hue, and color on my living room TV is with the remote. Programming the VCR, navigating satellite TV and DVD menus, titling my MiniDiscs, and managing active channels are all performed solely with the remote.

We all probably have a fair understanding of how a remote works, too: it sends a special infrared signal at the TV which the TV interprets as a command. If we want to change the channel, we press the "channel up" button on the remote and the remote sends the "channel up one" infrared signal. The TV picks it up and interprets it, then changes the station up one channel just as if we'd pressed the "channel up" button on the TV itself. This happens within a split second.

MIDI happens to function in the same way. An action on one device is translated into a signal that is transferred to another device. The receiving device decodes the message and takes the appropriate actions. This way, if a keyboard is connected to a sound module by MIDI, the sounds from the sound module can be played with the keyboard. When a key is pressed, say middle-C, the keyboard will send the "play middle-C" message to the sound module. When the sound module receives the message, it will produce the proper sound. This happens instantaneously just like the changing of TV channels.

The most powerful application of MIDI is the sequencer. A sequencer is a device that records MIDI messages and plays them back—like a tape machine for MIDI data. A sequencer can take the form of a hardware box with controls while some synthesizers have sequencers built right into them. You can also use a computer as a sequencer. By recording a list of MIDI messages transmitted from a keyboard while being played, the sequencer can then play the messages back to the keyboard at the same speed causing the keyboard to recreate the original performance. As you delve into the program, you'll see that Live is a full-fledged MIDI sequencer. Actually, Live is more like hundreds of little sequencers inside one big one, but we'll get to that a little later.

You may ask, "If we're going to record a performance and play it back, why do we use a sequencer? Why don't we just record the performance directly

What Is This Gear?

Typical MIDI gear can be divided into a few categories: keyboards/workstations, sound modules, controllers, and sequencers. Keyboards and workstations are all-in-one musical solutions. They will have a keyboard for you to play and an internal sound generator to create the sounds you play. Quite often, these keyboards will also have built-in sequencers allowing you to compose and arrange entire songs from one convenient unit.

Sound modules are basically just the guts from a keyboard/workstation—without the keyboard. Since all the hardware (plastic keys, springs, sensors, etc.) necessary to make a keyboard can present a great cost to the musician, sound modules offer you the tonal flexibility you'd achieve with a workstation without the extra hardware costs of the keyboard. These units are controlled completely via MIDI messages.

Controllers are the exact opposite of sound modules: they are keyboards that output MIDI messages, but have no sound generating capabilities of their own. While a silent device may seem like a worthless hardware category, controllers are actually extremely useful. They're much lighter than a keyboard/workstation making them perfect choices for musicians on the go. They also come in a much greater variety of sizes and configurations. See Chapter 3, "Getting Live Up and Running," for examples of control surfaces that are especially suited for Live.

Finally, a sequencer is a device with neither a keyboard nor sound generating capabilities. The sequencer's purpose is to record, edit, store, recall, and play back MIDI data to other MIDI devices. Usually, the sequencer contains all the data to play your song while the sound modules and keyboards generate the sounds.

Live can be thought of as a workstation—without the keyboard.

to tape?" The reason is that after we've recorded the MIDI messages into the sequencer, we can change (edit) them to improve the performance. Imagine playing a melody into a sequencer. As you're playing, you hit one wrong note about two-thirds of the way through. This performance, including the wrong note, is now stored as a list of messages in the sequencer. Before you play the melody back, though, you change the wrong note message to the correct pitch so the melody will be correct. This type of edit is not possible on tape since the tape does not contain notes. If we were using tape, we'd have to rewind the tape and re-record the whole melody over again until we got it right, or try to "punch-in" at that location to re-record the bad section.

Aside from fixing pitches of notes, we can change how loud they are, their timing, and their duration, as well as a myriad of other parameters, such as pitch bend and aftertouch. Groups of MIDI messages can be copied and pasted elsewhere in the list so we can repeat sections of our composition without recording the same thing again. This allows us, for example, to take a chorus and repeat it later in the song.

As you can see, the benefits of MIDI are intriguing. Being able to meticulously edit a performance is a level of power that can save some serious time. It's also welcome news to those of us who don't happen to be as technically accurate with our instruments as we'd like. Some of you may even be learning a new instrument right now! One could even argue that we're *all* learning a new instrument—Live—thanks to the innovative minds at Ableton.

What Is the Language of MIDI?

As the name Musical Instrument Digital Interface implies, MIDI messages are comprised of numbers. These numbers are used to represent functions within synthesizers, such as "turn up the volume," "change the sound," and "play a note." This makes MIDI work very much like your TV's remote control.

Though we wrote the text you're reading on a computer, the letters of the words we typed are not what are stored on our computer's disk drive. Instead, numbers are used to represent the letters we typed. In fact, everything a computer does—whether it's writing an e-mail, watching a DVD, playing a video game, or writing music—is all done and represented by numbers. It would then come as no surprise that MIDI messages are represented by numbers, too. That sounds like a whole lot of numbers, right? It definitely is, and it's mind-boggling that the computer can manage all of this while using only two digits.

Binary Numbers

Binary (bi- meaning "two") is the numbering system used by all computers and digital devices. It consists of only two digits, 0 and 1, whereas our standard decimal system (deci- meaning "ten") consists of ten digits: 0, 1, 2, 3, 4, 5, 6, 7, 8, and 9. Does that mean that the computer can't count any higher than one? Of course not. We can count higher than 9, can't we? The way it's done in decimal is that we group digits together and give unique multipliers to their values to attain greater values (Figure 2.2). For example, the number 37 is equal to 37 because there is a 3 in the "10s" column and a 7 in the "1s" column. When we add 3×10 to 7×1, we get 37.

Figure 2.2

This figure shows the value of each column in a decimal number. Multiply each digit by the value in each column then add the results together to find the value.

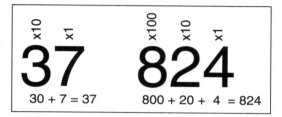

While the previous example may be seen as some sort of circular reasoning, it will make sense when we examine the same number, this time represented in binary. In Figure 2.3, we see the binary representation of the number 37 is "100101."

Figure 2.3

This figure shows the number 37 represented in binary. You'll see that the columns in a binary number have different values than those in a decimal number.

Of course, you don't need to know the ins and outs of binary computation in order to use Live effectively.

While the column multipliers in a decimal number are easy to remember (1, 10, 100, 1000, etc), the column multipliers for a binary number are different. Instead of being based on powers of 10, binary multipliers are based on powers of 2. So, the first column (on the left) is worth 1, since 2 to the power of 0 equals 1. The next column is 2 to the power of 1, which equals 2. The next column is 2 to the power of 2 (which equals 4) and so on. This means that the multipliers for an 8-digit binary number are: 128, 64, 32, 16, 8, 4, 2, and 1. When we apply the formula from the decimal example using these new multipliers, we get $1\times32 + 1\times4 + 1\times1 = 37$. And, since we'll never be multiplying any value with a number higher than one while using binary, we can just add up the values of the columns containing 1s; thus, $32 + 4 + 1 = 37$. Easy! Want to try another one? How about "11011010?" Again, we just add up the values of the columns that contain a "1." The result is: $128 + 64 + 16 + 8 + 2 = 218$.

Bits and Bytes

In computer language, each digit of a binary number is referred to as a *bit*. Binary numbers are usually expressed in groups of eight bits, therefore "00100101" would be the correct notation for 37. These groups of 8 bits are referred to as a *byte*. If you've used a computer for more than two seconds, you're probably familiar with bytes; it's how file sizes are expressed on a computer, though usually measured in larger amounts known as *kilobytes* (1024 bytes) and *megabytes* (1024 kilobytes). And no doubt you've heard the word "bit" thrown around, too, when discussing video game consoles, such as 32-bit and 64-bit systems. If you pay attention, you'll find these terms permeating conversation everywhere these days.

What's in a MIDI Message?

A MIDI message is, on the norm, composed of three bytes, meaning each message is 24 bits (24 binary digits) in length. Each of these 3-byte MIDI messages describes one *event*. An event is when something changes in a device, such as pressing a key, twisting a knob, moving a slider, or stepping on a pedal. The TV remote has events, too, like turning on the power, adjusting the volume, and choosing channels.

Let's talk about the TV remote for a moment. When you press the power button on the remote, the TV turns on. The TV will stay on, even if the line-of-sight between the remote and TV is obstructed. This is because the TV remote is not sending out a constant signal to keep the TV on. Instead, the remote only sends a signal when the power state of the TV should change. So, when the TV receives another "power" message from the remote, it turns itself off.

The same is true for MIDI. When you press a key on a keyboard, that action generates an event known as "note on." Along with the "note on" message, the keyboard will send the number of the key that was played (note number) in addition to a number representing how hard the key was struck (velocity). This comprises the three bytes of a MIDI message. The receiving sound module or device then follows that MIDI instruction and plays the note represented in the message at the indicated volume. At this time, the note will continue to play indefinitely. In fact, one can disconnect the MIDI connection between the keyboard and sound module, and the module will continue playing its sound. Just like the TV, the sound module is waiting for a command directing it to turn the sound off. So, when you release your finger from the keyboard, the keyboard generates another event, a "note off." Attached to the command is the number of the key released and the strength at which it was released. The module then responds in kind by stopping the sound.

Maximum Velocity

In music, it is a common technique to vary the loudness at which notes are played. On the piano, you can play quietly by pressing the piano keys gently. The harder you strike the keys, the louder the sound. In MIDI language, this striking force is known as *velocity*. Velocity is expressed as a number (big surprise) from 0 to 127. A "note on" message with a velocity of 127 means the key was struck with full force.

After note on and note off messages, the most common MIDI command sent is a *control change*, which is usually generated by moving a controller (knob, slider, button, etc.) on your MIDI device. Examples of controllers include the mod wheel, foot pedal, breath control, volume, and pan. Let's look at the mod wheel a little closer: when in its lowest position, the value output by the wheel is zero. When the wheel is moved up, its output value increases. Moving the wheel downwards causes the value to decrease. Just like the MIDI note events, the mod wheel, or any other controller for that matter, will only output a message when its position changes. So, when the wheel is moved to its full upward position, it will output its full value. The wheel won't output another value until you start moving it back down again.

Putting It All Together

We've talked about binary numbers and we've talked about MIDI messages, so how are they related? As we mentioned earlier, a MIDI message consists of three bytes of data (see Figure 2.4). Each byte can be a status byte or a data byte. A status byte is the first byte sent when a new event is triggered. The status byte contains a couple pieces of information, but most importantly, it includes the MIDI command name, such as note on, control change, poly aftertouch, etc. The two following data bytes will contain infor-

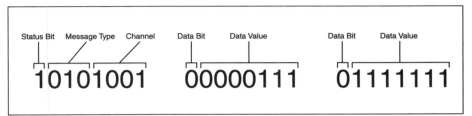

Figure 2.4
This MIDI message contains 3 bytes: 1 status byte and 2 data bytes. The status byte is signified by a "1" in the far left column of the byte while the data bytes contain a "0" in the far left column.

mation regarding the command. As previously stated, a note on message will have two additional values: the note played and the force used to play it. The purpose of the data bytes will change based on the status byte. If, for example, the status byte signaled a control change, the following two data bytes would contain the number of the parameter to change, such as 7 for volume or 10 for pan, and the value to change it to.

The status and data bytes are distinguished from one another by looking at the first bit in the byte. When the first bit is a "1," we have a status byte. A data byte will begin with a "0." This means the remaining 7 bits of the byte contain the actual values of the message.

Let's decode the message shown in Figure 2.4. As we can see, the first byte has a "1" in its far-left position, meaning this byte is a status byte. When decoding a status byte, we look at two groups of numbers. The first group is the 3 bits just to the right of the status bit. These three bits will determine the type of event being processed. We decode the value by treating these bits as their own binary number. In this case, "010" decodes as the number 2, which is the number for a control change.

The remaining four bits of the status byte indicate the *MIDI Channel* intended to receive this message. This is extremely useful if we want to control 2 different MIDI devices, such as a sound module and a drum machine, from the same source, such as a sequencer. The sound module can be set so it only receives MIDI messages set to channel 1. The drum machine could similarly be set to receive only on MIDI channel 10. This way, a note sent to the sound module won't simultaneously trigger a sound in the drum machine. The MIDI channel is determined by treating the last four bits as their own binary number, just like decoding the MIDI command. In this case, "1001" decodes as 9, which is actually MIDI Channel 10. Why, you ask? The reason is that with 4 bits, it's only possible to count from 0 to 15. So, the MIDI specification adds "1" to the decoded MIDI channel, so the channels become 1 through 16 instead.

Okay, we now know that the event we're decoding is a control change intended for a device set to MIDI channel 10, just like the drum machine above; however, we still need to know some more information before we can complete the control change command, which is what the remaining data bytes are for.

The second byte in Figure 2.4 is a data byte because its first bit is set to "0." We then find the value of the remaining 7 bits to get the control being changed by this message. "0000111" decodes as 7, which is the MIDI number for volume. The last data byte, "1111111," decodes as 127. So, our complete MIDI message is: "Change control 7 on MIDI channel 10 to 127." This message will cause the volume of the drum machine to be turned to its maximum.

❄ Round Numbers

Have you ever wondered why such stupid numbers are used when it comes to computers? Why does RAM come in megabyte sizes such as 128, 256, and 512? It seems like nice round numbers such as 125, 250, and 500 would be a lot easier to remember, don't you think?

It turns out that those numbers actually are round numbers, at least they are for the computer. The reason for this can be seen when we fill all the bits of a binary byte with "1". The value of "11111111" is 255 (128+64+32+16+8+4+2+1=255), meaning "100000000", which looks pretty round, actually equals 256. This is the equivalent of 99 in decimal language, where adding another digit gives us 100. We like to think of 255 in binary as being similar to 99 in decimal and 256 in binary being similar to 100 in decimal.

In the case of MIDI, the first bit of a byte is always used to indicate "status" or "data" which leaves us with only 7 bits of information to use. Filling up the 7 bits of a data byte with "1" yields a value of 127 (64+32+16+8+4+2+1=127), therefore the largest transmittable value with a data byte is 127. You'll find that almost all MIDI parameters are adjustable between 0 and 127 for this very reason. So, next time you go to turn up the volume or crank up some modulation, remember that MIDI goes beyond 100 up to 127.

Benefits and Pitfalls of MIDI

While throwing messages around between our gear will prove to be amazingly powerful, there are still a few quirks with MIDI you should be aware of. First of all, MIDI is not audio. It is impossible to hear MIDI. The only way to hear what is being transmitted is to have a device receive those messages and act on them. Since MIDI is only information about what pitches were played, what knobs were moved, etc., the sound of your MIDI information will be based entirely on the synthesizer that's being controlled by the messages. This means if I write a piano piece on my Brand X keyboard and record it as MIDI, it will sound slightly different when played back on my friend's Brand Y keyboard. The melodies will still be the same, as well as all the timing of the performance, but the sound and tone of the piano will be different. It's exactly the same as playing a piece on an upright piano and then playing it again on a grand piano. The musical piece is the same, but the instrument sounds different. While this may be an annoyance when collaborating with another artist who has different equipment than you, it can be a powerful production tool. For instance, if you write a bass part using a fretless bass sound on your keyboard, you can change that sound to something else (like a slap bass) to hear what another instrument playing the same part sounds like without having to re-record. Perhaps you'll discover that the bass part actually sounds best when played by a bassoon sound. This type of experimentation is possible only through MIDI.

Another useful quality of MIDI is that we can alter the pitch and timing of the MIDI messages independently of one another. This allows us to record a part at one tempo then play it back faster without changing the pitch—handy when you're doing some intricate parts. This doesn't work in the analog world, because recording something to tape then playing it back faster will cause its pitch to rise, possibly altering the tonal quality of the recording. Also, we can move the pitches of the MIDI messages without changing their timing allowing quick transposition of parts, or fixing bad notes. Furthermore, we can fix rhythmic timing issues without altering the pitches that were played.

What makes MIDI truly appealing is its file size. The amount of MIDI data necessary to reproduce a musical performance is only a fraction of the amount needed to play back a digital audio file of the same length. Therefore, projects that rely heavily on MIDI programming and control will be much smaller in size than one dependent on audio files.

Digital Audio Primer

If MIDI data is so small and efficient, why would we even concern ourselves with digital audio? One reason is that we may wish to incorporate non-MIDI instruments such as vocals, acoustic guitar, sitar, didgeridoo, and bagpipes into our compositions. Since we can't program these instruments (yet?), our only option is to record the real thing or use gigantic sample-playback libraries. Another reason we use digital audio is that its audio recordings capture the exact nuances of a performance far more accurately than MIDI.

For decades, major recording studios have been relying on analog tape machines for recording audio. Indeed, the sound of analog tape is amazing, but it comes at quite a cost. These professional multi-track tape machines are grossly expensive, extremely sensitive to environmental changes, a chore to maintain and operate, and are just plain huge. Moreover, the quality of the recording begins to degrade from the moment it was made and is helped further along by replaying the tape over and over, which is a necessary evil of overdub and mixdown sessions. Editing tape requires that a skilled professional make cuts (splices) in the tape with a razor blade, rearrange the pieces, then re-tape them together, something that needs to be done right the first time—there's no "undo" in the analog world.

Fortunately, with the increase in speed of computer processors and the expanding capacity of affordable storage mediums such as tape and disk drives, it is now possible to digitize sound waves so they may be recorded as a series of 1s and 0s. While this method has numerous benefits, some experts still dispute the quality of digital sound. To explain why, we'll take a closer look at how the digital audio process works.

What Is Sound?

Before we can start recording and digitizing sound, we must first understand what sound is. Basically, sound is the repeated rise and fall of air pressure. When these repetitions, or *cycles*, fall within a particular rate, or *frequency*, our ears pick them up and send impulses to our brains. Our brains then decode the impulses allowing us to "hear." Our ears are most sensitive to sound falling within the frequency range of 20 to 20,000 cycles per second. *Hertz* is the term used to indicate cycles per second, so you'll commonly see above frequencies listed as 20Hz to 20kHz (Hz is the abbreviation for Hertz; k is a prefix that means "×1000"). Frequency and pitch are directly related to one another; when the frequency of a sound rises, its perceived pitch rises as well.

Another quality of sound, besides its frequency, is its volume, or *amplitude*. The amplitude of a sound is measured as a *sound pressure level (SPL)* which is notated with units known as *decibels (dB)*. The quietest sound the average person can hear lies at the threshold of hearing which is where they set the 0 dB SPL mark. As the volume of the sound begins to rise, the decibels also rise. At some point, the sound is going to get so loud that you will start to feel physical pain in your ears. This is known as the threshold of pain and lies somewhere around 130 dB SPL. While some concerts may well exceed this loudness, it is recommended that musicians (or anyone who enjoys being

Figure 2.5
Pictured are three elementary waveforms of the same pitch: a) sine wave, b) sawtooth wave, and c) square wave. Though their shapes repeat at the same rate, they will each sound different to our ears.

able to hear) keep their listening levels somewhere in the middle ground, around 80dB SPL. Remember: without your ears, Live is no fun at all!

One final element of sound is the color or tone of the sound, called the *timbre* (pronounced TAM-ber). This quality is what allows you to differentiate between the sounds of a piano, trumpet, clarinet, guitar, or any other instrument, even if they're all playing the same pitch. The timbre of a sound is analogous to its *waveform*. In Figure 2.5, you'll see three different waveforms. All are at the same frequency and amplitude, but they have different shapes. Thus, while the sounds will have the same pitch, they will sound distinctly different.

The waveform drawings in Figure 2.5 were created by mapping sound pressure levels on the vertical axis of a graph while mapping time along the horizontal axis. An increase in air pressure is shown by the waveform being above the 0 dB line, and a decrease in pressure is shown by the waveform being under the 0 dB line.

How Is Sound Represented in the Computer?
By now we're sure you've anticipated that the computer must represent sound with numbers—the name "digital audio" gives it away. The computer

must use numbers to represent not only audio, but other forms of media such as movies (digital video) and pictures (digital imagery). Interestingly, the processes of digitizing an image and digitizing audio are remarkably similar, so we'll compare them both in our discussion. The digitizing process is known as *analog-to-digital conversion* (ADC).

You've probably heard the term "analog" before and you may feel it has a "vintage" or "old school" connotation. You'll find numerous artists and engineers who, when looking for "that fat, analog sound," reach immediately for old equipment. While many engineers prefer old analog circuitry, "old" is not what the word analog really means. Analog simply refers to something that has infinite variations and degrees. We can see the difference when we compare an analog thermometer with a digital thermometer (Figure 2.6). The analog thermometer can show temperatures between 70 and 71 degrees. As temperature rises, the mercury will slowly rise from 70 to 71. The digital counterpart, however, can only show 70 or 71 degrees—it can't show any value in between—so, when it's actually 70.6528 degrees outside, the digital thermometer rounds up to 71 degrees. Pretty close, right? Perhaps, but some people may want a more accurate reading. So, to get a more accurate temperature reading, we get a digital thermometer with the ability to display 10ths of a degree. Now, we see that instead of 71 degrees, it's actually 70.6. That's closer than 71, but it's still and always will be an approximation of the actual temperature, which could be varying at an un-measurable level.

When we digitize audio or images into the computer, the computer is similarly making approximations of the original. Actually, the computer is making thousands, if not *millions*, of approximations which are used collectively to approximate the original.

Sampling Process

When you want to get an image into a computer, you use a scanner. This device usually looks like a super-thin photocopier and has a cable that connects it to your computer. To record audio into the computer, we use an audio interface (see Chapter 3 for examples of these) which is, in essence, a scanner as well, but one made for audio. Therefore, the processes of digitizing an image and digitizing audio are very similar, and the same parameters that affect image quality will affect audio quality. Since you're reading about all of this, we'll give you the visual example first.

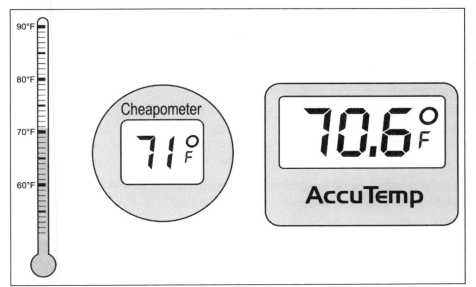

Figure 2.6

Here are three thermometers measuring the outside temperature. The digital thermometer on the right can provide a more accurate reading than the one in the middle.

Below in Figure 2.7, you see a black-and-white photograph. We want to scan this image into our computer using a scanner, so we place the image on the scanner and hit "start." We see some light moving around under the scanner lid and, after a few moments, our image magically appears on our screen.

Figure 2.7

This is a photograph that has been captured by a scanner.

Not bad, right? Perhaps, but when we look closer at the photograph, both the original and the one on the screen (Figure 2.8), we'll start to see that the computer version is "blocky." What's that all about? Why doesn't the computer image look sharp like the original? The reason for this is that the computer uses assortments of colored blocks, known as *pixels*, to create an image. The computer creates the pixels by looking at tiny areas of the picture and approximating the color there. The approximated colors are then laid out side-by-side and line-by-line on the computer screen. When we stand back from the screen, we see the image. When we get closer, we start to see the individual pixels.

This phenomenon can be experienced at a sports game when a huge group of people in the stands hold up individually colored cards to make a sign. When you're standing right next to them, all you see is people holding huge crimson and gold squares. But when you're on the other side of the stadium, all those little cards form a colossal sign that reads "Go Trojans!" This means that when the pixels, or blocks, used to make an image are small and close enough together, our brains will cease to see the individual pieces and will instead construct a single image. The trick is to record and store only as many pixels as are necessary to create an acceptable reproduction. After all, it's wasteful to record a whole bunch of tiny pixels if we'll never zoom in far enough for it to be an issue.

The process of digitizing audio is the same. The computer takes "pictures" of the incoming audio waveform and stores them in a list (Figure 2.9). Each of these little pictures is known as a *sample* and is analogous to the pixel used in images. A sample represents the approximate amplitude of an audio signal over a very brief amount of time. When it's time to play back the audio, the individual amplitudes are lined up side-by-side to recreate the waveform.

Figure 2.8

An enlarged version of the photograph (left) and computer screen (right) shows that the computer image is not as sharp as the original.

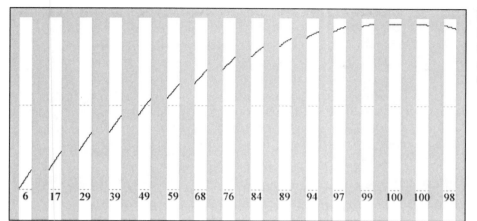

Figure 2.9

Here, an audio signal is broken into tiny little pieces so they may be numerically approximated by the computer.

6 17 29 39 49 59 68 76 84 89 94 97 99 100 100 98

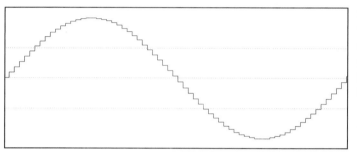

Figure 2.10

When looking at the digitized waveform in detail, we can see it is broken into steps similar to the way an image is broken into blocks (pixels).

If audio digitizing and image digitizing are so closely related, you can probably anticipate the next problem. When we zoom in on our digitized audio wave and compare it to the original (Figure 2.10), we can see that the computer's version is again very rough and blocky. Does that mean that it sounds rough and blocky, too? You bet. The good news is that there's a solution.

Sample Rate

One thing we can do to immediately improve the quality of our images and sounds is to capture more information when digitizing. If we use an even greater amount of smaller pixels to generate an image, the resulting picture will appear to be much crisper in detail (Figure 2.11). We have just increased the *resolution* of the image and have therefore packed a greater number of pixels into the same amount of space as our previous image. As a result, we can zoom in further to these higher resolution images before we start to notice the pixels.

✳ ✳ ✳

Figure 2.11

The picture on the right was scanned at a higher resolution (sample rate) than the one on the left, and therefore still looks decent after zooming in.

If we can increase the number of pixels used to compose an image, can we increase the number of samples taken for a sound wave? Absolutely! By taking more samples of the audio every second, we are increasing the *sample rate* of the recording, therefore producing a more refined waveform with a less pronounced blocky effect upon playback (Figure 2.12). Sample rate is defined as the number of amplitude readings taken every second and is expressed in Hertz.

While increasing the sample rate will have advantageous effects on audio quality, it is only doing half the job. In essence, we're taking more measurements per second, but we're still using a cheap thermometer.

Figure 2.12

Here, the waveform with the higher sample rate preserves the shape of the original waveform much more accurately.

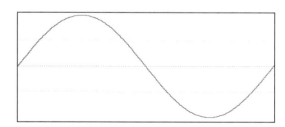

❄ Does It Really Sound That Bad?

Here we are telling you that low sample rate and low bit-depth sounds bad. Don't take our word for it, try it out for yourself! Included with Live is the Redux Device which specializes in reducing, decimating, or otherwise destroying audio using sample rate reduction and dithering techniques. Check out Chapter 9 for a walkthrough of Redux to hear this phenomenon firsthand (or is that first ear?).

Bit-Depth

At the beginning of this section, we looked at thermometers and the added accuracy of having additional digits to read. Our first thermometer only had two digits and could therefore only show values from −99 to +99 degrees (we're assuming that the minus sign doesn't constitute a digit). Our second thermometer had an additional digit, so it could accurately show readings from −99.9 to +99.9 degrees. Does that mean we only gained 1.8 degrees in range? That doesn't sound impressive.

While we haven't increased the range of our thermometer by much, we have increased its accuracy immensely. The name of the game here is not to get an expanded operating range. What we want is more sensitivity, more response to subtle changes in temperature. By taking this increased accuracy analogy and applying it to the scanner, it means the computer can make a closer approximation of color for each pixel since it is now more sensitive to subtle differences in shades (Figure 2.13). So, increasing the resolution of an image increases the number of pixels used, therefore creating a sharper image. By increasing the accuracy of each pixel, we've improved the color tone and depth to provide a more natural appearance.

So how do we do the same thing with sound? In order to increase the accuracy of our samples, each sample will have to be capable of representing a larger number of amplitudes. In essence, we need to use more digits for each sample. In our thermometer example, we added a digit to the right side of the temperature readout. This gave the thermometer the ability to register smaller changes in temperature. We can also add some digits to the sample value to achieve the same results. Since each digit in a binary number is called a bit,

Figure 2.13

By allowing each pixel to represent a larger number of shades, we can achieve a smoother tone across our right image.

Figure 2.14

You can see that the waveform with the higher bit-depth maintains detail even as the sound gets quieter.

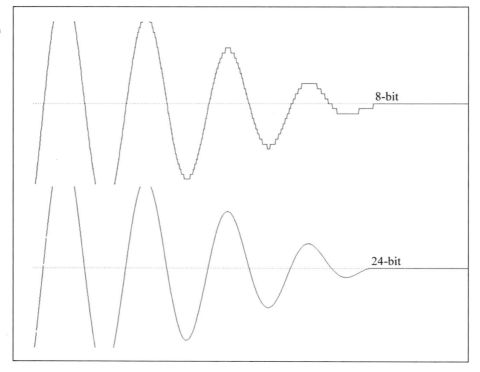

the number of bits used to represent a sample is called the *bit-depth*. Increasing the bit-depth will increase recording accuracy just as it did for the thermometer (Figure 2.14). Just as adding digits to the thermometer had a negligible impact on its range, but a profound impact on accuracy, increasing the bit-depth doesn't really let us capture louder sounds. Instead, the computer can now maintain a more accurate waveform at lower amplitudes.

The point of increasing the sample rate and bit-depth when recording audio is exactly the same as increasing the resolution and color depth when scanning an image. Just as the image grew sharper and more vibrant with the increase, the audio will also become smoother, deeper, and more detailed. Just as our eyes blend the tiny pixels into a large, crisp image, our ears will blend the tiny samples into a smooth, continuous waveform.

Benefits and Pitfalls of Digital Audio

Digital audio definitely has advantages over its analog counterpart. The recording media for digital audio, be it CD, digital tape, or hard disks, are cheaper than professional analog tape, and these digital mediums have sig-

❄ Quantify This!

We've been speaking in general terms so far, so we're now going to apply some numbers to all of this. As we mentioned, a lot of samples are needed in a short amount of time to yield quality audio. The standard CD format calls for 44,100 samples to be taken each second for both the left and right channels of audio. That's 88,200 samples a second being read from the CD. Furthermore, the CD specification also calls for samples to be 16 bits long. This means it takes two bytes of data to represent one sample of audio (8 bits equals 1 byte, right?). The binary number "11111111 11111111" (that's 16 ones) happens to be equal to 65,535, so that means a 16-bit sample can represent 65,536 different amplitudes. That's a pretty good number.

While CD standard is what most of us are used to hearing, audio professionals regularly use even higher sample rates and bit-depths to attain even more accurate audio recordings. A common recording format is 24-bit/96kHz. This means that the computer is now recording 96,000 samples every second for each channel of audio. On top of that, a 3-byte number is used for each sample enabling the computer to represent 16,777,216 different amplitudes!

nificantly higher capacity than tape. Also, once audio (or any data for that matter) has been stored as digits, it will suffer no loss of quality. The audio data can be played again and again for months and the last play will still sound identical to the first. This also means that copies can be made with no loss of quality since the computer merely transcribes the numbers (samples) from one location to another.

Since digital audio is just numbers, it's also easy to transport and distribute. Portable hard drives make it possible to take entire albums of working material from studio to studio with ease. CDs and DVDs are super-thin, yet hold hundreds of *megabytes* (that's 1024 kilobytes) of data. Audio can also be distributed over the Internet allowing instantaneous collaboration between artists, even when they're on opposite sides of the world.

Of course, the ease with which digital audio can be copied and distributed is also a pitfall. Though illegal, it is quite common for music files to be traded over the Internet between users. While this does wonders for spreading the work of artists, they receive no money for their efforts. Fortunately, a number of companies such as Apple and Napster have created online stores where users can buy songs individually at a fraction of the CD price and have them transferred (aka *downloaded*) immediately to their computer's hard drives. Since there is no CD production, packaging, or distribution costs involved, the price is reasonable for the consumer and the artists still get their share. There's one small catch, though: the downloaded files have a sound quality that is slightly inferior to that of a CD.

Why would these companies only allow you to download inferior quality files? The reason is simple: digital audio files are huge. Consider how many numbers are being recorded for every second of audio. At CD rates, there are 88,200 16-bit samples taken every second. That's 176,400 bytes of data per second. Multiply that out over a four minute song and you'll get 42,336,000 bytes—roughly 40 megabytes of sample data. Downloading 40 megs of data can be quite an undertaking, especially if you're confined to a dial-up Internet connection. So, to make transferring files easier, the files are *compressed* before being sent. The process of compression can vary from protocol to protocol. The most popular format, MPEG-1, Layer-3 (MP3), is what is called "lossy" compression. In an effort to reduce the file size, an MP3 *encoder* will remove what it considers to be extraneous data and will compact the remaining audio data into a file that is roughly a tenth the size of the original. Clearly, downloading 4 megabytes is much preferred to 40 megs. When the file is uncompressed after download using a *decoder*, an approximation of the original audio is produced which is usually acceptable for most intents and purposes. Some are still unsatisfied with the quality of MP3, and so additional compression formats have popped up including WMA, AAC, and Ogg Vorbis (is that a cool name or what?).

The last thing one should consider when working with audio is that the pitch and speed of the audio file are directly related to one another. This means that slowing down the playback rate of an audio file will also cause its pitch to drop. The opposite is also true—increasing the pitch of an audio file causes it to play back faster. Think of a record on a turntable. If you turn off the motor while the record is playing, it will begin to slow down. As it does, you'll hear the song also start dropping in pitch until the record finally makes a complete stop. DJs use this phenomenon to create new pitches and melodies by manipulating the record's speed while scratching.

We mention the relation of pitch and speed last, because it is a barrier that has been broken—by Live. You will see throughout the rest of this book how Live has turned digital audio data into complete goo, allowing you to re-pitch and morph the tempo of these files at will *in real time*. This capability is one thing that makes Live stand out from all the music applications available today. By removing this crippling limitation, Live has "opened up" audio for complete experimentation and creativity.

3 } Getting Live Up and Running

If you are accustomed to buying studio gear (hardware), you are probably like me—get the sucker home, tear open the box, and start making noise. Manuals are for other people after all and, well, who's got the time? When it comes to software, however, there is one fundamental difference: it is almost always up to you, the end user, to set up and configure the hardware properly, install the software the way it was designed, and set up the preferences so that the new application won't interfere with any legacy applications, cause strange hardware issues, or impair general functionality. In short, you become the final manufacturer. It is this sort of engineering control that is both the advantage and disadvantage of personally transfiguring your computer into a recording studio, a performance sampler, or a Live sequencing instrument.

Before we dive in and start producing hits, it is important to take a moment to verify that your computer system is up to speed and then to install Live properly to ensure maximum performance potential. This chapter will provide more than a few recommendations to help you through the lonely installation process and a few rarely mentioned tips for fine-tuning your Ableton Live studio. We will cover both Mac and PC setup and talk about several methods for optimizing your system. Also, remember that Ableton's technical support is an excellent way to get to the bottom of anything not covered in this book, as is Ableton's online user forum (got to www.ableton.com and click on "forum"), which is usually rich with tips, tricks, and advice (see Figure 3.1).

System Requirements

Listed below are Ableton's posted system requirements, dependent upon system make, and followed by my recommendations. For the record, I've tested

Figure 3.1

Ableton's user forum is packed with good information. Make sure you take full advantage by logging on (selecting a user name and password), so that you can receive private messages, converse with other members, and be notified when any of your posts have been responded to. Also, by using the forum's search window, you can usually find some reference to the problem you are facing and eliminate needless inquiries to commonly asked questions.

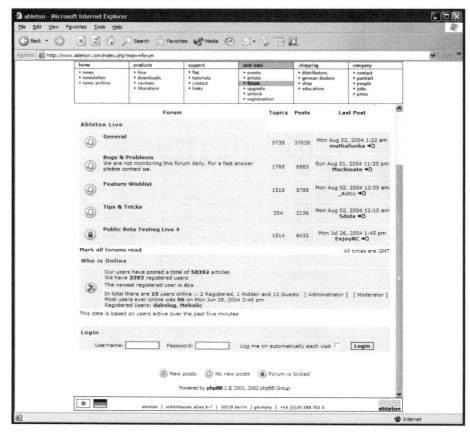

and composed music using Live on several different makes of Windows PCs and Macs running both OS 9.2.2 and OS X 10.3.4. Still, as mentioned above, every computer is customizable and this can lead to unforeseen problems. If Live is acting strange—for example, if the audio is stuttering or if each edit is taking a very long time—try running Live completely by itself. Make sure you are not running any other applications in the background, such as MP3 players, office suites, or (as we will cover in Chapter 8, "Using Effects") third-party plug-in effects, which can cause CPU performance problems.

Keep in mind that the vast difference in *Requirements* versus *Recommendations* could well mean the enviable difference between functioning and flourishing with your Ableton product.

Ableton Live's System Requirements for Macintosh

- ❄ Any G3 or faster
- ❄ 256 MB RAM
- ❄ Mac OS 9.2 or later
- ❄ Mac OS X 10.1.5 or later

Ableton Live 4.0 Power!'s Mac Recommendations

- ❄ G4 or faster
- ❄ 1 GB RAM
- ❄ Internal SCSI, ATA/IDE, or External 7200 RPM FireWire Drives only (USB hard drives tend to be slower and less reliable)
- ❄ Mac OS X 10.3.4 or later
- ❄ Sound card with MIDI interface

Ableton Live's System Requirements for PC

- ❄ 600 Megahertz CPU or faster
- ❄ 256 MB RAM
- ❄ Windows 98/2000/XP
- ❄ Windows compatible soundcard (preferably with a DirectX or ASIO driver)

Ableton Live 4.0 Power!'s PC Recommendations

- ❄ 1.5 Gigahertz CPU or faster
- ❄ 1 GB RAM
- ❄ Windows 2000/XP
- ❄ No USB hard drives
- ❄ ASIO compliant soundcard with MIDI interface

Installing, Running, and Updating Live 4.0

If you are brand new to Live and haven't yet picked up your copy, or have never installed audio software before, then this section is for you. Sometimes a little background information helps make for a more rewarding software experience. Here are a few general tips for installing, running, and updating Live 4.0:

- ❄ Live can be purchased via the Ableton Live Webshop or by ordering the packaged version through an Ableton distributor (M-Audio in the US, www.m-audio.com) or retail outlet (Guitar Center, Sam Ash, and others). No matter where you get it, Live 4.0 can run on Mac OS 9.2 and up, OS X 10.1.5 and up, as well as PCs running Windows 98, 2000, and XP. Note: if you have downloaded the Ableton Live 4.0 Demo, you should still check to see that your version is the latest update when you decide to buy the program. To check this, simply go to www.ableton.com and click on "downloads" to see the latest version. At the time of this writing, the Live 4.0 demo doesn't allow saving or rendering and is limited to 30 minute continuous sessions. The demo can be upgraded to the full version.

❋ To begin making music in Live, you will need samples, recorded music, or an audio interface that will enable you to record into your computer. If you picked up the boxed version of Live, you already possess over 600MB of royalty-free loops from Big Fish Audio. If you are anxious to get your hands on some more rights-free loops, please see "Where to Get Loops" in the FAQ (Appendix B). Also, there are literally hundreds of Web sites and other sources of free and inexpensive loops, as well as a couple hundred professional-grade companies that make high-end sounds, such as Ilio Entertainment, PowerFX, E-Lab, QupArts, Zero-G, etc.

❋ In terms of audio, Live supports ASIO and DirectX for PC, Soundmanager for Mac OS 9.2, and Core Audio for Mac OS X. If you don't have an ASIO- or WDM-compatible sound card, be prepared to hear some audio latency when recording and playing back recordings made in Live. A more detailed explanation of audio and MIDI latency and a discussion of all their trappings is presented later in this chapter.

❋ Also, aside from the infallible book you hold in your hand, it won't hurt to take a look at Ableton's Live 4.0 manual. All versions of Live contain a PDF version of the manual that can be viewed by going to the Help menu and choosing "Read the Live Manual." The boxed version of Live includes an analog (printed) owner's manual, which is still worth referring to even though you have wisely purchased *Ableton Live 4.0 Power!* It is worth noting that Ableton frequently updates Live, and when they do, Live's included PDF manual is always updated.

Live Installation Tips (Mac OS 9.2 and Beyond)

Though installing Live 4.0 in OS 9.2 is as easy as point and click, it can be advantageous to spend just a little time configuring OS 9's memory allotment. Live 4.0 tends to be more processor-intensive than RAM-intensive, due to the number crunching involved when warping audio files or applying dense effects, such as reverbs. A clean installation and proper RAM allocation setting can help smooth out Live's operation in Mac's OS 9.2. If you are new to Macs or new to setting memory allocations, here's how to do it:

1 Once you have installed Live, locate the Live 4.0 application on your hard drive. Note: this is *not* the shortcut (or alias) on your desktop! The best way to locate the app, if you don't know where it is, is to click on (highlight) the shortcut and select File > Show Original (CMND + R). Next, click one time gently on the application file and select File > Get File Info > Memory Settings.

2 You will then have the choice of constraining the minimum and maximum memory settings for your Mac. For standard use, we recommend about 100 MB of RAM for Live.

3 To check how much RAM your Mac is actually using, start up Live and begin playing the demo song (or one of your own compositions). Next, click on your desktop or the Mac finder window, and click on the apple in the uppermost left. Choose "About this computer" and a small box will pop up telling you how much RAM is being used and by which programs. Depending upon your system setup, there is a small degree of trial and error involved in determining exactly how much RAM you want to allocate to Live. Some actions will pull on the RAM a bit more than others, so you will want to leave some headroom. You will also want to save some RAM for running other applications such as Reason, in ReWire mode. We recommend trying a few different configurations depending upon your setup. Figure 3.2 shows the screen of a G4 titanium Powerbook (often called a TiBook) running Reason 2.5 and Live 4.0 and their relative memory allocations.

Figure 3.2

This screenshot shows the memory allocations for a G4 laptop running Reason 2.5 and Live 4.0.

Live Installation Tips (Mac OS X 10.1.5 and Up)

Due to Ableton's foresight, and Live's minimal dependency upon an operating system, Live was the first multi-track audio application on the planet available for Mac OS X! As you might expect, installing Live 4.0 (like all previous versions) on OS X is a breeze. Insert the Live installation disc, open the disc dialog, and drag the Live 4.x folder to the Applications folder on your hard disk. All pertinent files, including Live 4.0's manual will be contained here. For quicker access to Live, you may want to install a shortcut onto the OS X dock (if you are using it). This makes Live easier to open and a little more fun—you can watch the bouncing Live icon as the program loads up. To do this, simply open your applications folder, or the location on your drive where you decided to install Live, and drag the program icon to the dock. An instant shortcut is made. To remove the item from the dock, drag it to the trash or to the desktop and watch it go "poof."

Windows 98, 2000, and XP

Installing Live onto a Windows machine is much like installing any other Windows-based application. Once you click on Setup and follow the instructions, Live's installer will ask you where you would like to place the Ableton folder and its files. We recommend using the installer's default setting which will place Live in an Ableton folder in your computer's Program Files folder. You will want to pay special attention to where your VST plug-in folder exists. It is common practice to keep all VST plug-ins stored in one common location so every VST-compatible application will be able to use them. For instance, if you have Steinberg's Cubase SX installed on your computer, you can instruct Live to look for plug-ins in the Steinberg shared VST folder which is commonly located at Program Files > Steinberg > Vstplugins. After the installation, you will want to customize your preferences (see the "Setting Preferences in Live" section later in this chapter).

> ❋ **Mac Users Take Note**
> The centralizing of plug-in folders is useful in OS 9 and OS X as well, though OS X audio applications typically take care of this for you by installing VST plug-ins at the location Library > Audio > Plug-ins > VST.

Updating Live

To check what version of Live you are currently running under Mac OS X, click on Live > About. On a PC or Mac OS 9.2, go to Help > About Live. Both the version and serial number will be displayed (see Figure 3.3). Click anywhere on the pop-up screen to close this window. To see if there is an update for Live 4.0, you will need your serial number. Visit www.ableton.com and click on "downloads," then simply follow the instructions for downloading and installing the latest version. Or you can use "Check for Updates" in the Live Help menu if your computer is currently online. We recommend checking for updates as often as your time and interest allow. Updates seem to be posted approximately once a quarter. Ableton remains ambitious about tracking down even the smallest bugs in Live and posting software updates. Their user forum (click on "forum") is also of value and is a great place to pick up new tips, suggest ideas to Ableton, trade songs, and network with other Live users. (See Figure 3.1.) Be sure to sign up for Ableton's newsletter to be alerted to all major updates and general Ableton news and events.

Copy Protection

Ableton uses a challenge-response authentication system to protect Live from the ills of software piracy. Many companies are employing this method now because of both its effectiveness in deterring illegal copying and its ease for

Figure 3.3

This screen will confirm which version of Live you are currently working in. After you update your copy of Live, follow the steps described in Updating Live to make sure that the new version is running properly. You may need to swap out old desktop or dock shortcut icons because they will continue to point to (launch) the old version of the product.

the customer. I like it because you really don't even need to rely on the original system disk, which can become scratched or broken. With this system, you could be in the middle of a tour, notice a new update online, click on Live's About menu and jot down your serial number. Live 4.0 keeps track of all challenge and response codes internally, as does Ableton's database.

Here's how it works. After installing and launching Live you will be asked to enter a serial number. Live will then generate a unique (specific to your machine) number that coincides with your serial number. This new number is your challenge number. If you're connected to the Internet, simply click on "Authenticate" and Live will handle all of the challenging and responding invisibly—behind the scenes. This can also be done via e-mail. In fact, you have ten days to complete this authentication procedure before Live will not operate. If for some reason you don't have access to the Internet (if, for example, the computer with Live on it does not have a modem), you can obtain this information via fax or phone. You can then manually plug Ableton's response number into Live when the authentication dialog box emerges. Note: Live will only ask for this information immediately after the first installation, after major hardware upgrades, or until the information is provided within the first ten days.

Should you encounter problems authorizing Live 4.0, write a kind note to support@ableton.com and you will get an answer soon.

Basic Computer Specifications

When buying a computer, you're often faced with a dilemma centered around brand, timing, processor speed, and a ridiculous number of options. You can spend your entire life chasing processor speeds, and faster CD-R drives. Our feeling is that it is more important to get a functional machine rather than bending-edge technology that may or may not be 100 percent stable. Here is a list of the most important considerations when buying a PC, Mac, or laptop for using Ableton's Live 4.0 software.

Processor Speed

It is in our very nature to want the fastest and most efficient processor available. Business folks want to spend less time waiting for massive data crunching, musicians want to hear fewer digital "hiccups" in their music. Two or three years ago, a case could be made that Pentium III may have completely out-clocked a Pentium II, or now that the 1.5 GHz G4 PowerBooks have arrived, they should be light years ahead of last year's 500 MHz. This is not always the case, however, and although faster may be better, don't spend all of your time chasing processor speeds. Trust us, it can be an expensive proposition. Instead, set your sights just below the industry top dogs. For example, at the time of this writing, the 3.6 GHz PC chips and dual 2 GHz are the PC and Mac (respectively) top performers. Ableton Live doesn't necessarily require this kind of processor speed to perform basic functions. Sure there are limitations, and contrary to popular belief, there always will be. So instead of spending $3500 (or more) on your next industry champion, take a step back, save several hundred dollars, and invest in a quality sound card and a pair of professional speakers. Your music will be better for it.

Hard Drives

Fast hard drives, on the other hand, are essential. Say what you want about processor speeds, when recording audio, your hard drive spin and data throughput are terrifically important. Most drives run at 7200 RPM these days, but be wary of buying one of those 5400 RPM internal or USB hard drives. As for seek time, 9 milliseconds or less is the maximum I would tolerate. Super fast SCSI hard drives are the best option if money is no object, but I find that 7200 RPM FireWire or internal ATA/IDE drives are plenty fast enough for most mono and stereo recording and overdubbing.

RAM

In Live, most of your short samples (less than 5 MB) will sit in RAM as opposed to on the hard disk. Any samples used in your virtual instruments must also occupy memory space. 1 Gigabyte should be plenty for any serious computer musician, though more is always better if you've got the cash. You can make it with 256 MB for a while, but more RAM will help to ensure stability during live performances as well as help if you have other applications or plug-ins running in the background or in complement with Live.

Cache

Cache is generally thought of as ultra-fast RAM that handles mission-critical data even closer to the hardware level of a computer. The amount of cache and speed of the motherboard can enhance overall system performance. Laptop users want to be particularly careful not to get jilted out of their cache. Since it is pricey, many resellers will diminish its importance. Most of Macintosh's Titanium G4 Powerbooks now ship with Level 3 cache. When talking about cache, you will also hear talk of bus speed, which refers to the speed limits of your CPU's circuitry. Most Mac motherboards these days are clocking in at around 100 to 133MHz, while the PCs clock in at 400MHz, which is plenty fast enough for Ableton Live.

Audio Interface Specs

No piece of hardware is more important in determining the audio quality of your work than your audio interface. Almost invariably, the audio capabilities that come standard with your PC or Mac are lacking. Depending upon your needs and budget, you will want to either replace your computer's audio hardware or add a second interface to your system. Audio interfaces can connect in several different ways. PCI cards for desktop computers and PCMCIA (CardBus) cards for laptops are thought of as internal sound cards, while USB, FireWire (IEEE 1394), USB 2.0, and FireWire 800-connectable sound cards, can be thought of as external cards. Pro Tools TDM interfaces, in which the internal and external hardware are integrated, can be thought of as a combination of the two. Here are some items to consider:

What Kind of Audio Interface Should I Get?
Desktop computer users have the greatest number of choices when shopping for audio interfaces. These computers can normally accept PCI and PCI-X audio cards, external USB and FireWire connected interfaces, and hybrid internal/external audio solutions. PCI and PCI-X cards, which fit into slots inside your computer, will offer the best performance out of any format available. PCI offers high bandwidth and bus speeds which allow greater amounts of data (digital audio) to be passed back and forth between the CPU and interface.

The increase in speed and reliability of laptop computers has made them very attractive candidates for hosting Live. By running live from a portable computer, you have the convenience to take your instrument wherever you go, just like guitar, bass, saxophone, and harmonica players can. Also, since Live is a robust multi-track recording environment, a laptop gives you the ultimate remix and recording studio for the road or bedroom studio. We also like the fact that the laptop allows for and encourages spontaneous creativity, since your studio is never far from reach.

Laptops, due to their compact size, do not have room to accept PCI and PCI-X formatted audio interfaces. Instead, laptops are equipped with a PCMCIA, or CardBus, slot which allows small format cards to be added when necessary. Laptops also sport USB and, commonly, FireWire ports to facilitate the connection of external audio devices. FireWire and USB 2.0 are currently your best choices for low-latency audio. PCMCIA comes in second, while USB 1.x comes in a distant third. External sound cards are portable and efficient, but many feel that USB 1.x is just not fast enough. This is due to the fact that USB 1.x can transmit only up to 12 MB per second (Mbps) while FireWire and USB 2.0 cards push up to 30 or more Megabytes per second (called throughput). Playback is usually decent on USB cards because you are often just listening to a stereo mix (two channels), but when recording multiple tracks (more than three or four), USB 1.x can have some problems keeping up. You should consider carefully which applications (besides Ableton Live) you plan to use and then decide upon the best hardware platform. USB 1.x is fast enough for typical Ableton Live use, where typical is one or two inputs and a stereo output mix. Power users will want to take advantage of Live's multiple ins and outs (routing) to employ hardware mixers and outboard effects, and will therefore need an interface to support it.

How Many Outputs Do You Need?
The advantage to multiple outputs is an increased amount of control over your project. With Live, you may want to send drum and percussion tracks to outputs 1 and 2, while sending the vocals to output 3. These outputs are often routed through a hardware mixer (separate and apart from the computer). All sound cards that we are aware of provide at least two outputs as a stereo pair. Other common specs include 4, 6, and 8 outputs, and many provide outputs in other kinds of formats, such as S/PDIF (Sony/Phillips Digital Interface) and AES/EBU (Audio Engineering Society/European Broadcast Union) digital formats, analog XLR, RCA, and others. There are many different digital formats available, so always be sure the interface you get will work with the gear you currently have. If you have a keyboard with a coax S/PDIF connection, you won't want to buy an interface with an optical digital input—the two are not compatible.

How Many Inputs Do You Need?
Like outputs, the number of inputs you need will narrow the list of interfaces to consider. Generally, sound cards have a minimum of two input channels, a right and left input, summing into stereo. These can either be RCA, XLR, digital (S/PDIF or AES/EBU), or others (such as ADAT Lightpipe). Keep in mind that for more than two channels of input, FireWire, USB 2.0, and internal PCI and CardBus cards will be a more efficient means than USB 1.x in delivering the large amount of multi-track audio data to your hard drive.

Selecting the Right Sound Card

Road-worthy components, great sounding analog-to-digital converters, and responsive tech-support are the three most important qualities to consider when selecting your most vital piece of hardware outside of your computer: the sound card. Here is a short list of tried and true sound cards with quality, precision, and portability in mind.

M-Audio (www.m-audio.com)
M-Audio's Delta series has proven that professional specs can be affordable. (See Figures 3.4 and 3.5.) All of M-Audio's Delta series cards connect via PCI, and support the leanest audio drivers (ASIO and Core Audio); however, M-Audio's latest (2004) devices introduce FireWire connectivity. (See Figure 3.6.) FireWire is an excellent solution for laptop users as it offers an expanded bandwidth while maintaining the convenience of USB. Mobile users can now take advantage of multi-channel audio for previewing tracks or routing outputs to a mixing desk. M-Audio is a company committed to Live like no other; they are Live's U.S. distributor.

Figure 3.4

The Delta series of M-Audio audio cards are made with a variety of input, output, and MIDI options. They are both affordable and well supported. The Audiophile 2496, pictured here, is the Honda Civic of audio cards.

Figure 3.5

The Delta 1010 pictured is a powerful professional audio card that can handle eight analog inputs and outputs and an additional stereo input via S/PDIF. The pictured front and back rack-space portion of the unit, like many breakout boxes of this type, connects to the additional PCI card inside your computer (seen on top of rack unit).

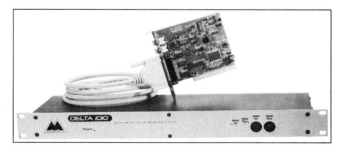

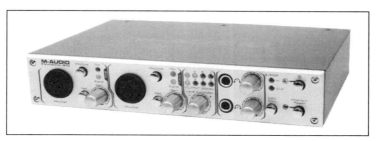

Figure 3.6

The FireWire 410 presents an excellent mobile solution for laptop users. The FireWire connection provides high-bandwidth and low-latency and can power the unit when connected to a 6-pin port.

Echo Audio (www.echoaudio.com)

With their newly revamped product line, Echo has its eye on the pro-audio crowd. With 24-bit/96 kHz sampling, the Layla line of desktop and laptop sound cards has garnered some excellent reviews. Echo's Layla24 and Gina24 are similar in design to M-Audio's Delta 1010 (seen in Figure 3.6), with professional hardware drivers and plenty of input/output options. If these boxes are too expensive for your budget, you might want to take a peek at their newest product line, the Indigo series, which is an inexpensive ($129 and up), high-end prosumer level PCMCIA card that could easily support small clubs or informal editing sessions. Indigo has two eighth-inch mirrored stereo outputs and ASIO drivers. (See Figure 3.7.) The Indigo DJ is specially suited for use with live as its additional output allows you to preview clips before sending them to the dance floor. The Indigo I/O ("I/O" means the card handles both input and output) swaps the second output pair from the DJ for an analog input pair.

Figure 3.7

Echo Audio's Indigo series audio cards provide consumer level audio support that is both inconspicuous and simple. No MIDI or digital transfer is supported, but what do you want for a couple hundred bucks?

RME Hammerfall (www.rme-audio.com)

As we prepped to write *Ableton Live 4.0 Power!*, Hammerfall's Multiface (Figure 3.8a front and 3.8b back) turned up again and again as the sound card most preferred by laptop aficionados. It has too many capabilities to list here, but if you are looking for a solid, professional solution, you will not be disappointed. The Digiface and Multiface breakout boxes (external audio interfaces with multiple inputs and outputs) add an exceptional level of professional audio support and flexibility to laptop producers, and connect via the RME's CardBus connection. For stand-alone PCs and Macintosh, RME offers a PCI interface, so that you can transfer either of the above two breakout boxes to laptop or your home/studio computer. RME has done a commendable job of making sure all possible digital formats are covered.

Digigram (www.digigram.com)

The "Pocket" series by Digigram is a family of pro-level cards that, as the name says, are small enough to fit in your pocket, though you really should just put them in your laptop card slot. Newer Digigram units feature on-board processing, which can really take the load off of a strained processor and free up headroom for more audio content. One other advantage to

Figure 3.8a

RME makes the most flexible, and possibly the most professional, laptop audio card on the market.

Figure 3.8b

The back of the multi-face. There are connections for eight inputs and outputs, S/PDIF, ADAT, word clock synchronization and more. Multiface is your top-of-the-line studio on the go.

Figure 3.9

Digigram makes several similar-looking cardslot pro-audio soundcards for laptops. The PCXpocket 440 supports onboard effects, which can take a good deal of the audio effect processing load off of the laptop CPU. Extra reverb, anyone?

Digigram's products is that the CardBus design (pictured in Figure 3.9), like Echo Audio's hobbyist-oriented Indigos (see Figure 3.7), is contained inside the laptop. There is nothing else to carry, power-up, or break as the case may be. Digigram's less expensive "pocket" series cards are known to sound great and are simple enough to use.

Aside from the above-mentioned sound cards, Emu (www.emu.com), Aardvark (www.aardvarkaudio.com), and Edirol (www.edirol.com) all make professional-level sound card products. It almost goes without saying that times change quickly and new technology emerges. So keep your eye on the latest reviews in magazines such as *Computer Music, Remix, Mix, Electronic Musician, Keyboard, EQ*, and non-biased Web sites such as Harmony Central (www.harmonycentral.com) for fresh product info. Also, it is extremely important to continually check your sound card manufacturer's Web site to be sure you have the latest audio drivers. Current and correct audio drivers can make a world of difference in how your software performs in your system. Depending upon your hardware vendor, drivers may be updated as frequently as once a month or more. Don't just trust that the included CD (that ships with your soundcard) has the most recent drivers. These CDs are usually packaged well before the final tweaks to driver software are finished, and well in advance of software innovations.

What Do You Need to Know About ASIO Drivers?

ASIO (Audio Stream Input/Output) was first invented by German software-slinger Steinberg (www.steinberg.de or www.cubase.net). Originally, ASIO drivers were created to help musicians and producers using Cubase to digitally record multi-track audio with minimal amount of time lag within their digital system. This time lag can be a real buzz-kill and is called *latency*. Latency occurs because the sound you are recording is forced to travel through your operating system, your system bus, and host application to end up on your hard drive. Like bad plumbing, the signal may be coming down the pipe, but there are unnecessary clogs and corners that must be navigated along the way. The gist is that your computer is performing calculations (remember, it's all numbers for the computer) and, though they are blazingly fast, it takes a moment for the processor to do so, and the result is latent.

Live 4.0 supports ASIO on both Mac OS 9.2 and PCs (ASIO is unnecessary on Mac OS X thanks to Core Audio). You'll be happy to know that most popular consumer and professional-grade audio cards support the format, too. It has become an industry standard, thanks to the fact that it works cross-platform (both Macs and PCs) and can cut latency down to barely detectable levels. Properly installed, ASIO drivers will make Live as responsive as a hardware instrument with less then eight milliseconds of audio delay. ASIO helps Live users hear the instantaneous results of MIDI commands, audio input/output, mouse moves, and keyboard commands. Someday we'll all look back and laugh that latency was ever an issue, but for now, count your blessings that there is ASIO. See the "Setting Preferences in Live" section later in this chapter for more on the infamous "L-word."

Choosing a MIDI Interface

Nothing makes playing Live 4.0 more rewarding than cranking real knobs and watching virtual faders move (or perhaps I should say *hearing* them move). You can move virtual faders, adjust the amount of effects and their settings, modify the tempo, and do just about anything else you can imagine, all by using a MIDI interface. Those wishing to exploit the power of Live's new MIDI sequencing features will also require a good MIDI control device. In the next section, we will take a look at several portable, affordable, yet full-featured MIDI controllers—a product category that has grown exponentially over the last couple of years.

One controller commonly found in use by Live users is the Evolution X-Session controller (Figure 3.10). This compact device is especially suited for Live as it sports a DJ-style crossfader among its 16 other controls. The ten programmable buttons also function perfectly as scene select and launch controls. You'll find it extremely easy to map filters, delays, feedbacks, and other parameters to the knobs for instant tweaking; plus it will fit just about anywhere. Take a look at the setup of either Junkie XL or Sasha and you'll see the X-Session staring back at you.

Figure 3.10
The X-Session is the choice for anyone seeking to dominate Live's crossfader.

Figure 3.11
Knobby Control features what else? Knobs! Eight to be exact. These come in handy with a program like Live and just like Live, Knobby can be updated on the fly.

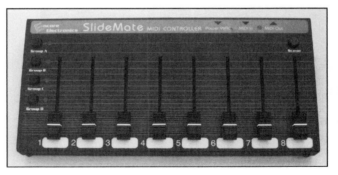

Figure 3.12
SlideMate's eight live-programmable sliders will comfort those missing their old analog desks (mixers). Slidemate programming is nearly identical to Knobby above, though some Live tweakers may want both.

Encore Electronics, www.encorelectronics.com, makes several basic MIDI-Controllers. The two shown here, Knobby Control in Figure 3.11 and SlideMate in Figure 3.12, are perfect for small stage setups, tight budgets, and minimizing programming hassle. Both the Knobby and the SlideMate can be programmed via a computer and can also send SysEX (system exclusive) messages—a great asset for those hard to reach MIDI parameters.

German-based Doepfer, www.doepfer.de, makes a mean blend of quality controllers with customizable parameters and a small footprint for inconspicuous fader-flippin'. The Pocket Dial's (Figure 3.13) endless rotary knobs make tweaking Live a blast. You can grab or turn a knob and not have to worry about its previous placement. 1-10 or 0-10 knobs can limit the creative possibilities in a program such as Live by causing unwanted spikes in whatever parameter you are adjusting. Endless rotary allows you to pick up wherever the value is at a given time, and modify it from that point. Of course, endless faders are not really an option, but Pocket Fader, pictured in Figure 3.14, helps to migrate software-based remixes to your desktop.

Figure 3.13

Our personal experience with Pocket Dial has been nothing short of a joy. Its small footprint and 16 knobs times 4 banks for 64 accessible presets make Pocket Dial one of the best all-around options where inexpensive MIDI-controllers are concerned.

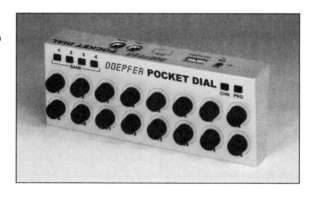

Figure 3.14

Fade outs and volume swells never really feel that great on a mouse, not to mention that it is hard to control multiple tracks (unless you are creating an aux bus). Pocket Fader is specifically designed to handle these kinds of tasks.

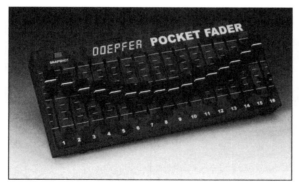

The FaderFox controllers are so compact and functional you'd think they came from James Bond's arsenal of gadgets. No larger than a guitar stomp box, the Micromodul LV1 and LX1 (Figure 3.15) are designed specifically with Live in mind, allowing control of the Session Mixer and Clip Slot Grid (both of which are discussed in Chapter 4). These self-powered units use standard MIDI connections, so you'll need a MIDI interface. A one-port

Figure 3.15
There are obviously some Ableton Live fans over at FaderFox.

interface will suffice, as the modules can be daisy-chained together. These controllers may soon be distributed in the US, but in the meantime you can order one directly from the manufacturer at www.faderfox.de.

The above MIDI-controllers begin to give you an idea of what is available for just a couple hundred bucks (or less). Virtually any MIDI controller, including MIDI-based Mixers, can work with Live. You can assign sliders, knobs, or faders in an infinite amount of creatively rewarding ways. In Chapter 5, we explore specific ways of making a MIDI map. There are literally millions of possibilities. Imagine mapping these controllers to adjust panning, effects, tempo, crossfader, frequency filters, EQ settings, and on and on.

MIDI Connectivity

Midi Controllers usually connect in one of two ways, either via USB or through your audio interface (if MIDI input is supported). Earlier, when we discussed USB for audio, I suggested steering clear of USB and recommended FireWire, PCI, or PCMCIA (on a laptop) when looking for a reliable audio card. With MIDI, however, USB is a safer route because MIDI information is much less cumbersome than digital audio when traveling over your system bus. MIDI information is so small that it can even be transmitted over serial port, but in recent times, we have become accustomed to pairing MIDI-controller information and digital audio through the same card. If your sound card does not support MIDI, USB is an efficient means to interface. Several companies, including Edirol and Midiman (the same company as M-Audio) make simple little single-input MIDI connectors, such as the UM-1S and Midisport (pictured in Figures 3.16 and 3.17, respectively).

Figure 3.16

UM-1S is a simple USB MIDI port that will allow you to quickly route your new sassy MIDI-controller or MIDI keyboard into Live 4.0.

Figure 3.17

Midiman has been making MIDI connectivity devices for as long as I can remember—well, at least since around the time MIDI was invented in 1984.

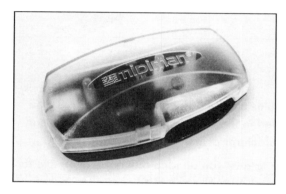

Figure 3.18

The design and release of Oxygen8 created quite a splash among laptop studio owners and other MIDI-happy musicians concerned with overall space.

One of the most popular combination MIDI-keyboard/controllers to hit the market was M-Audio's Oxygen8 (Figure 3.18). The original unit was cheaply made, with less than optimal controller knobs, but it represents the merging of two similar worlds (keyboard and MIDI controller), and has inspired competitors like Edirol to release their own knob-and-fader keyboard conglomerates, the PCR-30 (Figure 3.19) and the PCR-50. In response, M-Audio has attempted to outdo itself by releasing an improved version of the Oxygen8,

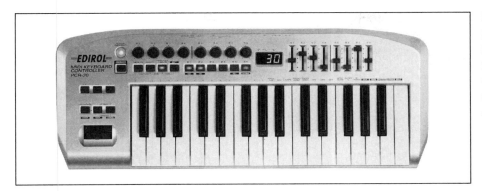

Figure 3.19
Edirol's hybrid PCR-30 sports keys, faders, and knobs, and is really made for musicians who think small, at least in terms of their desk (studio) size.

called Ozone, which also features a mic preamp and audio interface. As you can see, the only thing certain about the future is change.

Setting Preferences in Live

Optimizing Live 4.0's preferences is essential for smooth operation. You see, preferences are more than merely your personal whims about how you would like Live's interface to be colored, or where your files are automatically saved. Preferences are your primary control center for fine-tuning Live's ability to actually work in your customized computer/audio environment. From the Preferences menu, you will be able to control default loop traits, audio and MIDI interface settings, and audio/MIDI latency settings. Sound like too much to manage? Read on, and let's tame this beast. To call up the Preferences dialog box on a PC or Mac running OS 9.2, select Options > Preferences; on a Mac running OS X, select Live > Preferences. The emerging dialog box contains five tabs: Audio, MIDI/Sync, Plug-ins, Defaults, and Misc. We will discuss them in order, so click on the Audio tab if you are not already there.

The Audio Tab

The first section you will likely get to know is the Audio tab in Preferences seen in Figure 3.20. This tab's pull down menus and options will depend largely on what kind of sound card you have, whether it is correctly installed, and the operating system you are using. In Figure 3.20, you will see that we are using an Echo Audio card (an Indigo PCMCIA card to be exact) with ASIO drivers on the PC. It says "ASIO Echo WDM" because it is using the Echo audio driver.

Figure 3.20

Audio preferences will be revisited often as you seek out the perfect latency settings and audio interface setup.

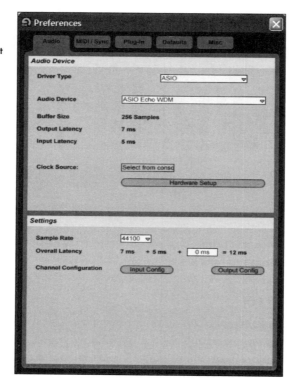

Driver Type and Audio Device

The first menu in this section allows you to choose the Driver Type you wish to use for your audio interface. On the PC, options will include MME/DirectX and ASIO, Mac OS 9 users will have Sound Manager and ASIO as selections, and Mac OS X will feature Core Audio. Once you select the Driver Type you wish to use, you will have a selection of audio devices to choose from in the second menu.

You may not find the audio device you wish to use when using certain driver types. For example, the built-in audio cards on laptop computers don't support ASIO, so you'll only find these cards listed when MME/DirectX is selected for Driver Type.

Please note that Live will always seek out the audio interface last saved in Preferences each time the program launches. If Live cannot find the sound card, such as when you have unplugged or swapped it out, Live will still launch, but with no audio enabled. In this instance, you will see a small warning message mentioning that Live cannot find the audio card and that audio will be "disabled" upon startup. You will also notice a second red warning on Live's actual interface (after the program launches) that says "The audio engine is off. Please choose an audio device from the Audio Preferences." After you do this, you will again be ready to set up Live for audio.

Buffer Size

You may or may not be able to adjust your sound card's Buffer Size from this Preferences menu. Most ASIO and other sound cards need to be accessed directly through their own driver interface which can be launched with the "Hardware Setup" button. If you are using a standard or consumer-level audio interface, such as Apple Core Audio or DirectX, you will see a buffer slider here. The lower your Buffer Size setting is (in samples), the less latency you'll experience, but more potential problems can arise. In other words, too much Buffer will increase the amount of undesirable latency, yet too little latency will most often result in your system choking and wheezing in the form of digital pops, audio dropouts, and the like. In the next section, we will take this latency discussion up a level and give you a couple ideas for possible workarounds.

Latency Settings

Latency: there is that dirty word again. Here is how to approach optimizing your Live software to work with your computer and sound card to achieve the least amount of audio latency. First, recognize that there is output latency, input latency, and MIDI latency. Each type of latency imposes a different kind of problem, and while there are some ways to combat these timing issues, zero-latency is still not really a viable option for applications reliant upon an operating system (such as Windows or Mac OS 9, OS X). Realize also that latency is designed to be a buffer for when you put extra strain on your system and your CPU is having trouble keeping up with all of the demanded processes.

Output latency is the amount of lag time between when you trigger a sound or action and when you hear it. Or if you add an effect, such as distortion or reverb, the extra time that it takes to actually hear that sound is output latency. Do not confuse this output latency with Clip Update Rate, described below. For instance, if your Clip Update Rate is set for 1/4 note, you may hear a small (1/4 note or less) pause before hearing many of Live's clip effects even with output latencies of only a few milliseconds. This can be remedied in the ways we'll discuss later.

⁂ **Who Dunnit?**

Many people blame their software for their latency problems, and this is just simply not the case. Another tip for hunting down latency issues is to make sure your audio interface (sound card) has been adjusted to the best possible settings, which can be done via Window's Control Panel, Mac OS X's System Preferences panel (click on Sound), or Mac OS 9.2's Control Panel > Sound. Try lowering your buffer settings to reduce the audible latency until you experience dropouts, digital pops, or other system-related problems. Then raise the buffer to just above the level where the problems occur and record your track. You may need to increase the buffer again when starting the editing/mixdown process. Some ASIO audio interfaces (RME for instance) do not support Sound Manager (in Mac OS 9.2), and will not show up in the Control Panel. If this is the case, you must use the audio interface's own ASIO drivers' "Settings" utility.

You can stress test your system for latency and alleviate the above-mentioned confusion. Here are the steps for the stress test:

1 Click on the Misc tab, and turn your clip update rate to 1/32 (1/32-note timing).

2 Load a decent size audio clip, preferably a stark drum loop, into the session view.

3 Load several Live effects and audio clips until your CPU meter in the upper right-hand corner reaches about 70 percent of capacity.

4 Then, while slowly reducing the Output Buffer Size, listen for pops or clicks in the audio. Adjust your final setting to a comfortable level above the popping level. Note, this buffer size may need to be adjusted from your sound card's settings or, if it is not grayed out, can be set in the Preferences' Audio tab.

Don't be surprised if you can get your latency time extremely low and detect no discernible latency. It is there all the time, but often miniscule when using ASIO, WDM, or Core Audio drivers, which is why these driver types are preferred.

Input latency arises for the same reasons as output latency. Audio is buffered on the way in to the computer, so Live receives this audio a little later than it should. Fortunately, Live knows it's behind and it takes this into account when recording. The result is a take that is recorded in time. When input latency starts becoming a problem, though, is when you try to monitor audio *through* Live. Now the audio has to pass through the input buffers, through Live and any potential effects that may be loaded, and back to the output buffers before it can reach your ear. Keeping your buffer settings as low as possible will keep this "double" latency to a minimum.

Most professional audio cards, like the ones mentioned above, feature "direct monitoring" which helps alleviate some of the problems of recording

with latency. Instead of having Live blend your input signal with its output signal and buffering it to the audio card, the audio card will blend your input
signal with the output from Live so the input signal doesn't have to travel all
the way through the computer and back out again. The result is instantaneous monitoring of your input signal—no latency. The drawback is that you
will not be able to use effects on a direct monitored signal since the audio
signal is not being sent from the computer. The audio interface simply routes
the input right to the output.

Audio interfaces are designed to report their latencies to Live so it can offset
its operations properly. However, in the case that a device reports its times
improperly, Live gives you the option to add or remove time from the overall
latency calculation by changing the value in the small data entry box.

MIDI latency can be divided into two camps, synchronization problems and
MIDI triggering delays. The latter has nearly disappeared with wide adapta-
tion of Steinberg's ASIO technology and the recent integration of Windows
WDM drivers in Windows 2000 and XP, plus the advent of AMS in Mac
OS X. MIDI sync issues will be covered in the MIDI/Sync Tab section below.

Sample Rate
The Sample Rate setting in the Audio preferences tab will determine the
recording quality of both Live's output and recorded input. A good basic
sample rate to start out with is 44,100, or 44.1kHz. As you learn more
about digital audio, or if you are pro already, the Sample Rate dropdown
box will give you a multitude of friendly choices. I never recommend using
anything lower than 44,100, but if you are long on system resources (including hard drive space), you might experiment with 96,000 or 192,000 so
long as your audio interface can handle it.

Channel Configuration
When you make music in Live, you have to send it to the outside world somehow. For simple audio interfaces, Live will automatically set this up for you
by sending a stereo master output to your audio interfaces master output;
however, if you have the good fortune to have an audio interface that supports multiple outputs, then you can take advantage of that here. In Chapter
13, "Playing Live...Live," we will talk about how to capitalize on Live's cueing ability via sound cards with multiple outputs. Also, if you have the option
of digital or analog output, this is the place to set up that output.

The MIDI/Sync Tab

This brings us to the second Preferences tab, shown in Figure 3.21, the MIDI/Sync tab. This is where we will specify which of our MIDI devices will serve as remote controls, MIDI inputs and outputs, and sources for synchronization; however, if you are not planning on synchronizing Live to work with a hardware or software MIDI sequencer, then some of the MIDI/Sync parameters will not be of much interest. The tab is divided into three subsections, MIDI Control, MIDI Synchronization, and MIDI Timecode. Beginners will want to step right up and tackle the MIDI control box, which is the place to assign any of the toys discussed in the "Choosing a MIDI Interface" section earlier in this chapter.

Active Devices

These two tables show a list of the MIDI input and output devices available on your computer. Each device is preceded by a square button which may be used to enable or disable the various ports. Click the button to toggle its

Figure 3.21

The MIDI/Sync tab found in Live's Preferences box. This is the logical place to handle how Live works with MIDI and syncs to the outside world and to resolve MIDI timing issues.

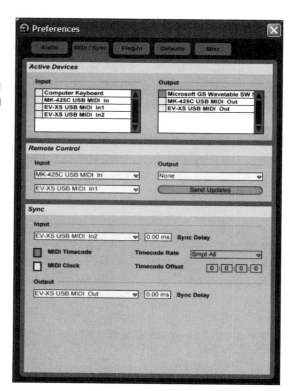

state; green is on and gray is off. Any MIDI device you wish to use with Live will need to be enabled here before it will be listed in any of Live's menus.

Remote Control

Live 4.0 allows for two MIDI devices to be used as remote controls for functions in Live. Remote control is used for assigning MIDI controllers to Live's mixer knobs and sliders and for linking MIDI notes to clips and buttons. Controls that can be commanded from MIDI can be easily discovered by clicking the MIDI button in the upper-right corner of the Live window. Anything that becomes superimposed with a blue box is a device that can be controlled via MIDI. You'll see that even the MIDI button itself can be controlled by MIDI!

Live also provides the ability to apply feedback to motorized MIDI controllers. If you have a control surface with motorized faders/knobs, you can choose that device from the Output menu of this section. Any time a fader or knob is moved on screen, Live will cause the associated control on the MIDI device to move as well. If, for some reason, the controls on screen don't match those on the control surface, press the Send Updates button to refresh the control surface with Live's current control values.

Sync

MIDI synchronization is a two-way street. Live can either drive or be driven. To drive Live from an external device, you will want to either send MIDI Timecode (MTC) or MIDI Clock (also called MIDI Beat Clock—MBC). The difference between MIDI Timecode and MIDI Clock is simple: MIDI Timecode is location information expressed in hours, minutes, seconds, and frames; while MIDI Clock is tempo, measure, and beat information, such as beat 1 of measure 5, moving at 120 beats per minute. MIDI Clock is best for interconnecting sequencers. It is also most useful when synchronizing two or more Live users as the tempo and beat location will be matched between all of the computers.

Most often, MIDI Timecode is used when syncing to an external hardware (or occasionally software) video device. While Live can do this type of work, it may be best used when run in tandem with any one of a number of programs adept at video work. In other words, we would recommend syncing Live to that application, also called running Live in slave mode. This is not to be confused with running Live in ReWire mode which is a form of audio and MIDI synchronization that runs transparently between two ReWire enhanced software applications. For more info on this, see Chapter 12, "ReWire."

When choosing the MIDI input port, you are also allowed to choose which type of sync Live will read, either MIDI Timecode or MIDI Clock. If you choose MIDI Timecode, you'll need to specify the Timecode Rate by choosing from the menu. You can also add a Timecode Offset if needed.

If you decide to use Live as the master clock source (other devices will receive their clock positions from Live), you'll need to choose an output port for the MIDI Clock. Unlike the incoming timecode options, Live can transmit only MIDI Clock.

In both cases, you may experience a slight misalignment when using sync. The Sync Delay value may be adjusted to bring Live and the external device into accurate sync with one another. For the best results, synchronize one machine at a time, using a process of elimination to figure out the hardware or software (usually the problem) culprit. Also, don't forget to try swapping out MIDI cables. They can easily go bad and will make you crazy if you don't check on them.

Hint: we have found that it is easier to sync two similar computers, such as two Mac Powerbooks of the same speed as opposed to a Dell and a Mac or some such other combination. Also, it is worth noting that when syncing machines, we usually have to give the second machine a negative value. The best results we have found after much trial and error is to activate the click tracks on both machines, with the preferences open, and then reduce the one machine's delay sync into negative territory. With luck on your side, you should hear the click tracks begin to flange or sound out of phase. This means they are sitting virtually on top of one another, or, right in sync.

Recently, when attempting this with a friend, we used two Mac Powerbooks, one with no sync delay (the master) and the slave with a sync delay of about −100ms. If you are attempting to sync hardware, you will want to adjust Live's delay, as many machines won't have a similar sync delay function.

The Plug-in Tab
Pictured in Figure 3.22 is the Plug-in tab. Here you can set preferences for displaying plug-ins and mapping out Live's VST and Audio Units plug-in folders.

Window Handling
The first two options determine how Live will display a plug-in's custom display window. When "Multiple Plug-In Windows" is activated, it will be possible to open more than one plug-in window at a time. When this is off, open

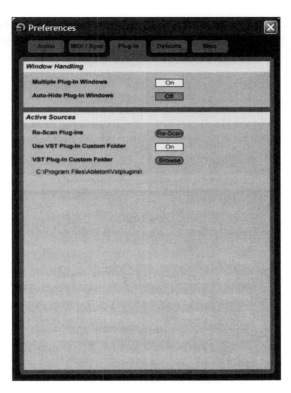

Figure 3.22
The Plug-in Tab allows customization of window han-
dling and plug-in location.

plug-in windows will be closed any time a new one is open. Keeping this option off can help minimize screen clutter.

The second option, Auto-Hide Plug-In Windows will make plug-in windows appear only for those plug-ins loaded on a selected track. For example, if you have a MIDI Track loaded with an instance of Native Instrument's Battery and another MIDI Track with LinPlug Albino, Battery will be hidden when the Albino track is selected and Albino will be hidden when the Battery track is selected. This can also help minimize screen clutter, especially useful for laptop users.

Active Sources
The VST and Audio Units (Mac OS X only) plug-in folders can be set to any folder on your machine that holds VST or Audio Units effects and instruments compatible with Live. The only sure way to know if Live is compatible with a plug-in is to try it out. To do this, place the plug-in in the appropriate folder and click the Re-Scan button. If you can see the new device listed in the plug-in section of Live's Browser, then chances are Live will at least be able to

load the plug-in. Live will occasionally not work with some plug-ins, possibly because they are incompletely developed. If this occurs, please do everyone a favor and send in a quick bug report to both Ableton and the third-party plug-in developer. Each time Live is started, the program scans your system for new VST and Audio Units plug-ins in the designated locations. If you notice an unusually long startup time (an extended view of Live's splash screen), you may have added a large number of new plug-ins, or unintentionally added an incompatible device that is having trouble "talking" to Live.

The Default Tab

Preference's Defaults tab (seen below in Figure 3.23) will likely be a place you visit as you discover your own preferences for working in Live.

Live Set

The Save button is used to save the current Live Set as the default or template Set that will be loaded each time Live is launched. This can be helpful for pre-

Figure 3.23

Live will automatically open loops the way you like once you tame the Default tab in Live's Preferences. Your settings in this tab will likely change as you experiment with how you most often use Live.

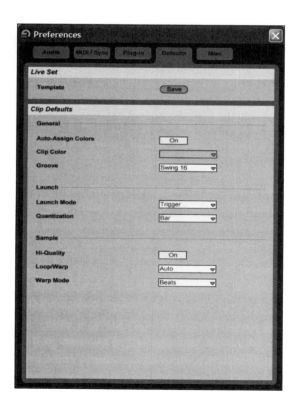

configuring commonly used settings such as MIDI assignments, input and output routing, and common effect patchwork (such as EQs on every channel). Note that at this time, you can save only one template in this Preferences tab. For additional templates, I recommend that you create a Live set folder called "templates," and save empty, yet configured, Live sets there.

Clip Defaults
The remainder of the Default screen determines the settings applied to a new clip when it is created in Live. As you begin performing with Live and have a chance to build a few practice sets, take note of how you tend to configure your clips. Are you always setting them to Tones mode? Do you prefer 1/4 note quantization? You can specify any of these parameters as defaults in the following sections.

General
First up are the Auto-Assign Colors toggle switch and the Default Clip Color selector. With Auto-Assign Colors on, Live will randomly choose a color for each new clip or recording. These colors can be changed at any time in a screen called Clip View, which will be covered later in the book. If Auto-Assign Colors is off, the Default Clip Color comes into play by determining which color Live will default to for all new audio. Of course, color will not affect the sound and is strictly a matter of preference.

The last option determines the Groove template associated with a clip. Groove Templates allow you to produce subtle or drastic re-quantization of audio and MIDI by offsetting certain beats to create different feels. See Chapter 6 for a detailed explanation of how to get your Groove on.

Launch
When triggering a clip to play, Live gives us some options known as Launch Modes. The full run-down on these modes can be found in Chaper 5. For now, we recommend leaving the mode on Trigger or Toggle.

The idea of launch quanitization is to force your performance to fit into the time grid of the current piece. Any time you launch a sample in Live (called a Clip), you have the option of launching it on the "one" of the next bar, or every second bar, every fourth bar, every eighth bar, or by picking a note quantifier to begin playback on the very next 1/32, 1/16, 1/8, 1/4, or 1/2 note after you trigger the sample. Of course this is a grand selection of choices and the right selection can depend upon the type of sound you are launching. For instance, an orchestral or ambient guitar sound might not

need as strict a quantization as a conga or cowbell loop. You can also opt
to turn Quantization off by default by selecting None from this dropdown
dialog box, or the safest bet for novice and/or careful Live musicians is
to select Global, which will assume the same quantization setting as the
project—a good way to keep every sound in line.

Sample

You will also want to pay attention to the Hi Quality default toggle button,
which (when activated) will make Live use a more complicated algorithm
when calculating Live's loop warping attributes. The reason to not use Hi
Quality is simple; it demands a bit more system resources and, when applied
to all of your loops, can really create a noticeable CPU spike. You can also
opt to leave Hi Quality off as a default setting, yet still use it on select loops
by double clicking on a clip and adjusting its clip settings—more on this is
found in Chapter 6.

The Loop/Warp menu is used to determine the default state of a new clip, be
it a loop or a one-shot sound. The Auto setting will cause Live to try and
determine the nature of an imported loop on the fly and set its loop and
warp settings accordingly.

Warp Mode, the next and last item on the Defaults tab list, is another story
entirely. In Live 4.0, there are four warp modes. The original product, Live
1.5, treated every loop as a beat, which can be problematic when treating
melodies, basses, drones, ambient textures, and, well, just about anything
without a well-defined percussive texture. Here is a DJ style breakdown of
the four warp modes in Live. This is a topic central to understanding how
Live works and will be revisited in chapters to follow. Remember, these are
merely the defaults; all can be changed once the clip is loaded in Live.

  * **Beats Mode:** Beats mode is the original Live warp mode. The program auto-
    matically breaks up the loop into sections determined by the Transients set-
    tings. For instance, Live can divide a loop into 1/32 notes, 1/16 notes, 1/8
    notes, 1/4 notes, 1/2 notes, and full measures. As long as the sound is rhyth-
    mic and fairly short in duration, Live does an impeccable job of making the
    loop sound as though it were recorded at your project tempo. Drum loops,
    dance grooves, and percussive instrument loops (bass, short synth, turntables,
    or funk guitars), can all be convincingly stretched in beat mode.

  * **Tones Mode:** This is the mode for bass and keyboard lines, melodies, pitched
    sounds that are not necessarily grooving in perfect time with a metronome, such
    as a legato horn line or harmonic chord progression or even vocals.

❆ **Texture Mode:** For sounds more complex than melodies and rhythms, Ableton has brought us Texture Mode. This is the mode to use for ambient effects, atonal pads, and indefinable sounds. Texture Mode bears the distinction of further tweaking possibilities with Grain Size and Flux (fluctuation) controls. These two new parameters determine the intensity, severity, and randomness of Live's slicing. This can be an excellent sonic deconstructing tool for any kind of loop in addition to the ones mentioned.

❆ **RePitch Mode:** For loops that just can't be sliced, or for samples that offer the right attitude only when they are sounding their fattest, Ableton's RePitch Mode removes all pitch correction, yet still corrects the loop's tempo to fit into the piece at hand. Some loops may sound funny at their new pitch, but this is a sure-fire way of eliminating strange artifacts that can sometimes appear when retiming and repitching a loop simultaneously.

Also, Live 4.0 allows you to turn any of the above four modes off entirely. This means that the sample/loop is played back exactly as is, at its original tempo and pitch. This no-warping mode can be achieved by deselecting the warp button at the bottom of the clip view, and is the preferred mode (non-mode) to use when setting up your tracks for a DJ set. For more on DJing with Live, see Chapter 13.

The Misc Tab

Just because this tab is titled Misc, don't assume these parameters are extraneous. Each of the four sub-sections, Appearance, Behavior, Audio Recording, and Samples are important in creating a smooth Live environment.

Appearance

The Appearance section (seen in Figure 3.24) allows you to choose the skin for Live. 28 skins are provided with Live 4.0 and artists such as Monolake (www.monolake.de) are developing new ones all the time. To test out which scheme you like best, simply click on the Load Skin window in the Preferences dialog box, and use the up and down arrows on your keyboard to scroll though the options. If you download a new skin or two, place these inside the Skins folder. For PCs, the skins are located in the Resources folder in the Live directory. For Macs, skins can be found in the Ableton Content/Skins folder. To add skins to OS X, control-click the Live 4 application icon, select "Show Package Contents" and then open the folder Contents > App-Resource > Skins. Then place the newly downloaded skins here.

Figure 3.24

Live's Appearance section. These two menus allow for customization of Live's Skin and Language settings.

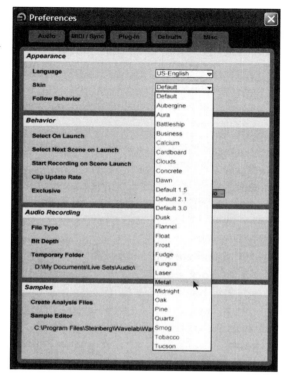

Also, it may be of interest to point out that Live's internal language settings, which affect its internal help menus, interface text, and informational messages, can be set to read in French, Spanish, and German as well as English. If you do not see one of these languages, you can visit the Ableton Web site and click on Download to find the Ableton Live application file with the languages you need.

The third option, Follow Behavior, determines the graphical style used when following the cursor (Now Line) in the Arrange and Clip views. When set to Scroll, the Now Line will stay in place while the window moves smoothly under it. When set to Page, the window will stay stationary while the Now Line moves. When the Now Line reaches the right edge of the screen, the

window jumps ahead so the Now Line appears again on the left. The Scroll
option is much harder on your CPU, so if you are experiencing dropouts or
sluggish response, set this option to Page.

Behavior
The second section, "Behavior," (Figure 3.25) determines how Live handles
loops once they are loaded (dragged or recorded) into Live. Select On
Launch will cause the Clip View of a newly added Clip to be displayed
immediately. This is useful when in the creation stage of your song as you'll
probably need to modify the new Clip to match all of your other pieces; however, when performing with Live, it may be more valuable to turn this option
off. During the performance stage, you've probably made all the adjustments necessary for a Clip and may wish to maintain a view of effects that
are loaded instead.

Select Next Scene On Launch greatly simplifies the performance of Live
Sessions. Any time a Scene is launched by keyboard or remote control, Live
will automatically advance the Scene selector to the one below it. If you've

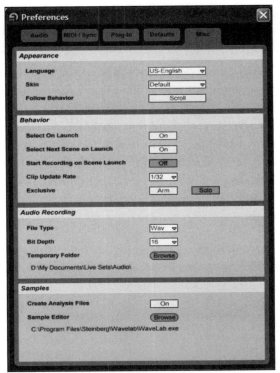

Figure 3.25
The Behavior section is for
specifying Live's treatment of
audio files.

already laid out the sections of your song in a top-to-bottom arrangement on the Session Grid, you can progress through the song with just one button.

Start Recording on Scene Launch determines if clips will begin recording when launched by a Scene. Having this option off will allow you to play an instrument live (track is armed for recording) while navigating through scenes. If this option is armed, a clip will begin to record in an armed track when the scene is launched. This can be powerful when used live by triggering a recording at a particular point in a piece. The recorded part can be instantly looped for building compositions in real time.

Clip Update Rate is the frequency with which Live re-calculates changes to the clip. For instance, if you transpose a clip in Live, while the Clip Update Rate is set to 1/32 note, you will hear nearly instant changes to the pitch of the loop in the clip. Conversely, choosing a Clip Update Rate of 1/4 note, or the even slower rate of "Bar" (meaning one update per measure), will result in changes occurring more slowly. This is meaningful during a live performance, in which changes may need to be heard as they happen instead of after the fact. For example, if you are working in the studio with Live, or if you're editing and noticing slow performance, turn down the Update Clip Rate to 1/4 note (its default setting), as seen in Figure 3.26. When performing, go for broke at 1/16 or 1/32 note settings.

The Exclusive buttons are used to determine the Live Mixer's behavior when engaging solos and arming tracks for recording. For example, when Solo Exclusive is on (green), only one track may be soloed at a time. If you click the solo button of another track, the previous track will have its solo status turned off. The same is true for Arm Exclusive. Only one track can be record-enabled when this button is active. To solo more than one track at a time in Live, simply hold down the CTRL (CMND) key and click away. You can also arm more than one track at a time for recording by using the very same method.

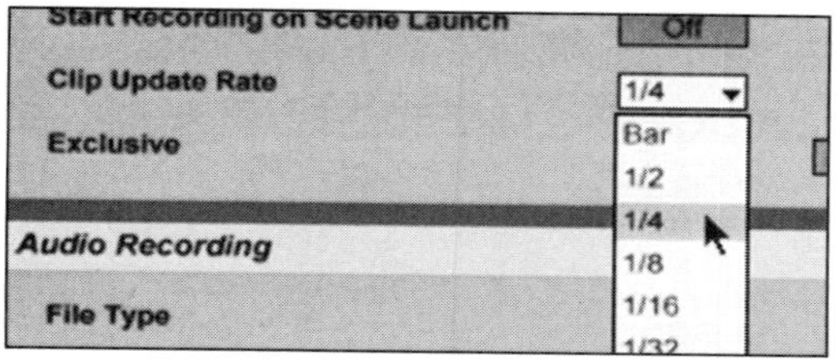

Figure 3.26

By adjusting the clip update rate, Live can change loops (per your direction) more quickly. An excellent advantage for the live laptop loopist.

Audio Recording

Other Behavior settings are more self-explanatory, but it is worth noting that a PC's native format is WAV, and a Mac's is AIFF. You can invert these settings, but if you want to have these files available in native applications, you may run into problems. I also recommend setting the bit depth to 24 when recording (the Record Bit Depth option), so long as your audio interface supports it. This ensures the maximum detail for newly recorded sounds. You can always render a file downward (to 16-bit), but cannot really go up, to add detail that is not there. Think of it this way: a color photo can easily be degraded to black and white, but the reverse is much more difficult, and requires some special technology.

The Audio Record Folder is the folder into which Live places all WAV and AIFF audio files once recorded. You will find that once you save a file (song), you can choose to place all corresponding audio into a designated (a.k.a. less confusing) location. So think of this folder as a temporary scrap heap that you can retrieve old files from, browse for hidden gems, or just flush periodically.

Samples

The Create Analysis Files option states whether Live will save its graphical display of audio waveforms for quick loading in the future. The first time an audio file is used in Live, the program will create a waveform display for use in the Clip View. When this option is enabled, Live will store the graphical analysis as a file on your computer's disk. The file has the same name as the sample it is associated with and has ".asd" as its extension. The next time the audio file is used in a Live Set, you won't have to wait for the graphical display to be rendered again.

The Sample Editor setting is for defining the location of your favorite wave editor, such as Sonic Foundry's Sound Forge, Steinberg's Wavelab, Bias Audio's Peak, or Syntrillium's Cool Edit Pro. Your preferred editor will then launch when you press the Edit button in an Audio Clip. For a more detailed look at wave editors, please refer to Chapter 14, "Live 4 Power."

The goal of Chapter 3 has been to get you up and running with Live and to give you a general idea about how the Preferences settings will affect your workflow. As we move throughout the book, we will again and again direct you back to the Preferences discussion in this chapter. In Chapter 4, "Live Interface Basics," we will proceed with the rest of your introduction to Live's two primary views.

Live Interface Basics

One of Ableton's software development team's crowning achievements is the creation of Live's simple, but elegant, interface. Only two views are needed to accomplish everything in Live: Session View and Arrangement View. Session View is geared for live performance, loop experimentation, and a quick multi-track recording sketchpad, while Arrangement View better facilitates studio editing, audio and MIDI sequencing, and song arranging. Each subsection of Live's paired-down interfaces is intuitive, easy to maneuver, and contains built-in help to remind you of any onscreen buttons or features that might be unclear in the heat of a mix. Ableton's Zen-like approach to audio software provides solid relief in a world full of gargantuan multi-track applications, with gaggles of resizable pop-up windows and confusing setup and routing schemes. Instead, Live is a breath of fresh air, boasting streamlined controls with easy-to-read menus, and discernible mixer and effect settings. Even with the fog machine blowing and lights down low, Live lets you get into the mix, rather than trying your patience with unnecessary system customization.

In the next few sections, we will break down each section of Live's two primary landscapes, as well as point out some timesaving ways to maneuver in Live. Later in the chapter, we will look at some of Live's more customizable viewing features, a few pertinent file saving schemes, and the permanent parts of Live's screen real estate. Feel free to skip around if you need help in a particular area. If you are a Live user, but are new to version 4.0, you will want to pay extra attention to the new MIDI Tracks and expanded signal routing capabilities.

Session View

Live's Session View (Figure 4.1) is where you will spend the greater part of your performing and composing time. With some practice, Session View can take on a musical life of its own, and may well be the software world's first "jam-friendly" songwriter's sketchpad. Even better is that after the jam, Live permits an infinite amount of additional recording, editing, and arranging, which we will get to later in this chapter. There are four main sections contained within the Session View:

* The Clip Slot Grid
* The Scene Launcher
* The Session Mixer
* The Input/Output Routing Strip

The grid-like screen in the upper-right corner of your monitor is the actual Session View, while the side and bottom retractable-rectangle views (such as Browser Info, and Track/Clip View) are present in any view when you want them to be. Session View is where most people experience the creative spark in Live, so if you should create something worth saving while you are working through this chapter, go to File > Save Live Set As, and name your new sketch of a song. We also want to point out that while we will cover each element in the interface, the Browser and Info View will be explained later in the chapter, while Track and Clip View will be saved for Chapter 5, "Making Music in Live."

This ordinary looking grid will be the launch pad for many a Live jam. Each cell—Ableton calls them Clip Slots—can be triggered to play or stop via the mouse, computer keyboard, or MIDI-controller, depending upon your settings. Each Clip can be played in similar fashion to an Akai MPC, drum machine, or similar phrase sampler. For example, artists such as DJ Shadow may lay out several sampled drum hits across the 16 pads of an MPC 2000, and then play them with the MPC's comfy rubber pads. Live's Clip Slot grid, which we will explore in detail below, is similar in design and can house an unlimited number of loops, samples, one shots, and MIDI parts. You will need to supply your own triggering scheme as we suggested in Chapter 3, "Getting Live Up and Running."

Clip Slot Grid

Session View's Clip Slot Grid (Figure 4.2) is actually the first tool you will use to organize your musical parts into a song. Live uses these rows and

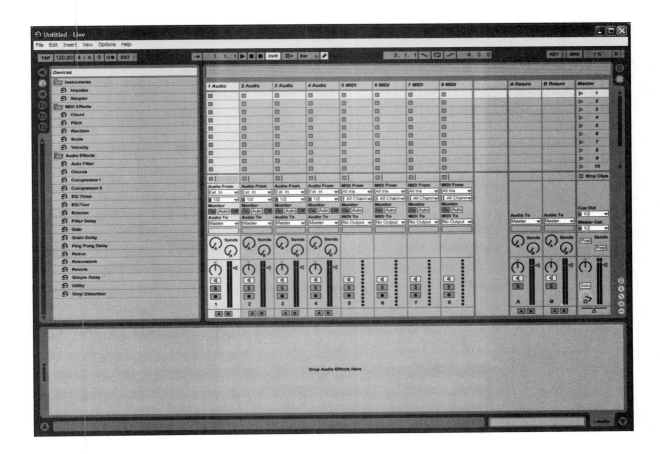

Figure 4.1

Pictured above is Live's Session View. This is the window used for live performance. Each Clip Slot (represented as rectangles beneath the Track Title Bar) is a placeholder for audio samples, loops, and MIDI sequences.

columns, referred to as "Scenes" and "Tracks" respectively, to give us different levels of control. What's important is that you begin to think of Live's Clip Slot grid as a palette upon which to place your sonic colors (in this case musical parts composed of audio files and MIDI data) for later sonic "painting" and further color exploration (sound combining).

Along the bottom of the Clip Slot Grid are the Clip Stop buttons. Clicking the square in one of these Slots will cause any Clip playing on that Track to stop. Also, there is another box labeled "Stop Clips" in the Master Track. This box, as its name implies, will stop all Clips—both audio and MIDI.

❈ **Space Out**

The Spacebar starts and stops audio in Live as it does in most other audio software application.

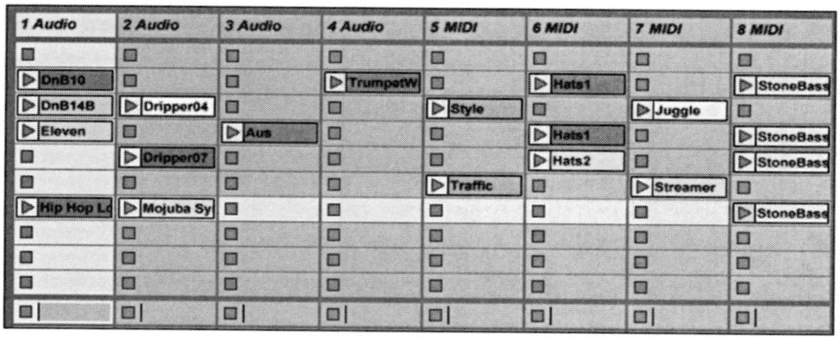

Figure 4.2

The Clip Slot Grid, shown with a few Clips loaded in some Slots.

By loading Clips into the Clip slot grid, you are arming Live with musical ammo. Next steps range from firing off parts in a live performance to creating new musical combinations (songs) to switching to the Arrangement View for more editing.

Some Live users prefer to build their entire song in Live by using several small, yet simple loops, and then utilize Live's Session View to organize, improvise, or compose. Other artists may show up to the gig with a blank slate, along with a stash of well-organized Clips, and practice building their mix from the ground up in more gradual, yet still improvisational way.

> ❄ **Knobby Digital**
>
> To adjust any of the virtual knobs found in Live, click on the knob and move the mouse forward and backward just like moving a fader. In other words, sideways mouse moves are a waste of time. Don't feel silly practicing how this feels; after all, it's your "Sequencing Instrument."

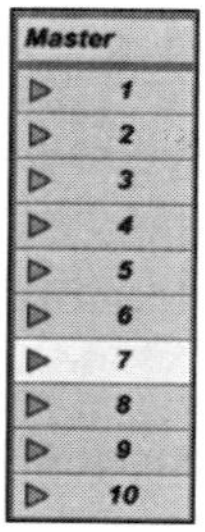

Figure 4.3

Click the triangle to launch all the Clips in the Scene (row).

The Scene Launcher

As mentioned above, the rows in the Clip Slot Grid are referred to as Scenes. Since Live can play only one Clip at a time in each Track, it makes sense to put each one you want to play in a horizontal line across the Grid. Live then offers us a way to launch all of the Clips in the Scene using the Scene Launchers (Figure 4.3) found on the right side of the Clip Slot Grid in the Master Track. As you get deeper into the program (especially in the next chapter), you'll see how using Scenes offers you a quick way of arranging and performing a song.

The Session Mixer

Live's Session Mixer, seen in Figure 4.4, approximates a hardware mixer in both concept and design; but since it's a software mixer, it is also completely automatable, MIDI-mappable, and expandable. Similar to its hardware

❄ ❄ ❄

cousin, Live's Session Mixer utilizes a set of individual channel controls and a master section.

Audio Tracks and Their Controls

The Track shown in Figure 4.5 is an Audio Track. This type of track has been with Live since the beginning. You can use Audio Clips and Audio Effects (both described in detail later) on this type of Track as well as record new Audio Clips.

The Audio Track outputs an audio signal that is fed into an audio channel of the Session Mixer below it. The audio channel controls give you control of the output volume, pan position, and effect sends for the Track. The buttons include the Track Activator (the speaker icon) which enables the Track when it's green; the Solo/Cue button which routes the Track to the Pre-Listen Bus; and the Record Arm button which enables the Track for recording as well as monitoring for Tracks set to Auto (monitoring will be explained in a few sections).

MIDI Tracks and Their Controls

A MIDI Track without a virtual instrument (Figure 4.6) does not output audio; thus, there is no volume, pan, or send knobs for them in Session Mixer. You still have the Track Activator, Solo/PFL, and Arm buttons which function the same as their Audio Track counterparts. When a virtual instrument is loaded onto the Track (see Chapter 8), the full Audio Track controls explained above will appear instead.

Figure 4.4

Live's Session Mixer looks similar to most other virtual mixers. Each vertical strip represents a channel with individual values for volume, panning, and routing.

Figure 4.5 (far left)

The Audio Track can house Audio Clips and process them with Audio Effects. The controls available on this Track are Volume, Pan, Mute, Solo, Record Arm, and Sends.

Figure 4.6 (left)

The MIDI Track does not have a Volume or Pan control if there is no virtual instrument loaded into its Track View.

❋ **P.F. What?**

PFL stands for Pre-Fader Listen. This is a function found on many mixers that allows the user to listen to the sound on a channel without letting the audience hear it. The process is "pre-fader," meaning that you listen to the channel before the sound enters the volume fader. You will therefore be able to listen to a channel that is muted or has the volume turned all the way down.

Figure 4.7

The Return Track is basically an Audio Track without Clip Slots.

Return Tracks and Their Controls

The Return Tracks (Figure 4.7) output audio, but unlike their Audio Track cousins, they can't hold any Clips. What good is a Track that can't hold Clips? While they may not add new parts to your song, they can still hold effects and can receive input from both the Send knobs and Audio Output routing. These can be used for send-style effects like reverbs and delays, or can be used to group Tracks together by routing the individual Track outs to the Return Track. Since Clips can't be used on Return Tracks, there is no Record Arm button. See Chapter 8 for a full explanation of Return Tracks and their uses.

> ❋ **Stereo on the Go**
>
> All channels in Live are both stereo- and mono-capable, depending upon the source that is playing. Panning works similarly for both stereo and mono Tracks (as you would imagine), but keep in mind that stereo signals may sound noticeably weaker when panned. Mono signals, on the other hand, will provide more "presence."

> ❋ **Function's Function**
>
> Your computer's first eight function keys (F1 through F8) double as channel mute shortcut keys for Live's Session Mixer. F1 works for channel 1, F2 for channel 2, and so on up to channel 8. This is an exceptionally handy tool for live performance when you are looking to mute and un-mute parts in a hurry—a technique employed by many DJs and Electronica artists. For those using Mac Powerbooks, you need to hold the "Fn" key while you use the function keys.

Figure 4.8

Your entire mix will generally pass through the Master Track, so it's a nice place to add final effects to your song.

Master Track and Its Controls

The Master Track, shown in Figure 4.8, is the granddaddy of them all. All Tracks outputting to Master will pass through this Track on their way to your speakers. You can't make or destroy the Master Track and it, like the Return Tracks, cannot house Clips. In place of the Clip Slots are the Scene Launchers explained earlier. The Master Track gives us one final point to treat our mix since it has a Track View that can be loaded with effects such as mastering EQ and compression. You'll also find the Solo/PFL volume knob here which adjusts the pre-listen level while browsing audio files and also sets the volume of the metronome.

> ### ※ Solo/Cue
>
> Here in the Master Track is the Solo/Cue volume knob and function button. The knob controls the volume of all pre-listen functions such as soloing tracks and previewing audio files in the browser. If you've selected unique outputs for your pre-listen bus (see the Audio Tab in Chapter 3), the Solo button above the knob may be switched to Cue. When Cue is active, the Solo buttons on the Audio Tracks will turn to Cue buttons (little headphone icons). When you press one of these Cue buttons, that track will be routed to the pre-listen output without muting the other tracks. You can use this feature to listen to a track before switching on its Track Activator—a helpful performance tool.

The Crossfader

Live features a weapon like none we have ever seen in audio software—the MIDI-mappable DJ-style crossfader (Live calls it just a plain old *Crossfader*). For over twenty years now, analog crossfaders have been making magicians out of DJs by enabling them to mix two or more tracks together, juggle those mixes, and break up monotonous loops with one simple gesture. Scratch DJs have also taken crossfader technique to incredible levels. The Live adaptation of the analog crossfader (seen in Figure 4.9) is the humble-looking horizontal slider just below the Master Volume section described in the preceding section.

Figure 4.9

Live's Crossfader adds a whole new set of performance (and mix) tools to Live's Session View. The A and B buttons assign their respective Tracks to one side of the Crossfader or the other.

To use the fader, you will have to assign Session Mixer channels to either A or B sides of the Crossfader. If you are new to crossfaders, think of it as a double-sided volume fader. As you move to B (to increase the volume of all channels set to B), you decrease the volume of all channels set to A. The reverse holds true when you come back to A—A channels get louder, while B channels get quieter.

Here are a few tips for jumping into Live's Crossfader feature:

※ **Assign a couple of channels to A or B sides of the Crossfader:** When selecting your Session Mixer channels to A or B, you don't have to designate all of your active Tracks (to A or B). By not assigning a channel to A or B, you have, by omission, selected both. This means that you will hear any non-specified channels all of the time. DJs often like to bring in a different groove under the same music bed and vice-versa. Simply leave all of your Tracks as they are and make one drum groove A and the other B. Now gradually flip back and forth on the Crossfader.

※ **Get your MIDI on:** By assigning a MIDI-controller to control Live's Crossfader, you can add a whole new performance element to Live. To do this, you will need a MIDI-controller or MIDI keyboard set up for your computer (see the X-Session controller in Chapter 3). Then all you need to do is press the MIDI button on the upper right-hand side of Live's screen. Click once on the Crossfader, and then move a knob or keyboard wheel (the modulation wheel works well).

❋ **Dry up the mix trick:** You can quickly "dry" up your mix (remove all audible effects) by routing each of your effects Returns to one side of the Crossfader. To do so, simply route all effect Returns to B, and leave all other Crossfader Assigns alone (no assignment). Assuming you have effects on your Aux Returns (we will describe how to do this in the following sections), moving the Crossfader to position A will have no effects, while the B position will be fully effected.

❋ **Hideaway**

Live can feel a little constrictive with its profusion of virtual controls. You can hide sections of the Session View by clicking on the small icons to the right of the Master Volume slider. You can also turn the same sections on and off by selecting them in the View menu.

Track Input and Output Routing

Live's Session Mixer is even more flexible once you get under the hood. The Input/Output Channel Routing is capable of routing any input imaginable into a Live Track from external audio and MIDI sources, ReWire clients, and other Live Tracks by merely clicking the menus (see Figure 4.10) and picking your source. Any multi-channel input, such as an eight-channel sound card or multiple-output software such as Propellerhead's Reason, can have inputs routed to correspond with any given channel. If, for example, you want

Audio From	Audio From	Audio From	Audio From	MIDI From	MIDI From	MIDI From	MIDI From				Cue Out
Ext. In	Ext. In	Ext. In	Ext. In	All Ins	All Ins	All Ins	All Ins				II 1/2
II 1/2	II 1/2	II 1/2	II 1/2	I All Chann	I All Chann	I All Chann	I All Chann				
Monitor	Monitor	Monitor	Monitor	Monitor	Monitor	Monitor	Monitor				
On Auto Off	On Auto Off	On Auto Off	On Auto Off	On Auto	On Auto	On Auto	On Auto				
Audio To	Audio To	Audio To	Audio To	MIDI To	MIDI To	MIDI To	MIDI To	Audio To	Audio To		Master Out
Master	Master	Master	Master	No Output	No Output	No Output	No Output	Master	Master		II 1/2

Figure 4.10

The Input/Output Routing strip. In Live, you have the choice of configuring Input Type and Channel, as well as Output Type and Channel for audio and MIDI Tracks. Return Tracks only have the output options.

microphone input number one to be recorded on Session Mixer channel one (or any other), the drop-down menus will accomplish this.

Any ReWire applications currently existing on your computer will also be seen in the Input drop-down menu. (ReWire is a software linking technology invented by Propellerheads that allows Live to run, control, or be controlled by programs such as Reason, Sonar, Cubase, Project5, Storm, and many others. See Chapter 12 for the lowdown.) By routing a ReWire application through Live's inputs, you will be able to monitor and record that application's audio output as you would another audio source.

You will also see "Resample" in the inputs section. This is available in case you want to send Live's own output to itself, for instance, when you have finished a track and want to render your song in real-time, or if you want to make a quick submix of more than one track. These various inputs and methods will be covered in the following three chapters.

❋ **Cloning and Grouping Tracks**

Live's Input/Output section allows us to use data from one Track to feed other multiple tracks. This is especially useful with MIDI Tracks since you can trigger multiple instruments from one Clip creating colossal layers. It is functionally the same as cloning your Track, Clips, effects, and all, and adding another instrument. However, this way allows you to control it all from only one set of Clips.

When performing this type of routing, your first instinct may be to set the output of your controlling Track to multiple destinations. However, the Output section of each Track only allows one destination to be selected. Instead, you'll need to set the inputs of the other Tracks to the control Track. If you're feeding multiple Tracks into one, such as when grouping Audio Tracks, the process is the opposite—you choose the destination Track for all the control Tracks.

Arrangement View

Beginners may think of it as merely Live's "other" window, but Arrangement View (seen in Figure 4.11) is the place for recording and editing your Live Session View jams, performing overdubs, automating additional effects, and rendering your final track. If Session View is the spontaneous right-brain-tickling creative screen, Arrangement View is the analytic, left-brain-stimulating, "finishing touches" side of Live. You may notice that Live's Arrangement View closely resembles many other multi-track applications' "Arranger" screens. Programs such as Acid Pro, Sonar, Cubase, Logic, ProTools and many are based on horizontal, left-to-right audio arrangers (also called linear-based arrangers). If you like this method of working, you will be right at home making music in Live, Arranger-style.

For those who didn't read the figure caption, here it is again: Each Track in Session View corresponds precisely with its Track counterpart in Arrangement View. If you have eight Tracks in Session View, you will have eight Tracks in Arrangement View. You can add a Track in either view, and it will appear in the other as if you are working on the same project—because you are.

There is, however, a very important distinction between Session View and Arrangement View. Once you record your music from Session View into Arrangement View, you will hear your new arrangement (playing from Arrangement View) until you override it by executing a control in Session View or by actively moving a previously automated control.

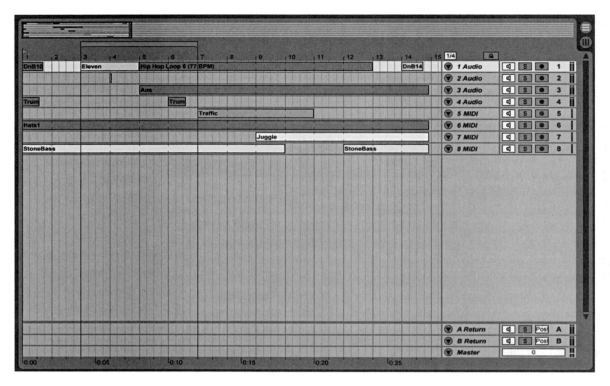

Figure 4.11

Live's Arrangement View will contain the results of your recorded Session View songs. Each horizontal line in Arrangement View represents a Track that will correspond to a vertical channel in the Session Mixer.

This is actually a great feature, but can baffle those making the switch from a traditional linear-based sequencer application. The idea rests on Session View being a palette for your musical "painting" in Arrangement View. You can record a single run through (a take) and then move to Arrangement View to edit your song to completion. Or you can do multiple takes or punch-ins by again activating Global recording and "overdubbing" additional song-parts into Arrangement View from Session View. This is also a great method for touching up previously recorded automation data.

This is an extremely important concept to grasp, so let's look at it a bit more closely by loading up the Live Demo song "1-Make Music With Live.als." After you have loaded the file found in your original Ableton Live folder in the subfolder entitled Demos and Tutorials, follow the steps below.

1 When you load "1-Make Music With Live.als," you will be looking at a completed song in Live's Arrangement View. Press Tab to switch to Session View.

2 Take a look at the Session Mixer and notice all the red markings. These markings mean that the knob, fader, and/or button has associated automation data in the Arrange View. (Automation data consists of the recorded movements of

every fader, knob, or button you moved when you did your Live recording.)
We will cover this in great detail throughout the book, but most notably in
Chapter 5, "Making Music in Live."

3 Now move the volume slider on Track 4. Notice that the red blip goes away,
   and the red light on the Back to Arrangement button (in the control bar) lights
   up. You have now told Live to ignore that specific fader's automation and use
   your manual setting.

4 To reinstate the automation—so you can listen to the song's original recording
   settings—simply press the red Back to Arrangement button on the control bar to
   the right of the record button. Notice how Track 4's fader level jumps back up
   to its original position.

5 Press Tab to go back to the Arrangement View.

6 Press Play or your Spacebar and hear/watch Live's settings move with the music.
   You will see panning and volume settings change on the right. Look at Track 3
   and start the arrangement around measure 6 to see the panner in action.

Important: Any time you move a control that has been automated, Live
ceases playback of that particular control's automation. By overriding the
control, Live assumes that you would like to temporarily listen to that particular control (or group of controls) as you have set them in Session View. In
any given project, you can only be sure that you are hearing the mix from
Arrangement View when the Back to Arrangement button is dark (Figure
4.12). If the Back to Arrangement button is on, you are likely hearing a mix
of both your Arrangement and Session View Clips and controls. If you
launch a Clip in the Session View, this will override playback of the corresponding track in Arrangement View Playing a Clip in Session View will also
result in illuminating the Back to Arrangement button. If you flip to the
Arranger, you'll see that the corresponding Track is faded out, symbolizing
its inactivity. When you press the Back to Arrangement button, all of the
Session View Clips will stop instantly (this does not wait for the Global
Quantization setting or anything like that) and the Arrangement Clips will
play. This is true for fader movements or manually changing the state of any
control with automation. Your new moves interrupt what should be playing
from the Arrangement's automation tracks, so the Back to Arrangement button lights signaling the divergence. Therefore, you should always double
check exactly which side you are hearing (either your programmed automation or manual mix
settings) if Live seems
to be "misbehaving."

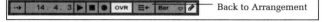 — Back to Arrangement

Figure 4.12

Whether you are in Arrangement View or Session View,
you can always revert to the
Arrangement View's mix
settings, which usually contain
automation, by pressing the
Back to Arrangement button.

This view-dependent mixer settings concept is a drastic difference from other applications you may be used to; the reasoning is simple: you will want to hear entirely different settings on your improvised remix or jam than you will on a finished piece of music. It can be handy to remove the automation, or, if you are in Session View, to hear the automation at a moment's notice. For this reason, and others we will delve into later, remember that Arrangement and Session View track settings are not always the same mix—hence they will not necessarily sound the same.

> ❋ **Icon Flip**
>
> In the upper-right corner of the Live window are two icons: one with three vertical lines and one with three horizontal lines. These icons can be used to switch between the Session and Arrangement Views. The Session View is accessed with the icon with the vertical lines (the Session View has its tracks oriented vertically) while the other icon, with its horizontal lines represents the Arrangement View.

Track Settings and Contents

The Arrangement View's Track settings are located on the right side of the screen and take up about one-third of the working portion of the Arrangement View, as seen in Figure 4.13. To maximize (view) a Track, click the downward-pointing triangle. Any Clips on that track will reveal their contents and several hidden track settings.

Figure 4.13

Each Track in Arrangement View has the same controls as the Tracks in Session View. This makes sense since the Arranger Tracks and Session Tracks are actually the same.

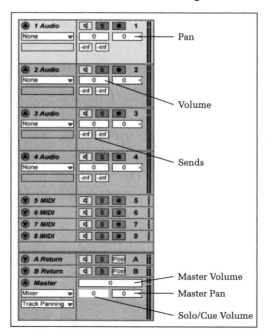

Each Arranger Track is still bound by the same rules as the Tracks in Session View. Only one Clip can be playing at a time in an Arranger Track. Clips can be added to Arranger Tracks in the same manner used to add them to the Session View. Simply drag the desired file from the File Browser into an Arranger Track. The Clip will appear and you will be able to move it, copy it, lengthen or shorten it, and perform other editing features described in the Arranger section of Chapter 5.

Volume, Panning, FX sends, Solo, Mute, Arm for Recording, and the same track routing features found in the Session Mixer are still accessible in Arranger. The only difference is visual: the controls have been turned on their sides and are represented by values instead of graphical controls. The Session Mixer's Master Settings are located on the bottom line of Live's Arrangement View.

Relation to the Session View

Though the Arrangement and Session Views seem like two different sections in the Live environment, they are actually closely related to one another. In Live, there are two places to arrange and play Clips: the Arrangement View and Session View; however, there is only one mixer in Live, and that is the Session Mixer. This means that the Arranger and Session need to share this mixer. Just like only one Clip can be playing on a Track at a time, only one Track—either from the Session or Arranger—can be fed into a Session Mixer channel at a time.

If you are playing Clips on a Track in the Session View, they will override any Clips in the associated Arranger Track. When you press the Back To Arrangement button, the Tracks in the Arranger will take over and all Clips in the Session View will stop.

This relation between the two views means you can arrange a song in the Arrangement View, but can begin improvising in the Session View. When your improvisation is done, press the Back To Arrangement button and your preset Arrangement will take over.

Overview

Standing tall above Live's Arrangement/Session Views and just below the control bar is the Overview (of your Live Arrangement). The Overview, which resembles a musical staff, is there purely for navigation and reference to show you where you are in your Arrangement. So long as you have Clips in Live's Arrangement View, it offers a bird's eye view of your entire track. You will see tiny colored lines representing your Clips in the Arrangement View. The Overview (Figure 4.14) can be seen in Session View, but is a permanent fixture in Arrangement View. You can hide the Overview (in Session View) by pressing CTRL + SHIFT + O on a PC, or OPTION + CMND + O on a Mac.

Figure 4.14

Live's Overview is quite literally a view from above.

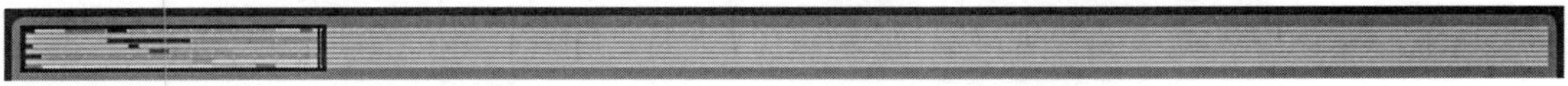

To use Overview to move to a new location, hover the mouse over the portion of the Overview bar you want to move to; the magnifying glass icon will appear; click once and you will be moved to the corresponding location in the arranger. To zoom in and out, hover over the Overview bar; depress the mouse button (left on PC), and move the mouse forward and backward to zoom in and out (respectively). You can quickly skip from the beginning to the end with one click of the mouse—though we should point out that you will still need to place your cursor in the desired location and then hit your Spacebar to start playback. Try this a couple of times; it takes some getting used to.

> ❄ **Tab = Flip**
>
> To see Live's other screen, simply strike the Tab key; for example, if you're in the Session View, strike Tab, and the Arrangement window will appear. Hit Tab once again to return to Session View and then just for fun, hit F11, to see Live's full screen view (F11 again to go back to Live's previous dimensions).
>
> Mac OS X users with Exposé enabled will not be able to use the F11 key for controlling Live's view since that key is used by Exposé. Enter your Exposé settings (in the System Preferences) and reassign the F11 function to another key. F11 will then control Live's full screen view.

The Live Control Bar

Headlining each one of Live's two different working views (Session and Arrangement) is Live's own version of a transport bar. Typically, transport bars function as the start/stop mechanism and track position finder all in one. Although transport bars are often free-floating in many other applications, in Live, the Control Bar (Figure 4.15) is fixed to the top of your screen. Still, most "power-users" default to keyboard shortcuts such as the Spacebar for starting and stopping playback rarely using the icons at the top of the screen. Also, many Live aficionados map Live's Control Bar functions to MIDI or computer keyboard controls. We will cover this in detail later in this section.

In the Control Bar, you will find pertinent song information such as time-signature, tempo, and processor load (a vital stat for the computer-based musician). Control Bar will also help you pinpoint your exact location within the track and determine Live's master quantize settings; and, a Tap Tempo and metronome make recording your Live projects from scratch just a tad more manageable.

Figure 4.15

Live's Control Bar remains constant at the top of both of Live's main views (broken into two pieces due to size constraints). Here you will find standard symbols for Stop, Play, and Record, as well as time/tempo information and other project parameters.

❄ ❄ ❄

Tempo, Time Signature, Groove, Metronome, and Sync

On the left side of the Control Bar you will find settings for song parameters (Figure 4.16). The buttons are (from left to right): Tap Tempo, Tempo, Time Signature, Groove Amount, Metronome, External Sync Switch, and External Sync Indicators.

Figure 4.16

This subsection of the Control Bar is devoted to time, including MIDI sync, tempo, and time-signature.

The Tap Tempo button is a handy song-starting feature in Live. For a quick test-drive of one of Tap Tempo's features, click the button four times and your project will begin at that tempo. This is a handy feature if you need to sneak in while another DJ is playing, synch up with your drummer, or match another device such as a turntable or CD player. You can also use Tap Tempo to help map out songs and better align groove clips. Sound confusing? Chapters 5 and 6 will clear it up.

Next up are Live's project Tempo and Time signature settings, which are found just to the right of the Tap Tempo button. Live can handle tempos ranging from 20 to 999 BPM (beats per minute), and time signatures with numerators ranging from 1–99 and denominator choices of 1, 2, 4, 8, and 16— a huge range of possibilities.

Moving to the right of time signature, you will come upon Live's Metronome button. This feature/function works complementary to the Tap Tempo. When engaged, you will hear a customizable click track (metronome) that can serve as a guide for new recordings and help with loop editing. The volume of the click can be adjusted using the Solo/Cue volume knob in Live's Master Track (the same knob you use for adjusting the preview volume when browsing for samples).

Lastly, the External Sync button and the External Sync monitoring lights show how Live handles the job of synchronizing to an external device. Provided that Live's Preferences have been set up correctly (to synchronize playback with another MIDI source), the External Synch Switch engages or disengages Live's MIDI-synchronization to an outside source, while the monitoring lights announce that the MIDI sync signal is being sent and/or received.

Follow, Play, Stop, Record, MIDI Overdub, Quantize, and Pencil

Most starting and stopping in Live is best handled with the Spacebar (tap it once to start, tap it again to stop); however, the second area of Live's Control Bar (Figure 4.17) sports official Start and Stop buttons. You will also find the

Figure 4.17

Here is the second element of Live's control bar. Keep your eye on the Quantization Menu. This is the key to sounding like a pro when you fire off your loops.

 — Global Quantize setting

Arrangement Record, MIDI Overdub, and Back to Arrangement buttons here which you will use during the track-editing process.

Other points of interest include the Arrangement Position box and the global Quantization Menu. The Arrangement Position box provides a continuous readout—in measures, beats, and subdivisions—of where you are in the song, whether you're listening or recording. You can manually enter a start time value into this box or drag up and down with the mouse to change the setting.

The global Quantization Menu, to the right of the Record button, sets the default triggering timing for Clips in Live's Session View that are set to Global quantization (more on this in Chapter 5). You have the option of selecting 1/32, 1/16, 1/8, 1/4, 1/2, and multiples of the full measure (called bars). What this means is that each Clip triggered in the Session View will "fire" at the very next subdivision you have selected. For instance, at the Bar setting, your "fired" Clip will not begin to play until the first beat of the very next measure. If your setting is 1/16, your Clip will begin playing at the next 1/16 note. You can imagine how this quantitative correction tool will clean up your performance. This can be a huge help and very cool trick for guiding rapid-fire sample sections, or just ensuring that your next Scene launches right on the first beat.

If quantization sounds sterile to you, and you want your music to breathe more, you can also set this menu to None for no quantization of any sort. Any Clip (set to Global) you fire while None is selected will sound the instant the sample is triggered.

Punch In/Out and Loop

Live provides several features that are built for both the (self-engineering) recording musician and the mad loop concocter. Punch In and Punch Out is just that type of tool. Using it, you will be able to record a select length of audio or create a sub-mix of Live's output. Recording in small segments like this can be an excellent way to make original loops for your collection, or add in just the right bit of music to your track. We will cover recording in detail in later chapters, so don't worry if this description seems a little overwhelming. The third set of tools in Live's Control Bar section, seen below in

Figure 4.18

Live's Punch In and Punch Out functionality makes recording Live's output or tracking some additional input a breeze.

Figure 4.18, includes controls for two loop points, the start and the end. If the Loop button is depressed, then Live's playback will loop (the

defined start/stop length) continuously, as opposed to playing through to the end of the song. If the two punch points are activated, Live can be set to record in typical multi-tracking get in/get out fashion. This tool is meant to provide a quick way of recording for a specified amount of time.

Key and MIDI Assigns, System Performance, and MIDI I/O

The fourth segment of the Control Bar (Figure 4.19) is the system-monitoring and Key/MIDI set-up area. We will cover the many ways to configure MIDI and computer keyboard triggering and controls in Chapters 5, 6, and 7; however, we want to point out that the Key (Key Map Mode Switch) and MIDI (MIDI Map Mode Switch) buttons are your entrance point to controlling Live with an outside hardware controller. Ableton was ingenious enough to make sure that all MIDI and Keyboard mapping can be done on the fly, without ever stopping playback—no small feat.

Figure 4.19

Pictured above is the fourth segment of Live's Control Bar. From here, you can monitor your hardware (CPU load and MIDI input/output action) and set up your Key and MIDI controls.

Knowing how much gas is left in the tank—or whether you're running on fumes—is important in the laptop world. Here to help, Live's CPU Load Meter continuously shows the amount of strain on your system for a given set of audio processing or loop playback. If for any reason, this bar is beginning to approach 100%, you may begin to experience performance degradation or audio dropouts. The D (Hard-Disk Overload Indicator) button just to the right of the CPU meter will begin to flicker red if your hard drive is not able to stream all the necessary audio files playing in the song quickly enough. This will also result in dropouts.

❅ **MIDI Prognosis**

The last two indicators, just right of the Disk Overload Indicator, represent MIDI Input and MIDI Output signal presence by lighting up (turning colors) when Live is sending or receiving MIDI signals.

The two similar indicators between the MIDI Map Mode and Key Map Mode buttons will illuminate when an incoming message is assigned to a MIDI Remote function.

Live's Custom Views

Live also hosts several concealable windows accessible in both Session and Arrangement Views. These secondary windows enable you to explore your loops and files, Live's Devices, Plug-in effects, and Live's integrated Info menu. Unlike most configurable software applications, these windows pop up or close with the click of a single triangle shaped icon (see Figures 4.20a and 4.20b). For instance, if you are working on a song arrangement, you will likely not need to have the File Browser open; or, if you are familiar with Live, you can close the Info View to give more space to the Clip and Track

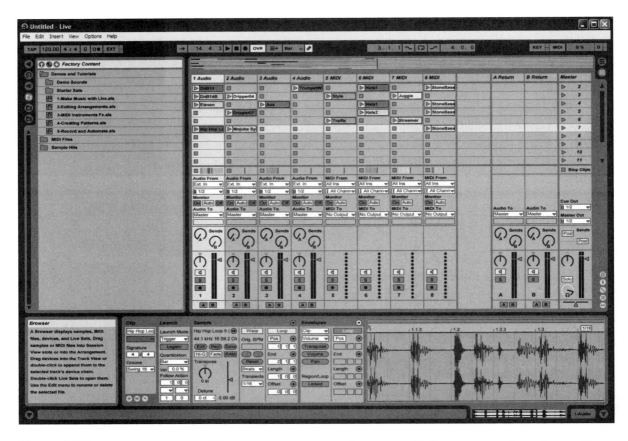

Figure 4.20a

Live's Session View with the
Browser, Info, and Clip View
(Chapter 5) maximized (open).

Views. After some experimentation, you will discover your favorite working
views in Session or Arrangement Views. The idea is that you may want to
hide collapsible windows in order to maximize screen real estate.

The Browser

The Browser window (Figure 4.21) is the means to access all of the prefab
elements you will add to a Live Set. It provides quick access to three different
locations on your hard drive for finding samples and MIDI files; houses the
collection of 17 Live Devices; as well as provide a listing of all Plug-in devices
located by Live. The Browser is retractable and located in the upper left section of either the Session or Arrangement View. By clicking the leftward-
pointing triangle-shaped arrow, you can hide this window. Conversely, if the
arrow is pointing toward the right, simply click once to view the Browser.

File Browsers

Warning! Do not underestimate the power of Live's browser. With it, audio can be previewed in real-time at the project tempo. Cakewalk's Sonar and Sonic Foundry's Acid Pro both do this for the PC, but all other programs require some pre-formatting before this can be achieved. Auto-previewing, or as Ableton calls it, "pre-listening," can be toggled off and on by clicking on the miniature set of headphones to the uppermost left of the loop browser.

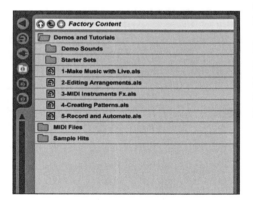

Figure 4.20b

With Browser, Info, and Clip View closed, Live's screen is wide open. You'll be able to see a greater number of Tracks and Clips this way.

Figure 4.21

Located on the far and upper left-hand side is Live's internal Device, Plug-in effects, and File browsers.

> ### ✳ Cueing the Mix
> You can adjust the volume of loops heard via Live's pre-listening feature by rotating the virtual solo/pre-listening volume knob on Live's mixer. In Session mode, you will see this control near the bottom of the master channel in the lower right corner of your mixer. In the Arrangement View, you will need to maximize the master channel (at the bottom of the track display) and adjust the pre-listening level in the box in the lower right-hand corner.

Drag and Drop

If you happen to like the sounds you are hearing when previewing loops, simply drag and drop the loop(s) into either the Session or Arrangement Views. You can place it in a clip slot in Session View, or onto a track (at any point you like) in Arrangement View. The sound file can then be accessed immediately in Live's Clip View. In Chapter 5, "Making Music in Live," we'll discuss Clip View in detail.

Navigating the Browser

 The default position of Live's File Browser will be the exact same position that you were searching when you last closed Live. To facilitate faster manual searches, Live enables you to set up shortcuts within three different File Browser placeholders (seen in Figure 4.22). These will save you time as well as aid in the time-consuming process of organizing your loops for a live show.

Figure 4.22

The File Browser placeholders. They may be tiny, but they are a mighty big time saver.

At the top of the browser, just below the tap, tempo, and time signature information, are three key icons. They will be just to the left of the name of your current folder (Figure 4.23). You will see a set of headphones (Live's Pre-Listening button) and two separate arrow markers—one hooking up (the Move Up button), the other pointing down (the Root button). The Move Up and Root buttons help you to locate the file you are looking for, and then designate the browser position, to save you time.

Figure 4.23

The Pre-Listening, Move Up, and Root (place-setter) buttons.

Earlier, we touched on the importance of pre-listening to your sounds in the browser before bringing them into your project. The Pre-listening (headphone-shaped) icon will engage or disengage Live's loop pre-view function. We generally leave this on while we're composing and experimenting, and then turn it off when it is time to go to the gig. The logic is simple in that we don't want to accidentally pre-view (hear) the wrong loop during a performance unless we are routing our pre-listening output through a separate sound card. Generally, when prepping for a live performance, our loops and samples will be organized and named descriptively enough that we will not have to hear them before importing them into my project.

✳ ✳ ✳

The next two icons, Move Up and Root, will help you by place-setting or bookmarking your location in Live's browser so that each time you open Live you can begin looking in the same folder. Since you have three separate File Browser Choosers, you can set three different bookmarked locations. Here's how to do it:

1 Open Live's Browser and click on one of the File Browser Choosers (the file folder icons numbered 1, 2, and 3).

2 Next, click into the folder you would like to browse sounds from by cycling down the file folder tree. You may need to click through several folders to get to the one you are after.

3 Now click once on the folder you would like Live to default to (your new desired bookmarked location for this file browser).

4 Press Root (the downward-pointing arrow-shaped icon in the browser). Once you click Root, the browser will move that folder to the top (starting position) for all future browsing. If you change your mind, or want to go back to a folder that you cannot see, click on the Move Up button (the upward-pointing arrow-shaped icon). The Move Up button simply moves your browser's view up one folder level at a time.

Organizing Your Sounds

In an effort to keep workflow smooth, you can rename your loops inside the browser. This can be an enormous time saver and creative tool when composing in Live. To rename a loop, simply highlight the loop in the browser (shown in Figure 4.24) and then press keyboard shortcut keys CTRL (CMND) + E. You may also do this via the menu, by highlighting the loop and selecting Edit > Rename.

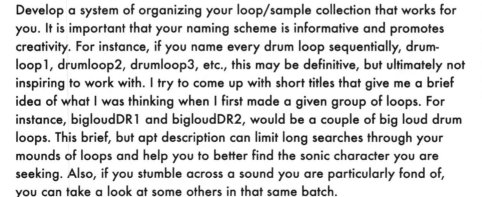

Figure 4.24

By highlighting a sound or loop in Live's browser, you can rename the file. Simply press CTRL (CMND) + E, and begin typing the new file name. If you change your mind at any point while typing, press ESC (escape).

Develop a system of organizing your loop/sample collection that works for you. It is important that your naming scheme is informative and promotes creativity. For instance, if you name every drum loop sequentially, drumloop1, drumloop2, drumloop3, etc., this may be definitive, but ultimately not inspiring to work with. I try to come up with short titles that give me a brief idea of what I was thinking when I first made a given group of loops. For instance, bigloudDR1 and bigloudDR2, would be a couple of big loud drum loops. This brief, but apt description can limit long searches through your mounds of loops and help you to better find the sonic character you are seeking. Also, if you stumble across a sound you are particularly fond of, you can take a look at some others in that same batch.

The Device Browser

Live's Concealable Device Browser (see Figure 4.25) contains Ableton Live's own brew of Effects and Instruments. Each Device type has its own folder in the Browser, one each for Instruments, MIDI Effects, and Audio Effects. The Device Browser is accessed through the button with the Live icon at the left edge of the Browser window.

Figure 4.25

Live's Device menu. To add an effect or instrument, highlight the Track you want to receive the Device, and then double-click the Device in the list.

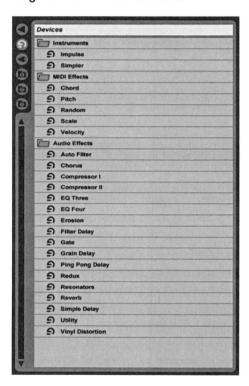

We will explore each of Live's wonderful plug-ins and learn how to incorporate VST (which stands for Virtual Studio Technology) effects and instruments in Chapter 8, "Using Effects." For now, it's enough to know that when you double-click on one of Live's Devices, you'll instantly add (or plug-in) an instance of the selected Device into the channel you have highlighted.

The Plug-in Browser

Plug-ins have become wildly popular in the last few years as a result of the efficiency that VST and Audio Units plug-ins are capable of delivering (in terms of system performance) over DirectX and Soundmanager Plug-ins. One reason VST development is so rampant is that the development information remains free to download from the Steinberg Web site. While this open-source philosophy sounds fantastically carefree, be forewarned: free code can spell danger. There are some incredibly smart, well-intentioned, software developers who are building innovative and interesting audio software (even for free), but with only the smallest of beta test pools. That means you should be wary of any plug-in, regardless of how expensive it is until you have tried it on your system, with your sound card and your Live song, in several different situations/combinations. We will recommend some safe plug-in tips in Chapter 8, but for now, recognize that Ableton's "house" plug-ins are capable of handling most common audio situations (and do an excellent job at it). Unless you are absolutely certain there is a plug-in available that you "need" or have thoroughly tested, don't assume all external plug-ins are trouble-free.

All of your VST plug-ins need to be in the VST folder Live searches at each startup. If you've been following along, we set this folder up during Preferences. We recommend giving Live its own VST folder and simply copying all VST plug-ins you would like to run in Live into that folder. Any Live-compatible plug-ins in this folder will be visible by clicking on the small "power plug" icon to the left of the Browser window as shown in Figure 4.26. See Chapter 8 for the rundown on using external plug-ins in Live.

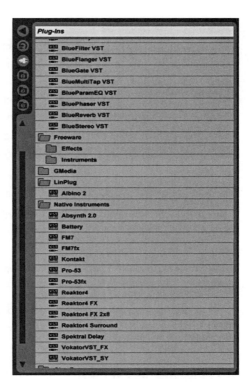

Figure 4.26
The Plug-in Browser will look different for everybody since it reflects your own unique collection of effects and instruments.

✳ **I Want My VST**

Any VST plug-in that cannot be seen via Live's browser cannot be used in Live—even if it is located in the correct directory on your PC or Mac. Be sure to move (delete) these plug-ins out of the VST folder that Live searches each time the program launches. Remember, this is the folder that we told Live to look in when we set up Live's initial preferences (see Preferences > Plug-in > VST Plug-in Folder). As a result, Live will start up faster. Also, if you notice a plug-in not working properly in Live, you should also take these out of the plug-in directory, write down the settings or combination of events that created the error, and send Ableton and the third-party plug-in manufacturer the feedback. By doing so, you may just help some small software developer zero in on a problem that would otherwise take months to figure out.

Saving Your Work

If you are new to audio software, that is a good thing. This means you come without preconceived notions of how difficult it can be just to organize all the files necessary for a given audio project. If you are a Pro Tools or Logic veteran, you know that calling up last week's session from a CD you burned that night might not be so simple. Live features an enhanced file-saving scheme sure to reduce at least some of the frustrating missing file searches and "which version am I working in?" blues.

Saving the Live Set

Live offers four ways to save project files: Save Live Set, Save Live Set As, Save a Copy, and Save Set Self-Contained. If you are familiar with common computer documents such as word processor applications, Save and Save As work in exactly the same way. Save, which can be done by pressing CTRL (CMND) + S, saves the document (in this case a Live song file called a *Set*) in its present state, under its present file name. This is the most common way you will save while you are working on a new song, especially when you like the results.

Save Live Set As, done via CTRL (CMND) + SHIFT + S, is the command for saving the current song file in its current state under a *different* name, and is usually done only when you want to begin a new song or modify an existing song without changing the original version. To do this, select File > Save Live Set As, select the location where you would like to place the file, and type the song's newest name.

If you are modifying a song, but would like to preserve the original, or if you would like to make a backup just for safety's sake, File > Save Copy will automatically add the word copy to the end of your file name.

Saving the Set as Self-Contained

The greatest save method is undoubtedly Save Set Self-Contained. If the very idea of a self-contained file makes you smile, you are no stranger to compu-ters. It is a terrible inconvenience (to put it mildly) to lose a file. Save Set Self-Contained eliminates this problem by guaranteeing that all related audio files, as well as Live's proprietary analysis files (recognizable by the file extension .ASD), are stored in a single folder (called sounds) as a brand spanking new copy of the original. Note: Saving Set Self Contained will *not* make your song into a single file (such as a Word document or text file), but will create a single folder for all of your sound and sound-analysis files. To play/load your song you will need this folder (automatically labeled *Song Name* Sounds by Live) *and* the Ableton Live Set (.ALS) song file that con-tains all of your song-specific information.

Saving Face—Keeping Your Files Intact

When saving as self-contained, Live saves the song file in the designated folder and then creates a corresponding Sounds folder just beneath it (one folder level down). For instance, if your song is called "Eye of the Tiger," you will notice that Live will create a folder with all of the sounds for your song and automatically title it Eye of the Tiger Sounds.

Sounds great, doesn't it? Imagine never ever having a problem again locating a file, opening a song on a different computer, e-mailing a track to a buddy, or just coming back two days later and not having any trouble recalling your song just as you had left it.

To save your Live set as self-contained, select File > Save Set Self-Contained, and then navigate to the folder where you would like to place the song (and all of its related audio files).

Even though saving as self-contained sounds all-encompassing, and it does wonders for keeping all of your audio files in the same easy-to-locate folder, there are still some items to keep in mind.

- ❄ **VST and AU Plug-ins:** While Save Self-Contained can be an effective way of keeping all of your audio files together, any external plug-ins (VST and AU) used in a given song will not be saved inside your file. This means that if you transport your song to a different computer or uninstall any effect or instrument plug-in that is present on the song you are saving, the plug-in will be missing upon loadup. If this is a free plug-in, this isn't too big of a problem; simply download a new version from the site where you originally got it; however, a shareware or store-bought plug-in is an entirely different matter—keep your installation CDs and registration numbers in a safe place!

- ❄ **Multiple copies:** Long (large) audio files will eat up a lot of hard drive space so be conscious of how many copies you make when saving as self-contained. This can be a real problem on smaller laptop hard drives, or if you are planning on sending a song over the Internet, or even setting up FTP downloads for collaboration. We recommend burning any song worth saving to a CD or DVD once you have saved all pertinent files via Save Set Self-Contained.

- ❄ **Don't forget the Song file:** When you are making a backup of your song, you will need to save both the song file *and* its associated folder full of sounds. This fact is critically important when transporting, backing up, or otherwise relocating your Ableton Live song files. Remember: the song file will never be placed into the Sounds folder (created by the Save Set Self-Contained feature), only the sounds, samples, loops and recordings go into the Sounds folder. Repeat: you must have the Live song file *and* the folder full of sounds to open up your complete song.

One other nice thing about Live's Save Set Self-Contained feature is that upon subsequent saves, Live will make sure that all files in the Sounds folder are being used. For instance, if you delete a Clip and are no longer using its sound file in the project, Live will notice this and, the next time you save, will ask,

> *"Remove unreferenced sample x, y, and z (whatever your files are called) .wav or .aif? This sample is contained in the Sounds folder C:\your directory\your folder\song name Sounds\ but the Set doesn't use it anymore. Please consider the sample might be accessed from other Sets."*

What to answer at this point depends on what you've done since the very moment you began working on this Set. Throughout your creative process in Live, you may be creating new audio files, possibly from recording an external audio input or resampling Live's output. What Live is telling you in the above message is that it can *technically* play this Live Set when you reload it if it deletes the unreferenced samples, which is true. After all, if there are no Clips in the Session or Arrange Views, nor samples in Impulse or Simpler, that need the audio file in question, the file would never be played even when playing the whole set in its entirety. Live's question may sound like a no-brainer (who would want files taking up space on their hard drive if they won't be used?), but you may still want to keep them. Consider this:

* If you deleted a Clip from your Session or Arranger *assuming* you could always drag it back from the Browser (that is a normal work method in Live, after all), this is one point where answering "Yes" to the above question will have you screaming, "No! No!" later on. Answer "No" and Live will leave the (temporarily) unused audio files where they belong so you'll find them there the next time you need them.

* If you've been having a heyday with effects and doing multiple layers of resampling in the process, you've probably achieved a copious assortment of interim audio files—building blocks in your quest for the perfect sound—but are only using the final few in your Set. If you still want to keep these files as a pseudo-Undo, answer "No" to keep them safe.

* Multiple takes on vocals and instruments are usually edited into one "super take" and are the results of using small sections of various files. While you may have achieved what is thought to be the perfect edit now, you may wish to revisit some of the other takes, possibly to create vocal doubling or a natural chorus (playing nearly identical takes simultaneously). This vault of archived audio will come in handy for that. Answer "no" if you want to keep this stuff on hand.

Saving as self-contained is the best method for saving any Live song. You can try just saving the file and keeping your audio where it is, but our experience and that of many expert audio users is that if you do, you will inevitably be referring to the section that follows.

Finding Missing Samples

It's going to happen. You can count on it. No, we're not psychic, but if you work in Live over an appreciable length of time, you will lose a beloved audio file, loop, and/or sample. This usually happens when files are moved, saved quickly (using the standard quick save, CTRL (CMND) + S), or after adding audio from a sample CD or temporary hard drive (and then ejecting/ detaching the disk).

Here is what to do (if you are unsure of where you moved the file):

1   Click on your Mac or PC desktop.

2   For Mac OS X, Press CMND + F. For OS 9, activate the Sherlock Search tool. For Windows select Start > Search > For Files or Folders.

3   Type the file name you are looking for and make sure you are looking on all possible hard drives.

4   If the file is located, jot down its location so you will be able to direct Live to the correct folder.

5   If you cannot find the file, pray that you have backed up your sounds to CD/DVD and will find it there. If not, well...back to the old drawing board.

Working with Multiple Versions

By now you can guess that we're going to heartily recommend that you save multiple versions of every song, creation, loop, or other chunk of digital data that is near and dear to your heart. Every time we do this, we feel just a little bit of reassurance that our creative work is safely documented and will not be lost by some idiotic press of a button, or some random Bill Gatesian infection, etc.

To do this in the most effective and least confusing manner, set up a folder entitled Backup. Copy your files into the Backup folder. Don't change their names or anything else. Sounds simple enough doesn't it? It is, but many people create elaborate backup file names that can be hard to remember.

If you have a multiple-partition hard drive, make sure to put your Backup folder and files on a different partition (a different drive letter) than the original song and sounds files. Or you may wish to back up to a different hard drive altogether. This will ensure their safety if your original partition gets corrupted.

Getting Help

The software world is big on searchable help menus, online help files, and gazillion-page PDF manuals. Between Google.com and online forums (such as Ableton's), the challenge is in the sifting.

The Info View

Are you having trouble locating what you need quickly enough? Once again, Ableton has anticipated the needs of their end user—this time in the form of many methods to seek out help in Live. Built into the very interface of Live is the

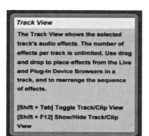

"Info View"—a retractable and informative window in the lower-left corner of the Live window that will discuss whatever topic correlates with the control your mouse is hovering over. (See Figure 4.27.) This won't always provide enough information to satisfy the power user you are becoming, but in a pinch or sudden memory lapse, it is the perfect thing to remind you of, "oh yeah, that's what this button is for."

Figure 4.27

The Info View can be hidden or expanded to give you quick bits of pertinent Live wisdom.

Feel free to pop this baby open any time you are unsure about a specific element of Live. You can easily hide it again, to protect your reputation, when your friend looks over your shoulder.

Getting Help On-Line

We all know the Internet holds an amazing amount of random and erroneous content. Finding precisely what you are after can be more elusive than Elvis' ghost. Thankfully, Ableton knows this better than most and remains faithful to their customers by providing the Live user forum, and reliable technical support. You can also feel free to drop corporate headquarters a note and tell them what a great job they've done.

All you need to do is click on Live's Help menu and you will see these options:

※ **Read the Live Manual:** The new manual is in Adobe PDF format and only takes up about five megabytes of hard drive space. Most of the information is expanded upon in this book, but sometimes a point in the right direction may do the trick. Go to the Help menu and choose "Read the Live Manual" to automatically open the document.

❋ **Visit Ableton.com:** Ableton's Web site is easy on the eyes and full of neatly organized goodies. If you are looking for some helpful distraction, the Artist page hosts scores of interviews, loops to download, and insightful hardware and setup tips. You'll also notice that Ableton prides themselves on acknowledging bugs as they are reported instead of denying their existence. After all, bugs are a part of software and Ableton's admissions and frequently provided workarounds, will tell you that you are not alone with your problem.

❋ **Join the User Forum:** Ableton Live users are some of the more savvy audio software heads on the planet. Try posting your question and set the option for e-mail notification (you'll get an e-mail message when someone responds to your post). Nearly all sensible inquiries are answered, even if they are repeats, or misnomers. In fact, once in a while, real live Ableton employees will jump in on the discussion. Now that's team spirit.

❋ **Talk to Ableton:** This link is really more about general inquiries, ideas, and feedback. If you're looking for information, try the "Get Support" option (see next bulleted item). However, if you just want to put in your two cents or share an idea or a complaint, then drop a line here.

❋ **Get Support:** Every so often, the user board isn't fast enough, or a problem is just plain weird enough that you really need a direct line to the author. Realize that Ableton, like most specialized software houses, is small and they may need a couple of days to get back to you.

❋ **Get Downloads:** In the realm of leading edge software, Downloads can be your lifeline. Check back on this link every month or so to see what's cooking, what's the latest update, and to be sure you have the latest version number. There is nothing more embarrassing than hounding your sound card or computer manufacturer about some strange conflict only to realize you have yet to download Ableton's latest patch. Trust me, somehow I know.

The Course Technology Web Site

Because we do make music with this software, we have developed a few different template ideas that help inspire us to get creative in Live. Course Technology has been gracious enough to grant us a small loft in cyberspace for the express purpose of sharing some of these ideas with you. And since there is a good chance Ableton will make some small changes or upgrades to the software that may affect this book, not to mention any additional information we think of (the day after the final edit is sent), we will be using the site to post corrections and changes. New artist tips and Live working strategies will also end up on this site.

The site will also be updated with templates, loops, and feedback about the book and future versions of Live. We will place news, corrections, and any suggestions you might offer (should they be sharable). To check in on what's going on in the world of *Live Power!*, check out www.courseptr.com.

Charlie Clouser

Who's Using Live?

Charlie Clouser—Musician/Producer/Remix Artist

Charlie Clouser got his start in a Manhattan music store around the dawn of MIDI. By making it his business to know the ins and outs of each new keyboard, synth, and piece of electronic gadgetry, Clouser became the "call-guy" for anyone playing New York and looking for a synth. A short time later, Clouser went on to play keyboards and design sounds for the seminal industrial act Nine Inch Nails. He has become one of the world's most inventive and sought-after remix artists and composers. His recent projects include a Rob Zombie remix for *Enter the Matrix* and scoring the high-impact television show *Fastlane*.

A self-proclaimed "Mac guy," Charlie likes to multi-track several different Macs running various software into his Pro-Tools and Logic rigs. Because of the sheer size of his sample/loop library, Clouser relies heavily upon Ableton Live's instant loop synchronization and preview features. In an interview hosted by Ableton, Charlie explains, "I use two dual processor 1GHz Macintoshes side-by-side; one running Pro Tools, the other Ableton Live and Reason. The Ableton computer has an RME Hammerfall card in it with Lightpipe over to the big guy and a Midiman 4 port MIDI interface, slaved by a beat clock tied to a master sequencer. There's no analog inputs or outputs on my Ableton rig at all, it's strapped to 24 channels of ADAT bridges on the Pro Tools system. When I'm working in Ableton, I break out to 12 stereo pairs, which come up on Pro Tools' screen faders. Basically, I think of Ableton as a drum machine. It's as simple to operate as a can of soda. It works all day long and it will not crash. I'm old school—I still have stacks of drum machines. You hit the spacebar on Pro Tools and everybody lights up and runs—old style. I treat Ableton in that same manner. Certainly I do complete performances on it, but I am always recording its output as though it were a performance instrument, which I then record on my multi-track, which just happens to be another computer.

"Quite literally Ableton is the holy grail of software. I've been waiting for 15 years for a method to preview my loops, one at a time, in sync to my song. One mouse click, one button. I even had a cash bounty on the problem. Several of us were going to chip in $5000 to get someone to write it! Then Ableton came out—I drove 60 miles to go pick up the first copy the day it hit the streets in America. Just the ability to choose loops and hear what they will sound like in context to my song has revolutionized the way I work."

5 } Making Music in Live

At last, the time has come to begin making music in Live. In this chapter, we'll cover how to analyze and prepare files for use in Live. We will explore the common areas of Clip View and, through practical examples, discover some of the most common ways music is made in Live. We'll also take a look at software configuration and general working methods for the Live musician.

Whether you are playing a popular hotspot or working in the privacy of your own home, the basic Live configuration and performance concepts are the same. Before writing this book, we spent a good amount of time interviewing Live "Power-users," the Ableton Live team, and conceptualists Robert Henke and Gerhard Behles. Through these discussions, and our own practice, we have discovered that nearly everybody is using Live just a little bit differently, depending upon their musical style and live performance needs. DJs demand different things out of Live than do producers working in studios. Film and television composers may be looking for different kinds of sounds than a musician playing Live in a band. As you read this chapter, think about how you want to use Live and focus on the areas that make sense for your situation. After all, there is no reason a DJ can't borrow techniques from a film composer and vice versa. As we proceed through the various ways to work in Live, take a minute to try some of the provided examples. As with learning any musical instrument, discovery will lead to inspiration, additional detail will bring delight, and a little practice never hurt either.

We will warn you now that this is a long chapter—we will be covering a lot of information. You'll find it interesting, though, that each concept we explain will introduce the next. This parallels the way Live's working process is based on a hierarchical structure of principles starting from small musical pieces up to a finished masterpiece. The basic procedure goes like this:

* **Create individual musical parts**—Record bass parts, guitar riffs, keyboard lines, drum grooves, MIDI instruments, or import samples and MIDI sequences. These become *Clips*.

* **Create song sections**—Arrange the Clips side by side in the Session View to make *Scenes*. Each scene represents a section of your song, such as intro, verse, chorus, bridge, and outro.

* **Record an Arrangement**—Live will record your actions in the Session View while you trigger the Scenes on the fly to record your song into the Arrangement View.

* **Finalize the song**—Edit the arrangement, add effects to the mix, layer additional parts, finalize the automation, and render the song to disk.

Each element of Live's interface is optimized for one of these tasks. You'll see that Clips are manipulated in the Clip View, Scenes in the Session View, song arrangements in the Arrangement View, and mixes in the Session Mixer and Track Views. This logical approach and use of only one window makes Live a streamlined composition environment. Furthermore, the same tools you use for writing are available for performing—there's a blurry gray line between composing and playing in Live.

You'll notice that the steps above are not numbered. This is because the creation process can always be in flux when using Live. You can record multiple layers of a part in the Arrangement View and bounce the results to a Clip in the Session View. You may begin mixing the song as you're composing it. In any case, Live is flexible enough to suit your style.

Working Methods

One of the remarkable things about Live is that no two people use it the same way. Some musicians come to use Live as a quick and flexible multitrack recorder that allows them to explore their own music in deep and original ways. Other artists use Live as a way to quickly integrate their samples and loops into a performance or group environment. Some will use Live for the entire production process—concept to mixdown. Recent television and movie music composers such as Charlie Clouser (Ex-Nine Inch Nails keyboardist), Klaus Badelt (*The Thin Red Line, Mission Impossible 2, Hannibal, Pirates of the Caribbean,* and other big-budget films) as well as Rick Marvin (*U-571, Six Feet Under,* and many more) have been using Live's time-stretching capabilities to enable them to synchronize their music to video images. DJs are using Live to play their favorite tracks, as well as to integrate their own material and pre-produced loops. In other words, DJs are producing and remixing full-length tracks on the fly; while producers are acting more and more like DJs all the time by mixing unusual textures, rhythms, and styles into a single track. On that note, one of the most popular uses for Live will be from remix and dance music producers, who take a pre-produced track, break it down, and rebuild it in another musical style. Let's take a closer look at each of these methods, to better understand each one's perspective and see why Live is the perfect application for each approach.

Using Live to DJ

Today, DJs make music using CDs, MiniDisc players, MP3 players, turntables, and computers. Their artistry involves selecting their own mix of music or musical components (beats, samples, etc.) to entertain, explore, or make something altogether new. Live fits into the DJ world perfectly, as it allows for WAV or AIFF files to be synchronized to other tracks and other playback devices. Additional parts, such as beats and basslines, can be made on the fly using MIDI instruments, which also lock perfectly to the beat. Many of the DJs we've talked with use Live in conjunction with turntables, CD players, and other computers. Often, they will spend a good deal of time configuring their songs for use in Live. This can involve editing tracks in a wave editor, mapping any necessary Warp Markers (see Chapter 6) in Live's Clip View to time align the track, or merely cropping their favorite portion of a larger track to be used as one in a collection of many time-synced loops. The bottom line is that DJs are benefiting from the flexibility and choices Live offers. DJs can use different parts of the same song looped against one another at the same time, or take advantage of multiple tracks (as opposed to being limited to a finite number of turntables, CD players, or mixer channels). Besides, a digital DJ doesn't ever have to worry about wearing out precious vinyl and irreplaceable acetates or scratching a CD surface.

Using Live with a Band

The organic nature of bands may seem like an unfit environment for computers. Every gig has a different energy and playing to the same old backing track every time could end up sucking the life out of a stage performance. Many bands have a free-form approach that doesn't follow a preset number of bars in an arrangement. Whatever the case, Live has some exciting news for you: the parts from the computer *can* be different every time and can be placed under full control of the band.

⁕ Live performers, especially jazz musicians, may feel that using a sequencer removes a level of freedom that is essential for improvisational music. Many times throughout this book (with more to come), we've referred to Live as a sequencing *instrument*. Live can be played in a live setting and it leaves the musical arrangement completely under user control. Perhaps your band always practices a song with an 8-bar solo section for your guitarist. When you are playing the show, your guitarist basically "catches on fire" and you all feel that the solo needs to be longer. By having the song arranged as Scenes in the Session View, you can extend the solo section by *doing nothing*; thus, allowing the solo section Clips to loop, naturally extending the section. You finally trigger the next section once the guitarist signals to move on.

⁕ The Tap Tempo features of Live will keep Live playing to the band, rather than the band playing to the sequence. A drummer could assign a trigger pad or foot pedal (anything that outputs MIDI) to the Tap Tempo button and could tap out quarter notes from time to time to keep Live in time with the band. Starting a song is also under the drummer's control as they can issue four taps while they count off the song resulting in the band and Live starting together.

⁕ When playing a gig, it may be necessary for some of the musicians to hear a click track from Live, possibly when the song calls for two bars of silence with everyone (including the computer) then coming in together. Live can provide this by means of its cue and multi-channel output functions (see the following note).

⁕ Click Track

A click track is nothing more than a metronome that a band or musician plays along with, just like the one in Live's Control Bar. Usually, the click is piped into the headphones of the person(s) who is recording. By playing along with the click track, the musician performs the musical parts in synch with parts of the track that have been previously recorded. In the studio, click tracks are often replaced by percussive loops, which are less monotonous and generally more musical. This can easily be accomplished with Live by assigning a Track with a fitting loop to Cue (see "Audio Tracks and Their Controls" in Chapter 4).

Multi-Tracking

Crafting songs by multi-tracking can be one of the most rewarding and creative activities a songwriter can take part in. Whether you are a solitary artist composing a demo in his bedroom, or a band with limited input channels, multi-track recordings can allow you to add many layers of music to the same piece without erasing previous tracks. In today's age of unlimited audio tracks, we take for granted the power of layering ideas on top of one another and auditioning different digital arrangements. Live can be a perfect composition tool or arrangement auditioning tool. We have shown several songwriters Live's ability to easily and musically rearrange a song (whether it was recorded to a click or not). Often their eyes are wide with disbelief. While Pro Tools, Logic, Cubase, and other multi-track studio applications are powerful, their audio flexibility cannot match Live's instant audio warping ability. In the next few years, watch for your favorite songwriters to be employing Live instead of their ratty old tape decks.

Producing and Remixing Music

Since the beginnings of computer-based music, remix and dance music producers have been the driving force behind many of the industry's most impressive innovations. Of course, "producer" is a loose term that usually refers to any remix artists, consultants working with bands or vocalists, or musicians with a penchant for hard disk recording and editing. Whether they are set up in a fancy studio or holed up in their college dorm room, producers using Live may be the largest and most feature-savvy group of them all. Many producers have already tapped into the exciting prospect of remixing another artist's work, as well as creating new music, when using Live's instant time-stretching and unprecedented sample manipulation ability. Producers want to compose, make music, put together unusual elements, find the "right" hook, etc. Live allows them the creative freedom to stick to the task at hand while keeping the process simple enough to remain focused on the music.

Scoring for Video

They say timing is everything. Nowhere is this more evident than in scoring music for the moving image. Whether you are attempting to add sound effects or mood music or creating a complete soundtrack, Live's ability to stretch audio in sync with MIDI is the perfect tool for the job. As we begin to discuss Live's unique "elastic audio" ability in the next few sections, you will see how Live is built to make sound behave in ways that were simply not possible before. Film and television music composers often run into problems when trying to synchronize audio and video. For instance, the audio track may need to speed up and then slow down; the music then must reflect this tempo change. Movie and TV music also need to be done quickly and Live's ability to be played, rather than only programmed, is a huge advantage.

While we have pointed out some of the typical ways creative people like you are making use of Live, we have by no means covered it all. New uses for Live continue to emerge. In fact, you will invent a few of your own. As an example, check out this brief excerpt from an interview with Film Composer Klaus Badelt (taken from the Ableton Web site). In the "Who's Using Live" section at the end of this chapter, we will gain even more perspective on how Badelt is employing Ableton Live in his motion picture soundtrack work.

Fair Use

New ways to use Live are popping up all the time. Here are a couple of ideas by film music maestro Klaus Badelt.

"Ever since Live came out, it changed my life. It enabled me to use our whole library of percussive loops. I'm not talking about loops (only) in the sense of just electronic loops, but all kinds of orchestral or ethnic percussion loops. I'm finally able to use them all very quick and try them out in tempo. It makes it possible to work much faster, especially when you only have a few days to write a whole score.

"I don't actually use (Live) in the way it was originally intended. I'm playing it from my sequencer. I trigger the program from the other computer as Live runs on its own machine. It holds the library. I drag in the loops I'm using and trigger them from the keyboard. I use the effects in there, but basically sub-mix and then send to the mixer. I basically use it as a synthesizer."

—Klaus Badelt is credited with *The Thin Red Line, Mission Impossible 2, Hannibal, Pearl Harbor, Pirates of the Caribbean,* and many other award-winning films. (Taken from www.ableton.com.)

In the next section, we are going to take a brief but important sidestep to explore the more practical side of Live's interface, Clip View and Track View, as well as several tips for working with loops and samples. Later in the chapter we will return to the idea of working methods, and different approaches for using Live. The combination of both practical knowledge and tried and true examples should put you well on your way to discovering your own particular way of harnessing the power of Live.

Live's Musical Building Blocks: The Clip

Within a musical composition, the parts involved can be broken into smaller pieces, such as "verse 1 bassline," "chorus backing vocals," "intro percussion," or whatever terms you might use. Each of these pieces is suited perfectly for a *Clip*—the musical building block in Live. Everything in Live is based on the creation, editing, arrangement, and playing of Clips. By having the pieces of your song assembled in Clips, you can then arrange the song on the fly and intermix different sections, whether for a live performance or as a means for programming the Arrangement View.

The Clip

Clips are the colored rectangles scattered throughout the Session View (Figure 5.1a) and the Arrangement View (Figure 5.1b). Each one plays an audio file or MIDI instrument. Playing Clips in the Session View is done by clicking the small "play" triangle at the left side of the Clip. Clips in the Arrangement View will be played when the Now Line passes over them.

Clips can be thought of as small, independent MIDI sequencers and audio samplers that all play in relation with one another. This is similar to pattern-style sequencing, except that the patterns can all be different lengths from one another. This offers the convenience of creating anything from small musical units to larger evolving parts, and using them in any combination together.

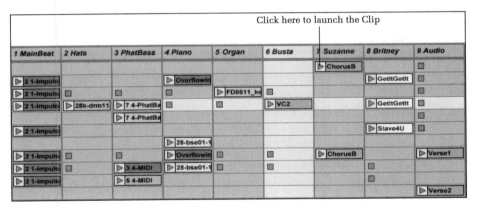

Figure 5.1a

Clips, as they appear in the Session View.

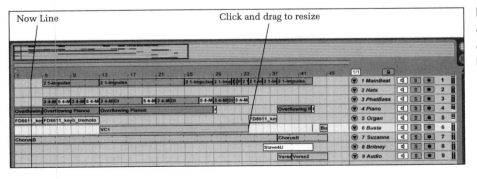

Figure 5.1b

Clips in the Arrangement View can be resized to change how long they will play.

While a Clip can be copied from one place to another, either by copying it from the Session View to the Arrangement View (or vice versa), or by creating multiple instances in both Views, each resulting Clip is independent from the others, even if they contain the same musical data and share the same name. This means that a Clip that was recorded into the Session View can have its parameters modified in the Arrangement View while leaving the original Session View Clip intact. This separation will become clearer as we look closer at the Session and Arrangement Views later in this chapter.

What Do Clips Contain?

Clips come in two forms: Audio and MIDI. Audio Clips (Figure 5.2a) contain references to audio files while MIDI Clips (Figure 5.2b) contain MIDI data for playing MIDI instruments (either virtual or hardware instruments).

Figure 5.2a

An Audio Clip plays an audio file on the computer. A graphical representation of the audio can be seen in the Clip View waveform window.

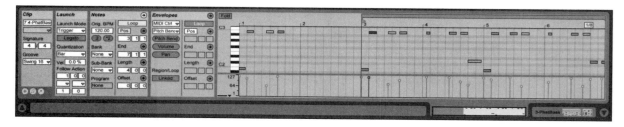

Figure 5.2b

MIDI Clips contain sequences of MIDI notes and data, which can also be seen in the Clip View.

What Audio Clips Don't Contain

While you can easily think of all the little Clip boxes as containing audio loops and such, it should be remembered that the audio file used in those Clips is not actually part of the Clip or Live Set. A Clip merely contains the information necessary for Live to play an audio file from disk—it is a pointer to your sample.

Should that file (sample) become altered by another application, such as a wave editor, each Clip that used that file will now play with the same alteration. If you delete the sample that is referenced by a Clip, the Clip, and any other Clips that used that file, won't play any more! See Chapter 4 on how to save your Set as Self-Contained to keep the audio files you use in a safe location.

Where Do Clips Come From?

Clips are created in two ways: By adding an audio or MIDI file from disk to the Session or Arrangement Views, and by recording new audio and MIDI performances into Live. When learning the first concepts of Live, you'll more than likely begin with Audio Clips created from audio files on your computer. Live comes with a library of loops for this purpose and you'll also find sample libraries from companies such as East West, Big Fish Audio, Power FX, M-Audio, and more, to arm you to the teeth with audio loops for musical inspiration. Of course, Live can work with audio files that aren't loops—any audio file (in WAV, AIFF, and SDII format) on your computer is fair game for manipulation in Live.

What's also great is that new Clips can be made by recording audio from external sources. If you've found a drum loop and bass loop that you want to use as the foundation for your song, you can plug in your guitar and record your own riffs on top, which are instantly turned into Clips.

The same is true for MIDI Clips. Tracks from MIDI files can be added from the File Browsers or new performances can be recorded directly into the Session or Arrangement. Unlike Audio Clips, the MIDI information in a MIDI Clip is saved in the Live Set file itself. Even MIDI Clips created from MIDI files will be independent from the original files.

Because the methods for recording Audio and MIDI Clips are different, they will be covered separately in the next chapters. What's important to understand at this point is how Clips work and how they integrate into the production process in Live. Whether they came from a sample CD or from your own voice, both Audio and MIDI Clips behave the same; most importantly, once you have a full understanding of using Clips, you'll be able to record better Clips yourself.

The Clip View

While there are two distinctly different types of Clips in Live (MIDI and Audio), there are a number of behaviors and settings that are common to both types of Clips, all of which will be discussed next. The common behaviors of MIDI and Audio Clips help blur the line between audio and MIDI in the Session and Arrangement. After all, when you're performing, you don't really care if a piano part is coming from an audio file or being triggered from a MIDI instrument. When you launch the piano Clip, you expect to hear the piano part with nothing else to worry about.

❋ ❋ ❋

Obviously, your understanding of Clips will have a tremendous impact on your ability to use Live. If Clips are not set up properly, many of Live's other functions, such as the ability to play multiple Clips in sync, will be compromised. The settings determining Clip behavior are accessed and edited through the Clip View (Figure 5.3) which appears at the bottom of the Live window whenever you double-click a Clip.

Figure 5.3

The Clip View contains multiple sections that can be shown and hidden using the icons at the bottom-left corner of the window. Turn them all on now so you can see all the options in Clip View.

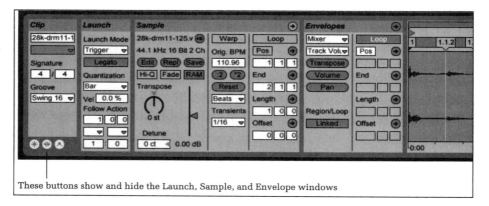

These buttons show and hide the Launch, Sample, and Envelope windows

There are different sections within the Clip View that can be accessed with the icons in the lower-left corner of the window. A few of these sections are common to both MIDI and Audio Clips. Those common properties will be explained in this chapter while the type-specific parameters and features will be explained in detail in their own chapters (see Chapters 6 and 7).

The sections we'll be concerned with at the moment are the Clip and Launch sections as well as the Loop settings found in the Sample window (for Audio Clips) or Notes window (MIDI Clips).

Clip Name and Color

The first two settings in the Clip section (Figure 5.4) are purely cosmetic—

Figure 5.4

Give your Clips useful names, like "synth1" or "vrs1Vox." You can also give similar Clips the same color to help organize your Views.

they have no impact on the behavior or sound of the Clip. The first field is the Clip name which can be any name and as many characters as you want. You'll only see about the first nine letters in Session View Clips, but you may see more of the name if you extend the Clip in the Arrangement View.

Clips are automatically named when they are created (they're also given a color based on your Preferences). If you create a Clip by dragging a file in from the Browser, the Clip will be named the same as the file. When you record a new Clip, it will be given the name of the Track it is created in.

To help keep multiple takes (recordings) in order, Live tacks a number on in front of the Clip (and file) name as each new one is created.

When changing the name of an Audio Clip, you should be aware that the name of the associated audio file is not changed. If you drag a file from the browser called "DnB Loop07 (168 BPM)" into the Session View, the resulting Clip will have the exact same name. If you change the Clip name to something more useful, like "MainBeat," the original audio file on your hard drive will still be named "DnB Loop07 (168 BPM)."

Time Signature

The Clip's Time Signature determines the numbering of the grid markers and quantizing grid (discussed separately in Chapters 6 and 7, respectively). It also affects the Launch Quantizing behavior, which we'll explain in a moment.

Groove Template

The Groove section is probably one of the most mind-blowing features you'll ever witness in an audio program. Using Groove Templates and the Groove Amount value in the Control Bar, you can add a shuffle or swing feel to your songs. The idea of morphing between straight and swing feels is not new. Many classic drum machines, like Roland's TR-909, have a shuffle control. The shuffle control delays certain beats of a sequence to create a swing or triplet feel—the further the control is turned, the more dramatic the effect.

While a swing control on a drum machine isn't news, swinging audio tracks is unheard of, or should we say, was unheard of. Since Live already has the whole time-stretching thing down, it's not really surprising that it can make such a surgical change on the fly to an audio file. After all, if MIDI sequencers just delay certain beats, Live can delay portions of an audio file (using short expansions and compressions of time) to yield the same results. Indeed, Live can swing your audio and MIDI performances in perfect sync with each other.

Choosing your Quantize Template will determine which beats get delayed. The Groove Amount (Figure 5.5) will set the intensity of the shuffle from 0 to 99. For example, the "Swing 8" setting is for 8th note swings and shuffles. Setting the Groove Amount to "50" will cause a straight 16th note groove to morph into a 6/8 feel. The "Swing 16" setting will take a straight 16th feel and delay the even numbered 16th notes, resulting in a nice swing to get everybody dancing. Of course, you don't have to set the Groove Amount to

Figure 5.5

The Groove amount is the tiny, unlabeled number in the left section of the Control Bar. Click and drag, type in a number, or assign it to a MIDI control to change it.

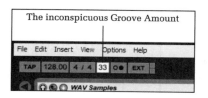

The inconspicuous Groove Amount

"50." Smaller amounts will make the swing less pronounced and less machine-like at the same time. If you're looking for a natural swing feel, set the Groove Amount to about "34." Any Clip with "Straight" selected for the Groove will be impervious to the Groove Amount setting. Going beyond "50" will give your Clip a crazy hip-hop "over-swing" that you'll want to hear for yourself!

One of These Clips Is Doing Its Own Thing

While the Groove Amount value sets the intensity of the swing applied by Live to your Clips, remember that each Clip has its own Groove setting. If you're increasing the Groove Amount but are getting weird results, be sure that all of the playing Clips are set to the same template. If some Clips are set to "Swing 8" while others are set to "Swing 16," the time shifts will not be in sync with each other, which can result in strange poly-rhythms (of course, if this is what you're after, don't mind us).

It may seem strange that Ableton didn't just use a global Groove setting; however, by having each Clip follow its own Groove settings, it's possible to have part of the song (perhaps Clips at the beginning) in "Swing 8" while another section of the song (maybe the bridge) is in "Swing 16."

Quantize

There are two types of quantizing that can be performed with Live. One method will line up stray notes in a MIDI Clip. This is called Note Quantization, which will be explained in Chapter 7. The other method is Launch Quantization, which is the topic of this section.

Launch Quantization determines when a Clip will start playing or recording after it has been triggered. Proper Launch Quantization settings will ensure that Clips will start on time and in sync with each other, even if they are triggered a little early by us sloppy humans. The default setting for this value is set in the Preferences. Most people choose either "Global" or "Bar" as their default values.

The available choices for Launch Quantization range from 1/32 notes up to 8 bars and are selected from the dropdown menu shown in Figure 5.6. There are also two additional settings, Global and None, which will cause the Clip to follow the Global Quantize setting (in the Control Bar) or ignore quantization, respectively. Any Clips set to "Bar" will only start playing on the downbeat of a measure, even if they were triggered before that. This means you can click (launch) a number of new Clips, but they won't start playing until the next measure. You can therefore launch a new bassline, drum part, and guitar riff halfway through the bar and Live will wait until the downbeat before playing them all.

When you trigger a Clip before its quantize setting will allow it to start, its green "play" triangle (the *fire button* or play button) will start to blink indicating that the Clip is standing by to play. Once the beat for the quantize setting is reached, the play icon will turn solid green and the Clip will begin playing. It's at this point that the previous Clip playing in the Track (if there was one) will be cut off in favor of the new one.

Figure 5.6

The Quantize settings for a Clip.

Of course, you may not always want to start a Clip on the downbeat of a measure. In these cases, a smaller quantize setting can be selected. A setting of 1/4 will force a clicked Clip to start on the next beat rather than waiting for the bar. Any Clip set to None will start playing the instant it is launched.

✳ **Bar Length**

Bar is another term for measure, which is the length determined by the time signature. In the case of 4/4 time, a measure (bar) is four beatslong with the quarter note equaling one beat. 12/8 is twelve beats long with the eighth note equaling one beat. This means that the length of time determined by a Bar quantize setting is dependent on the time signature.

If the time signature is 3/4 and your Quantize is set to Bar, you'll be able to launch new Clips every three beats (each measure is three beats long). When the time signature is 4/4, you'll be able to launch the Clips every four beats.

A special condition can arise when you're using Clips with time signatures different than the Live Set. If our project is set to 4/4, but our Clip has a time signature of 3/4, a setting of "Bar" in the Clip View will allow the Clip to launch every three beats. This means that while 4/4 Clips will launch on the downbeat, the 3/4 Clip will launch on bar 1, beat 1; bar 1, beat 4; bar 2, beat 3; and bar 3, beat 2. In this case, the length of the "Bar" setting is determined by the Clip's time signature.

If, on the other hand, the 3/4 Clip has its quantize set to Global, the quantize setting in the Control Bar will be used. If this value is set to "Bar," the 3/4 Clip will launch every 4 beats (on the downbeat with the other 4/4 Clips) because the length of the Global Bar setting is determined by the project time signature (4/4 in this case).

Launch Controls

To add more creative possibilities when using Clips, Ableton has given us four launch modes (Figure 5.7) to add extra control to our performances. In all of our discussions so far, launching a Clip has caused it to start playing (once the quantize time has been reached) at which point it continues to

Figure 5.7

Launch Modes: Choose, but
choose wisely . . .

play indefinitely (if looped) or through its entirety (when unlooped). This is the default behavior for Clips, and one that makes quite a lot of sense, but times may arise when you may want a different level of control.

Launch Modes will allow you to change not only the Clip playback state when the Clip is launched (either by clicking with the mouse or pressing an assigned Key or MIDI note) but will also determine the action taken (if any) when the mouse or key is released. The four available Launch Modes are as follows:

❄ **Trigger Mode**—The most common Launch Mode for use in most performance situations is Live's Trigger Mode. Each time you fire a Clip, it will launch. Once a Clip is launched and playing, you will be able to stop its playback only by pressing one of the Clip Stop buttons located in the same track. This mode ignores the up-tick (release) of the mouse button, computer keyboard key, or MIDI note. Each Clip can be fired as rapidly as the Quantization will allow (more on this in the "Launch Quantization" section that follows) and each time the Clip is fired, it will restart the Clip from the beginning, even if it was already playing.

❄ **Gate Mode**—When triggering a Clip in Gate Mode, you will only hear the sound for as long as your mouse or keyboard key is depressed. This is an excellent setting for dropping in snippets of sound without playing the entire Clip. In short, holding your left mouse button (or MIDI/computer-keyboard key) down will continuously play the Clip until released.

❄ **Toggle Mode**—With Toggle Mode engaged, the fire button basically turns into an "on/off" switch for the Clip. If you "launch" a Clip that is playing, it will stop. Launch the stopped Clip, and it will begin playing. This also works at the Scene level if you trigger a Scene with Clips set in Toggle mode. Each time you trigger the Scene, Clips that are playing will stop and stopped Clips will start. It is this functionality that makes Toggle Mode our personal favorite since each Clip Launch button can now have two functions: Start *and* Stop.

❄ **Repeat Mode**—Repeat mode is a way of re-triggering a Clip by holding down the mouse or assigned key/MIDI note. Any time the mouse or key is held, the Clip will continuously restart itself at the rate specified by the Clip's Quantize setting. If the setting is 1/4, holding the mouse/key will cause only the first beat of the Clip to play over and over again. When the mouse or key is released, the Clip will play through its entirety like normal. This mode can create fun stutter effects, but should be used sparingly. This mode is probably not a good choice for default behavior.

Velocity

Just below the Quantization box is the Clip Velocity scale setting (Figure 5.8). This value only works for Clips launched by MIDI. It uses the incoming velocity level of the MIDI note to set the playback volume of the Clip. At 0%, the velocity has no effect on Clip playback volume—it plays at its original level. At 100%, the Clip will respond as a velocity sensitive Clip. For settings in between, lower velocities will have less of an attenuating (quieting) effect. This works for both Audio and MIDI Clips.

Figure 5.8

Velocity scaling based on the MIDI velocity of the Clip's trigger note.

Follow Actions

Live's Follow Actions allow a new level of automation to be achieved within the Session View. Basically, using Follow Actions, you can set rules by which one Clip can launch another. Any particular Clip can launch Clips above and below it, replay itself, or even stop itself; all based on odds and a time period that we can program. We like to think of Follow Actions as a virtual "finger" that presses Clip Launch buttons for us. While that may not sound that impressive yet, it's just another example of Ableton's ingenuity in bringing us simple, generalized tools that can unleash the imagination. In fact, Follow Actions open up so many creative possibilities that you'll find a long list of possible applications listed in Chapter 14, "Live 4.0 Power."

Follow Actions work on groups of Clips, which are Clips arranged above and below one another in the same Track (Figure 5.9). If an empty Clip Slot is between two Clips, they are in separate groups. Follow Actions will allow automatic triggering of other Clips in the group and cannot be used to trigger Clips in different groups or Tracks.

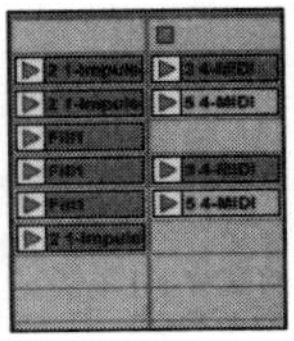

Figure 5.9

The track on the left features one group of Clips while the track on the right has two groups.

The time and conditions for a Follow Action are set in the three sections at the bottom of the Clip's Launch window (Figure 5.10). The first section, the Follow Action Time, determines how long the Clip plays before it performs the Follow Action. If the time is set to 2.0.0, the Clip will wait for two bars before "clicking" on another Clip.

Figure 5.10

These parameters determine the Follow Action behavior of the Clip.

Instead of just doing the same action over and over again, Ableton gives you the ability to create two different possible Follow Action scenarios for each Clip. Live will randomly choose between the two actions selected in the drop-down menus in Figure 5.11 (one on the left and the other on the right). The possible Follow Actions and their effects are:

❊ **No Action**—The empty menu selection refers to No Action, and is the default Action for all new Clips. In fact, Clips are always performing Follow Actions, but with No Action selected in both menus, Live will never trigger any other Clip.

❊ **Stop**—This action will stop the Clip. This allows you to make a one-bar loop play for eight bars every time you trigger it, for example.

❊ **Play Again**—Essentially re-triggers the Clip just as if you'd clicked on it again with the mouse.

❊ **Previous/Next**—These options will trigger the Clip either above or below the current one. If the Clip at the top of a group triggers the Play Previous action, it will "wrap around" and trigger the bottom Clip of the group and vice versa.

❊ **First/Last**—These will trigger the top or bottom Clips in a group no matter how many Clips are in the group. If the top Clip in a group triggers the Play First action, it will re-trigger itself.

❊ **Play Any**—This action will trigger a randomly chosen Clip from the group. It is possible to re-trigger the same Clip with this option.

Figure 5.11

The left Follow Action will trigger the Clip above this one while the right Follow Action will trigger the Clip below this one.

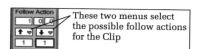

These two menus select the possible follow actions for the Clip

Which Action Live chooses to perform is based on the odds set in the numerical boxes below each Follow Action. By default, the odds are 1:0, meaning that the Action in the left menu will always be performed. Odds of 0:1 will cause the right action to always be performed. Odds of 1:1 will give you a 50–50 chance of either the left or right Action being performed. You can put in any values you like, such as 2:3 or 1:200.

❊ **Playing the Odds**

It should be noted that odds are calculated fresh every time a Follow Action is performed. If you have a Clip with Follow Action odds of 1:1 and Live chose the left Action the first time, it does not mean that Live will choose the right Action the next time. Just as it is possible to roll the same number on a die time after time, it is quite possible for Live to choose the left Action five times in a row, even with 1:1 odds.

When looking at the Follow Action choices, some of you may be scratching your heads at the "Play Clip Again" selection. What is the point of this one? To explain, let's look at a practical example:

You have two drum loops, one is the standard beat while the second is a variation of the first. We really like the standard beat, but from time to time, we want the variation thrown in to keep things from getting too repetitive. Consider Figures 5.12a and 5.12b. Both may appear to be the proper setups for this situation, but one has a flaw.

Follow Actions are performed only after the specified time has passed since triggering the Clip. Thus, in the case of Figure 5.12a, after one bar, the Clip performs the Follow Action. If the option on the left, "do nothing," is chosen, no Follow Action will be performed and the Clip will keep playing (infinitely if set to loop). In Figure 5.12b, when the left option is performed, the Clip will be retriggered, causing the Follow Action time to start counting down again. After the specified time, odds will be calculated and the appropriate Action will be performed. By using "Play Clip Again," we have basically looped the Follow Action.

Figure 5.12a

Here, if the left Follow Action is chosen, the Clip will loop indefinitely.

Figure 5.12b

In this example, when the left Action is performed, it will relaunch this Clip causing the Follow Action to be performed again.

❄ **Quantize Still Rules**

When triggering other Clips with Follow Actions, the target Clip will still follow its Launch Quantize setting. If a Clip has a Follow Action time of 1 beat and triggers a Clip with a "Bar" quantize setting, the new Clip will still wait for the downbeat before playing. If the Clip is set to "Global" or "None," the Clip will begin playing immediately when the Follow Action triggers it.

Tempo Settings

A Clip's Tempo is used to determine the timing grid for the Clip. This timing grid affects the grid markers and Warp Markers in an Audio Clip and the playback speed of a MIDI Clip. This Tempo is also what Live uses to keep Clips in sync with each other (if Live doesn't know the original tempo, it won't know the proper amount to speed up or slow down the Clip to match the current Tempo).

The tempo settings work a little differently in the Audio and MIDI Clip Views. For one, tempo is only available in Audio Clips (Figure 5.13) when the Warp feature (see next chapter) is engaged. If Warp is off, Live will simply play the audio at its original speed and perform no time-stretching on the Clip, therefore its original tempo is irrelevant; however, with it engaged, Live will be

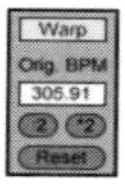

Figure 5.13

A Clip's Tempo setting is crucial to the proper operation of Live. Without the proper value here, the Clip will not match the speed of other Clips in the project.

able to Warp the audio as necessary to match the tempo of the Set. Secondly, the Clip tempo and the position of the grid and Warp Markers are related. As you make timing adjustments with the Warp Markers, you may notice the Original Tempo change slightly (or drastically) to compensate for the change in file playback speed. We will look into this further in Chapter 6.

MIDI Clips do not have Warp Markers, so the original tempo is solely controlled by the user. When a new MIDI Clip is created, it will take on the current tempo of the Live Set. This is usually sufficient and you probably won't need to change it; however, if you do (perhaps an imported MIDI track is playing at the wrong speed), changing the tempo value will scale all of the MIDI data in the Clip accordingly to make it play back faster or slower.

Below the Tempo value are two icons. The left "divide by 2" and right "multiply by 2" buttons will quickly double or halve the playback speed of both Audio and MIDI Clips. If the original tempo was 120 BPM, pressing the "divide by 2" button will result in a new tempo of 60 BPM. If the tempo of the Live Set is 120, Live will play the Clip twice as fast to bring the 60 BPM up to 120 BPM. The "multiply by 2" button will effectively cut playback speed in half. Reset will erase all Warp Markers and return the Clip to default values.

Clip Loop/Region

The size of the actual data in a Clip versus the size of the portion that you choose to use can be vastly different. In other words you may have a 4-bar Clip, but decide to use only the first bar of the part. You may have a five minute song from which you can isolate a great drum fill in the middle. Clip Loop/Region defines the area and length of the sound that is played. This is the tool to use for specifying your loop points, but it can also be used to simply set the beginning and ending of a one-shot Clip. In the example below (Figure 5.14), we are using only a portion of a larger sample. To do this, we constrained the length of the loop by adjusting the Clip Loop/Region brackets to the location we wanted. Note: you can make these adjustments while you are listening, or even recording, in Live.

Remember, Live is streaming audio files from disk as opposed to playing them from RAM. This means that using ten seconds of a ten minute file is no different than using ten seconds of an eleven second file. Don't worry about chopping off the ends of an audio file that you're not using—you may want

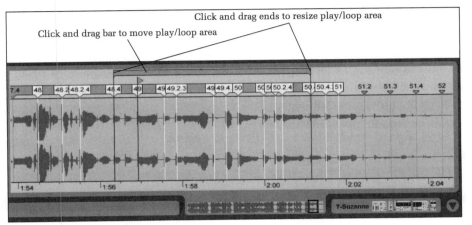

Click and drag ends to resize play/loop area

Click and drag bar to move play/loop area

Figure 5.14

You can adjust the endpoints of the loop or sample by moving the brackets, or shift the entire region by grabbing the top region marker.

❊ Region to Region

One trick employed by DJs and remix artists is to skip around to various regions of the Clip by clicking the Loop/Region Markers in the Clip View, then using the keyboard's up and down arrow keys to change its location. If you have lots of measures containing the same region length, you can skip around the sound to create some musical or wild effects. You can even record this to the Arrangement by pressing Record and then Play.

to use those parts in another song in the future. Moving the region markers around your desired section is all that's necessary.

Loop Settings

Loop Settings (in the Clip View), seen in Figure 5.15, often proves to be a more informational than practical way to change a loop's start, end, length, and offset. You'll probably just find it easier to drag the Loop/Region Markers with the mouse in the Clip View. Still, it is worth noting its features and considering how you may jump to certain parameters by making use of each parameter's three boxes. You may also find it easier to type exact values into these boxes when dealing with long Clips.

Figure 5.15

Each of these Loop Settings can be specified by clicking on the square and moving the mouse up and down or by typing into the boxes, where the digits correspond to measures, beats, and subdivisions.

Pay special attention to the Start/Position Toggle button (usually in the Start position). If Start is active, changing the value of the top boxes will move the Loop Start marker. When Pos (Position) is selected, you can move the entire Clip Loop/Region (both the start and end markers) to a new position within the track by scrolling within the boxes via the mouse.

Also, the arrows beside each locator are a shortcut for zooming to that exact position in the Sample Display. For instance, you may be working on a specific portion of the loop, such as the beginning or the end, and then want to quickly view the entire length of the loop. To do this, press the right-facing arrow beside Length (the third value in this panel). Similarly, you may wish to jump to the end or beginning of the loop. Simply press the Start or End arrow buttons to make this happen.

> ❊ **Red Digits**
>
> When loading new Clips, you may find that some of the numbers in the Loop Settings display are red. This means that the number being displayed is not exact. For example, if the Clip length is listed as 1.4.4 with the last 4 in red, it means that the Clip is not exactly that length and may actually be 1.4.45 beats long. Since Live cannot display values smaller than the sub-beats, the digits show up red when there are further numbers that can't be seen. Re-setting the Warp Markers (next Chapter) will fix these red digits by defining the exact size and timing of the Clip.

Loop Offset

Like a sentence, the point from which you start a musical phrase can make a huge impact on getting your meaning across (so says our editor). Live's Clip View has been expressly designed for this sort of audio rewording. To quickly hear what we mean, load a couple of drum loops into a few Tracks and launch them. Double-click one of the Clips to open its Clip View, then direct your attention to the Sample Display. Next, grab and drag the small black triangle just above the graphic wave file (just above the Sample Display window) shown in Figure 5.16. Drag this triangle (called Loop Offset) right. By changing the Loop Offset, you are defining a new start location for the Clip. Live will alter the current playback position to reflect this new start position, so you will hear that the altered Clip is now playing from a different position while still staying in time with the other beats. Sampleheads will know this trick as changing a sample's starting point. This can be done during playback or while editing and works for Audio and MIDI Clips. You can also change a Clip's playback point when editing your arrangement (while viewing Arrangement and Clip Views at the same time). This is one of our favorite music tweaks because of the incredible amount of variety it can create.

To quickly "turn the beat around" (kicks on beats two and four with snares on one and three), all we need to do is to move the Loop Offset to the second beat of the bar (position 1.2). Check out Figure 5.17 to see this simple yet powerful trick.

The groove will now begin on beat 1.2 and play though the bar back to beat 1.2 again, centering the loop at this new starting location. If you try this example with one of your drum loops you may think that the loop sounds exactly the same. It does. The only difference is the starting point, so you will need to hear it in context (against other loops or music) in order to determine the impact of shifting your start point. Here are a few of the most common ways to creatively use Loop Offset:

✳ **Drum fill**—Drummers (and drum programmers) typically rearrange their main drum part or pattern to add variety or to signal that the song is changing, building, etc. By changing the starting point of a loop, you can make it seem as though the drummer or drum machine is making a musical statement.

✳ **Limit loop**—Sometimes you may not want to use the whole portion of a loop. When changing a Clip/Loop's region, it is often necessary to adjust the Loop

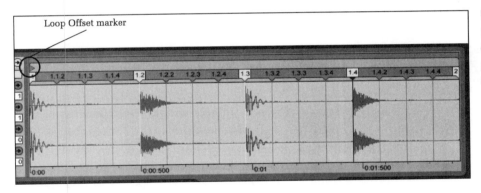

Figure 5.16

Here is a basic drum loop with the loop offset squarely placed on the one, along with the first kick drum.

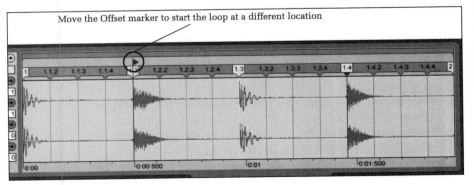

Figure 5.17

In this figure, we have moved the loop's start point to beat two. In Live, this is called adjusting the loop offset.

Offset as well. For instance, if we are using the last half of a Clip, the loop off-set gets automatically moved (when you adjust the region) to beat 3.

✳ **Instrument turnaround**—Like the drum fill idea above, adding variety to a Clip's playback parameters (such as loop offset), can alleviate the monotony in repetitive loops. Also, you may create some interesting section transitions or "turnarounds."

The Track

Moving up the totem pole from the Clip is the Track. The Track is a pathway for signals, audio or MIDI, to enter a channel of the Session Mixer and is also a place to arrange related Clips for playback. There are four different types of Tracks in Live (Figure 5.18) and each one serves a specific purpose in the way audio flows through your Live project.

Figure 5.18

The Session View with one of each type of Track.

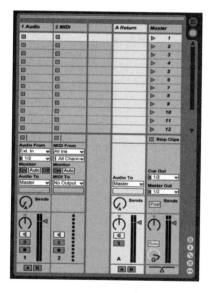

The Audio Track

An Audio Track (the leftmost Track shown in Figure 5.18) is where you will place Audio Clips so they can be routed through effects and fed into the Session Mixer. As we've mentioned before, only one Clip can be playing at any time on a Track, therefore it is wise to place similar Clips that won't need to play simultane-ously on the same Track. For example, "Verse Gtr" and "Chorus Gtr" are two guitar parts from different sections of the song. They won't be played at the same time so putting them on the same Track makes sense. You can trigger the verse guitar part and it will play until you trigger the chorus part. This gives you instant control of the arrangement since you can switch between the verse and chorus parts with a click of the mouse (or push of a button if you've assigned external control).

To create a new Audio Track, choose "Insert Audio Track" from Live's Insert menu. You can also press CTRL (CMND) + T for the same results. Double-clicking an Audio Track will display its Track View. It is here that you'll place plug-in effects for processing the Clips as they're fed to the Session Mixer (Chapter 8 explains the usage of effects in Live).

The MIDI Track

A MIDI Track is the same as an Audio Track, except it holds MIDI Clips, MIDI Effects, and Instruments. When you create a MIDI Track (Insert > Insert MIDI Track or CTRL (CMND) + SHIFT + T) it will output MIDI information, which can't be fed into the Session Mixer. Instead of seeing the normal volume and pan controls in the Mixer, you'll only see a status meter. These MIDI Tracks can send their data to external devices, such as sound modules, or to other MIDI Tracks using the Input/Output Routing section.

Double-clicking a MIDI Track displays its Track View. MIDI Effects can be added to this view for performing operations on the incoming MIDI data. More importantly, virtual instruments, such as Live's built-in Simpler and Impulse, can be placed on the Track to convert the incoming MIDI data to audio. Once an instrument has successfully been added, you'll see that the MIDI Track now has audio controls in the Session Mixer. This essentially turns the MIDI Track into a hybrid MIDI/Audio Track, one that functions as MIDI from track input through the Clip Slots and into the Track View, but functions as Audio from instrument output through the Session Mixer. This means Audio Effects can be added to the Track View any place to the right of the virtual instrument.

The Return Track

A Return Track does not hold any Clips, audio or MIDI, but can host Audio Effects. Each Return Track is fed by a mix of the Send knobs corresponding to the Return (Figure 5.19). As you'll discover in Chapter 8, the Return Tracks allow us to add additional effects to multiple tracks without overly taxing our CPUs.

By default, there are two Return Tracks in a new Live Set. You can add more, up to eight, by choosing Insert > Insert Return Track from Live's menu, or by pressing CTRL (CMND) + ALT + T on your computer keyboard.

The Master Track

The final track, the Master Track, is created automatically with every new Live Set and cannot be deleted. This Track does not feed into the Session Mixer. Instead, the Session Mixer outputs its audio into this Track to give us one last chance to add effects and adjust output volume and position.

The Master Track has its own Track View, and this is a fitting place for master compression or EQ to put the final touches on your mix (see Chapter 8).

Figure 5.19

The Return Track has a corresponding Send knob in each audio channel of the Session Mixer. Here we have three Send knobs for three Return Tracks.

Also, the Master Track will not hold Clips, but instead houses the Scene Launchers, which are explained in the next section.

The Session

You'll quickly find the Session View to be the most spontaneous section of Live. It is here that Tracks are arranged side by side and broken into tiny cells called Clip Slots. This Clip Slot Grid (Figure 5.20) becomes a huge organizer for our musical ideas (all nicely encapsulated in Clips) where we can begin to create the structure of our songs as well as perform live arrangements.

❋ Clip Stop Buttons

In Figure 5.20, you'll see that only some of the empty Clip Slots have small squares in them. These are the Clip Stop Buttons. If you click or trigger one of these buttons, it will stop the Clip playing on that Track. The Clip will stop according to the Global Quantize setting.

Removing Clip Stop Buttons from a Scene will leave any playing Clips on the Track untouched when the Scene is launched (no new Clip will start and any playing Clip will continue). You can toggle a Clip Stop Button on and off by selecting it (or a group of them) with the mouse and pressing CTRL (CMND) + E.

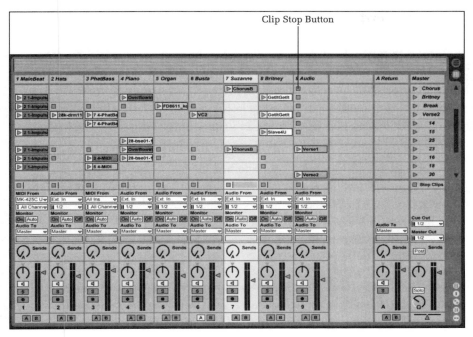

Clip Stop Button

Figure 5.20
This Session View is populated with an assortment of Clips ready for us to start playing. You can see some of the Clip Slots are completely empty— their Clip Stop Buttons have been turned off.

Adding Clips to the Session

Adding new Clips to the Session is as easy as dragging a file from the Browser into one of the Clip Slots. Audio files are dragged into the Slots of Audio Tracks and MIDI files into the Slots of MIDI Tracks. You can also grab multiple samples from the Browser (hold SHIFT to select an area or CTRL (CMND) to select individual files) and add them as a group to the Session View. By default, the Clips will be created on the same Track. In fact, you'll see transparent versions of the Clips as you drag them into the Session. To have Live arrange the samples in the same row, press and hold CTRL (CMND). You'll see the transparent Clips change their arrangement and you can then choose their final destination.

New Clips can also be created directly in the Session by recording our performances, either audio recordings or MIDI recordings. Recording new Clips is covered in the Recording sections of Chapters 7 and 8.

Drag-and-Drop Techniques

Clips can be added, moved, and duplicated in the Session View using a variety of key and mouse combinations. Clips already on the Grid can be moved to other slots just by clicking and dragging them, then releasing the mouse button once the Clip is over the desired location. A group of Clips can be moved by first selecting the area of Clips you want to move, then dragging the group to a new location in the Grid. Groups can be selected by dragging an area around the Clips with the mouse. If there isn't any room around the Clips, you can click one corner of your desired area (selecting the Clip) and then click the other corner while holding the SHIFT key. By defining the corners of the area you want, all Clips within that area will be selected.

You can also duplicate Clips by selecting them (click once) then dragging the new copy to the desired location while holding the CTRL (Option) key. By holding the CTRL key when we click and drag, the original Clip will stay in its original location. This is the same as selecting a Clip, choosing Edit > Copy from the menu, clicking the destination, and choosing Edit > Paste. This duplicating technique also works with groups of Clips like above.

Editing Commands

The Clips in the Session View (and Arrangement View, for that matter) all respond to the standard Cut, Copy, Paste, and Delete editing commands. You can select a group of Clips, choose Cut (CTRL [CMND] + X) to remove them, then Paste them (CTRL [CMND] + V) in a new location. You can also Copy (CTRL [CMND] + C) Clips and Paste new versions elsewhere in the Session. If you merely wish to create a new copy of some Clip to be moved later, you can use Duplicate (CTRL [CMND] + D) to instantly create a copy of your Clips below the originals. Of course, you can always select Clips and press Delete to erase them.

Using Scenes

Scenes are horizontal rows of Clips in the Session View that can be triggered all at once, meaning that several Clips can be triggered with a single action. Musical arrangements in Live often work best if you think of your music as starting in Scene 1 (the top row) and then progressing downward, Scene by Scene (row by row). In other words, Scene 1 may be an intro section, Scene 2 may be a verse, Scene 3 may be a chorus, and so on. Of course, don't get caught in the idea that your song has to work this way—you can set up and skip scenes in any manner you see fit. As you read on, this concept will begin to make sense.

Notice that in Live's Session View, the Scene Launcher is located just to the right of the Clip Slot Grid. By pressing the sideways triangles in the Scene Launch strip (under the Master Track column), called "Fire Buttons" in Live, you can launch simultaneous playback for all Clips in the given Scene. If there are any Clip Stop Buttons in the Scene, they will stop any Clip in their Track. Fire Buttons prove useful when composing live, "on the fly" arrangements, during which you may want to jump from one song section to the next, and then back again. Figure 5.21 shows a single Scene (row) in Live's Session View.

❊ **Two Scenes Are Better Than One**

One of our favorite shortcuts is the one for duplicating scenes. This command will insert a new scene directly below the scene you are working in, and copy all present loops—a huge time saver! To do this, press CTRL (CMND) + SHIFT + D. By using this technique, it is easy to build basic song progressions for a more varied sounding musical composition. Incidentally, you can duplicate the contents of a single clip slot by pressing CTRL (CMND) + D.

Different Live users will explore their own creative ways to use Live's interface. For the laptop DJ, Scenes may represent complete songs or pieces of music (as opposed to short loops), in which one Clip Slot could contain a Clip that is really an entire song. In this instance, a "Scene" change is more like swapping vinyl than moving to a new part of the song. Back in Figure 5.20, you can see eight Clip Slots in a single row, all playing a separate clip at the same time. These all happen to introduce the section of the song known as "Act II." These new Clips are launched with the simple click of the "Act II" Scene Launcher.

❊ **Insert Scene**

To insert an additional Scene (row) in Session View, or to insert a Scene at a given point, select the Scene above the desired location where you would like the new Scene to appear, and press CTRL (CMND) + I. Additional Scenes can also be added by choosing Edit > Insert Scene. If you create a new Scene in the wrong place, see the "Moving Scenes" Tip.

Click here to launch all Clips in this Scene

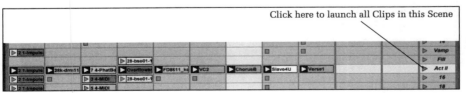

Figure 5.21

Scenes can be used as song sections, such as the verse, chorus, or bridge.

❊ ❊ ❊

※ **Moving Scenes**

To move a Scene, simply grab the Scene's title with the mouse and drag it up or down to the preferred location. All Clips in the Scene will be included in the move.

Figure 5.22a

Eight clips in a column, a.k.a. Track. Each Track is a channel in Live's virtual mixer.

It is worth repeating that triggering any Clip or Clip Stop Button will halt the playback of any other Clip on the same Track. Figure 5.22a shows an example of eight Clips in a column, while Figure 5.22b shows eight Clips in a row. Note: in Figure 5.22a, you can play only one of the Clips at a time, while in Figure 5.22b you can play all eight at once.

The fact that a Track can play only one clip at a time, rather than being a limitation, is actually a tool that can be used to your advantage in a couple of different ways. For instance, by using variations of the same drum loop—each in its own Clip Slot, stacked in the same Track—you can make more realistic-sounding, or at least more interesting, drum fills, "breakbeats," and rhythmic turnarounds. This is also a great method for organizing other instrument tracks that change parts when moving from Scene to Scene (such as two different bass guitar loops, one for the verse, the other for the chorus). By dedicating a single Track for variant Clips of one particular instrument (one Track for drums, one for bass, one for piano, etc.), you will create a more common mixer setup, one that will feel more like an actual recording studio.

Figure 5.22b

Each row can house whole musical sections, new song directions, or merely a slight modification in the piece currently playing. Many Live users think of their songs from top to bottom, advancing their song as they move down the grid, one row at a time.

※ **Channel Strip**

Live's Session Mixer approximates its analog cousin in a couple of important ways. For starters, any mix, panning, or effect settings on a given channel will be applied to any sound on that channel. If you plan carefully, you can take advantage of this fact by keeping similar instruments on the same Track. For instance, if you apply an EQ to Track 1 and boost the highs, all highs on all Clips on this channel will be boosted. As you move from Scene to Scene, verse to chorus, the settings remain the same. We will see in later chapters that Live's Arrangement View allows us to automate effects, toggle them on and off in the middle of a song, etc.

You can therefore set up Live's Session Mixer to resemble an analog studio mixer: Track 1 is designated for drums, Track 2 is designated for guitar, etc. The difference is that you will have several drum Clips vertically aligned on the same Track in each Scene. Here is a more complete song (Figure 5.23). Notice how the same loop is copied multiple times on each Track (in multiple Scenes).

 RAM Tough

All of these copied loops will not strain your CPU more than the one instance of the loop playing. Live "knows" that the clips all reference the same file for playback.

In order to move downward easily, row by row, you can take advantage of the Scene Launcher in the Session View. Scenes can be triggered by pressing one of the Fire Buttons in the Scene Launch vertical strip (with mouse, computer keyboard, or MIDI keyboard) on the right-most side of Live's Clip Slot grid (Figure 5.24). You can also trigger a Scene by pressing the Enter (Return) key so long as the Scene number/name is highlighted. Changing the highlighted Scenes can be done with the arrow keys, and then triggered again with the Enter (PC) or Return (Mac) key. Live also features a Preferences setting (see Chapter 3) that will automatically advance the Scene Highlight down to the next Scene every time the Enter key is pressed. Note: if you select another Clip Slot or parameter on the mixer, you will need to highlight the Scene again to begin triggering with the Enter/ Return key.

Figure 5.23

This more complete-looking Clip Slot grid shows how a more developed song might work. You will move through the song sections by clicking the Scenes, which are named in the Master column. As you can see, you don't need to use every row—Scenes can skip rows if you like.

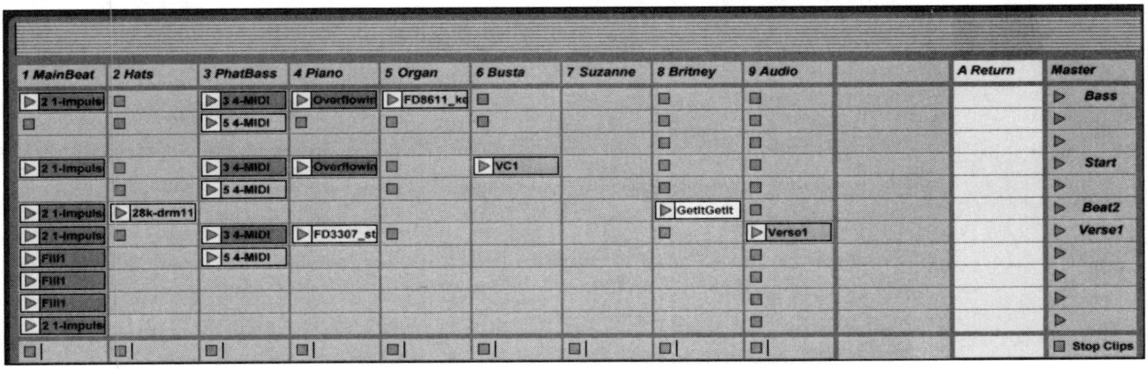

1 MainBeat	2 Hats	3 PhatBass	4 Piano	5 Organ	6 Busta	7 Suzanne	8 Britney	9 Audio		A Return	Master
▷ 2 1-Impuls	▢	▷ 3 4-MIDI	▷ Overflowin	▷ FD8611_ke	▢		▢	▢			▷ Bass
▢	▢	▷ 5 4-MIDI	▢	▢	▢		▢	▢			▷
							▢	▢			▷
▷ 2 1-Impuls	▢	▷ 3 4-MIDI	▷ Overflowin	▢	▷ VC1		▢	▢			▷ Start
	▢	▷ 5 4-MIDI	▢	▢			▢	▢			▷
▷ 2 1-Impuls	▷ 28k-drm11						▷ GetItGetIt	▢			▷ Beat2
▷ 2 1-Impuls	▢	▷ 3 4-MIDI	▷ FD3307_st	▢			▢	▷ Verse1			▷ Verse1
▷ Fill1		▷ 5 4-MIDI						▢			▷
▷ Fill1								▢			▷
▷ Fill1								▢			▷
▷ 2 1-Impuls								▢			▷
▢	▢	▢	▢	▢	▢	▢	▢	▢			▢ Stop Clips

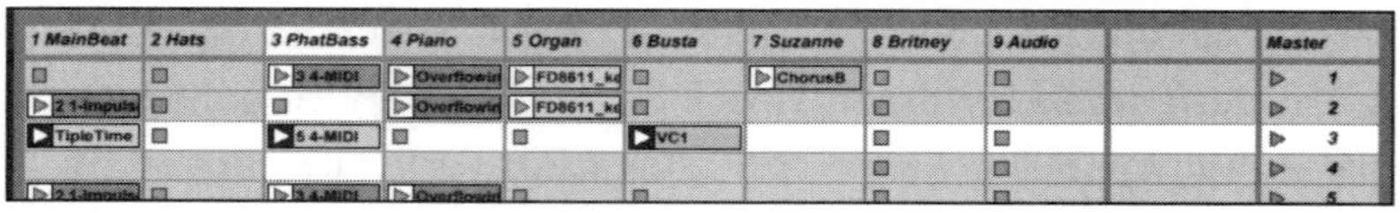

Figure 5.24

Live's Scene Launch strip (titled Master) appears to be just another column in the grid, yet these are the triggers for firing multiple Clips at once. Here, Scene Launch 3 is triggering three loops.

1 MainBeat	2 Hats	3 PhatBass	4 Piano	5 Organ	6 Busta	7 Suzanne	8 Britney	9 Audio		Master
		▷ 3 4-MIDI	▷ Overflowir	▷ FD8611_k		▷ ChorusB				▷ 1
▷ 2 1-impuls			▷ Overflowir	▷ FD8611_k						▷ 2
▷ TripleTime		▷ 5 4-MIDI			▷ VC1					▷ 3
		▷ 5 4-MIDI								▷ 4
▷ 3 1-impuls		▷ 3 4-MIDI	▷ Overflow							

Capturing Scenes

When experimenting with random combinations of Clips in the Session View, you'll come across combinations that work well together. You can press CTRL (CMND) + SHIFT + I, or select Insert > Capture and Insert Scene, to create a new Scene that is populated with the currently playing Clips. You can quickly build a collection of potential Scenes this way that you can experiment with to build a song arrangement.

Naming Scenes

Scenes can be named and renamed as many times as you like (the default name is simply a number). Many Live users label their Scenes by song section, such as "verse," "chorus," "bridge," and/or "breakdown," in order to remind them of what section they are triggering. To rename a Scene, click on its current name or number, press CTRL (CMND) + E, or choose Edit > Rename, then type in whatever you like. Press Enter, or the Return key, to accept the new name or ESC (escape) to leave it as it was.

Programming Scene Tempos

From time to time, you may want to make instantaneous jumps to different tempos while in the Session View. By naming a Scene using a special convention, you can cause Live to change tempo when the Scene is triggered. To switch the tempo to 85 BPM, name the Scene "85 bpm" and launch it. The Scene can be empty; you don't need to trigger any Clips when you launch this Scene, if you merely wish to change tempos. You can remove all the Clip Stop buttons (select them an press CTRL [CMND] + E) so none of your Clips are stopped.

One instance where programming Scene Tempos is particularly helpful is when organizing a large batch of clips into a set so that a single Live set contains multiple songs. One group of Scenes may belong to one song at a given tempo while another group of Scenes represents a different song and tempo and so on.

MIDI and Computer Keyboard Control

There sure is a lot of mouse clicking going on in Live. Thankfully, we can off-load a lot of these tasks to a much more intuitive interface, such as our MIDI keyboards or our computer's keyboard. Once you get Live under external control, you'll really be able to feel the musical power at your fingertips.

Controlling Live from external devices is called *Remote Control*. Before we start, select your desired control devices in the Remote Control section of the MIDI/Sync Preferences pane (Chapter 3). You can have two different control devices selected at a time. Live will remember these settings, but loading Live without one of your devices connected will require you to re-select it when it's available again.

First, click the MIDI Assignment button in the upper-right corner of the Live window or press CTRL (CMND) + M (Figure 5.25). You'll see a bunch of blue squares and rectangles appear above Live's Clip Slot Grid, Session Mixer, Effects, and a variety of other parameters, such as Tempo and Groove in the Control Bar.

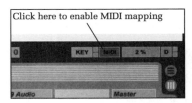

Figure 5.25

Clicking the MIDI Assignment button exposes the MIDI layer where control can be assigned to elements of Live.

The superimposed blue squares indicate controls that can have a MIDI message assigned to them. If you click on one of your Clips in the Clip Slot Grid and press a key on your MIDI keyboard, you'll see a white box appear in that Clip Slot showing the MIDI channel and note assigned to that Slot. Clicking the MIDI Assignment button again will exit assignment mode and return Live to normal. Now, when you press the assigned key on your MIDI keyboard, the Clip will launch, just as if you'd clicked it with the mouse.

You can also assign knobs and sliders on a MIDI controller to the knobs and sliders you see on Live's screen. If you like, you can assign a knob to control a slider and vice versa—whichever suits your style. To assign MIDI controllers, press the MIDI Assignment button, click on the dial or fader you wish to control, then twist or move the control you wish to use. Exit MIDI Assignment Mode and you'll be ready to go.

❄ **With the Push of a Knob**

Live will allow you to assign MIDI knobs and sliders to its buttons as well as assign MIDI buttons to its sliders and knobs. In the first case, the button in Live will turn on when your MIDI control passes 64. It will switch off when you move the control back under 64. If you assign a MIDI button or key to a slider or knob, pressing the button or key will make the slider or knob toggle back and forth between its lowest and highest settings.

Just to the left of the MIDI Assignment button is the Keyboard Assignment button. This works the same way as the MIDI button, except it assigns Live's controls to keys on your computer keyboard instead of the keys on your synthesizer or other MIDI control device. Press Key (or CTRL [CMND] + K) and orange highlight boxes will appear. Click and press a key to assign, then exit Key Mode.

Key and MIDI assignments are saved in each Live Set, so every song can have a different control scheme. If you find yourself always making common assignments, such as buttons for the Transport, you can assign them and save them as part of your Live template (see Chapter 3).

> ✻ **Who's Your Relative?**
>
> When assigning knobs to control Live's on-screen dials, you may use a MIDI controller that features endless knobs, also known as rotary encoders. These knobs are unique in that they will spin around and around without stopping like a normal potentiometer would.
>
> Rotary encoders transmit a special form of MIDI message known as *relative control*. Instead of transmitting an exact value like the mod wheel on a keyboard, they simply transmit how far they've been turned and in what direction.
>
> Unfortunately, there is no standard in the MIDI specification for relative control, so many different schemes have popped up from various manufacturers. Live does, however, read a variety of different relative control schemes.
>
> When you assign a control to a slider or knob, a menu will appear at the bottom of the Live window. It will be set to Absolute, but you can change it to one of the relative schemes listed. If you don't know what scheme your device uses, you'll have to experiment.

The Arrangement

Even though we've been touting Live's unique "on-the-fly" arranging style possible in the Session View, we still have the Arrangement View to consider. We've hinted a few times at what the Arrangement View does and how it shares channels on the Session Mixer with the Session View; but how does the Arrangement View augment our compositional workflow in Live? Some of you may think that the Arrangement View is a step in the opposite direction from Live's real-time capabilities; however, because of the unique interrelationship between the Session and Arrangement Views, you'll find the Arrangement View is just as creative a space to work in as the Session View, and it can be used to enhance a live performance.

❄ **Look Both Ways**

You can zoom and scroll through the Arrangement View using the same method as navigating the waveform display of the Clip View.

Any time your mouse turns into a magnifying glass, you can click and drag to change your view: dragging up and down changes the zoom setting while dragging left and right pans the view.

You can also use the condensed Overview, located at the top of the Arrangement View, to locate sections of your arrangement. You can drag the left and right edges of the Overview Box to choose the area you want to view.

What Is an Arrangement?

Briefly, an Arrangement is a predetermined playback scheme of Clips and mix automation (to be explained in a moment). The Arrangement View (Figure 5.26) has horizontal Tracks (unlike the vertical Track layout of the Session View) and Clips are placed in these Tracks so they can be played in order from left to right. The Arrangement View is almost exactly like the time-line views of other sequencer packages such as ProTools, Logic, Cubase, etc. For those with experience in those programs, the Arrangement View will be instantly familiar.

Just like other sequencer programs, the Arrangement View has a *Now Line* (the thin vertical line that moves from left to right when Live is running) that shows the current playback location of the Arrangement. When you press the Play button in Live's Control Bar, it will start the Arrangement running. In fact, *any* time Live is running, even when just playing Clips in the Session View, the Arrangement will be running as well.

Controlling where you'd like to begin playback within the Arrangement, as well as starting and stopping it, is handled a little differently in Live than it is in other programs. First, when starting Live's transport, the Arrangement will start playing from the location of the Start Marker (Figure 5.27). If you press

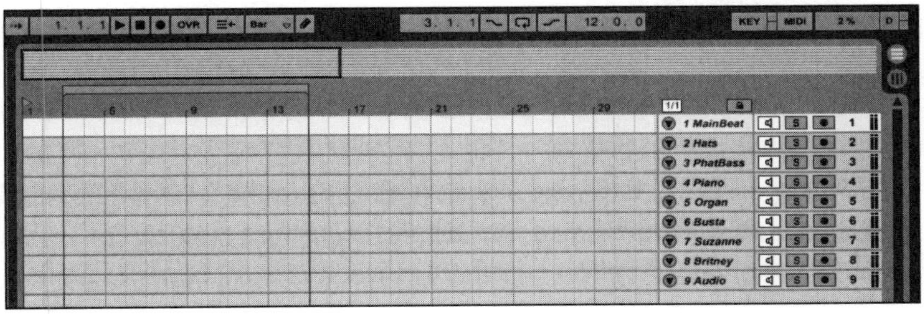

Figure 5.26

The Arrangement View is where you can start putting the arrangement of your song into stone.

Figure 5.27

The Start Marker is signified
by the small triangle "flag" at
the top of the Arrangement
View.

Figure 5.27

The Start Marker is signified by the small triangle "flag" at the top of the Arrangement View.

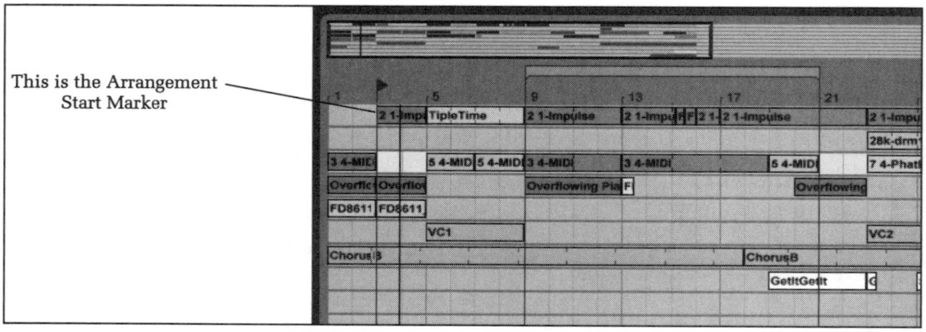

Stop then press Play (or if you press the spacebar once to stop followed by another press to start again), the Arrangement will restart from the Start Marker. If you wish to have the Arrangement start from its stopped location, you'll need to hold down SHIFT while you press the spacebar. The SHIFT + SPACEBAR command means "continue" instead of "start." If you want to start the Arrangement from a different location, you'll need to move the Start Marker. If you move your mouse over the triangle at the top of the Start Marker, your mouse will change to a similar triangle allowing you to click and drag the Marker to a new location. If the Start Marker is not on screen for you to click and drag, you still have another technique at your disposal. Move your mouse up into the timeline while holding CTRL (CMND). When your mouse is just above the numbers in the timeline, it will change into the same triangle shape, allowing you to click the new location for the Start Marker.

Recording From the Session Into the Arrangement

Because the Session and Arrangement Views are so closely related, it's possible to program the Arrangement by recording your performance from the Session View. With the Session View open, press the Arrangement Record button in the Control Bar and then perform your song as usual. When you're finished, press Stop and take a look at the Arrangement View (press Tab). It will now be filled with an arrangement of Clips (Figure 5.28). Press play and this Arrangement will begin to play. You'll hear your entire performance played back for you exactly as you recorded it, including all control movements, such as tempo changes, volume adjustments, and effect tweaks. Easy!

If you find you like a different selection of Clips in the Session View better than what you'd programmed into the Arrangement, you can press the Arrangement Record button and the Session Clips will begin replacing the

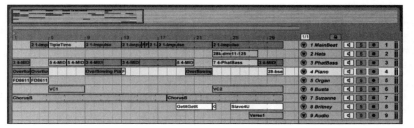

Figure 5.28

The Arrangement View is filled with Clips after we recorded our performance from the Session View. Pressing play will play back our performances just like the original.

❊ Back to Arrangement

Since the Session and Arrangement Views share the same channels in the Session Mixer, it is possible to override what has been programmed into the Arrangement by launching Clips in the Session. These newly launched Clips will play in place of what is programmed into the Arrangement. When this happens, the Back to Arrangement button (Figure 5.29) will light up red. Clicking this button (turning it back to gray) will stop any Clips playing in the Session View and will re-engage the Tracks in the Arrangement. If you're working on an arrangement and find you're hearing something different than what you see in the Arrangement View, check this button and be sure it's gray.

In the case of an empty Arrangement View, *anything* you do in the Session View will cause the Back to Arrangement button to light. This is because you're hearing something different from the Arrangement—which is silence. You'll see that if you click the Back to Arrangement button in this situation, all of your Clips will stop in order to "play" the silence programmed into the Arrangement.

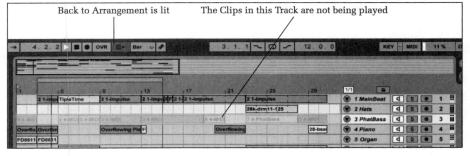

Figure 5.29

We can see that the Back to Arrangement button is lit. We can see that Track 3 of the Arrangement is not playing because the Track is slightly transparent. Clicking on the Back to Arrangement button will make Track 3 solid again so we can hear it.

contents of their Arrangement Tracks. This is just another way Live makes it easy to experiment and capture our ideas quickly without stopping the flow of music.

Adding Clips to the Arrangement

While recording from the Session View is one way of quickly filling the Arrangement View with Clips, you can create new Clips using the same methods employed in the Session View. You can either drag files from your Browsers to create new Clips, or you can record new Clips from external sources.

Drag a file from the Browser into an Arrangement Track. *Voila!* A new Clip appears. This is exactly like dragging a file into one of the Clip Slots in the Session View. You can double-click this Clip to see its Clip View where you can make all of your adjustments just like in the Session View. Indeed, Clips in the Session View and Arrangement View are identical. One does not have more functions than the other; however, one thing you can do with an Arrangement Clip is determine its play length. When a Clip is added from a file, it will appear as only one repetition of the file (i.e., a one-bar drum loop will appear as a Clip that is one bar long). By clicking and dragging the right edge of the Clip, you can lengthen it, which will cause the Clip to repeat as it's played. This will only work for Clips with Loop engaged. If your Clip is not stretching past a certain point, check the Clip View and make sure Loop is enabled.

Editing the Arrangement

By editing the contents of the Arrangement, you can fix mistakes you may have made while recording your performance. Perhaps you launched a Clip a bar early when recording from the Session View. Maybe you coughed during the middle of a vocal take. You can remedy these mishaps using the techniques explained below.

You can also use the tools of the Arrangement View as a step in the creative process as well. The meticulous editing and manipulation that can be achieved at this level can be used as a stylistic element of your music. In fact, the Arrangement View is often used as a "cutting table" for assembling new Clips for use in the Session View. Beats can be spliced together and combined into new Clips, or multiple vocal takes can be assembled into one perfect take.

Cut, Copy, Paste, Duplicate, Delete
The standard Cut, Copy, Paste, Duplicate, and Delete commands work as expected in the Arrangement View. Copy (CTRL [CMND] + C) will copy the selected Clip(s) to the computer's "clipboard," which is a temporary memory location for items being copied. You can then place a copy of the Clip(s) at a new location on the timeline by first clicking the destination location for them in the desired Track. A flashing red line will appear, indicating where the new Clip(s) will be added. Use Paste (CTRL [CMND] + V) to copy the Clip(s) from the clipboard to this new location. The Clip(s) will still be in memory, so you can paste additional copies anywhere you like. The Clip(s) will remain in the clipboard until replaced by other ones, or until you quit Live.

The Cut command (CTRL [CMND] + X) works like the Copy command, except that it removes the selected Clip(s) when copying to the clipboard. You can then use Paste to place the Clip(s) to a new location in the Arrangement. Duplicate (CTRL [CMND] + D) will simply take the selected Clip(s) and make a new copy directly to the right of the selection. This is handy for repeating a section. If you simply want to remove a Clip or Clips without copying to the Clipboard, select the Clip(s) and press the Delete key.

Dragging Techniques
You can move a Clip or group of Clips from one location in the Arrangement to another by simply clicking the middle of the Clip and dragging it to a new location. Select a group of Clips and click-drag one to move the whole group. You can even drag the Clip(s) to a different Track if you want. Furthermore, you can change the length of a Clip by moving your mouse to the right end of the Clip. When your mouse turns into a bracket (it looks like "]"), click and drag the Clip to your desired length. You'll be able to extend the Clip beyond its original length only if the Loop button for the Clip is on.

Using Copy and Paste, explained above, to create multiple Clips is a technique that you will probably use a lot. Because of this, Live gives us a simple way to copy Clips without using the multiple key commands. If you click on a Clip while holding the CTRL (OPTION) button on your keyboard, you can drag the Clip to a new location and release the mouse button. A new copy of the Clip will be made while the original stays in place.

Splitting Clips
You can break a Clip into smaller Clips using the Split function. Perhaps your guitarist recorded the verse part and the chorus part all in one take. You'd

like to split that Clip so you'll have one containing the verse part and another containing the chorus. To do this, you'll need to view the contents of the Clip in the Arrangement View, by pressing the Track Unfold button, which looks like a downward-pointing triangle just before the Track Name. Once the Track is unfolded, you can find the point at which you want to split the Clip. Click (with the Pencil tool turned off) the location for your cut and press CTRL (CMND) + E. The Clip will be split into two Clips (Figure 5.30). These new Clips are completely independent of one another, meaning they can have their own unique Transpose, Gain, Warp, Loop, and Envelopes.

Because the resulting Clips are all independent, you can modify each Clip at will. If you want your Clip to change from Beats Mode to Tones Mode at a certain point in the song, Split the Clip and set the second Clip to Tones Mode. If you want to do a slew of effects on tiny slices of audio, Split the Clip into tiny pieces and retune each one with different Transpose, Gain, and Loop settings.

Consolidating Clips

After breaking Clips into smaller ones for editing purposes, you can re-join the Clips into one Clip for easier use. Select the Clips that you want to join and select Consolidate from the Edit menu, or press CTRL (CMND) + J. Live will quickly render a new Clip containing all the parts you had selected (Figure 5.31).

When Live consolidates a Clip, it is creating a new audio file on your hard drive. This new file is what Live will use when playing the new Clip. The pieces that were used to assemble the new Clip are removed from the Arrangement View. If these audio files are not used anywhere else in the Live Set (either in the Session or Arrangement Views), Live will ask if you

Figure 5.30

Just click and split to break Clips into smaller ones for independent editing.

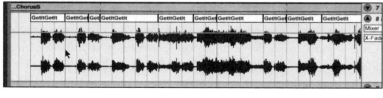

Figure 5.31

Consolidating all the "micro edits" from the previous figure gives us one single Clip to work with.

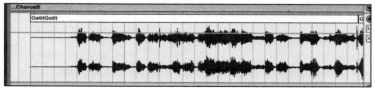

want to delete them when you save or exit. If you know you'll never use those smaller Clips again, go ahead and delete them; however, if you plan to assemble some more Clips from the same pieces in the future, you'll want to keep them on hand.

Another good use for the consolidate command is to trim a larger file down to just the section you actually want to use. This isn't necessary to do since Live is streaming audio from your hard drive, but we find that it can be a good way to clean up files on your hard drive. For example, let's say you record a ten minute vocal recording but decide that only five seconds of the entire take are worth using. In the Arrangement View, simply select the five second region of the Clip that you would like to keep and then consolidate that portion of the clip. Once you delete the larger portions of the Clip from the Arrangement, Live will ask if you would like to delete these files since they are no longer in use.

Cut, Paste, Duplicate, Delete, and Insert Time
While copying and manipulating Clips are achieved with the Cut, Copy, Paste, and Delete functions, we can use the Cut Time, Duplicate Time, Delete Time, and Insert Silence commands to make broad edits to the whole Arrangement. When using these commands, it is only necessary to select (by click-dragging) the area of time you wish to manipulate. These commands work on all Tracks simultaneously, selected or not.

The Cut Time command (CTRL [CMND] + SHIFT + X) works like the regular Cut command, except that it cuts a section of the Arrangement away and stores it to the clipboard. An eight-bar chorus can be chopped to four by selecting the last four bars and choosing Cut Time. You can place the cut time in a new location, if you wish, by clicking the desired insert point in the Arrangement and selecting Paste Time (CTRL [CMND] + SHIFT + V).

Duplicate Time (CTRL [CMND] + SHIFT + D) works the opposite of Cut Time: Extend an eight-bar chorus to sixteen bars by selecting the first eight bars and using Duplicate Time. The selected time is duplicated and inserted directly to the right of the original area. Delete Time will remove a section from the Arrangement without copying it to the clipboard.

Insert Silence (CTRL [CMND] + I) will insert an amount of silence where you click-drag an area. Selecting the first two bars of an Arrangement and executing Insert Silence will shift the entire Arrangement to the right by two bars, thus giving you two bars of silence before the song starts.

Automation

Along with the Clips in the Arrangement are tracks of *automation*. Automation is programmed or recorded movements for controls in Live's Session Mixer, Devices, and Plug-ins. For example, if you want to fade out the volume at the end of your song, you would *automate* the Master Volume so Live will perform the fade every time the end of the song is reached.

Just about every parameter in Live can be automated. One rule of thumb: if you can control a parameter by MIDI Remote, you can automate it in the Arrangement View. If you're wondering if a particular control can be automated, click the MIDI Assignment button in the upper-right corner of the Live window. If your control gains a superimposed blue square, it can be automated.

Recording Automation

The simplest and most intuitive means of automating your Arrangement is by recording the desired control movements in real-time while the song plays. For example, to program the fade out we explained above, you'd activate the Arrangement Record button in the Control Bar and press Play. When the song reaches the point you want to start fading out, start moving the Master Volume control downward. You can either click and drag with the mouse or use an external MIDI controller—both methods will be recorded the same way. When you're done with the fade, press Stop. You'll now see a red dot in the Master Volume control. This red dot will appear over every control that has automation recorded in the Arrangement. You can go back and re-peat the recording process as many times as you like to build your automation in layers. For instance, you can control the volume of a synth part on the first pass then make another recording to automate the pan. Live will per-form the previous pass of volume automation while you make the new recording of pan movements.

Viewing Automation

You can see the automation for a Track by first unfolding the Track (click the downward-pointing triangle next to the Track's name) then selecting the parameter you wish to view. The parameter is selected by using two menus: the first menu selects the general category of automation, such as Mixer, Send, or any Plug-in that is loaded onto the Track. The second menu selects a specific parameter from the general category selected. For example, to see the

Track's volume automation, you'd select "Mixer" in the first menu and "Volume" in the second menu. If an Auto Filter effect is loaded onto the Track, you can view its Cutoff automation by choosing "Auto Filter" and "Cutoff Freq."

Automation is displayed as a line-graph superimposed over the Clip's data (Figure 5.32). The meaning of the line shown in the automation track is determined by the parameter being controlled. In the case of level controls such as Volume or Send, volumes increase as the line moves toward the top of the Track. For other controls, such as Pan, a line in the center of the Track represents a center pan position. Lower values cause the pan to move left while higher values cause the pan to move right.

Editing Automation
We can change the shape of the automation graph by using two techniques. When the Pencil tool is off (toggle the Pencil tool with CTRL [CMND] + B), you will be using the *breakpoint editor* (Figure 5.33). The automation will be displayed as lines with little circles at each "elbow," known as a breakpoint. You can click and drag these circles to new locations to reshape the graph. You can double-click a circle to delete it, or you can double-click a line to create a new breakpoint in that location. You can also select an area of the automation graph (click and drag the desired area) and then move a whole section of automation around.

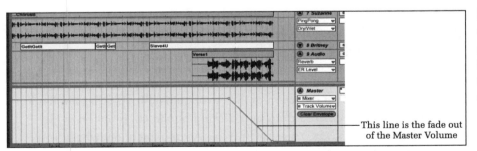

This line is the fade out of the Master Volume

Figure 5.32
We can see the final fade out of our song represented by the downward-sloping line in the Master Track of the Arrangement.

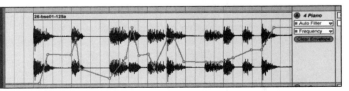

Figure 5.33
The breakpoint editor is great for creating smooth ramps between values.

Maintain Ctrl

When editing automation curves, you'll frequently be making only small modifications, such as increasing volume by 1 dB or making a mute happen a little sooner. By holding the CTRL (CMND) key while moving points of the graph, your mouse movements will be minimized, allowing you to make subtle and specific changes with ease.

By switching the Pencil tool on, you will be working with Live's step editor. By drawing with the pencil in the automation graph, you'll create flat "steps" that are each the same width as the current quantize setting (Figure 5.34). This will allow you to create tempo-synched automation effects such as volume gates or timed effect sends. The Pencil will overwrite any ramps that may have been made in the breakpoint mode in favor of its flat step style.

Quantize Keys

You can change the value used for the quantize grid with these keystrokes:

CTRL (CMND) + 1: Makes the quantize units smaller.

CTRL (CMND) + 2: Makes the quantize units larger.

CTRL (CMND) + 3: Toggles triplet mode on and off.

CTRL (CMND) + 4: Toggles the quantize grid on and off. When the grid is off, you will be able to draw values anywhere.

Region Markers

The Region Markers, found in the Arrangement View, serve two purposes. They function as loop points, and they also mark the start and stop points for automatic recording.

Creating a Loop

You can loop, or repeat a section of the Arrangement by placing the Region Markers around the desired area and clicking on the Loop button in the Control Bar (Figure 5.35). You can start the Arrangement anywhere you like, but if playback ever reaches the right Region Marker, playback will

Figure 5.34

Using the Pencil tool, we can create tempo-synched steps in our automation graphs.

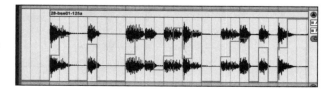

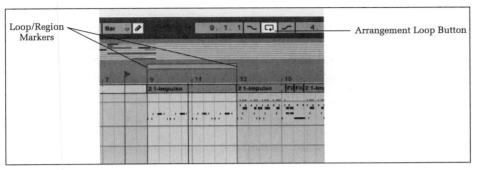

Loop/Region Markers — Arrangement Loop Button

Figure 5.35
Playback will loop repeatedly between the Region Markers while the Loop button is engaged.

jump back to the position of the left Region Marker. If you switch the Loop button off while the Now Line is between the Region Markers, playback won't be affected except that the song will continue after it reaches the right Marker.

You can move the loop region while the Arrangement is playing. Playback will not follow the Region Markers as you move them, but the song will begin to loop again once it reaches the new location of the right Marker. This means you can loop one section then just move the markers to the new location once all the desired repetitions are played. Once Live reaches the next region, it loops. This can help you to zero in on problem spots, automate mix settings, or merely give a section a good listen. If you happen to move the loop region to a position to the left of the Now Line, playback will continue until the end of the song. The Now Line will not jump back to the location of the Markers.

Auto-Punch

In the next two chapters, we will discuss recording audio and MIDI into Live. The process is nearly identical for both Audio and MIDI Clips. We will cover how to record both into the Session View and the Arrangement View.

However, when recording to the Arrangement View, Live can be set so that it automatically begins recording at a specified point in the Arrangement and stops at another. This is the second function of the Region Markers. This auto-recording function is referred to as *auto-punching* and is controlled by the two buttons on either side of the Loop button (Figure 5.36). Punching-in is when you start recording, punching-out is when you stop. Normally, punching is used when you need to replace only a section of a recording. Perhaps your bassist put down an amazing take, but happened to rush an intricate part leading into the last chorus. You can use the auto-punch feature to

Figure 5.36

We've placed the Region Markers around the bar right before the last chorus. With the Punch-In and Punch-Out buttons, we can start playback before the bad measure, but Live will only record the section in between the Markers.

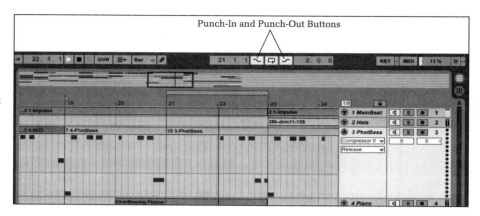

begin recording right where the bad part is and then stop right before the chorus.

As you can see, the Punch-In and Punch-Out buttons can be set independently. This means you can have Live start recording at a specific point and continue until you stop it. This will allow you to punch-in part way through the song and record until the end. You can also have Live stop recording in the same spot every time. This is helpful when trying to nail down a tricky intro part.

Render to Disk

Once you have finished your Live song—and you are liking the way it sounds—it is time to get it out of your computer, burned to CD, and onto the street. Though Live cannot burn CDs, it can help you prepare your song with an intermediary step called *rendering*. Figure 5.37a shows the Render to Disk menu that appears any time you press the render command CTRL (CMND) + R. Note Figure 5.37b is the same menu in the Arrangement View with one exception. Since you manually select the length of the section to be rendered, you will not see the top Length [Bars.Beats.16th] settings.

In both the Session and Arrangement View Render to Disk Menus, you have several important decisions to make. To begin with, you will need to know the exact length of the section of audio you are rendering. If you are rendering from Session View, then you are likely only rendering a 4-, 8-, or 16-bar section; whereas in the Arrangement View, you may well be rendering an entire song and can select the amount of desired rendering time by click-dragging on any Track to highlight the desired length of your render. For instance if you want to render a four minute song, simply drag (highlight) the

Figure 5.37a

The Render to Disk Menu in Session View.

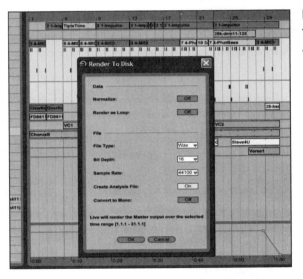

Figure 5.37b

The Render to Disk Menu in Arrangement View.

entire length of the song on any Track. Explicit directions for rendering are found in the "Rendering Techniques" section later in this chapter.

Normalize

When the Normalize setting is set to On, Live will raise the level of audio to the maximum level possible without distortion. We recommend leaving this setting Off for full songs and relegating all mastering/normalizing tasks to your wave editor. Most wave editors, such as Sonic Foundry's Sound Forge,

Bias' Peak Audio, and Steinberg's Wavelab (to name a few) have a good deal more flexibility than Live in the matter of normalizing; however, if you are merely rendering a quick loop, or small selection of audio, you may switch Live's normalization setting to On (when rendering) to save time.

Render as Loop

Upon first glance, Render as Loop may seem like an insignificant option; however, this is a very important box if you have used any reverbs or delays in your soon-to-be-rendered loop, or selection of audio. Normally, any loop with delay or reverb will have a tail, or specified amount of decay, until the sound completely dissipates. The problem arises in the first few notes of a given loop, where the delay or reverb has not had time to kick in—those early notes are dry in comparison to the rest of the loop. Each time the loop cycles, you will hear the dry notes at the beginning and then a gradual swell in the effects. By activating the Render As Loop option, Live will actually render the file twice—once placing in all the reverb, delay, and effect tails, and twice to actually render the sample(s). You should be aware that this option is not desirable for complete songs. It's doubtful that you would want any sort of tail at the beginning of your compositions.

File Type

When rendering, you have a choice between saving your audio in either AIFF or WAV file formats—either of which are capable of being burned to CD. AIFF is usually the preferred format for Apple Macintosh computers, while WAV is the Windows audio standard. When it comes time to actually burn your music onto a CD, you will need to use either Apple's iTunes, Microsoft's Windows XP burning utility, or a third-party CD burning utility such as Ahead Software's Nero (www.nero.com), Roxio's EZ CD Creator (www.roxio.com), Cakewalk's Pyro (www.cakewalk.com/products/pyro), or Adaptec's Toast (www.adaptec.com).

Bit Depth

The Bit Depth drop-down menu gives you two choices: 16- or 24-bit. Bit-depth was discussed in Chapter 2, but we want to reiterate that unless you are short on hard drive space, you should usually render to 24-bit. Why not have a little extra detail to scrape away later if you so choose? Since Live can work with 24-bit files, loops, and samples, any loop you render can be re-imported into Live at a later time. If, on the other hand, you plan on burning the rendered file directly onto CD, you'll want to choose 16-bit, as this is the proper bit-depth for CD sound.

Sample Rate

Typically, you will only use sample rates of 44,100 (the CD standard rate) and up. 48,000 and 96,000 will provide more accurate sampling at the expense of hard disk space in similar fashion to Bit Depth selection. The lower sample rates (22,050 and 32,000) will most often be used for creating lo-fi special effects popularized by older first- and second-generation hardware samplers.

Create Analysis File

Each time Live sees a WAV or AIFF file, it has to draw a visual waveform, determine the positioning of the Warp Markers, and analyze the pitch and tempo. To do all this, Live uses a small pertinent secondary file called an Analysis File that will retain the master sample or loop's file name with the added file-extension .asd. When this setting is activated, Live will also create an ASD file in addition to the rendered audio file. This is helpful when creating loops that will be re-imported back into Live. Otherwise it is really not necessary to create the added file.

Convert to Mono

Though this heading is fairly self-descriptive, we want to point out its usefulness. Many Live musicians have found that Mono loops/samples are preferable when working in a limited environment such as a laptop computer set up. The reason is that stereo loops are actually two channels of audio running on a single track. Therefore, they require roughly twice the system resources of a mono file—we say roughly because Live can forgo all Warp Marker and file analysis since it has already been done for one side/channel of the file.

Mono loops can also be a great way to render loops or samples that you are planning to use again in an Ableton Live song. They will often have more presence than their stereo counterparts. If need be, you can always pan or use some kind of stereo simulation effect to widen the stereo field of the sample.

Rendering Summary

Okay, this is not an official control, but we do find it helpful to look at the summary provided by Live at the bottom of the Render To Disk menu. Here you will see a description of what you are about to print. For instance you might see, "Live will render the Master output over the chosen length," or "Live will render the Master output over the selected time range [1.1.1–9.1.1]." If you get in the habit of watching this splash of text, you may cut down on mistakes in the rendering process.

> ❊ **Watch the Levels**
>
> As you are adjusting and automating your mix, pay close attention to Live's level meters. They will tell you when your overall or individual track levels are peaking. Any peaking channels will result in a nasty digital glitch. To remedy the problem, you either adjust (decrease) the peaking channel's volume, or, if the channel has already been fully (and intricately) automated, you can employ the Utility Device (see Chapter 9) to reduce the output volume of the channel.

Rendering Techniques

It is worth pointing out that rendering can be done with any portion of the song, at any time you are working with Live. In other words, if you want to render a loop or section of a song, you can do this from either Session or Arrangement Views. Why would you do this? Listed here are some common reasons for rendering a portion of a complete song. What follows is an explanation of how to complete the process.

* **Grab a loop**—We often render small loops for later use with a different piece of music, or make a complete file out of several edited clips.
* **Submix a section**—Occasionally, you might have added so many plug-ins to a particular section or Track that Live can no longer run smoothly. At this point you may want to consider rendering a single track or a subsection of the song (such as a verse or chorus), in order to lighten the processing load on your computer.
* **Export a completed song**—By far, the best feeling is rendering a completed song. This is nearly always done from the Arrangement View.

Grab a Loop
Follow these steps to Render/Save a loop.

1 Determine how long you want your loop or rendered audio section to be. There is no need to render more than one repetition of the audio segment; however, you can often make your music more interesting by embellishing the repeated loop, and then rendering both the original and the varied loop as two loops.

2 Determine whether you are going to render in Session or Arrangement View, and go to that View.

3 Highlight the Clip(s) to be rendered. In Session View, highlight the Clips or Scenes that you would like to render with the mouse. In Arrangement View, highlight the desired length (on any track), at the appropriate location. Note: Live will render whatever is coming through on the Master Track. If you want to render the loop on Track three only, you will need to either mute the other Tracks (by turning of the speaker-shaped Track Activator icon), or solo all pertinent Tracks, such as Returns and the Track(s) you want to render.

4 Press CTRL (CMND) + R to call up the Render Options menu; or, you can select File > Render to Disk. Note that in Session View, you will need to type in the length of the file to be rendered determined in step 1.

5 Here your choices may vary, but we will recommend for small samples that you do the following: Normalize = On; Render as Loop = On; File Type = AIFF for Mac, WAV for PC; Bit Depth = 24; Sample Rate = 44,100; Create Analysis File = On; Convert to Mono = Off (usually).

6 Click OK or press Enter and select the drive/folder where you want to save your new loop.

Submix a Section

When creating a sub-mix of several tracks, or one effect-laden track that is too processor-intensive to continually keep playing, there are some slightly different options to select in the Render to Disk Menu. Follow these steps to create a track to be re-imported into Live.

1 In the Arrangement View, select and highlight the entire Track or Tracks that you would like to render. This may include several drum and percussion Tracks, multiple vocal takes, or the compiled genius of your guitarist pal's efforts.

2 Solo all tracks and sends you are planning to render by activating the Solo/Cue button labeled S in the Arrangement View. You may also mute all other tracks (by turning off the speaker-shaped Track Activator icon). Remember: Live will render whatever is routed through the Master Track.

3 Press CTRL (CMND) + R to call up the Render Options menu. Or, you can select File > Render to Disk.

4 Select these settings: Normalize = Off; Render as Loop = Off; File Type = AIFF for Mac, = WAV for PC; Bit Depth = 24; Sample Rate = 44,100 (or the setting you are accustomed to); Create Analysis File = On; Convert to Mono = Off.

5   Click OK, or press Enter, and save the rendered file (and analysis file) some-where that makes sense with your current song. We suggest saving it in the same sounds folder as the other loops from your song. When you add the sub-mixed track back into your mix, don't forget to mute all of the original tracks, or else you will hear an intense phasing effect.

Export a Completed Song

Finally the time has come to render your completed song. Don't expect this to be a one-time process. You may find that there are subtle tweaks you'd like to make to the mix after burning your song to a CD, and listening to it on different stereo systems.

1   On the Master Track in the Arrangement View, highlight the entire length of the song.

2   You may wish to place a bit of leader, or space, at the beginning of your track. To do this, use the mouse to highlight the first couple of seconds of your track, and then add the leader by selecting Edit > Insert Silence. Remember that you can always clean up the beginning and end spaces on your track in a wave editor.

3   Press CTRL (CMND) + R to call up the render options menu. Or, you can select File > Render to Disk.

4   For a final mix, we recommend setting Normalize = On (Off if you have a wave editing application); Render as Loop = Off; File Type = AIFF for Mac, = WAV for PC; Bit Depth = 24; Sample Rate = 44,100 (or the setting you are accustomed to); Create Analysis File = Off; Convert to Mono = Off.

5   Click on OK, or press Enter, and carefully save the file to a location where it is safe for final mixes.

Summary

We covered quite a lot of topics in this chapter—everything to bring your song from the tiniest musical fragments to fully arranged compositions. It is appropriate, therefore, to summarize the process once more just to help solidify it in your mind.

Here is a *general* idea of how a song is built in Live:

1   You start, for example, in the Session View by making a MIDI Track named "Drums." You load an Impulse instrument (Chapter 11) onto the Track and quickly build a drum kit from samples on your hard drive. You program a MIDI Clip for the main groove of your song and set it looping.

2 You might then make an Audio Track titled "Bass." You pull out your P-Bass and plug it into the instrument input 1 of your audio interface. You select input 1 of your interface on the Input/Output Routing strip and Arm the Track. You can now hear your bass blended with the drums, though you're not recording anything. You fool around for a moment on the bass until you come up with a part you like. You click one of the record buttons in a slot on the Track and start playing on the next downbeat. You put down the jam along with the drums. When you're done, you click again on the Clip and it begins to play. You move the right loop marker to the left since you didn't stop the recording on the downbeat (your hands were full playing the bass).

3 You keep recording new Clips, such as guitar and MIDI synth parts. You search your loop libraries for things that augment the song. Once you find a good combination, you use Capture and Insert Scene. You now have one Scene in your Session arrangement.

4 You record a new bass part for the next section of your song. You write some new drum Clips. You record the parts of other members in your band. You start tweaking Clips with Envelopes. You keep building more and more sections and capturing them as Scenes.

5 Once you have a pretty good set of Scenes to build a song from, you start listening to them and move their order around on screen into a fashion that starts resembling your song (it's OK if you don't use all the Scenes you captured). You enable Record in the Control Bar and start performing the song as it's arranged in the Session View. You can, of course, trigger any Scene in any order that you want (you don't *have* to go top to bottom) and can also launch any Clip you want.

6 You'll now have a skeleton of your song in the Arrangement View. You now start making multiple passes over the song to program volume fades, mutes, pans, effect modulations, or any other automation you want in your song. You also edit the Clips in the Arrangement, changing their length, volumes, etc., and also split and re-arrange them.

7 Throughout this process, you are adding effects to the mix and bouncing the results to new Clips when necessary.

8 You then start to experiment with new parts against your Arrangement by launching new Clips in the Session View. You try out some new synth loops and record new guitar riffs—they'll all play synchronized with the Arrangement. When you want to hear your original Arrangement again, you click Back To Arrangement.

9 You finalize your song's Arrangement, putting the last tweaks on your mix. You render the final Arrangement to a WAV file. In WaveLab, you apply mastering plug-ins and maximize the quality of your song. You render the results to a 16-bit, 44,100 stereo file which you burn to CD. You take the CD and put it in your car and drive all around town with it turned up as loud as possible!

Of course, the process of creation in Live is entirely up to you. You may decide that, instead of building the song from little pieces, you're going to multi-track your whole band playing at once, thus capturing the song in one pass. You then use the creative editing and mixing features of Live to finalize the mix. Afterwards, you may take those large recordings and split them into small Clips so you can make a live remix in the Session View. The creative flow is all up to you. Isn't that nice?

❊ Who's Using Live?

Klaus Badelt—Film Composer

Klaus Badelt got his start in film music by working with the prolific soundtrack and score creator Hans Zimmer. Since that time, Badelt's grand scale soundtracks include *Gladiator, Mission Impossible 2, Pearl Harbor, Hannibal, Pirates of the Caribbean*, and many more. When using Live in a film setting, Badelt uses his main sequencer on one computer to trigger Live (running in sync with Propellerhead's Reason) on a separate computer—for more on Reason Live sync, which is called ReWire, see Chapter 12, "ReWire."

Klaus Badelt

"I then drag in the loops I'm using (into Live) and trigger them from the keyboard," says Badelt in an interview conducted by keyboard magazine's Greg Rule (and found in its entirety on the Ableton Web site). "I use the effects in (Live), but basically sub-mix and then send to the mixer. I basically use it (Live) as a synthesizer. I have to be able to use Reason and Live at the same time. They're always integrated."

Explains Badelt, "Reason turned out to be fantastic because it's basically a rack of synthesizers. I can plug in, load samples into, create sounds, store them, and recall them immediately. I use a lot of these built-in synthesizers in Reason, especially the new Malström, which has fantastic, weird sounds." Klaus also spoke of his affection for Live, "I have to say that ever since Live came out, it changed my life. It enabled me to use our whole library of percussive loops. I'm not talking about loops in the sense of just electronic loops, but all kinds of orchestral or ethnic percussion loops. I'm finally able to use them all very quick and try them out in tempo. It makes it possible to work much faster, especially when you only have a few days to write a whole score."

Badelt goes on to explain that computerized music technology has eliminated the need for racks of samplers, synths, and outboard gear. "I don't have a single sampler anymore," says Badelt, "I used to have 28 EMUs, 21 Rolands, and four Kurzweils. We needed all these samplers to hold the orchestral library. But now we have switched more or less completely from the hardware samplers into software. I still have a few hardware synthesizers, especially old analog ones, but I'm probably not going to buy hardware synthesizers any more because software synthesizers are much more flexible. In our world, we have to be very fast. We have to change from one musical style to another within the minute. So the total recall is very important." This total recall is a natural part of Live. In later chapters, we will see exactly how you can link Reason to Live, and stream huge amounts of samples from your hard disk.

6 The Audio Clip

The Audio Clip has been the basic building block in Live since version 1. The Audio Clip is a reference to an audio file on your hard drive. When you trigger the Clip to play, it plays the referenced audio file according to the settings of the Clip. The parameters available to you are numerous, yet simple to understand. Using the tools of the Audio Clip, you can make any audio file play back in perfect sync with your song as well as play them in the proper key. You can also use the Audio Clip settings to mangle your sounds and generate new ones.

Of course, you can also record new Audio Clips from virtually any source. You can use the inputs of your audio interface for recording vocals, guitars, drums, pianos, horns, and synths—anything that can be picked up with a microphone or connected directly to the audio interface is fair game. You can also record from other computer programs, bounce other tracks in your set, or even re-record Live's own output. All of these recordings can be performed with the precision of Live's Launch Quantizing allowing perfect loops to be recorded on the fly.

Before you start recording hordes of Audio Clips, take a moment to familiarize yourself with the unique parameters of Audio Clips. Drag an audio file from the Browser into a Clip Slot or load one of Live's Demo Sets so you can follow along and try tweaking some of the parameters that follow.

Audio Clip Properties

The properties of an Audio Clip are edited through the Clip View (Figure 6.1). Double-click an Audio Clip to see its Clip View. Every Clip in Live has common settings, such as those found in the Clip and Launch windows of the

Figure 6.1

The Clip View for an Audio Clip.

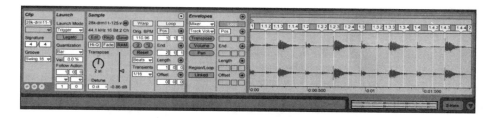

Clip View; however, things will start to differ as we look at the windows entitled Sample and Envelope.

Figure 6.2

The Sample window contains controls concerning audio file playback speed, pitch, volume, and loop region, plus the settings for the Warp Engine.

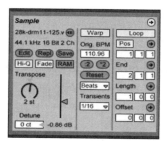

Buttons

In the Sample window (Figure 6.2) is a group of six buttons which are used to load and set playback quality for samples.

Edit

Pressing the Edit button will launch the external wave editor selected in the Default tab of the Preferences. The Clips audio file will be loaded into the editor so you can perform any off-line processing you wish. When you are finished editing the audio file, close the editing software. It will ask if you want to save your changes. Click Yes and the new changes will be saved and loaded into Live.

> ❋ **Self Destruct**
>
> Unlike every other process in Live, editing the source audio file will result in a change to the original audio file. If this file is also used in another Live Set, the Set will inherit the same edit (both Sets use the same file). Please pay special attention to this when using the Edit button. For safety, first save your Set as Self-Contained. Any edit you then perform will only alter the sound file in the Sounds folder for that project.

Using an off-line editor can be helpful when making microscopic edits to audio. Perhaps the vocalist's lips smacked as she began singing the first verse. The lip smack could be easily silenced in the external editor. Furthermore, every Clip referencing that same file will have its offending lip smacks removed, too.

An off-line editor is also helpful for layering effect plug-ins. While you could build a chain of plug-ins in the Track View then resample the output, some may prefer to use the off-line method to only effect part of the audio file. Furthermore, some audio editors will allow you to use plug-in formats not supported by Live. For example, Sony's Sound Forge supports DirectX plug-ins on the PC which are not supported by Live. Using Sound Forge as your external editor will allow you to process your Audio Clips with any plug-in you may have that are DirectX only.

Replace

The Replace button allows you to use a different audio file as your sound source while keeping all of your Clip's playback parameters the same. Imagine having an Audio Clip as a part of a chain of Follow Actions. After listening to the chain, you decide you want to use a different audio file for the third Clip. Instead of deleting the Clip, loading a new one, then setting the new Clip's Follow Actions to the previous settings, you can click Replace, then choose a new audio file. The Follow Actions, Pitch, Quantize, etc., will remain the same.

✳ **Drag-n-Replace**

As with almost everything in Live, there's another way to pull off the function listed above. Dragging an audio file from the Browser into the waveform display of the Audio Clip will just replace the audio while leaving the other parameters unchanged (you will have to re-assign your Warp Markers, though).

Save

When adjusting the parameters of a Clip, you may want your changes to become part of the audio file. For example, if you have to Warp Mark a certain beat every time you load it into a Clip Slot, wouldn't it be nice if the Warp Markers could be remembered the next time you import the file? By pressing Save, information regarding the playback settings of the audio file will be saved in a special file with the extension ".asd." The ASD file contains the peak information of the audio file (used for the Clip View waveform display) but can also contain information regarding Warp Markers, tempo, tuning, and Warp Modes. Pressing Save updates the ASD file with the current settings of the Clip. Next time you create a Clip from the file (dragging it from the Browser), the Warp Markers will already be in place and the proper tunings and Warp Modes will be set.

Hi-Q

This button simply switches the Audio Clip between high-quality and low-quality interpolation (used for time-stretching). If this button is on, the Clip will play using the better time-stretching algorithms, but will also place a heavier strain on your CPU. We recommend leaving this option on (even setting it on in the Default Preferences) and only turning it off when the CPU starts to overload.

Fade

To help an audio file loop seamlessly (no clicks or pops when the file loops around), Live can perform a quick volume fade at the ends of the Clip. We recommend leaving this option on (as default, too) unless the downbeat transient seems too quiet. It is possible that the fade can soften the initial attack of the downbeat (for instance, shaving the attack of a one-shot sample), so you may need to turn this off from time to time.

RAM

As we've mentioned before, Live streams audio files from disk as they play. With each additional Audio Clip that plays, the computer will have to stream another file from disk. Your hard disk can only stream a finite amount of data per second and when Live requires more than the disk can provide, audio dropouts begin to occur (Figure 6.3).

Figure 6.3

When the hard disk is not able to stream the necessary amount of audio for the playing Audio Clips, the "D" icon in the Control Bar will blink signaling a disk overload.

To alleviate this, you can load Audio Clips into your computer's RAM memory, which is accessed much faster than the hard disk. Pressing the RAM button for an Audio Clip will cause Live to load the associated audio file into RAM and cease streaming it from the hard disk.

Remember to be conscious of the size of the files you're loading into RAM. If you have five Clips that are four minutes long and two Clips that are loops of only a few seconds, it would be better to load the short Clips into RAM. Even if you're using only ten seconds of an eight-minute file, Live will still load the whole file into memory if you press its RAM button! Unless you have multiple gigabytes of RAM available on your system, you should try to only load short files into RAM.

❄ **A Moment of Trouble**

When performing live, there was a section of the show (one Scene to be particular) that had sixteen Audio Clips playing simultaneously. The only way the computer could do this was by running a couple of the Clips from RAM. Even though the kick drum Clip had streamed from disk throughout the performance up until this Scene, it was necessary to run it from RAM for this one point in the show. So, the kick drum Clip was set to RAM only in the offending Scene with sixteen Clips. When the next Scene was launched, it triggered the kick drum from disk again. Therefore, it's possible to have some instances of a Clip in RAM with other instances of the same Clip streaming from disk.

Transpose and Detune

When adding a new Audio Clip to your Live Set, more than likely it will not be in the right key. If you're writing a song in the key of E, but you import a Clip that's in B-flat, the new Clip will be out of tune with the rest of the set even though it's playing in sync with the song. The Transpose and Detune controls (Figure 6.4) allow you to change the playback tuning of the Clip (without changing its playback speed) to move it into key with the rest of the song.

You'll use the Transpose knob to shift the playback pitch of the Audio Clip. In case the Audio Clip is still slightly out of tune, the Detune knob can be used to fine-tune the pitch by raising or lowering it in small steps known as *cents*. Cent means one-hundredth, which is why a centimeter is one-hundredth of a meter. In music, a cent is one-hundredth of a semi-tone.

Figure 6.4

The large Transpose knob will shift an Audio Clip up or down in semi-tone amounts. The Detune value below the knob can make micro-adjustments to the tuning by moving it up or down within 50 cents (100 cents = 1 semi-tone).

> ❄ **Going Way Out**
>
> Though the tuning features of an Audio Clip are generally used to make a loop match the key of your song, don't forget that new sounds can be found by tweaking the tuning up or down by multiple octaves. Once a sample is altered this much, new textures and sounds can emerge. Take time to experiment!

Gain

The Gain slider is used to adjust the individual volume of a Clip. If you grabbed three different drum loops for a song, it's possible that the loop for the bridge is quieter than the other two. Instead of trying to automate a volume change at the bridge, you can simply turn up the volume, or *gain*, of that Clip to match the others.

When you adjust the Gain, you'll see the waveform display change to reflect the new playback volume. Even though you see the waveform display change, remember that the original file has not changed. You're only telling Live to play the file at a different volume. Keep an eye on your levels as you increase the Gain of the Clip since it's possible to turn the volume up so much that the Clip will begin to distort.

Cranking up the volume also provides you with a way to zoom in vertically on a waveform. You can always extend the Clip View window vertically (Figure 6.5), but it still may not show enough detail.

Figure 6.5

By dragging the top edge of the Clip View upward, we can see the waveform in better detail.

If enlarging the Clip View still doesn't show enough detail, turn up the gain and you'll have a larger waveform to edit in the waveform display (Figure 6.6). When you're done editing and adjusting, don't forget to turn the Gain back to its original level or the Clip will play extremely loud (watch those ears!).

Warp Control

Warping is the term used to describe Live's time-stretching and compressing technique. The method of Warping an audio file to match the tempo, groove, and pitch of a song is determined by many parameters. The most basic controls are the Warp button and the Original Tempo value.

Live's time-warping features will be available only when the Warp button (Figure 6.7) is on. If this button is off, the Original Tempo box will be grayed out and you will not be able to use Warp Markers, nor transpose the pitch of the file. With Warp off, the Clip plays at the audio file's original tempo

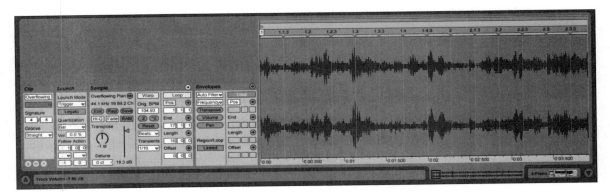

and pitch, end of story; however, once Warp is engaged, a whole world of possibilities opens. You can change the playback speed and pitch of the Audio Clip as well as make adjustments to its timing and groove.

Figure 6.6
The waveform is much larger once we increase the Clip's Gain setting.

Original BPM

This value is used by Live to set the playback speed of an Audio Clip in beats per minute. If the Project tempo is 120 BPM and the Clip's Original BPM is 120, then Live will not change the playback speed of the Clip. If the project tempo is 100 BPM, Live would know (from looking at the Original BPM value) that it needs to slow down the Clip so it will match the rest of the song.

Figure 6.7
Engage Warp to "open up" your Audio Clip.

When you have multiple Warp Markers (explained below) in a Clip, the Original BPM window will display the BPM from one Warp Marker to the next. If you have four Warp Markers in a Clip and you click on the second one, the Original BPM window will show the tempo between Warp Markers two and three. When you click on the third Warp Marker, another tempo will be displayed that reflects the playback speed from marker three to four.

You'll see that when adjusting grid and Warp Markers that the tempo listed here will change. This is helpful because, after setting the Warp Markers appropriately, Live will be able to tell us the exact BPM of the Clip. Quite often, this is not a round number, like 120 BPM, but more like 119.72 BPM.

Half/Double Original Tempo

The two buttons below the Original Tempo window will either double or halve the tempo of the Clip. Pressing the "*2" button will multiply the Original Tempo by two. The result is that the Clip will play at half speed. Pressing ":2" will have the opposite effect. This is helpful when Live incorrectly guesses the length and tempo of a new Audio Clip. Loops at a drum and bass tempo of 160 BPM will frequently import as 80 BPM Clips. A simple click of the "*2" button will fix this immediately.

Warp Modes

As we mentioned earlier, Live's Warp Modes make for cleaner, more musical warping. Warp Mode affects the way in which Live approaches Warping. Four different Warp Modes are possible in an Audio Clip's Warp Settings section: Beats, Tones, Texture, and Re-Pitch. Each mode also features a special set of controls that will appear below it in the form of a Transients drop-down menu, Grain Size box/knob, and Flux box. We will cover these in each subsection below. Also, don't forget that you can simply turn off Live's Warp engine altogether and play the sample at its default speed and pitch. Here's a list of what kinds of different sounds you can expect when switching between these four Warp Modes.

Beats Mode

Beats Mode is a great mode for rhythmic loops, percussive samples, and even entire songs. You will usually want to use Beats Mode with percussion, drums, drum machines, and sounds characteristically containing minimal decay (sustain). When importing songs (or long wave files), the same rules apply. Occasionally, if the sound is too textured, or lacks rhythmic definition, you may hear artifacts. Artifacts happen when Live tries to Warp a non-percussive file, such as a drone or flute melody. Live's transient settings, just below the Warp Mode settings, allow you to zero in on busier patterns or to relax the Warp Engine for more sparse-sounding loops.

You'll choose the proper setting for the Transient value based upon the rhythm of the audio file. If the beat doesn't have anything smaller than an 1/8 note subdivision, set the Transients to 1/8.

The way Beats Mode works is by cutting the file into slices the size of the Transient setting. If you have a one-bar loop with the Transient value set to 1/16, the file will be cut into sixteen slices (Figure 6.9). The positions where these slices are taken are determined by the grid and Warp markers in the waveform display. If your markers are aligned perfectly with the transients in the file, the Beats Mode will be cutting the slices at the appropriate locations. If the markers are out of place, the slice points may be after a transient, making it disappear upon playback.

❋ Definition of Transient

The Transient setting is a critical element of Live's warping functionality. But what is a transient to begin with? A transient is the short, sharp attack portion of a sound. An acoustic snare has a huge transient, which is the "crack" we hear (and see, as in Figure 6.8) right when the stick hits the drum. The soft attack of strings has no transient.

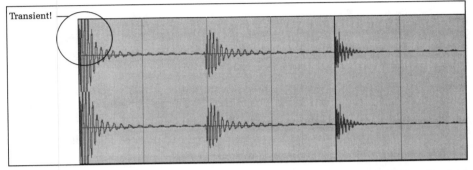

Transient!

Figure 6.8

Drum parts have easily identifiable transients.

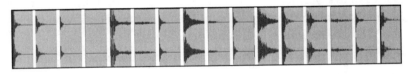

Figure 6.9

Our beat split into sixteen slices.

If the beat being Warped needs to be sped up to match the tempo of Live, the slices will be moved closer together (Figure 6.10). As this happens, the end of each slice will be cut off by the next slice, which needs to play sooner because of the faster tempo. If your beat only contains transients of the subdivisions you specified, only the tail end of every sound will be getting cut off, which is hardly noticeable.

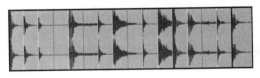

Figure 6.10

The slices start overlapping as they move closer together. Each slice cuts off the previous, so the tail end (right edge) of each slice gets shorter.

However, if you specify a Transient setting of 1/8 for a beat that has 1/16-note transients, the beat will only be cut into 8 pieces. Since a slice is an 1/8-note wide, it will contain two 1/16-note transients each (Figure 6.11).

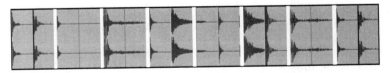

Figure 6.11

The same beat in eight slices.

Figure 6.12

1/8-Note slices moved closer together. The resulting beat has uneven spacing between the individual 1/16 -notes.

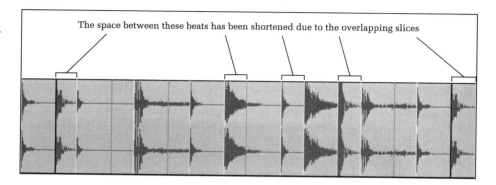

The space between these beats has been shortened due to the overlapping slices

When the slices are moved closer together, the space between the two transients on each slice stays the same, but the distance from the second transient to the first one on the *next* slice gets shorter (Figure 6.12). This means the even timing of the 1/16 notes in the audio file will be lost since the space between *every other* 1/16-note changes. If you do this right, you can turn a straight beat into a swinging beat! Check out the Beats Mode tutorial file on the Web site to hear how this is done.

The slicing mechanism in Beats Mode is a special form of granular synthesis. Instead of using miniscule "grains" of audio, Beats uses large slices. Instead of repeating each grain when filling the space between pieces that are moved apart (slowing down a file), Beats Mode only loops the last portion of the slice—the fading sound of the transient. This means that the wrong setting for the Transient value, such as 1/8 for a 1/16-note loop, will have undesired effects as Beats Mode will loop the second transient on the slice in an attempt to fill the space, which will sound weird.

Tones Mode
Tones Mode is standard granular resynthesis. As a file is played back, it is broken into tiny pieces called *grains*. The idea is that when you loop each tiny grain, you get a continuous tone that represents that sound "frozen in time." By splitting the audio into grains and spreading the grains apart, we slow down the tempo of the audio playback; however, since each grain is still played at its original pitch, there will be empty space between each grain. By looping each grain to fill the space, we achieve granular time-stretching.

Of course, looping each grain isn't necessary when speeding up playback of a file. As the grains are brought closer together, they will overlap one another. Each grain will therefore cut off the one before it, resulting in a continuous sound, but one playing faster than before. For this reason, you'll probably find that you have better success speeding up loops or transposing them down (both methods use the same process) than slowing them down or pitching them up, which requires looping the grains.

With careful setting of the Grain Size value, you can achieve nearly transparent Warping. Tones such as bass guitars, synthesizers, vocals, keyboards, or other long-sustaining instruments will usually sound much less processed when playing in Live's Tones Mode. You can adjust Live's Grain Size to help reduce undesirable audio artifacts. Ableton advises, "For signals with a clear pitch contour, small grain sizes work best. Larger values help avoid artifacts that can occur when the pitch contour is unclear, but can result in audible repetitions."

Texture Mode

Texture Mode is built for using orchestral samples, field recordings, thick keyboard pads, and similarly dense audio textures. Like Tones Mode, Texture Mode is based on granular resynthesis. In an effort to cloud the repetitive artifacts from looping grains, a Flux value is added which, when increased, allows Live to randomly change the Grain Sizes used in the process. This also adds a sense of stereo imaging to mono files!

Re-Pitch

Re-Pitch mode is more like true vinyl DJing—Live will alter the pitch of the sample depending upon the playback speed. This mode will produce no artifacts, especially if the warped, looped, re-pitched sample is played close to its original tempo. Re-Pitch basically turns off the granular and slice based resynthesis and merely alters the file playback speed which results in pitch changes. Since resynthesis is off, you will not be able to use the Transpose adjustments in this mode.

Reverse

Live's sample reverse feature is not instantaneous—don't expect it to be. It is, however, a whole lot of fun when used properly.

The process is simple: Click the Reverse button (Figure 6.13) and Live will calculate a new audio file which is a reversed version of the original. This new audio file will be named the same as the original but will have the letter "R" added to the end.

Figure 6.13

That tiny little icon is the Sample Reverse button. You can see the transients of the drum beat are now backwards.

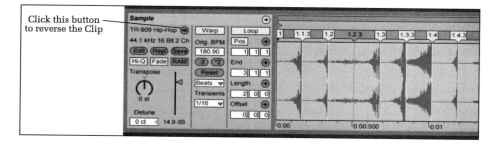

Okay, so it's not a Reverse button as in "play the sample backwards." Instead, the Reverse button means "play a backward version of the sample." This means you'll have to wait for the "R" file to be made the first time you Reverse, but from that point on, Live will just choose the original or reversed file to play allowing you to switch directions almost instantaneously.

❁ On the Up and Up

When controlling objects on the screen with the mouse, they almost always respond when you release your mouse button, not when you first click on them. The Reverse button is no different. You may think that the Reverse response is sluggish because you expect it to reverse right when you click; however, reverse won't take effect until you release your mouse button.

Because of the nature of the Reverse feature, we don't suggest that you use this button during live performances. You'll lose all control while the "R" file is being calculated and the timing of the reverse isn't tight with the mouse (you can't control it with MIDI Remote, either).

Instead, we recommend you make two Clips: One normal and one reversed. Enable Legato mode and you'll be able to switch between them in the Session View for the same results, with the aid of Launch Quantization if you wish.

❁ Waiting for R

When you click the Reverse button for the first time, a new audio file is created on your computer. If you switch the Clip back to normal playback, you will technically have an unused file on your computer (the reversed file with the "R" at the end). If you save or quit, Live will ask you if you want to get rid of the unused reverse file. If you say yes, you will have to wait for Live to recalculate the file the next time you click Reverse. If you were just experimenting and don't plan on using the reversed version of the file, go ahead and delete it. Otherwise keep it so Live can still switch to the reversed version quickly.

Warp Markers

You've heard us mention Warp Markers time and time again throughout this book so it's about time we explain what they are. The principle behind Warp Markers is simple, but still manages to confuse some long-time users; however, using them properly will have a profound effect on Live's ability to lock your Audio Clips together, and they are essential when dealing with live (human) players.

Purpose of Warping

In a nutshell, you use Warping to alter the playback timing of an audio file, usually to match the tempo of our song. You've already witnessed how Live can quickly change the playback tempo of an audio file dependent on the Session Tempo. When you lowered the tempo, the audio files slowed down immediately. Since Live is performing all its Warping in real-time, it can respond to instant changes anywhere during audio playback.

If you have an audio file that has improper timing, such as a drum part where the drummer played a beat late (Figure 6.14), you can fix the timing using small changes to the Warp parameters. If the snare drum on beat 1.2 is late, playing through the first beat of the file at an increased rate will cause the snare to move earlier. Playing the second beat of the file slower will allow the rest of the file after beat 1.3 to stay in the same place. By adjusting these two speeds, you can correct the timing of individual beats in a file. Fortunately, we don't have to alter these playback speeds numerically. They are computed for us as we manipulate Warp Markers.

Figure 6.14

The snare drum hit on beat 1.2 is late. Damn those human drummers!

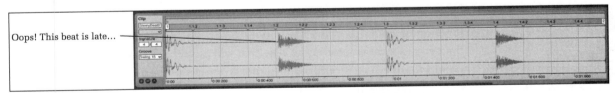

Oops! This beat is late...

Creating and Erasing Warp Markers

Click on the Sample window Title Bar in the Clip View to view the Clip's Marker. The Markers show where Live thinks the beats are in an audio file. The lines that appear with numbers above them are the grid markers. The lines with the green handles at the top are Warp Markers. Any grid marker can be turned to a Warp Marker by double-clicking its beat number (Figure 6.15). Double-click a Warp Marker to switch it back to a gray grid marker.

Figure 6.15

There is always at least one Warp Marker in an Audio Clip. It's the Marker at beat 1. You can make others by double-clicking grid markers.

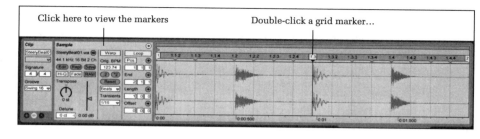

Figure 6.16

As Warp Marker 1.2 is moved right, the grid markers to its left spread apart while the markers to its right get closer together.

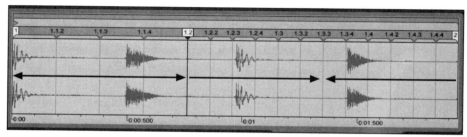

The difference between Warp and grid markers is that Warp Markers will stay where you place them. When you create a Warp Marker, you can click and drag it to a new location in the waveform display. The Warp Marker will stay in this location even if you move other markers around it. Grid markers will always stay evenly distributed between neighboring Warp Markers (Figure 6.16). Moving a Warp Marker will make all the surrounding grid markers move as well.

Correcting Timing Errors

If you turn grid marker 1.2 into a Warp Marker and move it right so it's lined up with the beginning of the snare drum, you are telling Live the new location of beat 1.2 in the file (Figure 6.17). Since you are showing Live that the second beat is later in the file, Live will play the file quicker up until this point to make sure it reaches this later transient on beat 1.2.

When you move the Warp Marker over to its new location, it causes all the grid markers to its right to move as well. This means beat 1.3 now needs to

Figure 6.17

Creating a Warp Marker and moving it in line with the snare drum will cause Live to play this section of the file in time.

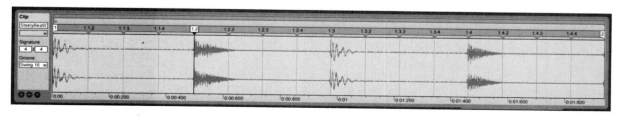

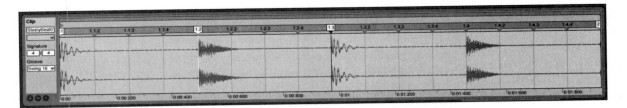

be lined up. Changing grid marker 1.3 into a Warp Marker and moving it left to the proper location fixes this (Figure 6.18). Since the location of beat 1.2 is now closer to beat 1.3, Live will play that section of the file slower so it doesn't arrive at the third transient early.

To potentially fix all of the timing errors in a file, you may need to make lots of Warp Markers (Figure 6.19). In cases like this, you'd probably want to click the Clip's Save button so the Warp Markers will be loaded in future imports of the file.

Figure 6.18

Moving Warp Marker 1.3 into position with the third transient corrects the rest of the file.

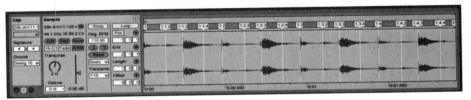

Figure 6.19

You can manipulate Warp Markers down to small subdivisions to correct multiple timing problems.

Creating New Rhythms

If you can use Warp Markers to align audio to the proper beat, can you use them to align audio to the improper part of a beat? Of course! You can change your beat by having Live play the snare later in time, perhaps on beat 1.2.2. If you remove Warp Marker 1.2 and create Warp Marker 1.2.2, you can align this new marker to the transient of the snare (Figure 6.20). By doing so, you have told Live that the snare drum falls on beat 1.2.2. Live will now play the audio file from 1 to 1.2.2 much slower than normal. By playing slow, the snare won't sound until later—beat 1.2.2 in this case. Since the snare was pushed so far back in time, Live will now have to play from 1.2.2 to 1.3 quickly in order to keep the rest of the file aligned.

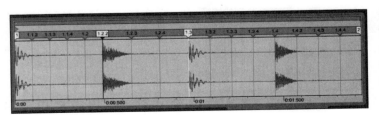

Figure 6.20

Though the waveform hasn't changed, this beat will sound significantly different when it plays back.

171

Clip Envelopes

The final window in the Audio Clip View is the Envelopes window. Before we go too far, some of you may be wondering what an envelope is. To start with, it's nothing that you will put in a mailbox. Rather, it's a graphical representation of values that change over time. The envelopes appear as a line graph superimposed over the audio waveform and represent anything from volume and pitch changes to effect tweaks. To understand how envelopes function, it helps to actually manipulate them and hear the results, so play along with us here.

Volume

The easiest Clip Envelope to understand is the Volume Envelope (Figure 6.21). In the figure below, the envelope is the ramp that rises from the bottom-left corner of the display window to the upper-right corner. When this Clip is played, its volume will rise over its two-bar length. When the Clip repeats, the volume will immediately jump to silence and will begin to rise again.

To access the Volume Envelope for your Clip, press the Volume shortcut button in the Envelope window. The Volume Envelope will superimpose itself over the Clip.

When you first make a Clip, its Volume Envelope will look like the one in Figure 6.22. Clip Envelopes are always working, so this "fully up" envelope allows you to hear your Clip. This means there's no such thing as a Clip without a Volume Envelope—it's just set to full level so it appears to have no

Figure 6.21

The upward ramp will cause the Clip's volume to rise over two bars as it plays.

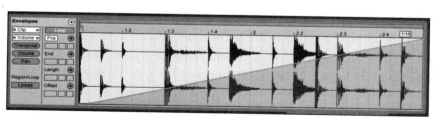

Figure 6.22

This is the default Volume Envelope for a new Audio Clip.

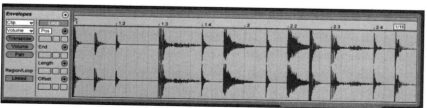

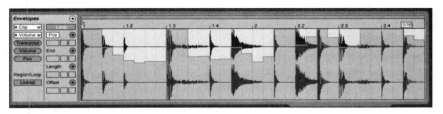

Figure 6.23
These steps will change the
playback volume of the Clip.

effect. In other words, all the Envelopes are always present, they're just set to do nothing by default.

Let's edit the Envelope to hear its effect on your Clip. Click on the Pencil tool in the Control Bar so its icon is on. Then, click in the Envelope window to create some "steps" (Figure 6.23). You'll hear Live adjust the volume of the Clip according to these steps when you play it.

It's important to realize that the Volume Envelope (as well as any other Clip Envelope) is affecting the playback volume in a relative way. If you look closely at the Gain slider in the Sample window, you'll see a small dot by it that moves up and down along with the volume changes. This dot shows the volume of the Clip based on the Volume Envelope. We like to think of this dot as the Envelope's "finger" on our controls showing us what it's doing. If you change the Gain amount, you'll hear an overall volume change while the steps drawn in our Volume Envelope continue to incrementally change the volume. You'll notice that the volume didn't jump back up to its previous location because of the Envelope. Instead, the Envelope scales its range based on the location of the Gain slider. This is because the Clip Envelopes work relative to a control's current position. This way, you can create repetitive volume patterns, but still adjust the overall level of the Clip in the mix.

Pan

Another simple envelope to master is the Pan Envelope, which is accessed with the Pan button in the Envelopes window. Instead of seeing a "full up" envelope like you saw for Volume, you'll see a "flatline" going through the middle of the window (Figure 6.24).

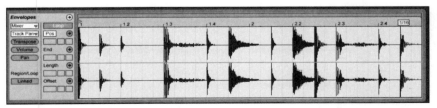

Figure 6.24
The Pan Envelope doing
nothing.

Figure 6.25

This ramp will cause the Track to pan from right to left during playback.

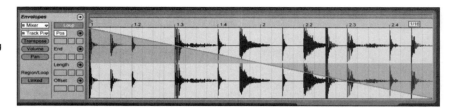

Remember how we said that Clip Envelopes work relative to a current control's position? In the case of the Pan Envelope, the flat line down the middle means no panning left or right. If the Envelope is above this center line, the pan position of the Track will be moved right. The Track will pan left when the line is below center. This means creating a ramp from the upper-left corner of the window to the bottom-right (Figure 6.25) will cause the Clip to pan from right to left as it plays.

If you turn the Pan knob in the Session Mixer to the left, you'll hear that the panning doesn't start fully on the right. It now starts partway to the left and continues fully left. This is because the Envelope is changing the pan position relative to the current location of the Pan knob. In fact, if you look closely,

Figure 6.26

The colored section of the Pan knob shows the actual output position as a result of the Pan Envelope.

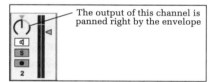

The output of this channel is panned right by the envelope

you'll see a colored indicator appear around the Pan knob as the Envelope changes its position (Figure 6.26). This is how the Envelope's "finger" is represented on a knob.

Transpose

The third envelope accessible through shortcut buttons is the Transpose Envelope. This envelope will modulate the location of the Transpose knob, allowing you to program pitch changes, slides, or entire harmonic progressions for the Clip.

The Envelope begins as a flat line, just like the Pan Envelope. Every line above zero is one semitone up while every line below zero is a semitone down (Figure 6.27).

Figure 6.27

This envelope transposes the Clip up through the notes of the major scale.

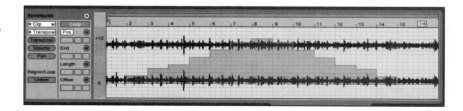

The Envelope affects the Transpose knob in a relative way, meaning that after you've programmed in your progression, such as a major scale like Figure 6.27, you can still select the root note of the scale with the Transpose knob.

Sample Offset

While there are only three shortcut buttons in the Envelopes window, there are many more Envelopes available for us to program. In fact, there's a Clip Envelope for nearly every parameter of the Clip and its containing Track.

To select an Envelope other than the three available as shortcuts, you use the two drop-down menus at the top of the Envelopes Window. These menus work in a similar fashion to the pairs found in the Input/Output Routing section. The top menu will choose the device you want to view and the bottom menu selects the parameter. One of these additional Clip Envelopes takes a little explaining—the Sample Offset Envelope. This Envelope can be found by selecting "Clip" in the top menu then choosing "Sample Offset" in the lower menu. This option is only available to Clips in Beats Mode. If this option is grayed out, switch to Beats Mode or find another Clip that's in Beats Mode already.

The Sample Offset Envelope (Figure 6.28) is another one of those "flat-liners" like the Transpose and Pan Envelopes above. It can be thought of as a step sequencer for your beat. Each line above zero is worth +1 1/16 note. Each line below is worth –1 1/16 note.

Remember how Beats Mode splits an audio file into multiple slices? Well, when playback of an Audio Clip reaches a non-zero value in the Offset Envelope, it signals Live to jump to a different slice of the file relative to the current location. In Figure 6.28, there is a value of +1 at beat 1.1.4. When playback reaches this point, Live will play the slice of audio located 1/16 note ahead of the current position, which is the slice for beat 1.2. So, when playback reaches 1.1.4, you'll hear the snare that occurs on beat 1.2. On

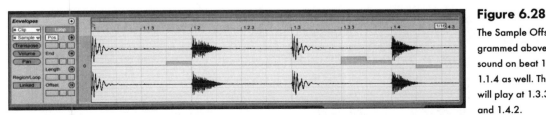

Figure 6.28

The Sample Offset programmed above will cause the sound on beat 1.2 to play on 1.1.4 as well. The sound at 1.4 will play at 1.3.3, 1.3.4, 1.4, and 1.4.2.

the next beat, 1.2, the Offset Envelope is zero. This means Live plays the audio slice at its current location. In this case, you'll hear the snare on beat 1.2 again. The additional steps around beat 1.4 will cause two hits before 1.4 and one after. By creating patterns of Offset motions, you can rearrange the slices of an audio file into any order you wish. Try it—take the pencil and scribble all over the Sample Offset Envelope and listen to the random results.

The Sample Offset Envelope rearranges the slices in a Beats Mode Clip. Because of this, the Transient setting for the Clip will determine the smallest Offset that can be performed. If Transient is set to 1/4, you will be able to offset the beat only on the quarter note. This also means that the finest resolution for the Sample Offset is 1/32 (the Clip's Transient setting can't get any smaller). However, if you're looking to do some meticulous micro-editing of your beats, using the Sample Offset Envelope may not be the best solution, but it can definitely get you started. Really tight and complicated edits are better suited for the Arranger (see Chapter 14 for the "Beat Wreckin' Clinic").

Sends and More

Another fun Clip Envelope is the Send Envelope. Select Mixer in the top device menu then choose Send 1 in the lower menu. With this Envelope, you can control the level of signal sent to the various Return Tracks.

The Send Envelope (Figure 6.29) is a "full-on" envelope like Volume. This makes sense because the Send knobs are just special volume controls themselves. Editing the Envelope will scale the output level of the associated Send knob. In the Envelope below, the Send only works on beat 1.4.

To hear this work, you'll need to have an effect loaded onto the Return Track (see Chapter 8) and the Send knob for the Track turned up. Since the Send Envelope is relative, the Track has to have its Send turned up at least a little before the Envelope can scale the level. The result is that the Send knob will

Figure 6.29

The Send Envelope sending on beat 1.4 only.

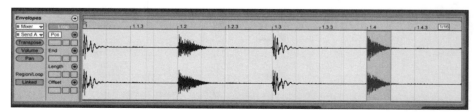

actually send on beat 1.4 only. The rest of the time it will be muted even though the Send knob is up.

You'll find even more Clip Envelopes as you explore the drop-down menus in the Envelopes window. In fact, as you add effects to the Track (see Chapter 8), Envelopes for the plug-in's parameters will also appear in this list so you can modulate them. That's quite a lot of modulation available at your fingertips!

Unlinking Envelopes

Until this point, we've been talking about editing loops of a given length. After all, a loop is, by definition, a repeating sample or phrase. That is just what loops do—they loop. And by default, each Envelope in a Clip is the same length as the Clip itself, allowing you to create repetitive modulation patterns that recur every time the Clip repeats itself.

Sometimes, however, you may wish to extend a given loop beyond its original borders. For instance, you have a repetitive two-bar drum loop and you really wish that you had an eight-bar loop to make it sound more lifelike and less repetitive. Enter unlinking Envelopes. By changing the length of the Clip Envelopes so that they are different than the length of the Clip that contains them, you can introduce just this kind of variation to your loops.

By pressing the Unlink button (Figure 6.30), the audio peak data is removed from the waveform display. This is because the Envelope you create may not occur at the same place in the Clip anymore, especially if you set the Envelope length to a value other than a multiple of the Clip length.

If you have a one-bar Clip and you unlink its Volume Envelope, setting its Envelope length to 3 beats will cause the Volume Envelope to repeat sooner than the Clip itself. If you've muted the volume at any place in the Envelope as in the figure below, this mute will begin to occur at different places as the Clip loops. The Envelope shown below will remove one 1/16 note every three beats. This means beat 1 will be missing, then beat 1.4 (it's three beats later, see?), followed by beat 1.3 the next time through the Clip. The third

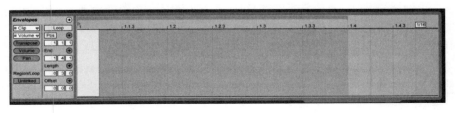

Figure 6.30

Unlinking the Clip Envelope will allow you to create more "random" sounding modulations because the various Envelopes can repeat at independent times.

time through the Clip, beat 1.2 will be muted. With the fourth repetition, the pattern starts again. It therefore takes three bars for the Volume Clip to repeat itself, thus the resulting Clip also repeats in a pattern three bars long.

To make things more complicated (and fun), other Clip Envelopes can be unlinked and set to their own unique lengths. If a Pan pattern is programmed into an Envelope that is set to be 3.3 beats long, it will take seven bars for the pattern to repeat itself. Most of your listeners would probably think the motion was totally random, especially with mutes occurring every three beats!

Breakpoint Editing

In our examples, we edited the Envelopes using the Pencil Tool. The Pencil Tool creates steps which are as wide as our quantization setting; however, step-style modulation is not always proper for some situations. For example, you may wish to make a smooth panning ramp to cause the Clip to swirl around your head. These ramps can be achieved by turning off the Pencil Tool. With this tool off, you will edit the Envelope in "breakpoint style."

When in breakpoint mode, each "elbow" in the Envelope will be marked with a tiny circle or *node*. Nodes are created by double-clicking with the mouse on the Envelope. Double-clicking an existing node will remove it (Figure 6.31). By moving the nodes around, complex modulation curves can be created.

You can also select an area of the breakpoint curve and move all the selected nodes together as one unit. You can also click and drag segments of the Envelope causing its attached nodes to move as well. With a little clicking around, you'll quickly learn how to create your desired ramps.

Figure 6.31

Double-click to create and destroy nodes. Click and drag to reposition them.

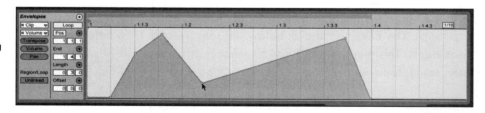

❋ Warp Modes and Clip Envelopes

The behaviors of some of the Clip Envelopes may seem incorrect when in Beats Mode. Remember that Beats Mode is treating sections of the audio file as independent slices. These slices are not processed through granular resynthesis and are therefore limited in their capabilities.

For example, when Transients are set to 1/8, the Transpose Envelope will only have an effect every 1/8 note. Each slice will play at the pitch determined by the Transpose Envelope as the slice starts to play. If the Transpose Envelope changes value during the time when the slice is playing, it will be ignored. The next slice to play will sound at the pitch dictated by the Transpose Envelope at the new point. Therefore, even smooth ramps in the Transpose Envelope will create audible steps when re-tuning Clips in Beats Mode. To decrease the size of these steps, increase the Clip's Transient setting. To hear a smooth Transpose curve, switch the Clip to Tones or Texture Mode.

Recording New Audio Clips

Now that you've got a grip on Audio Clips, let's really start putting them to use. While Audio Clips will frequently be created by dragging an audio file into Live from the Browser, you can also record live audio input directly into a new Clip. This means you can pick up your guitars and start throwing ideas into Live to be sorted out later. You can start putting out vocal fragments to begin sketching the structure of a song. You can record multiple Clips of percussion to create multi-layered poly-rhythms. Since you're recording anything that can be fed into your computer's audio interface, anything you can hear can be a potential piece of your song.

. . . In the Session View

New Audio Clips can be recorded in the Session View, even while the others are playing. First, select the source you're recording from in the Track's Input menus. The top menu lets you select the source device which includes options such as "Ext. In" (the inputs of your audio interface), "Resample" (for recording Live's Master output), ReWire applications (for recording the output of external programs such as Reason), and the outputs of the individual Tracks in your Live Set. When you arm the Track for recording, all of the Stop Clip Buttons in the Track's Clip Slots will turn to circles (Figure 6.32). These are individual Clip Record buttons—click one of them to start recording a new Clip in that location. You can stop recording by either clicking the Clip again, clicking the Stop button in the Control Bar, or by disarming the Track.

What's fantastic about recording in the Session View is that Live can create perfect loops from the recordings with ease. Just as a Clip will wait for the Launch Quantize setting before playing, Clips will also wait for the same setting before recording. If you have "Bar" selected as the Global Quantize

Figure 6.32

Select an active audio input, arm the Track, then click one of the circular Clip Record buttons in the Clip Slot Grid. Recording will commence at the time specified by the Global Quantize setting in the Control Bar.

value, Live will wait until the downbeat of a measure before it begins to record. If you click the red Play button in the Clip while it's recording, it will stop recording at the downbeat of the next measure. Furthermore, if your default launch mode is Trigger, the Clip will immediately start looping when recording ends.

Please keep in mind that recording will stop following the Global Quantize setting only if you click the Clip's Play button while recording. If you press Stop in the Control Bar or disarm the Track, the recording will stop immediately.

Doing multiple takes (repeated recordings of the same part of the song) is as easy as triggering additional Clip Record buttons in the Track. Every time a new recording starts, the previous one will end. You can then go back and listen to each take individually to find the best one. You could then move the Clips to the Arrangement View to edit the multiple takes together into one perfect "super-take" that is a consolidation of the best parts of each of the individual takes.

Of course, the nicest thing about this workflow in the Session View is that it allows you to quickly build layers and sections of a song without ever stopping Live. You can then go back and audition all of your new Clips and capture Scenes to start arranging the sections of your song.

✻ Sound on Sound

Since Live makes recording perfect loops so easy, you can build sections by doing multiple layers of recorded loops. For example, you can begin by recording some congas for four bars. When you stop recording, the Clip immediately starts to loop. Move the Clip to an empty Audio Track and it will continue to play. You can then trigger another recording in the first track and play along with the congas. Perhaps you record a shaker part for the second loop. When you stop recording, the congas and shaker will both be looping in sync with one another. You can keep layering additional Clips in this fashion then resample the output into one final Clip when you're done.

. . . In the Arrangement View

To record an Audio Clip directly into the Arranger, select the channel input and arm the Track just like when setting up recording in the Session View. This time, instead of pressing one of the Clip Record buttons, press the Arrangement Record button in the Control Bar (Figure 6.33). When you start

❄ **On the Level**

Before you start recording, check your input signal level to make sure it's not too high or too low. The Track's meters will show the volume of any incoming signal as soon as the Track is armed. Play the part to be recorded as loud as you plan to while watching Live's meters. If the signal is too loud (the meters reach the top), you may distort, or clip, the recording. If the level is too low, your sound may become grainy when turning it up to match the rest of your song. Even if you're recording a part that should be quiet in your song, always record it as loud as possible without distorting. You can then turn down the part in the mix when you play it back.

Figure 6.33

We're recording a new Audio Clip in Track 9 of the Arranger. You need to arm the Track for recording and enable Record in the Control Bar to record new data into the Arranger.

Live's transport, it will begin recording a new Clip into the corresponding Track of the Arranger while playing back the other tracks in the Live Set. Stop the transport, disarm the Track, or turn off the Record button in the Control Bar to end recording.

You can also automate Arranger recording using the Punch-In/Punch-Out values in the Control Bar. Set the Start and End markers around the area you wish to record. Engage the Punch-In and Punch-Out buttons (Figure 6.34) and press Record then Play in the Control Bar. Live will start running, but will wait for the Punch-In time before starting to record. Recording will continue until the Punch-Out point is reached. You may, of course, use just the Punch-In or Punch-Out feature by themselves if you choose.

❄ **Who Named You?**

When you create new Audio Clips, new audio files will be created on your hard drive. These files will be named the same as the Track they're being recorded on plus a number signifying the number of individual Clips that have been recorded for the Track. To change the name of a recorded file, use the Rename feature of the Live's File Browser.

Figure 6.34

Live will automatically begin recording on Track 7 at bar 9 then stop recording at bar 13. This leaves your hands free to play your instrument instead of trying to trigger the recording.

❄ **Recording Effects**

If a Track's monitoring is set to Auto while it's armed for recording, Live will play the incoming audio through the Session Mixer and out to your speakers or headphones. You can place effects onto the Track for real-time processing of your input, but Live will still record the part without these effects.

If you want to record the sound of your incoming part *with* the effects, you'll need to use another Audio Track. On the second Track, set its audio input to the first Track. The sound of your incoming audio will be processed by the effects on the first Track which you can then record on the second Track.

Editing Audio Clips

After you've recorded your new Clips, you may need to edit them. Perhaps you rushed a part or breathed too loud between your vocal lines. There are a variety of ways to alter our Clips once they're recorded, and these are a few you'll want to check every time.

Clip Timing and Rhythm

Live's functionality is dependent on your ability to adjust the timing of audio files to match playback of others. Whether an Audio Clip is created by dragging a file into Live or by recording something new, the method for fixing the timing of the file is the same: Warp Markers. After you've recorded your part, look it over and see if it needs to have any Warp adjustments made. You may see that you played a few notes a little early with one note late near the end. Whatever the mistakes are, you can quickly fix them with a few clicks using Warp Markers. Then, check your Warp Mode and set it to something appropriate for the Audio File as explained at the beginning of this chapter. Press the Save button in the Sample window so your markers and tunings are saved with the audio file in case you use it in another project. Making a habit of doing this now will help keep future creative sessions running smoothly.

Destructive Sample Editing

Some of the mistakes in an audio file may be so minute that they are more appropriate for a detailed offline sample editor like Steinberg Wavelab, Sony Sound Forge, Bias Peak, etc. Within these specialized editing environments, you can make edits more detailed than could be achieved with Live alone. When you save your changes, the new audio file will be ready for use in your Clip.

Editing in the Arrangement View

While using the Session View to record new pieces of audio, the Arrangement View can be used as a "splicing block" for editing multiple Clips together. If you want to use the first 2 bars of Vox A and the last bar of Vox B, you can arrange them as such in the Arrangement View then consolidate the Clips into one new one (Figures 6.35a and 6.35b).

The resulting Clip will contain the parts from Vox takes A and B all wrapped up in one convenient Audio Clip. We can copy this Clip from the Arrangement View to the Session View for use in the developing song structure. If we need to change the edit, the original Audio Clips remain so we can always do it again.

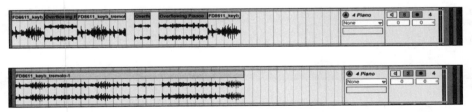

Figure 6.35a

Arrange and edit an assortment of Clips on a Track ...

Figure 6.35b

Chose Consolidate from the Edit menu to render the Track into one new Clip which can be moved back to the Session View.

Tips for Great Loops

Looping audio files is a little art all its own. You're trying to make something that was only played once sound like it's playing over and over again in perfect time with the rest of the parts in your song. While Live does an exceptional job of looping imported files (especially loops that are already cut to the right lengths), there may be times when Live is unable to determine the proper tempo and length of a file, especially in the case of a long audio file (like a whole song). When Live fails to identify a loop, you can quickly tell it where the loop points should be and figure the original tempo. The tools to do this are simple, and the concepts are just as easy:

* **Set Warp Marker 1:** Always be sure that the loop is actually beginning on the downbeat of the sample. Zoom in at the beginning of the sample (Figure 6.36) and make sure there is no silence before the sound starts. If there is, slide Marker 1 over to change the start location.

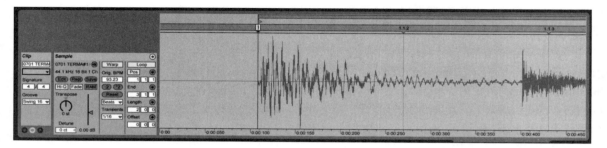

Figure 6.36

Make sure there's no dead air before the sample starts.

* **Do the same zoom-in check at the end of your sample:** Make sure there is no extra noise from a following beat (Figure 6.37). Just like above, move the last marker in line with the beginning of this noise if it's present.

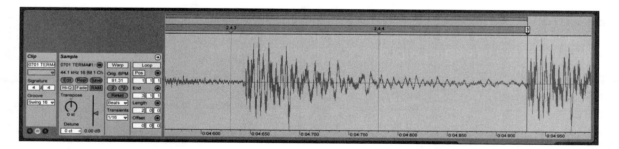

Figure 6.37

Check the end of the loop for any extraneous noise that shouldn't be there.

* **Check the beats in between:** If the beginning and end Markers are in the right place, there's still no guarantee that every beat of the loop will be locked in with the rest of your parts (Figure 6.38). Check all the major beats and be sure that the sounds are lined up properly. Create Warp Markers to compensate when necessary.

* **Make sure that the Fade button is on:** This will perform a quick fade at the beginning and end of the audio loop to remove any "clicks" that can occur at the loop point.

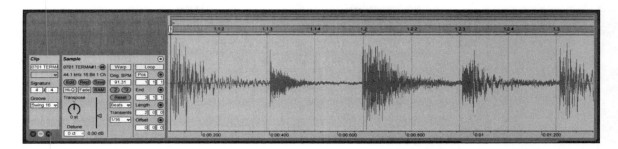

❊ **Experiment with all of the Warp Modes:** While Beats Mode will be rhythmically accurate, it may cause sonic artifacts that outweigh the rhythmic precision. You may find that some of your loops sound better in Tones Mode. Don't forget to check Repitch mode as well—some drum loops will sound better with no Warp processing at all.

❊ **Play with the Warp Markers!** The elastic audio possibilities of the Warp Engine are staggering. While you can fix timing errors with Warp Markers, try messing things up a bit by "shifting" some beats. Is there a Warp Marker on beat 1.2? What happens if you put the 1.1.4 Marker there instead? The sound will now play a 1/16 note early! Use this in combination with the Sample Offset Envelope in Beats Mode to reorder the slices in your loop. Then layer a Transpose Envelope, then an unlinked pan envelope, then whatever other parameters you dare to experiment with!

Figure 6.38

You can see that the sub-beats of this loop are not lined up even though the first and last markers are in the right place. Additional Warp Markers will be necessary to fix the timing of this loop.

❊ ❊ ❊

7 The MIDI Clip

One of the highlight additions to Live 4.0 is the integration of MIDI sequencing into Live's outstanding audio sequencer. Users of earlier versions of Live had been begging for this feature since its first release—everyone could imagine how well MIDI would integrate into Live and expand the creative possibilities. Ableton listened and delivered.

As expected, implementation of MIDI in Live is leveraged from the concepts set forth by Audio Clips. Each MIDI Clip is its own, self-contained, sequencer with its own data. Just like Audio Clips, every MIDI Clip is independent of all the others. MIDI Clips with the same name can all be edited independently, allowing collections of infinitely varied Clips to be generated effortlessly.

The good news is that MIDI Clips are actually simpler to manipulate than their Audio Clip brothers. MIDI Clips don't use any files on the hard drive for playback. Instead, the MIDI data for the Clip is saved in the Live Set project file itself. Unlike audio files, MIDI data does not need to be fed through any sort of Warp Engine when matching its playback speed to the project tempo, so we won't have to worry about Warp Modes nor any of the related settings, such as Warp Markers; nor do we have to worry about Hi-Q interpolation, RAM modes, locating audio files, or hard drive speeds. As a result, there are only a few parameters for MIDI Clips, compared to the amount required for Audio Clips.

However, if you've learned anything about Live so far, you'll know that the apparent simplicity of the MIDI Clip actually belies an extreme amount of power. You'll find that tossing MIDI notes and commands at your virtual instruments and external hardware can be just as powerful (if not more so) than Audio Clips, especially since they both behave the same in regard to Launch Modes, Launch Quantization, Follow Actions, and Envelopes. For this reason, using a combination of audio and MIDI in a Live Set is not confusing—Audio and MIDI Clips look and respond the same in both the Session and Arrangement Views. The differences aren't apparent until you start digging into the Clip and Track Views. In Chapter 5, we discussed a good portion of the Clip View, such as naming and coloring Clips, defining loops, and Follow Actions. These properties exist for both Audio and MIDI Clips. We then covered the additional areas of the Clip View that were unique to Audio Clips in Chapter 6. Now it's time to look at the sections of the Clip View for MIDI Clips.

MIDI Clip Properties

The list of unique properties for a MIDI Clip is abbreviated, compared to Audio Clips. As explained above, manipulating MIDI information is not limited to the same constraints found when dealing with audio files. In the MIDI world, pitch is not related to time. We can speed up a MIDI Clip without causing the MIDI notes to rise in pitch. The opposite is also true—we can transpose the notes in the MIDI Clip without changing its playback speed. Because all these changes are possible by editing the MIDI data, there is no need for special functions in the MIDI Clip View like the Transpose and Warp functions in an Audio Clip.

Furthermore, MIDI and Audio Clips approach controlling sound from different directions. While Audio Clips manipulate an existing sound (an audio file), MIDI Clips manipulate ways to actually *make* the sound by triggering another sound-creating device—be it an external device or a virtual instrument. This means the "sound" of a MIDI Clip is based entirely on the sound created by the device that receives the MIDI data from the Clip.

 Best of Both Worlds

If there is an Audio Clip-specific function that you want to perform on your MIDI part, such as reversing the sound, you can record the output of the MIDI instrument into an Audio Clip and then tweak this new Clip.

The MIDI Clip View is much smaller than the Audio Clip View. The only properties that are unique to the MIDI Clip are the Bank, Sub-bank, and Program selectors (Figure 7.1). Bank and Program Changes are used to recall particular sounds on the destination MIDI device. Most MIDI devices have the ability to save their settings, such as filter parameters, LFO speeds, modulation

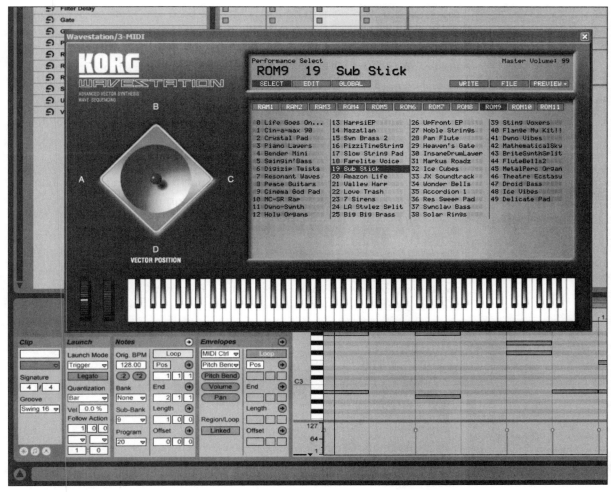

Figure 7.1

The above settings will recall the twentieth sound in the ninth bank of the associated Wavestation instrument. When using the factory default sound bank, these settings will load the "Sub Stick" sound.

sources, etc. These saved settings are referred to as a programs, patches, presets, sounds, or instruments depending on the manufacturer's nomenclature. Regardless of what the company calls its saved sounds, they are always accessed with MIDI Program and Bank Change messages. By setting the Program and Bank values in the Clip View, each Clip can recall a different patch from the instrument when it is launched.

A Program Change is a number between 0 and 127 (that's no surprise, is it?) and refers to a memory location in your MIDI device's sound bank. The way a manufacturer maps the Program message to the memory slots is entirely up to them, but generally a Program Change of "0" will cause the first sound on the instrument to be loaded. In the case of a General MIDI synthe-sizer, this will load a piano patch (the General MIDI specification includes a list of standard instruments and their associated Program numbers). So, using the Program Change message, we can recall a sound from our instrument's 128 choices. But what if our device has more than 128 sounds? That's where the Bank Change message comes into play. A bank holds 128 programs. So, we can recall any sound in our MIDI device by first specifying the containing bank followed by the program number.

Again, the way instrument manufacturers choose to assign sounds to banks and programs is entirely up to them. For example, Waldorf's MicroQ has three banks of 100 sounds. This means that Program Changes 100 through 127 aren't used by the MicroQ. Furthermore, the first sound is labeled as "Bank A Sound 01." This means that a Program Change of "0" will recall sound "A01." A Program Change of "15" will recall "A16." Therefore, if we want to use sound "B01," we'd first have to send a Bank Change message to switch from bank A to bank B, then issue a Program Change of "0" to recall the first patch in that bank (number "01").

So, you will probably have to consult the manual for your MIDI instrument to find out how the manufacturer is using the Bank and Program Change mes-sages. Some will even require that the Bank Change be done with two num-bers, thus the presence of the "Sub-bank" setting in the MIDI Clip properties.

While this may sound confusing, figuring out how your MIDI instruments re-spond to these messages will open up a level of flexibility where each Clip in a MIDI Track can "sound" different. This is because a new sound will be loaded when you launch a new Clip. When using the Waldorf mentioned above, we can make one MIDI Clip that is a string part while another Clip (in the same Track) is an arpeggiated blip sequence; however, if you do not wish to change the patches of your instrument during your song, you can just load the patch you want directly in the instrument's interface and Live will recall it each time the Set is loaded.

Recording New MIDI Clips

To harness the power of MIDI Clips, we'll need to make some first. The easi-est way to make a MIDI Clip is to simply record a part from a MIDI device, such as a keyboard, EWI (electronic wind instrument), MIDI guitar, or a con-troller, though you can also record the MIDI output of other MIDI Tracks and external sequencers. You'll need to have a MIDI interface (discussed in

Chapter 3) to record an external MIDI source. Some audio interfaces include MIDI ports making them especially handy in this situation. Once you have your MIDI device connected, you're ready to record.

. . . In the Session View

In the Session View, recording a new MIDI Clip is almost identical to recording an Audio Clip. The fact that the procedures are similar means there is less for us to learn and remember when using Live. It makes the composition process more transparent because you'll use the same motions every time you record, be it audio or MIDI.

To begin, make a MIDI Track (CTRL [CMND] + SHIFT + T). Then, specify the MIDI input you'll be recording. This is done in the Input/Output Routing strip, shown in Figure 7.2, by selecting the MIDI input device followed by the channel you want to record. Live has a setting called "All Channels" that will record any MIDI data entering the selected input regardless of the MIDI Channel assigned to the data. If you only have one device connected to the MIDI device you selected, then All Channels will be an appropriate setting; however, if you have multiple instruments entering the selected MIDI port, you may want to specify the channel you want to record to prevent data from another instrument being recorded in your Clip. Of course, in order to hear your MIDI data, you'll need to select an output destination for the MIDI Track. You can simply load a virtual instrument onto the Track, or you can specify an external device and channel to play the MIDI.

Figure 7.2

The Evolution MK-425c has been selected as our MIDI input device. Since the MK-425c is just a controller keyboard, we can listen to all incoming MIDI channels. This Track will end up controlling channel 4 of Waldorf's MicroQ which is hooked up to MIDI Out port of M-Audio's FireWire 410.

In the example above, the input and output has been specified for our Track, so we can set the Track for recording by activating the Arm button in the Session Mixer. With Monitor set to "Auto," we'll now be able to play the MicroQ from the Evolution keyboard (MIDI data enters the Track from the MK-425c and is then immediately sent out to the Waldorf). The Track is now ready to record.

You'll notice that all the Clip Stop buttons in the Track have changed to circles. Clicking one of these circles will begin recording a new MIDI Clip in that slot. Just like Audio Clips, recording will wait for the time specified by the Global Quantize setting. Once recording has commenced, start playing. Everything you do, including pitch bends, aftertouch, knob tweaks, etc., will be recorded into the MIDI Clip. When you're done, click the play icon in the Clip to stop recording (if your default Launch Mode is Trigger, the Clip will begin playing back your new recording). You can start recording additional takes by clicking the circles in any of the other Clip Slots.

. . . In the Arrangement View

If recording MIDI Clips resembles recording Audio Clips in the Session View, you can probably already guess how to record MIDI Clips in the Arrangement View. Indeed, it is the same procedure used with Audio Clips in the Arrangement View. You'll first need to set up your MIDI input and output as explained in Figure 7.2. You'll also Arm the Track, but instead of using the circles in the Clip Slots to start recording, you'll click the Record button in the Control Bar. When you then press Play in the Control Bar, Live will start playing your Arrangement while recording your new MIDI Clip (Figure 7.3). If Live is already playing, recording will begin the instant you press the Record button. By arming multiple Tracks, you can record multiple Clips simultaneously, allowing Live to work as a multi-track MIDI recorder. You can, of course, also record multiple Audio Clips at the same time, too!

> ### ❈ Multi-Recording
>
> Can't seem to arm more than one Track at a time for recording? Don't worry, you're just being stopped by Live's new Arm "exclusive" behavior. To Arm multiple Tracks, hold down the CTRL (CMND) key then click the Arm buttons. This is just like selecting multiple files on your computer. If this behavior annoys you, you can turn it off in the Preferences (Chapter 3).

Quantizing Your Performance

Nobody's perfect. We can't always play our instruments with the rhythmical precision of a drum machine; but, with judicious use of quantizing, Live can

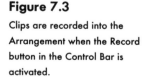

Figure 7.3

Clips are recorded into the Arrangement when the Record button in the Control Bar is activated.

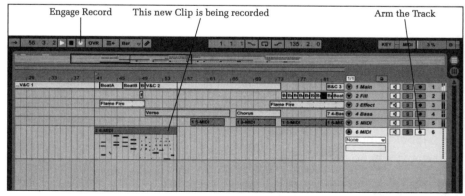

Engage Record　　This new Clip is being recorded　　Arm the Track

make you sound like you're dead-on the beat. *Quantizing* is the process of aligning events to a timing grid. In the case of Launch Quantizing used in the Session View, we're making sure our Clips start playing on a division of our timing grid. When Quantizing a MIDI Clip, we're making sure *every note* is aligned to the grid.

Live, by default, will automatically quantize any MIDI Clip you record. If you record a part and immediately play it back, it will be perfectly aligned to the rhythmic subdivisions currently selected (see Figures 7.4a and 7.4b). This is great as it keeps you from having to manually quantize every MIDI Clip you make. This is a dream come true when programming drum beats since every recording will be rhythmically tight. The size of the subdivisions used for the Quantize function is set in the Edit > Record Quantization menu. Live can quantize notes to a grid of quarter notes, sixteenth note triplets, and everything in between.

Of course, not every style of music demands strict rhythmic quantization. In fact, many musicians prefer to keep the natural feel of their performances in

Figure 7.4a

Here are some unquantized MIDI notes.

Figure 7.4b

The same notes after quantizing. Notice how each note's left edge is aligned with one of the grid lines.

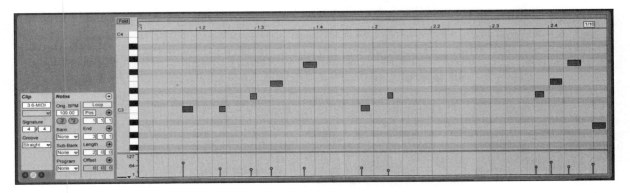

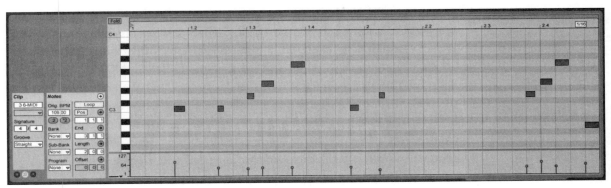

their takes. You can turn off Live's automatic Quantizing by choosing "No Quantization" from the Record Quantize Menu. If you decide later that you do want to quantize the part, press CTRL (CMND) + U to force all notes to line up with the MIDI Clip's current quantizing grid. If you want to quantize only a section of notes, select them first, then press CTRL (CMND) + U.

> ❋ **The Undo Two-Step**
> When Live is set to automatically quantize a recording, you'll still be able to undo the quantizing in case you left it on by accident. The first time you press CTRL (CMND) + Z after recording, the recorded notes will move to their original, unquantized locations. The second Undo will erase the Clip, allowing you to make another.

Overdub Recording

Overdub recording is a function available only for MIDI Clips; it allows you to record additional MIDI data into a Clip without erasing what's already there. This is an awesome feature when it comes to programming drum beats, since you can build them one piece at a time. You can make a 2-bar loop with a hi-hat, then play the additional parts (kick drums, snares, cymbals, etc.) layer by layer as the Clip continues to loop.

To enable MIDI Overdub recording, click the "OVR" button in the Control Bar (Figure 7.5). When you launch a Clip, it will start playing and its play triangle will be green. Once you Arm the Track for recording, the MIDI Clip will keep playing, but its play triangle will turn red. This signifies that the Clip is playing *and* recording at the same time. Anything you play at this point will be added to the current MIDI Clip (it will be quantized on the fly, too, if Record Quantization is enabled) and each iteration of the loop will contain the new data you recorded.

Combined with the drag and drop techniques of the Session View, programming variations of beats can be accomplished in moments instead of minutes. You can start with a simple drum pattern (perhaps just kick drum and hi-hat for the intro of your song), drag-copy (use the CTRL [CMND] key while dragging) the Clip to a new location, then use the MIDI Overdub to layer the snare hits on top of the kick and hi-hat. You'll now have two MIDI Clips, one with just kick and hats and the other with a snare added. You can drag copy the new MIDI Clip and layer on an additional part, such as a shaker or congas. Using this technique, you can quickly build a collection of drum variations for your song which you can then trigger on the fly.

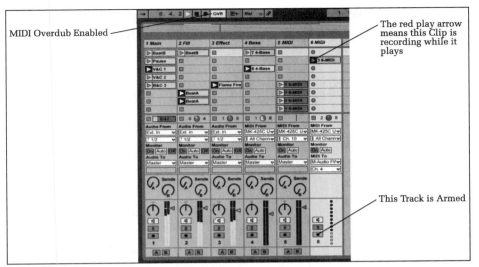

MIDI Overdub Enabled

The red play arrow means this Clip is recording while it plays

This Track is Armed

Figure 7.5

MIDI Overdub recording allows parts to be built in layers while a MIDI Clip is playing. Note that recording occurs for any playing Clip on an Armed Track.

Of course, you can use Overdub recording for more than drums. If a piano part is really tricky, you could record the left-hand and right-hand parts separately. Perhaps you'll perform the left-hand part on the first pass then overdub the right-hand on the next pass.

✸ **MIDI on MIDI**

You can have Overdub enabled when recording new MIDI Clips. When you record a new Clip, the process is the same as if Overdub were off; however, once you click the Clip to stop recording, it will start looping and immediately enter Overdub mode (the play triangle will be red). You can then start layering additional parts immediately without having to stop the music.

Editing MIDI Clips

One of the most attractive features of MIDI is the ability to edit the MIDI data in order to create a perfect part. Recorded notes can be effortlessly transposed to different pitches, extended or shortened, and moved to a different location in time. This can make recording MIDI parts a little easier because you don't have to worry about getting the part *exactly* right. You only need to get it close so you can make final adjustments to the MIDI data.

When we edit MIDI Clips in Live, we have the ability to not only change the notes that are recorded, we can create new ones by hand. In fact, many producers prefer to draw parts directly into the Clips instead of playing them. It allows them to create specific performances, such as perfectly repeating sixteenth notes that are all the same duration and velocity. Editing data by hand also allows you to create precise automation, such as perfect volume fades and quantized filter modulations.

Adjusting the Grid

All editing in a MIDI Clip is governed by the timing grid. Any time a note is created or moved, it will snap to the grid values. If your grid is set to 1/4, you'll only be able to align the MIDI notes to the quarter note of the Clip. You can, of course, change the grid settings, allowing you to make more precise rhythmic adjustments. You can even turn the grid off completely for free-form editing.

Adjusting the timing grid in the MIDI Clip View is performed in the same manner as changing the grid in the Arrangement View (see Chapter 5). It is accomplished with a set of key commands outlined below. As you execute these key commands, you'll see the quantize value change in the MIDI data window (Figure 7.6), reflecting your modification.

- ❋ **CTRL (CMND) + 1**—This will decrease the value of the grid. If the grid was set to 1/16 before, it will be 1/32 after using this key command.

- ❋ **CTRL (CMND) + 2**—This has the opposite effect of the command above. A grid value of 1/16 will change to 1/8 after using this command.

- ❋ **CTRL (CMND) + 3**—This key command toggles triplet mode on and off. A previous setting of 1/8 will turn to 1/8T (eighth-note triplet) after pressing these keys. Use this key command again to switch triplet mode off.

- ❋ **CTRL (CMND) + 4**—This turns the entire grid on and off. When the grid is off, the grid value display will turn gray. You will be able to place MIDI data anywhere you like while the grid is off. To re-enable the grid, press this key command again.

Figure 7.6

The current grid setting is 1/16. This means all notes we manipulate will lock to sixteenth-note timing.

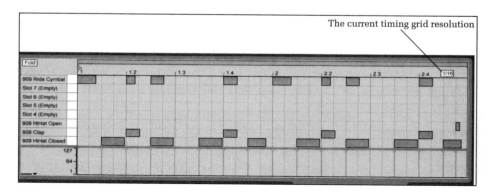

The current timing grid resolution

Editing Notes and Velocities

Once you've got your desired grid timing selected, you're ready to start manipulating MIDI notes. Live displays MIDI notes in a style known as a "piano roll." This term comes from the old player-pianos that were programmed using rolls of paper. These rolls had small slots cut into them, each representing a specific note on the piano keyboard or one of the other instruments mounted inside. A note that played for a long time was triggered by a long slot in the paper. As the paper rolled by mechanical sensors, it triggered servos to play notes on the piano.

Viewing MIDI Data

The piano roll view in Live features a lane for each note in the MIDI scale. When looking at Figure 7.7 below, you'll see an image of a piano keyboard at the left side of the window. From each of these keys is a lane extending to the right where notes can be placed. Notes placed in these lanes trigger their corresponding key in the scale.

You can zoom in and out of the vertical piano keyboard, thus allowing you to see more or less of the 128 possible notes in the MIDI scale. You can zoom by moving your mouse over the piano keyboard at the left of the window. When the mouse changes to a magnifying glass, you can click and drag to zoom. Since the view is vertical instead of horizontal, the zooming moves have also been turned on their side. Dragging the mouse left and

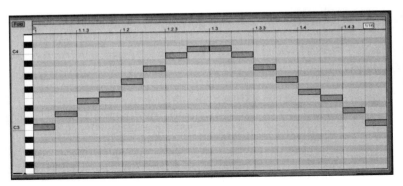

Figure 7.7

The MIDI data here is a C major scale. You can see that only the white keys are being triggered by the MIDI notes.

197

❄ **Into the Fold**

Live's MIDI display has a unique feature that hides any lanes that don't contain MIDI data. When the "Fold" button is activated, the display will be condensed and you'll only see the lanes that contain notes in the Clip. This is perfect for programming drums since many synths and keyboards map their sounds over a wide range of octaves. You may be using a kick drum sound at D1 while using a hi-hat sound three octaves higher at E4. So, instead of scrolling up and down repeatedly to see the two parts, you can press "Fold" and you'll see only the lanes for D1 and E4, making editing a snap. Turn "Fold" off to see all the lanes again.

right will now adjust the zoom while dragging up and down will scroll through the piano keyboard. If you zoom out too far, the piano keyboard will disappear. Zoom in to see it again.

Editing MIDI Data with the Pencil

There are two methods for editing MIDI data: with or without the Pencil. When the Pencil is on (activate it in the Control Bar or press CTRL [CMND] + B), you can quickly add notes to the MIDI note window and set their velocities. Clicking in the grid will cause a note to appear that is the length of the current grid setting. If you continue to hold the mouse button after you create the note, you can drag up and down to set its velocity. If you click and drag horizontally (Figure 7.8), the Pencil will create a series of notes in that lane, great for hi-hat patterns (you can also drag up and down to set the velocities of the whole group). Clicking an existing note with the Pencil will erase it.

Editing MIDI Data without the Pencil

While writing notes with the Pencil can be extremely efficient, there are a few things that can't be done with the Pencil such as changing the start time and length of a MIDI note. These advanced edits can be performed by switching the Pencil tool off (click the icon in the Control Bar or press CTRL [CMND] + B to toggle it). When the Pencil is off, your mouse will appear as a standard arrow.

Figure 7.8

We used the Pencil to quickly draw in a series of sixteenth notes for the "909 HiHat Closed" sound.

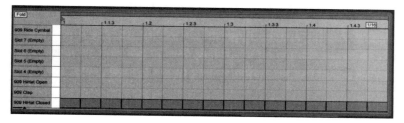

To create a MIDI note in this mode, *double-click* an empty slot. After the note has been made, you can click and drag it to a new location. This will let you change the pitch and time for the note in one maneuver. When you move the mouse to either end of the MIDI note, the mouse will change to a bracket (it will look like "[" at the beginning of the note and "]" at the end). Clicking and dragging in this location will stretch the MIDI note, making it either longer or shorter. Double-clicking the note again will erase it.

To adjust the velocity of a note when you're not using the Pencil requires exposing the velocity lane in the MIDI note window. This lane can be viewed by dragging the lower boundary upward (Figure 7.9). The velocity of each note is represented by a vertical line with a small circle at the top. The taller the line, the greater the velocity. Since multiple notes can occur in different lanes at one time in a MIDI Clip, it's possible that the velocities for multiple notes will be stacked on top of one another. As you move your mouse over one of the circular handles at the top of the velocity lines, you'll see its corresponding note become highlighted in the upper window, showing you which note you're about to edit. We actually recommend doing the reverse, however, by selecting the note in the upper portion of the window first to ensure you will edit the right velocity. If you do decide to use the Pencil tool in the velocity lane, you will not be able to specify which note to edit when two or more occur at the same time (vertically aligned). Instead, the Pencil will set these notes to the same velocity.

Another benefit of not using the Pencil is we can select groups of MIDI notes to edit. We can click and drag around the area of notes we want, or we can select them individually by holding SHIFT and clicking. Once selected, you can perform edits on multiple notes at once. You can drag the notes to a new location, changing their pitch and timing. You can lengthen or shorten

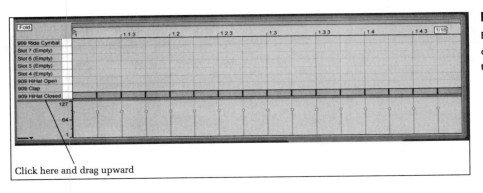

Click here and drag upward

Figure 7.9

By dragging the bottom border upward, we've exposed the velocity lane.

them as a group. You can copy them using all the standard Cut, Copy, and Paste commands (even the dragging techniques of the Session View work here), or you can scale their velocities all at once in the lower window.

MIDI Clip Envelopes

Once your MIDI notes are straightened out, it will be time to look at your Clips envelopes. That's right, MIDI Clips have Clip Envelopes just like Audio Clips—some are even identical. These envelopes will be used for creating controller data to be sent to your MIDI devices. When effects and instruments are loaded onto the MIDI Track, the Clip Envelopes will be able to control those devices, too.

MIDI Ctrl Envelopes

In a MIDI Track with an empty Track View, the only category of envelopes that will be available are the MIDI Ctrl Envelopes. These are controllers such as Pitch Bend, Modulation, Volume, Pan, and Sustain, and are all shown as graphical envelopes in the Clip View (Figure 7.10). These envelopes generate values that are translated to MIDI data then sent to the destination MIDI device.

Figure 7.10

The movements of the mod wheel are represented by an envelope that bears a striking resemblance to a roller-coaster.

When you look through the list of available MIDI controllers, you'll see some of them have already been named, such as volume, breath, pan, and expression. This is because part of the MIDI standard defines certain controller numbers for certain musical tasks. Controller 10 is generally pan. Controller 7 is usually volume, and so on. Whether these controllers actually have any effect or not will be determined by the MIDI device on the receiving end. If you have an old analog synth with MIDI, it may respond to notes and pitch bend, but it might not be able to do a pan. Others may not respond to Controller 7 for volume. You'll need to look at your MIDI device's manual,

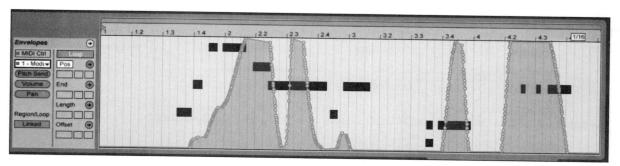

specifically the MIDI implementation chart (usually at the end of the manual), to see a list of the MIDI controllers and messages for the instrument.

The MIDI Envelopes are edited in the same fashion as the Clip Envelopes in the last chapter. You can edit them with or without the Pencil tool, and you can unlink them for interesting rhythmical results.

Mixer Envelopes

If you happen to load a virtual instrument onto your MIDI Track, a few more envelope categories will be available for your tweaking. Once the virtual instrument is in place, the Track now behaves like an Audio Track. You'll see that you have a "Mixer" category available with Volume, Pan, and Send Envelopes. There will also be a category for the virtual instrument you loaded. This means you can modulate the parameters of the virtual instrument while it plays. Furthermore, any Audio or MIDI effects loaded into the Track will be available for tweaking.

✳ Shortcut to Confusion

We found a situation that had us scratching our heads in confusion for a moment. We started programming a MIDI Clip on a Track with no virtual instrument. We clicked the Pan button and programmed some movements. Everything was good.

Later, we loaded a virtual instrument onto the Track. When we pressed the Pan button, we were presented with a flat line! We could hear the part panning around, but we couldn't see the automation anymore.

In a moment, we realized we were looking at the *mixer pan* control. When we originally programmed the pan, we did so at the MIDI level—we sent MIDI controller 10 messages to the synth. The Pan button had brought up "MIDI Ctrl" and "10-Pan" in the Envelope menus. With the virtual instrument in place, the Pan button was now loading the "Mixer" and "Pan" menu selections.

When we manually switched the menus to "MIDI Ctrl" and "10-Pan," we could see our envelope again. This same behavior is true of the Volume button as well.

Virtual Instruments and Effects

You can draw and edit envelopes for parameters of the Live Devices and plug-ins loaded onto a Track by selecting them from the Clip Envelope menus. The top menu will select the Device or plug-in, which can be an instrument or an effect (both audio and MIDI effects). For each device selected in the top menu, you'll get a list of device-specific parameters which can be edited.

> ❄ **Is This Thing On?**
>
> All controller values are represented as Envelopes in Live. If the parameter you are controlling is a switch, values above 64 usually turn it on and values below turn it off. You'll need to make sure your envelope only passes above 64 when you want your parameter "on."

Importing and Exporting MIDI Files

Live stores all MIDI data and parameters for MIDI Clips within the Live Set itself. While Audio Clips must play an audio file stored on a hard disk, the MIDI Clips don't require any sort of external support file that you need to keep track of. When you import a MIDI file, Live copies the data from the MIDI file into the Live Set. Live will never use the original MIDI file again. Should the file be changed or lost, the Live Set will still play perfectly.

Standard MIDI Files

Live imports MIDI parts from Standard MIDI Files (SMFs). SMFs come in two flavors: Type 0 and Type 1. Type 0 won't do us any good in Live—all the parts are squished into one track. Type 1, on the other hand, has the MIDI parts split into separate tracks for each instrument. There will be a track for the bass, some for the drums, and tracks for any other part in the song. Live lets us import one of these tracks into a new Clip.

Importing MIDI

In Live's Factory Content folder, there is a folder named "MIDI Loops by KeyFax." Open this folder and you'll find what looks like the directory of a sample CD. Open the first folder named "BRK_120." You find five different MIDI files inside (MIDI files end in the extension ".mid"). When you open the "BRK-Bass.mid" file, it will open to reveal a track which you can drag into a Clip Slot on a MIDI Track. Of course, you'll need to have a MIDI instrument to play this bass part before you'll hear anything. Load a Simpler or your favorite bass synth into the Track View and launch the Clip. It will play your instrument perfectly in time with the project tempo.

Each of the KeyFax loops are only one track per MIDI file; however, Standard MIDI Files can have multiple tracks in them. When they do, each one will be displayed below the MIDI file when you open it in the Browser (Figure 7.11). Drag the tracks in to create new Clips.

If you've got a song in another software, or perhaps something stuck in an older hardware sequencer, and you want to transfer it to Live, Standard MIDI Files will usually take care of the job. The format has been around for a long time so you can be assured of compatibility; however, SMFs don't retain everything from a computer project. When exporting songs done in other programs, you may have been utilizing application-specific features that are beyond the scope of MIDI. This can include mixer and effect automation as well as the port and channel assignments of the MIDI Tracks. This kind of information gets saved in the application's native file format, but usually won't appear in a Standard MIDI File export. That type of automation will have to be reprogrammed.

Figure 7.11

This MIDI file has multiple tracks that can be individually added to the Live Set.

Exporting MIDI

If you need to take the MIDI part from a Clip and send it to another Live Set or a different program, you can export the MIDI data as a Standard MIDI File. Select the Clip and choose "Export Selected MIDI Clip" from Live's File menu. You'll be prompted for the name and destination for the exported data. Choose a location and name and click "Save."

Now that we have a handle on the ins and outs of Audio and MIDI Clips and how to arrange them, it's time to start adding effects. The next chapter will show how effects, if used properly, can add another dimension to your music by introducing elements of sound design. You'll also learn how to use virtual instruments and put them fully under hardware control.

8 Using Effects and Instruments

Effects can have a profound effect on your music. They can be used in a variety of ways; possibly to remove unwanted frequencies from an audio track (EQ), to create the sound of a room for a vocalist (Reverb), or to completely destroy and mangle a sound into something totally new (Distortion). Effects put a lot of power at your fingertips. Those new to these toys will more than likely run hog-wild the first few times they get their hands on them. Hey, effects are fun—we know that. As with all things, practice will help you determine which type of effects will help your mix the most. Don't forget that sometimes having no effect on a sound can be the best decision.

Using Effects in a Session

What are effects and how do they work? In the simplest sense, an effect is a device that takes an input signal—either audio or MIDI data—performs calculations upon it, and spits the result out its other end. For example, a delay effect will take a sound into its input then wait a specified amount of time before sending it out its output. A filter effect can take a sound, remove all the frequencies below 500Hz, and spit out the result. We can chain multiple effects together for even more power by having the output of one effect feed the input of another, and so on.

The Track View

In Live, the graphical layout of an effect chain is surprisingly simple and logical. Double-click a Track name—either at the top of the Session View or at the right side of the Arrangement View—and you will see its Track View appear at the bottom of the Live window. Effects are placed in the Track View side by side to form a chain (Figure 8.1). A signal enters the left-most device and proceeds through each until it comes out the right-hand side.

The Effect Browsers

We gain access to our collection of effects through the two device browser icons seen in Figure 8.2. The top icon activates the Live Device Browser while the lower icon activates the Plug-In Device Browser.

The Live Device Browser contains three folders which can be opened to view the built-in Audio Effects, MIDI Effects, and Instruments, which will be individually discussed in a moment. The folder layout of the Plug-In Device Browser will depend entirely on the current configuration of your system and the plug-ins that are available to Live.

Adding an Effect to a Track

Adding an effect from one of the Device Browsers is as easy as it gets. In fact, there are three different ways to load an effect onto a track, all of which may be used interchangeably:

※ The first method is to click and drag a device from the Browser to the desired track, as shown in Figure 8.3. This will cause the new effect to be added to the right side of the effect chain if there are any pre-existing devices on the track.

※ The second method involves first selecting the destination track (click on the track's name) then double-clicking the desired effect in the Device Browser. Just as above, the selected effect will be loaded into the far-right position in the track's effect chain.

Figure 8.1

An arbitrary arrangement of audio effects in the Track View. The input signal is processed by each device in order from left to right.

Figure 8.2

These two buttons are located in the upper-left corner of the Live window. Click the top button to gain access to Live's built-in effects and instruments. The bottom button displays a list of all the plug-ins, both VST and AU, currently available to Live.

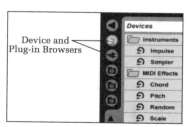

❋ The final method involves double-clicking the name of a track to expose its Track View. You may then drag and drop effects from the Browsers directly into the Track View (Figure 8.4). The benefit of this method is that you may choose where in the device chain the new effect will be loaded instead of always defaulting to the last position, as in the previous two methods. If you decide that you need some EQ before your compressor, you can simply drag it into this location.

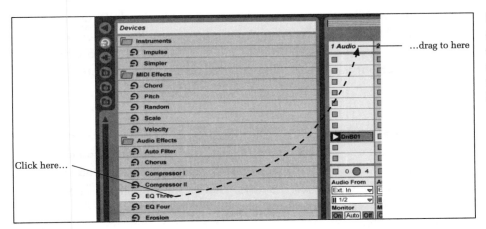

Figure 8.3

Click and drag an effect from the browser to the title of a track. When you release your mouse button, the effect will be loaded into the track.

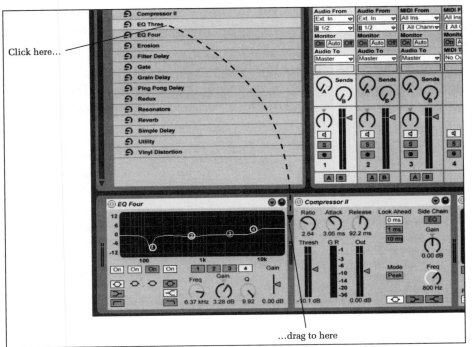

Figure 8.4

By dragging Devices straight into the Track View, you can choose to insert them at any point in the chain that you wish.

❋ ❋ ❋

All three methods explained above work identically in both the Session View and Arrangement View. Just remember that in the Session View, the track names are found at the top of the window while the track names are found on the right side of the Arrangement View.

Plug-in Types

There are two types of effects to deal with in Live: Audio Effects and MIDI Effects. As you would assume, Audio Effects process and alter only audio signals while MIDI Effects perform calculations on passing MIDI data. It also makes sense that a MIDI Effect can't be used on an audio track or vice versa. There is a special case, however, in which MIDI and Audio Effects can exist on the same track—when using the third device type, an instrument, on a MIDI track.

Audio Effects

Audio Effects have existed in Live since the program's first release. Audio Effects can be used to correct tone problems, add ambience to sounds, or shape noise into completely new textures—the possibilities are staggering. Audio Effects include equalizers, delays, choruses, pitch shifters, flangers, compressors, phasers, gates, distortions, and limiters. There may be a few more esoteric effects not categorized here for sure, but the majority of audio plug-ins will be of these types. Live includes a collection of seventeen Audio Effects for your perusal, use, and abuse. A complete dissertation on said effects appears in the next chapter.

Audio Effects can be used only on audio tracks. An attempt to place an audio effect on a MIDI track will be only somewhat successful. The effect will be loaded, but it will be preceded by a warning message (Figure 8.5).

Virtual Instruments

When Live tells us to "Drop Instrument Here," it's not directing us to drop our keyboards. Instead, it is referring to a *virtual instrument*, which is another type of plug-in. While an instrument is not an effect by definition, it exists in our effect chain. What's unique about an instrument device is that it takes MIDI input but spits out audio. This allows us to create MIDI data in the Session or Arrangement and feed it into an instrument to hear the results.

Live comes with two instruments of its own, Impulse and Simpler (see Chapter 11 for the scoop on these), plus supports any plug-in instrument conforming to the VSTi standard. Mac OS X users also have the ability to use Audio Units instruments, too. When we place an instrument onto a MIDI track, everything to the left of the instrument is MIDI and everything to the right is audio (Figure 8.6).

By adding an instrument to a MIDI track, we convert it into a hybrid audio/MIDI track. The result can be seen when looking at the I/O routing section of the Session Mixer (Figure 8.7).

MIDI Effects
The last type of effect used in Live is the MIDI Effect. Placing these on a MIDI track will alter the MIDI messages being passed on through the effect chain. These alterations can range from subtle, such as smoothing out velocity

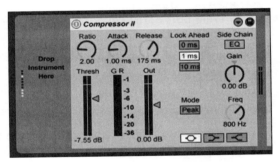

Figure 8.5

Here's a Compressor II sitting on a MIDI track. Notice the "Drop Instrument Here" message before the plug-in. Do you think something should go there?

Figure 8.6

We've added Live's Impulse instrument to the MIDI track. This track will now function properly and the output of Impulse will be compressed by Compressor II.

Figure 8.7

The I/O section on the left is for our track seen above. The Impulse has caused the router to change the output format of the track from MIDI to Audio. The track on the right does not have an instrument loaded so MIDI is never changed to audio. Thus, the right track still outputs MIDI.

response, to drastic, as when remapping notes to different pitches. Keep in mind that MIDI Effects do not alter what you hear, they alter what an instrument is told to play. Consider the following:

You load your favorite piano plug-in onto a MIDI Track. You record a short riff into a Clip and set it looping. You then load the Pitch Effect onto the track right before the piano plug-in. As you turn up the Transpose knob on the Pitch Effect, the notes being sent to the piano plug-in are shifted upward. The result is that the piano plug-in now plays the part in a higher register. You'll also notice that as you continue to increase the Transpose knob further, the piano will play higher and higher *while still sounding natural*. This is because you are not shifting the sound of the piano upward, you're moving the MIDI notes used to trigger the piano. It's exactly as if you'd moved your hands to a different part of the keyboard and played the part again. Now, you remove the Pitch Effect and record the piano part into an Audio Clip. As you transpose the Audio Clip higher, there will be a point at which the piano starts sounding artificial. This is the difference between changing pitch in the MIDI and audio domains. The Pitch Effect changes what the instrument plays, which results in a more pleasing transposition.

This distinction also has its "gotchas" that can result in seemingly confusing behaviors for MIDI Effects in certain scenarios. If we use the Pitch Effect (Figure 8.8) to transpose the MIDI messages sent to the Impulse up two octaves, we will not hear our drums sounding higher in pitch. In fact, you won't hear any drums at all! This is because the MIDI notes being sent to the Impulse are now two octaves above the notes that are used to trigger the samples. If we wanted to play Impulse on our external keyboards, we'd now have to play the notes 2 octaves lower in order to trigger the sounds. When the sounds are triggered, they will still be at their original pitch. If this situation doesn't make sense, take a look at the "Impulse" section in Chapter 11. It gives a full account of the MIDI notes used to trigger the samples. A full MIDI Effect reference can also be found in Chapter 10.

Third-Party Plug-ins
While Live offers an impressive collection of twenty-four devices right out of the box, you may still prefer to use plug-in effects and instruments from other manufacturers. Live fully supports the VST and Audio Units (Mac OS X only) plug-in standards, allowing limitless expansion possibilities for your virtual studio.

While all of Live's plug-ins can be edited entirely from their graphical interfaces in the Track View, the nature of VST and AU plug-ins and their fully customizable graphical interfaces requires that a separate window be used to display the effect. When an external plug-in is loaded, a generic X-Y object will be displayed in the Track View (Figure 8.9), allowing access to more detailed functions.

Re-ordering and Removing Effects

Live allows us to easily change the order of effects within a chain. This ability provides a way to experiment easily with different device arrangements. Does it sound better to run a vocal through a reverb then into a delay or the other way around? To find out, just drag and drop the pre-existing effects within the Track View to change their order (see Figure 8.10). The results will be heard immediately. When dragging an effect between existing effects, you'll see a dark line appear, indicating the insert point for when the mouse is released.

Figure 8.8

The Pitch device is transposing the MIDI data out of the operating range for Impulse. You can see the MIDI data entering the Impulse on its left, but there's no audio exiting on its right.

Figure 8.9

A VST plug-in shows up as a generic placeholder. Clicking the wrench icon opens up the plug-in's custom graphical interface.

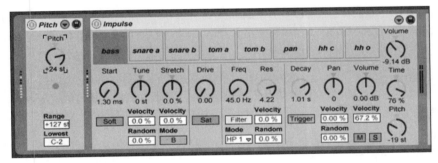

Click here to open plug-in window

Figure 8.10

Click and drag the Simple Delay to the left side of the Track View. When you release the mouse button, the two effects will switch positions.

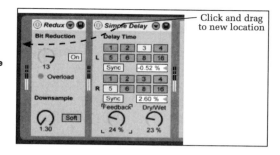

❄ **With or Without You**

If you want to compare the sound of a track with and without an effect, click the effect's power button located in the upper-left corner of the effect window. You can toggle the effect on and off without having to delete it. When the effect is turned off, audio will bypass the effect and continue through any others in your chain.

If an effect is no longer needed (perhaps you resampled this track and now wish to remove its effects) or it was loaded by accident, click on the effect Title Bar to select it and press Delete on your computer keyboard. The effect will disappear and any effect that may have been to the right will shift to the left to fill any space left behind.

Managing Device Presets

Live can store the current settings of a Device using the Preset icons at the top of the Device window (see Figure 8.11).

The icon with an arrow will open the Preset Menu, which contains a list of previously stored presets for the device including those provided as starters from Ableton (Figure 8.12). Selecting a Preset from the menu will cause it to be loaded and will replace the settings currently being used by the Device.

Figure 8.11

Preset management buttons found in each device's title bar.

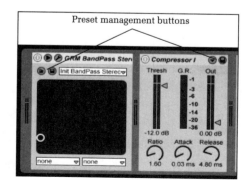

❁ ❁ ❁

The icon to right, which resembles a floppy disk, opens a dialog box for saving and deleting Presets. If you loaded one of the factory default presets, you will only have the option of saving a new Preset with a new name. If you loaded one of your user presets, the dialog box will offer options for overwriting the preset, deleting it, or saving it under a new name (Figure 8.13).

As you manipulate a given effect, you may discover a particularly useful configuration or sound that you want to use in another song or even in the same song on another track; the ability to save and recall effects settings makes such re-use of favorite effects simple.

Figure 8.12

Choose a preset from the drop-down menu to load it. Factory presets appear above the horizontal line in the menu and cannot be changed or deleted.

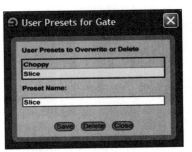

Figure 8.13

This dialog box offers you options for re-naming, over-writing, deleting, and storing new presets.

❊ **The Name Game**

Non-descriptive names will simply waste your time. Some examples of more useful, descriptive names might be Squashed Drums for a tough, quick compressor, Bass Erase for a hi-pass EQ Four, or Long Large Room for a washy and gradually decaying reverb.

Any saved presets can be recalled in any Ableton Live Set/Song file (ALS) on the same machine. The default file folders that the presets are saved to are as follows:

- ❊ **Mac OS 9:** System folder: Application Support > Ableton > Live X.X (version number)
- ❊ **Mac OS X:** Home > Library > Application Support > Ableton > Live X.X (version number)
- ❊ **Windows:** Programs / Ableton / Live X.X (version number)

When collaborating on projects with other artists, you may need to transfer your presets to their computers. Simply copy the necessary presets from the folders listed above and include them with the .als file and associated sounds folder. They can then copy your preset into their presets folder making them available in their copy of Live 4.0.

If you are backing up your system or migrating to another machine, it is a good idea to copy the folder that contains all of your presets. Or if you decide you would like to start fresh, you can delete this folder with no consequences.

Warnings

By using a plug-in, you are incorporating a new piece of program code into Live. This is very much like receiving a kidney transplant—it may work or your body may reject it. Plug-ins are available from a wide range of sources. Waves, Ohm Force, Nomad Factory, and PSP are a few companies that make terrific effects. Native Instruments, LinPlug, GMedia Music, Arturia, reFX, and VirSyn peddle some of the most cutting-edge virtual instruments around. A studious web-surfer can find an even greater offering of plug-ins to try, many of which are available as freeware downloads. In any case, the quality of programming put into the plug-in will determine its effectiveness and stability within Live. It's safer to use plug-ins from major companies as they have the resources to develop, diagnose, and improve their products quickly. Plug-ins developed by some guy in his basement may be the most imaginative of the breed, but commonly suffer from lack of optimization (one plug-in uses a huge chunk of CPU power) and instability (may cause crashes at the most inappropriate times). We are not saying that you shouldn't use these freeware and shareware plug-ins—quite the contrary; we just want to impress upon you the fact that problems may arise in this situation, so be ready (save often!). Most importantly, never use a brand new plug-in for the first time at a gig. Who knows what it may do. Take the time to thoroughly test the plug-in in the safety of your own home before playing out live.

Tips

When experimenting with new plug-ins, there are a few precautions to take. These hints can help keep you from loosing your work, crashing the system, and destroying speakers.

* **Save your Live Set before loading a virgin plug-in:** Should the plug-in cause Live to instantly crash, you'll be able to load your Set again and continue right from where you left off.

* **Back up the new Set:** Once you have a new plug-in running, save a copy of the set under a new temporary name, possibly the name of the song with "-test" added to the end. Then, quit Live and start back up again. Try loading the temporary Set to be sure the plug-in initializes properly. We've both had a

couple occasions where the plug-in worked when added manually, but the program would crash when trying to load the whole Live Set. Once you are sure
that the plug-in will load dependably, you can then re-save your Set under its
original name.

❋ **Watch your volumes:** Any time you add an unproven plug-in to your
Session, turn down your speaker and headphone volumes. A bad plug-in ini-
tialization can sometimes leave your computer outputting full-spectrum digital
noise which could rip both your speakers and eardrums to shreds.

❋ **Organize your plug-in collection:** We like to use the custom plug-in direc-
tories (see the "Plug-in Tab" section in Chapter 3) to keep a collection of plug-
ins that are confirmed to work with Live separate from the slew of freeware
and demo plug-ins that exist in our standard shared plug-ins folders. By only
having a small collection of plug-ins for Live to use, you will significantly reduce
the boot-up time for Live since the program performs a plug-in scan on every
startup. A shorter list is also easier to navigate when dragging and dropping
effects in a live performance.

❋ **Crash-Start**

If you find yourself trying to load a Live Set that keeps crashing, it could be one of the plug-ins causing the problem. Try removing (or at least relocating) the plug-ins from your folders one at a time
until the song loads successfully. When it loads, Live will tell you that it is unable to load one of the
plug-ins, but you'll be able to keep working. Try using a similar plug-in in place of the problem one
(i.e., try using Live's Reverb if a third-party reverb gives you problems).

Signal Path

While all signals pass through the Track View from right to left, there are still
a few ways we can vary the flow of signals through Live's mixer. Effects can
be used as *inserts* or they may be used as part of a *send and return*. This
routing is determined by whether we're placing the effect directly onto one
of our tracks or into a Return Track.

Using an Effect as an Insert

When we use an effect as an insert, we are literally inserting our device into
the normal signal flow of our Tracks. In Figure 8.14, an EQ Four has been
inserted on Track 1. All of the audio coming from the Clips on that track must
first pass through the EQ Four before it reaches the volume and pan controls
in the Session Mixer.

While all of the signal on Track 1 is forced to go through the EQ Four, some plug-ins allow you to set the balance of the original (dry) signal to the effect (wet) signal (Figure 8.15).

Effects best suited for insert use are EQ's, compressors, gates, and filters. When we EQ a signal, for example, we want to modify the frequency content of the whole signal, not just a fraction of it. Using an effect as an insert forces the entire audio stream to pass through the effect giving you full control of the sound.

Using a Send Effect

Send effects are used when we wish to *add* or *blend in* an effect to our sound as opposed to replacing it like an insert. This is achieved by sending a signal to an effect processor then blending its output with the final mix. In Live, we pull this off using a Return Track (choose "Insert Return Track" from Live's Insert menu). A Return Track is an abbreviated version of an audio track in that it cannot house Audio Clips, but Audio Effects may be added to its Track View. While it may seem weird to use something called a Return Track for send-type effects, the name is properly descriptive of the signal path since we send signal to the input of the track which then returns it to the Master Output via its loaded effects. In Figure 8.16, you'll see a Session with one Return Track. You'll also see a row of Send knobs labeled "1." You can now have up to 12 Return Tracks in a Set.

We use the Send knobs to dial in the amount of signal we want sent to the input of the associated Return Track. We can then add effects to the Track View of the Return Track (double-click the Return Track name) just as we would when adding them to a regular audio track. The portion of the signal being sent from the Send knob will be processed by the effects and output to the mix via the Return Track's volume and pan controls. You'll also see that the Return Track itself also has a Send knob. This allows you to output a portion of the returned effects to another Return Track for layering. The Return Track can also send back into itself allowing you to create feedback loops (watch your volume!).

Keep in mind that the Send knob does not divert signal to the Return Track, it copies the signal to the Return Track. This means that the output volume of the original track will stay the same regardless of the Send knob position.

So why would we want to use a Send/Return? There are a couple of reasons. First, some plug-ins, such as Reverbs and Delays, are meant to be

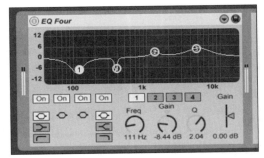

Figure 8.14

Placing an Effect on the Track View of an audio, MIDI, or Master track creates an insert.

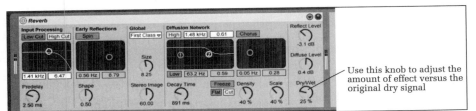

Use this knob to adjust the amount of effect versus the original dry signal

Figure 8.15

The Reverb plug-in allows us to add only a small amount of effect to our sound thanks to the Dry/Wet knob. When the knob is fully clockwise (100% wet), you will only hear the reverb signal generated from the original input. Setting the knob at 25% as shown will allow 75% of the original signal to still pass through.

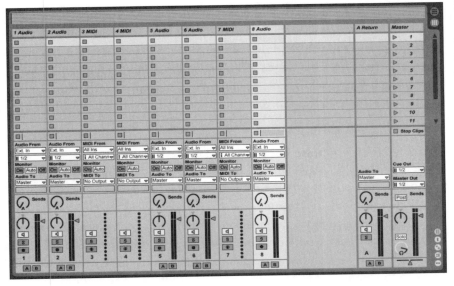

Figure 8.16

When the Return Track was added to this Set, a row of Send knobs was also automatically created.

> ### ❊ Pre or Post?
>
> On the right side of the Session Mixer, there is a button labeled Post for each send knob (Figure 8.10). These buttons determine whether the Send knobs take their signals *pre-fader* or *post-fader*. Post-fader is the default setting for each track which causes the amount of signal sent from the Send knob to be varied by the track's volume slider. If you're fading down a vocal part that is sending to a Reverb, the amount being sent to the reverb will also diminish, causing the Reverb to fade out as well.
>
> The Pre-fader position (click the Post button to turn it to Pre) causes the Send level to remain the same even if the track's volume is adjusted. This means, in the case of the example above, we would still hear the vocal reverb even after we had faded the track volume fully down. That could make for an interesting way to end a song.

blended with their original signals. For example, in order to add reverb to a vocal track, we would place a Reverb plug-in on a Return Track with its Dry/Wet knob set to 100% wet (every effect on a Return Track should be fully wet). While the vocal is playing, we start to turn up the Send knob. This will start sending a copy of the vocal to the Return Track armed with the Reverb. The Reverb will generate the proper ambience based on the incoming vocal and the result is mixed in with the original vocal. By adding Reverb in this fashion, our original vocal track remains unchanged; we've just added in some reverb to our mix.

Another reason for using a send effect is that it allows you to use the same plug-in to add effects to multiple tracks. If you have a lead vocal with three harmony parts, you can send all four vocals to the same Reverb. The incoming vocal tracks from the Sends will be mixed together as they enter the Return Track. The group vocals will then yield a group reverb which gets blended into the mix; therefore, it only takes one Reverb to effect four independent tracks, which is great news for your CPU usage.

Using Sends Only

There may come a time when you will want to combine the CPU-saving method of send effects with the complete sound replacement function of an insert. Perhaps you want to run a bunch of vocal tracks through one Auto Filter. If you were to place the filter on a Return track then turn up the sends on your vocal tracks, you'll only be combining the original unfiltered vocals with the filtered version being output from the Return Track, which will not allow us to completely filter out the vocals. What we need to do is silence the original tracks while still sending to the Auto Filter on the Return Track.

❋ Keep 'Em Going or Cut 'Em Off

Many modern productions, especially in the electronica-influenced genres, employ effect-muting techniques to add emphasis to particular moments in songs. Normally, if we add a reverb effect to a hand clap track, our ears would expect to hear the full decay of the reverb even if we were to suddenly mute the hand clap track. This is accomplished by placing the reverb on a Return Track and turning up the hand clap's Send knob. When the hand clap is muted, the signal stops being sent to the reverb as well; however, the reverb output remains unmuted, so we still hear the full decay of the reverb.

If we were to place the Reverb effect directly onto the hand clap track as an insert, we could then use the Dry/Wet knob to attain a similar balance of hand clap and reverb. Now, when the hand clap track is muted, the reverb will be muted, too, since we're actually listening to the output of the Reverb device on the track (that's why you have to use the Dry/Wet knob to hear the original signal). This can be extremely effective at the end of a build that stops abruptly. Also give this technique a try with delay effects.

We accomplish this by setting the output of the vocal tracks to Sends Only, as shown in Figure 8.17.

While the original tracks are no longer routed to the Master Track, the sends still remain active so we can funnel our sound over to the filter on the Return Track. We will then use the volume slider on the Return Track to adjust the level of the vocals in the mix.

❋ Mix Trick

Here's a common mixing technique employed by engineers that takes advantage of the routing explained above: Place a couple of drum parts on some tracks, preferably acoustic drums or percussion. Switch the track outputs to Sends Only and use the Send knobs to create a mix of the drums that can be monitored through the Return Track. Once you have achieved a nice blend, load a compressor onto the Return Track and dial up some heavy compression. By heavy, we'd say probably a ratio of 10:1, attack fully counter-clockwise, and a moderate release time of 25ms. Stop the clips from playing and switch the original track outputs to Master. Turn the volume all the way down on the Return Track and start playing the drums again. While the original tracks are playing, begin to slowly raise the volume of the Return Track. The compressed drum parts will start to blend in with the originals adding beef to the drums.

The reason this is so effective is that right when a transient occurs in the original drum tracks, the compressor on the Return Track kicks in and cuts off the transient (due to the short attack time), leaving only the original waveform in the mix. As the original waveform fades out, the compressor opens up again thus filling in the space between the transients. This keeps the drums sounding natural while adding the thickness characteristic of compression. Try this technique with other instruments that may need the assistance of compression while maintaining their original tone.

Figure 8.17

We have silenced the outputs of the vocal tracks by changing their output routings from Master to Sends Only. This keeps all the track functions intact, such as the insert effects (if any) and automation, but disconnects their outputs from the Master.

Control and Automation

As you've probably discovered by toying with a few effects so far, it's fun to tweak the knobs and parameters while audio is playing. Many new layers of musicality can be discovered by carefully manipulating effects during a performance. Live gives us a number of different ways to control plug-in parameters, either with real-time MIDI control or by automatic or pre-programmed automation. MIDI control is by far the most interactive way to control device parameters and offers an excellent way to program automation, too.

Controlling Live's Devices with MIDI

Controlling Live's Devices with MIDI is as easy as assigning MIDI control to the Session Mixer and Clip Grid (see Chapter 5 if you missed this). If the Device is on screen, press the MIDI Assign button in the upper-right corner of the Live window. A bunch of colored boxes will appear over the Device's controls just like they do for the Session Mixer. Click on the control you wish to assign, then move the control on your MIDI device. Live will instantly assign the moved control to that effect parameter and a small box will appear on the control stating the MIDI Channel and Controller assigned. Once you turn off the MIDI Assign button (click it again), the device parameter will now respond to the MIDI control. Piece of cake!

Common things to control with MIDI are the sample start and loop lengths in Simpler. You can create a morphing sound by moving through different areas of a long audio file with these knobs. For the Impulse, assigning a control to the global tune knob will allow you to tweak the pitch of the entire drum kit on the fly. You can also assign MIDI to the individual drum sounds— try adjusting the decay of the open hi-hat during a song.

Controlling Plug-in Devices with MIDI

Controlling the parameters of a plug-in device, such as a VST audio effect, is a little more difficult due to the fact that each plug-in has its own unique graphical interface. Because of this, Live cannot superimpose the little squares over the plug-in controls while in MIDI Assign mode. To solve this little problem, Ableton has included a small triangle located at the upper-right corner of a plug-in Title Bar. Press this triangle and the plug-in window will expand to the right and show a varying number of horizontal sliders (Figure 8.18 below).

Each slider corresponds to one of the plug-in parameters. Open up the plug-in graphical window and move a control. You'll see one of the controls in the Track View move as well. When you press the MIDI Assign button, you will see a box superimposed over the horizontal slider in the Track View. This is where you will make the MIDI Assignment. Once you have clicked the slider and moved your MIDI control, disable the MIDI Assign mode and you'll see that the plug-in parameter, including the control in its graphical window, is now under MIDI control.

❄ **Switch and Slide**

You may find that a parameter you wish to control in your plug-in is actually a button as opposed to a slider or dial; however, you will not find a button graphic in the small plug-in window of the Track View. This is because the plug-in's button is being represented by a horizontal slider, too. You'll see that after you drag the slider a certain distance, the plug-in's button will change state. When you move the slider back, the button will also change back. This allows you to assign a MIDI control to the slider to control the button.

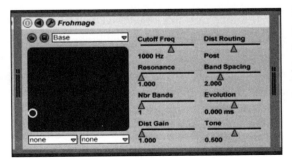

Figure 8.18

Pressing the small triangle in the corner of the plug-in window unfolds a collection of sliders which can have MIDI controls assigned to them.

Modulating Devices with Clip Envelopes

While tweaking the effects live is a blast, creating patterns and predefined movements for the effects can add a new layer of musicality to our songs. Perhaps you want the Cutoff of an Auto Filter to follow a sequence of movements that repeats every bar. Or how about a Resonator that re-tunes itself over 4 bars? Both, and more, are easily accomplished using the Clip Envelopes.

When we discussed Clip Envelopes back in Chapter 6, we learned that they provide a way to modulate the current settings of their destinations. The same is true for modulating plug-in devices. You will set the controls for the device to one position then you will use the Clip Envelopes to add or subtract values from those positions.

The process of creating a Clip Envelope for Plug-ins is the same as modulating any other parameter, such as volume and pan. Once a plug-in has been loaded into the Track View, it will be an available selection in the Envelope section of the Clip View in any Clip loaded on the Track. Figure 8.19 shows an Auto Filter's cutoff frequency being modulated by an Envelope.

Automating Devices within the Arrangement View

Just like the volume, pan, and mute automation we performed in Chapter 5, we can define the exact values for our Device's parameters by drawing envelopes into the Arrangement View. Every envelope shape we create in the Arrangement View will override the current value of the associated parameter. If you have a sweet effect dialed in, you may want to save it as a Preset before drawing in automation so you can retrieve the original settings if you need them.

Just like the process in Chapter 5, effect automation can be created by either entering Record mode in the Transport Bar and performing the desired movements or by drawing them into a track using the Pencil Tool and breakpoint editor. Just like their Session Mixer counterparts, any plug-in control with recorded automation will have a small red box in its upper-left corner. If you manually move a control, either with the mouse or by MIDI control, the automation for that control will stop until you press the Return To Arrangement button.

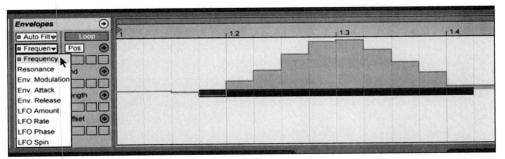

Figure 8.19

Use the two drop-down menus in the Envelope section of the Clip View to select the parameter to modulate.

Now that we know how to manage and control our effects, let's start sorting through the bevy of plug-ins already available in Live. The next three chapters are a reference section to get you up to hyper-speed with Live's Devices.

9 } Live's Audio Effects

When we perform a *mixdown*, we are attempting to create a sonic picture, a three-dimensional landscape of sound in which every instrument, voice, and noise has an individual place, yet they blend together in a cohesive fashion. This is not a simple task as there are many obstacles to overcome in the process. Instruments may have similar timbres and occupy the same frequency range making them hard to differentiate from one another. Some tracks may vary in volume so greatly that the part is inaudible at times and overpowering at others. We may be suffering the consequences of poor gear choice—cheap mics, audio interfaces, cables, and more could all be contributing to the degradation of our recorded sound. Audio engineers, being the clever people that they are, have devised a number of tools over the years in the form of signal processors and effects to overcome these problems and help us achieve the ultimate mix.

Effects used to exist only as hardware boxes that could be connected to a mixing console. Thanks to the increasing power of computer processors, it is now possible to recreate these effects using software. Software effects, commonly referred to as *plug-ins*, are extremely useful since one effect program may be used multiple times in a project. Normally, when dealing with hardware effects, we only get to use each box once. If we use an effect processor to generate a reverb, we will need to find another hardware box to generate a chorus. This can become quite costly if you need to use a large palette of effects in your mix. In fact, you've probably seen pictures of large recording studios with walls of rack-mounted devices for this very reason.

On a computer, we can use multiple *instances* of effects with ease. This means if we use a reverb plug-in to add some space to a voice, we can use the same plug-in again to create a reverb for our snare drum. In fact, we can

225
❋ ❋ ❋

use as many instances of the plug-in as we wish as long as our computer's CPU can handle the work.

The number of effects available to those with a modest computer system can be staggering. There are truly hundreds, perhaps thousands, of effect programs available from a myriad of developers and hobbyists. The quality of these plug-ins can be astounding; many software emulations rival their hardware counterparts. For convenience and power, Ableton has included a suite of effects integrated into Live to help bring your projects to life.

As we go through these explanations, please don't just look at our pretty pictures and take our word for it—drop these effects on a track and listen to how they alter your sounds. You will learn by doing.

We now present you with the ultimate guide to Live's built-in Audio Effects, all seventeen of them.

EQ and Filters
The first batch of effects we're going to dive into are the filters. These types of signal processors are used to attenuate (reduce the volume) and amplify (increase in volume) only specific frequency ranges within an audio signal. Engineers will use filters and EQs to finely craft the frequency distribution of their mixes resulting in beautiful, rich, and detailed masters (final mixes). Of course, these tools can also radically distort your sound, creating unique effects in their own right.

EQ Four
A parametric EQ is a powerful frequency filtering and timbre-shaping tool. While most hardware and software mixers usually have some variant of this equalization available on every channel, you will need to add an EQ plug-in manually to a Track any time it's needed in your Live project.

Live's EQ Four features four adjustable *bands* (frequency ranges) of EQ represented by the green-illuminated 1, 2, 3, and 4 buttons in the middle region of the plug-in pictured in Figure 9.1. The goal when using an EQ is to either boost or diminish certain audio frequencies, or a range (bandwidth) of frequencies, within a given sound. These frequency bands are often referred to as lows, mids, and highs; or other subdivisions such as low-mids or high-mids. High frequencies are found in the register we call treble while low frequencies refer to bass. Low-mids, mids, or high-mids make up the middle section (from left to right) of the sonic spectrum. With EQ Four's separate and select-

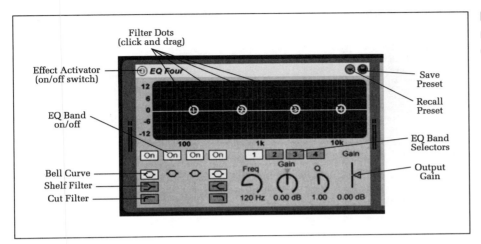

Figure 9.1

Here is Live's powerful if unassuming EQ Four.

able multiple bands, you will be able to meticulously sculpt the frequencies in the audio spectrum.

Many engineers like to *shape* or *carve* a sound's frequencies in a particular way for each song (or mix of a song). For instance, if the meat of a sound is in the bass, such as a bass guitar/synth, the track's high content and even high-mids may be uncomplimentary to the rest of the mix. Since you only have a finite amount of frequencies to work with (anything between 20Hz and 20kHz), you may want to save the song's high frequency content for your singer's lovely voice or your drummer's hi-hat. In this case, you'd want to use EQ to reduce the highs and boost the lows in the bass track.

Another frequency-shaping example would be to *shave* (remove) the mids and lows off of a crash cymbal sample (primarily a high frequency sound), so that no extraneous noise, such as mic or stand rumble, is heard. Therefore, some engineers may choose to *roll off* (eliminate) the lower frequencies using an EQ.

With EQ Four, each band specializes in treating certain audio frequencies by applying particular grades of slope, called *curves*. Bands 1 and 4 provide the option of using one of three different curves: bell, shelf, or cut. Actually, the last mode has a couple of names such as cut, roll-off, and high/low-pass. Filter bands 2 and 3 are simpler in that they are only bell curves.

A *bell curve* is a parabolic-shaped boost or cut of a given range of frequencies (see Figure 9.2). To change the grade or steepness of the slope, use the Q setting. To change the height or depth (the boost or the cut), alter the EQ band's gain setting.

Figure 9.2

This bell curve demonstrates a swell of the high-mid frequencies.

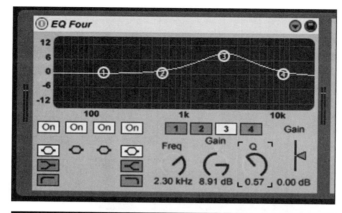

Figure 9.3a

A low-shelf curve. Often used to reduce background noise and rumble from audio tracks.

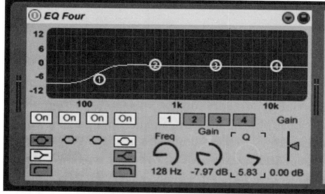

Figure 9.3b

A high-shelf curve. This type of curve would be especially useful to remove the highs from the bass track mentioned above.

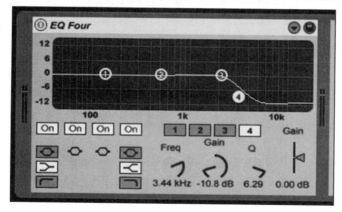

A low-shelf or high-shelf, possible with bands 1 and 4, respectively, provides an easy way to cut or boost all of the frequencies below or above a certain point, specified by the frequency setting of the EQ band. Figures 9.3a and 9.3b show an example of a low- and high-shelf curve.

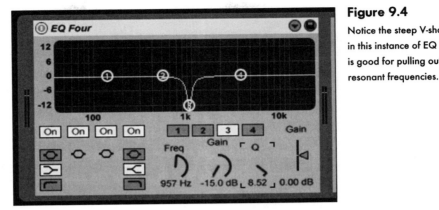

Figure 9.4
Notice the steep V-shaped cut in this instance of EQ Four. This is good for pulling out strange resonant frequencies.

As mentioned, you can zero in on specific frequencies by altering Q setting on each EQ band. Figure 9.4 shows a steeper, more acute frequency cut, accomplished by increasing the Q of a bell curve.

❄ Kick Me! (Part 1)

Here's a little something that gets pulled out of the ol' bag of tricks time and time again: how to get "that sound" for your kick drum. First, let us state that this is best for an acoustic kick drum, one that you may have recorded yourself. Synth kicks are a different species and don't suffer the same tonal complexities of a real bass drum but this trick may help with them, too.

Many will try to add bass with an EQ (it is the "bass" drum after all!) to get it to cut through the mix. This actually makes things worse by adding even more level to the bass frequencies, which can cause operating levels to clip. You end up feeling the kick more but not really hearing it any better. The reason the drum is muddy in the mix is because it is occupying space in the same frequency band as other instruments in the mix.

To get that deep yet punchy tone that will slice through the mix, try the EQ curve shown in Figure 9.4. Each bass drum is different, so you'll have to sweep the frequency around a bit. Around 150–200Hz, you'll hear a particular tone of the kick drum disappear, leaving behind that awesome kick sound we all love. The resonant tone that you pulled out may not be very strong on your kick, so experiment with the amount of gain you're removing—you may not need to cut all of it. By cutting this tone from the sonic space of the bass, guitars, etc., it now occupies its own space and cleans up the sonic image. Apply some compression (see below) and you've got your kick tone.

Now, in Figure 9.5, we will try a softer, more mellow/subtle bell curve by selecting a lower Q setting.

Filters 2 and 3 are always bell curves. Filter 1 can switch among bell curve, low-shelf, or low-cut modes. Filter 4 can switch among bell curve, high-shelf,

Figure 9.5

A more gradual, and therefore larger, curve due to a lower Q setting; nice for general, "broad-stroke," audio enhancement.

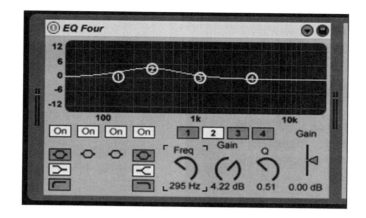

or high-cut modes. Each filter band can be turned on or off independently as well.

❅ **Gain**

While boosting and cutting various frequencies, you may notice that the overall volume has changed. Use the Gain slider to make up for any reduction in volume from serious cuts, or to pull back on extreme frequency boosts, especially in the bass frequencies.

To edit the filter curve, click and drag on one of the filter dots in the X-Y view. Horizontal movement changes the filter frequency, while vertical movement adjusts the filter gain. To adjust the filter Q (also called resonance or bandwidth), hold down the ALT (PC)/OPTION (Mac) modifier while dragging the mouse. You can also use the numbered filter selector buttons to select a band for editing, then edit parameter values with the Freq, Gain, and Q dials (and/or type specific values into the number fields below each dial).

❅ **Double Stack**

For more drastic cuts, boosts, and effects, try stacking EQs by assigning the same parameters to two or more filters, or use more than one EQ Four on the same track.

❅ **Power Miser**

Ableton suggests that you turn off any unused EQ bands to save CPU (processing) power. To do this, simply disengage (click) the On/Off button corresponding to the band not in use. For example, the first band is the first On button, the second band the second, and so on.

EQ Three

While EQ Four specialized in precision frequency crafting, the EQ Three is designed for more drastic EQ effects. Modeled after the EQ banks found on many DJ mixers, the EQ Three allows you to "cut holes" in the frequency spectrum and make broad adjustments to the overall sound of a track.

The EQ Three is only concerned with three frequency bands: lows, mids, and highs. As you can see in Figure 9.6, the EQ Three has 3 main dials, GainLow, GainMid, and GainHi. The frequency range of these dials is determined by the FreqLow and FreqHi knobs at the bottom of the effect. The GainMid knob will boost or cut all frequencies between FreqLow and FreqHi. The GainLow will adjust all frequencies below FreqLow and the GainHi knob will handle everything above FreqHi. The 24 and 48 buttons determine the slope, either 24 dB/octave or 48 dB/octave, at the edges of the frequency bands.

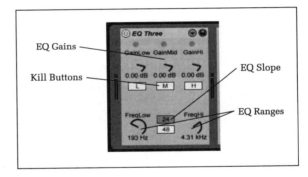

Figure 9.6

Lows, mids, and highs are under our complete control with EQ Three.

What makes the EQ Three uniquely different from other EQ plug-ins, including the EQ Four, is its ability to completely remove, or *kill*, entire frequency ranges from our audio. You'll see that as you turn the gain knobs down, they'll eventually reach –infinity, meaning the frequencies are completely cut. If you wish, you can use the green *kill buttons* (labeled L, M, and H) located below each gain knob to toggle that frequency range on and off with ease.

This effect is especially useful on the Master track in Live. Assign MIDI controllers to the EQ Three's controls and have fun sucking the bass out of the mix right before a huge drop, or slowly remove the upper elements of the music until only the gut-shaking bass is left.

※ **Sonic Jigsaw Puzzles**

Try placing three different drum loops on three different tracks, each armed with an EQ Three. Then, isolate the bass in one track, the mids in another, and the highs in the remaining track. You'll now have one hybrid beat consisting of kicks, snares, and hi-hats from different loops. Try swapping or automating the kills for other rhythm combinations.

Auto Filter

Quite possibly Live's greatest live performance effect, Auto Filter (seen in Figure 9.7) is a virtual analog-style filter with three selectable classic filter-types (high-pass, low-pass, and band-pass). Each of these can be controlled via the effect's X-Y controller and modulated by envelopes, rhythmic quantization, and any of three different LFO shapes. As you may have gleaned from the EQ Four explanation, suppressing certain frequencies allows you to carve out specific problem or overdone frequencies so your mixes sound more professional. The Auto Filter can do this as well, but it can also accentuate the cutoff frequencies for groovy effects.

Figure 9.7

Live's Auto Filter Device. If you've just been reading so far, you really need to get up and try this one. No, really.

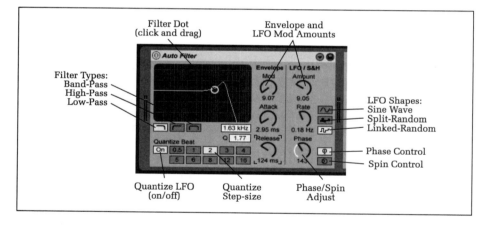

A common DJ trick is to mix two beat-matched songs, one with a low-pass filter and the second with high-pass filter (one on each turntable). The result is more than simply mixing two songs—the creation of an entirely new song is made from the combined frequencies (highs from one, lows from the other) of the two tracks. Without cutting some of the frequencies, the two songs could sound like a jumbled mush. Keeping the best frequencies does require some practice and will vary depending upon the musical content. If you are new to this concept, it can be a huge ear opener. See the following note called Filter Frenzy.

✳ Filter Frenzy

Low-pass, high-pass, band-pass . . . what does it all mean?

Low-pass simply means that the low frequencies pass through the filter, but nothing else does. For instance, your bass guitar and kick drums will be heard, though a little dulled out from the lack of highs. Some sounds will be gone completely, such as hi-hats. Conversely, a high-pass filter will allow shimmering cymbals and sparkly guitars and synths to pass, but will suppress basses and any other instruments in the lower frequency range. How low is up to you. Band-pass filters are basically high-pass and low-pass filters put together, thus only frequencies falling between the two filters will pass, sounding similar to a telephone at times.

To get going with Live's Auto Filter, you will want to select a filter—low-pass is a good starter—then use the X-Y controller to dial in Frequency (X-axis) and Q (Y-axis). The frequency range for the Auto Filter is adjustable between 46.2Hz and 12.5kHz. The Q control (also called resonance or emphasis) can range from .20 to 3.0 and will affect the volume of the filtered sound. We like to think of Q as the intensity of the filter, where low Q values will generate broader, less dynamic curves, and higher Q values will result in a more narrow, direct, and in-your-face kind of sound. If you really crank up the Q, you'll get those super-squelchy, screaming techno sounds as the filter begins to resonate. This can be lots of fun, but watch your volumes when this happens!

To the right of the X-Y controller are two strips of controls: Envelope Mod and LFO/S&H. The Envelope Modulation section determines how Auto Filter's envelope changes affect the filter frequency. In other words, it directs how much of the filter's variance or movement is audible, and how the changes are applied. Attack and Release work in tandem to determine the speed of the modulation. The shorter the attack, the quicker the modulation will be heard once the signal is present. Longer attack times will be slower to shift the filter. Similarly, small (quick) release parameters will tend to cut the modulation in and out more often. Long release will hold the modulation more steadily.

Hint: start out with quick Attack (5 milliseconds) and a medium amount of Release (200 milliseconds). Then gradually increase the modulation effect (Mod) to your liking. You will hear the sound get steadily brighter and louder.

You will also want to check out the Quantize Beat section at the bottom of the Auto Filter effect. The default position is off, so you will need to click the switch on to hear Auto Filter modulate your filter to the sixteenth note of your choice. Depending upon the rhythmic quality of your sample, you may or may not want to use the Quantize Beat settings. Short times can sound very choppy, while longer times can have strange shifts that may or may not

> ❄ **Filter Definitions**
>
> **Envelope**—A signal (used to be electric) that evolves over time to shape the timbre and amplitude of a sound.
>
> **LFO**—Low Frequency Oscillator generates a periodic waveform that affects—usually adding vibrato-type movement to—the envelope filter.
>
> **Modulation (oversimplified)**—The act of changing a sound with a signal. An example of *modulating the amplitude* would be turning up the volume of an amplifier with your hand (the control signal). More common modulations, as in Live's Auto Filter, involve using an LFO to modulate oscillator pitch. Frequency Modulation is the use of a control device to change the frequency of a sound.
>
> **S&H**—Sample & Hold uses randomly generated pulse waves (square waves of varying values) as modulators. The middle wave (on the right side of Live's Auto Filter) looks like a filled-in random pulse wave and is actually two independent (left and right channels) non-synced random pulse modulators. The third (lowest) button is a single (L/R-synced) random pulse modulator. When using the S&H modulators, the Spin and Phase functions are not relevant; thus, they have no effect.

make musical sense. Each loop will react differently, so try to listen closely to how the filter moves.

LFO stands for Low Frequency Oscillator (see the Filter Definitions note) and can help add further expression and movement to your original filter in an imprecise but rhythmic fashion. The Amount knob controls LFO's effect, while the Rate control designates the speed of the oscillation (movement)—the range is .01 (slow) to 10.0 (fast). Next to the Rate knob are three separate waveforms from which to choose. The top is a sine wave and will dictate fairly smooth sailing in terms of frequency modulation. The second and third waveforms are Sample and Hold variations—the middle wave is mono while the bottom wave creates different values for the left and right channels.

To help rein in the wild waves created thus far, the selectable Phase/Spin knob (located at the bottom right half of the plug-in) will add stereo dimensions to your frequency modulation. Phase will keep both right and left side LFOs at the same frequency. Of course, you can then gradually knock them out of phase by turning the knob toward 180 degrees. The Spin setting, which trades places with the Phase knob when activated, offsets the right and left channel LFOs, so that each channel is filtered at a different frequency.

Compression and Gate

Compression and gating can add clarity and power to your mixes if done properly. Done wrong, they can suck all life from what was a brilliant track.

Compression is one of the hardest things to learn to use properly and the use of compression is one element that separates the big fish from the little guppies.

Many people think that compression makes a sound louder. This is not true. What compression actually does is prohibit a sound from getting louder. As we explained in Chapter 2, we have a limited amount of dynamic range, or *headroom*, when dealing with digital audio. There is a limited range in the analog world, too, but analog equipment is a little more forgiving when headroom is exceeded. Digital distortion, on the other hand, is harsh and abrasive. Even one millisecond of this type of distortion can make a perfectly good take unusable. Compressors can be used to keep a sound recording from exceeding the ceiling (notated as 0 db in the digital world), thus saving our ears and our takes. Compressors can also be used to keep a wily vocal part in check. Got a singer who likes to switch from a delicate whisper to a death-yell within the same verse? No problem. A compressor will allow the nuances of the whisper to pass through unaffected, but will turn down the scream to keep the listener's head from being ripped off. As you're about to see (and hear—you're playing along at home, right?), compressors have a number of uses and many ways to abuse them.

Compressor I

One of the most popular methods for mix-boosting is to add compression. A compressor allows you to reduce (squeeze) the gain of an audio signal by a user-configurable amount any time the sound exceeds a certain cutoff point (again, user-configurable) called the threshold. Mastering engineers often apply a compressor to the whole mix (on the master track/outputs), but compression can also work wonders on individual tracks, especially if you are looking to add volume, punch, and clarity to your mix. Skillfully tweaked compression can help quell spikes, or sudden peaks, in a track so that the quieter portion of the sound can be comfortably elevated. Acoustic drum tracks are one of the most popular applications for compression, as are vocals and solo instruments such as guitars and horns. Figure 9.8 shows Live 4.0's Compressor I.

To apply compression to your mix, you will want to determine at what gain level (threshold) you would like the compressor to start working. The Threshold slider, Gain Reduction (G.R.) meter, and plug-in Output are the three meters that respectively help you to configure the gain level at which the compression will begin, how much gain is being lopped off of your original audio, and the overall output of the plug-in. Before we talk about how to use these three controls/meters, let's take a look at the ratio control.

Figure 9.8

Live 4.0's compressor plug-in.

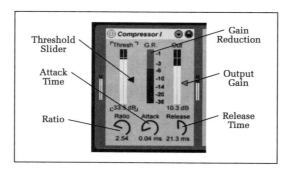

The compressor's Ratio control determines the amount of compression expressed as a ratio of the input volume to the output volume. For instance, 2 to 1 compression means that when a sound increases by 2 dB going into the compressor, we will only hear a 1 dB increase at the output. 4 to 1 would mean that for a 2 dB increase, only a 1/2 dB change would be heard. You may also notice that for larger ratio settings, the sound may become muffled or muted sounding as a result of the volume squashing that is going on. As you dial in your compression for a given track, you will want to watch the downward-spiking red indicator on the Gain Reduction meter. Extreme gain reduction, such as –12 dB and below, will often cut the life out of your sample—although you may occasionally want to over-compress an instrument as a special effect.

The compressor's other two controls, attack and release, determine how soon after a sound crosses the threshold compression will begin to work, and how long the compression remains active after the sound has dropped below the threshold. Ableton's manual recommends that using a small amount of attack time (5–10 milliseconds) is best for retaining some sense of dynamics (varying degrees of loud and soft in the music). Short attacks are great for instruments like drums and percussion, as well as vocals. Longer attacks are most often used with horns, bass, and longer sorts of sounds where the volume increase (crescendo) is also slower.

In contrast, a compressor's release settings are often better (less noticeable) when long. Basically, a long release time means that the compression continues to work for a given length of time (in milliseconds) after it has been engaged and the signal level has dipped back below the threshold. Typically, a short release time will force the compressor to repeatedly engage and disengage (start and stop), and a listener would be more apt to hear the repeated contrast (sometimes referred to as *pumping* or *breathing*). Short release times can still be a cool-sounding effect when used on drums and diced up pieces of audio (where the signal repeatedly crosses the threshold).

❄ **Kick Me! (Part 2)**

After you've used the EQ Four to dial in a nice kick drum tone, place a Compressor I on the track. We'll use the compressor to shape the amplitude of the kick sound just like using an ADSR envelope on a synth (see Chapter 11 and the Simpler Instrument).

The setting for the ratio dial is dependent on the amount of attack already present in the kick sound. If there's already a decent amount of punch, a ratio of 4:1 may be all that's necessary. If the kick is flat and has no life, a 10:1 ratio may be in order.

A fairly short attack time will need to be used, somewhere in the neighborhood of 5 to 20 milliseconds (ms). If the attack is too short, the drum will sound short, snappy, and clipped.

A slightly longer release time, 25 to 50ms, is used depending on the length of the bass drum. If the drum has a long tone (perhaps there was no padding inside the drum), a longer release will keep the tail end of the tone from popping up in volume after the loud transient of the drum has passed. If, on the other hand, the drum has a short tone or if the drum is played quickly, a short release time will allow the compressor to fully open before the next drum hit. If the release time is too long, only the first kick drum hit will sound right while the others that follow shortly after will not because the compressor is still attenuating the signal.

The threshold should be at a point where every kick played at normal volume will trigger the compressor. If it's too low, the compressor will squash the volume and never let go!

❄ **A Little Goes a Long Way**

Compression can create its own kind of special effect, but can sound unnatural when over-applied. Like EQ, a little goes a long way when adding compression.

Compressor II

New in Live 3.0 was the Compressor II plug-in, which has more parameters and options than Compressor I. Compressor II works the same as its predecessor, but the additional controls allow us to be more specific with our compression and timing (see Figure 9.9).

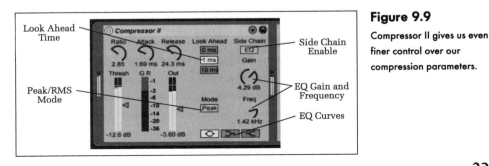

Figure 9.9

Compressor II gives us even finer control over our compression parameters.

❄ ❄ ❄

One of the additional sections added to Compressor II is the *side-chain*. This allows us to specify the frequency range that will trigger the compressor. For example, if we're trying to compress a snare drum, but we've got the sound of a kick drum bleeding through onto the same track (this usually can't be avoided when miking an acoustic drum kit), we can specify the snare frequencies as the trigger signal for the compressor. This is done by using the EQ on the right edge of the plug-in. If we focus the EQ on the high frequencies, Compressor II will start attenuating the signal when the amplified frequencies exceed the threshold. Please note that the side chain only determines what the compressor hears—the output signal will not be processed by the EQ.

Another frequent use of the side chain is for *de-essing*, which is the process of softening the sharp "sss" sound that can occur in vocal parts. By focusing the frequency control of the side chain on these sibilant frequencies (8kHz and higher), the compressor will drop the output volume any time a strong "sss" escapes the vocalist's lips. The rest of the vocal content below the side chain frequency will not cause the compressor to kick in.

You'll also see that Compressor II has a Look Ahead amount which allows the compressor to start reacting to sounds that are 1ms or 10ms in the future. This will help tame extremely sharp transients as the compressor will already be attenuating the signal before it arrives at the input.

The last control, simply labeled Mode, switches the compressor between Peak and RMS detection. Peak detection is best used on audio tracks with lots of transients. It will cause Compressor II to react to the loudest moments of the sound. RMS, on the other hand, creates an average amplitude based on the incoming audio and uses that to control the compressor. This smooth type of compression is best suited for vocals and strings as it will generally keep the audio levels in check while still allowing brief transients (consonants, string plucks, etc.) to pass through the compressor unaffected.

Gate

Gates can be thought of as backwards compressors, and therefore the two are often discussed (and used) together. Where compressors focus on reducing volume spikes above a certain threshold, Gates help weed out low-level noise beneath a certain threshold. The result of using a Gate is usually a cleaner, less cluttered, and overall more pleasing audio signal. Gates are a natural for reducing quiet hums, microphone bleed, and background noise

❋ Vocal Compression

Pay attention class, this is how to compress a vocal for a pop song. This works for rap, rock, R&B, grunge, electronica, or anything else that's got a nice full musical arrangement.

Drop a Compressor II onto your vocal track. Crank the ratio up all the way then twist both the attack and release knobs fully left. Engage Peak mode and disengage the Sidechain. Start with the threshold all the way up and begin the vocal track.

As the vocal plays, begin to turn down the threshold. Once the input level of the vocal passes the threshold, you'll see the gain reduction meter start to move. Keep reducing the threshold so the compressor is reducing only 1dB or so from a normal voice. A whispered voice should not make the gain reduction meter register at all. A loud passage, on the other hand, will make the compressor squash the vocal. Since the attack and release times are nearly instantaneous, the compressor kicks in immediately when the vocal passes the threshold. It then opens up again right when the vocal is back to normal levels. This means that the vocal will always be at a full level allowing it to sit nicely in the front of your mix.

(like your singer yelling for you to turn up his headphones). That said, Live 4.0's Gate plug-in is an excellent utility for this kind of work.

A Gate operates just like it sounds. Certain audio can make it through the Gate while other audio cannot. The threshold, or minimum requirement, to get through an audio gating effect is set by the Threshold Slider. Any incoming sound quieter than the threshold will cause the gate to close, thus attenuating the signal. Gating can be an excellent effect to apply when attempting to eliminate excess noise, hiss, hum, or undesirable reverb decay. You may find that a slight Gate can really clean up your drum loops. Many producers use Gate on drums like toms or snares so that they can capture the essence of the instrument at its highest volume point and eliminate all weaker background sounds. Other producers will use just a touch of Gate to clean up a noisy track. Figure 9.10 shows Live's Gate effect.

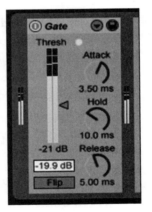

Figure 9.10
Live's Gate effect.

The small triangle next to the Threshold bar can be dragged with the mouse to set the minimum level of output (required to pass through the Gate). The lower the threshold, the more sound gets through the Gate. As sound passes through the Gate, you will see the small circular LED light flicker.

All or Nothing?

So far, we've only discussed a Gate as a tool for completely removing quiet audio signals from our tracks. From time to time, we may desire more of a semi-gate where some sound still gets through even while the Gate is closed. This is commonly used for toms so part of the decay and tone from the toms still sits quietly in the mix even after the initial attack has passed. If the gate closes completely, it may sound like the toms are overdubbed or pasted into the composition as they pop in and out of the mix. To remedy this, the Gate has a numerical value right below the Threshold slider. The default setting is −40 dB, which means the Gate will reduce the incoming sound by 40 dB when it's closed. Try raising this value while the Gate is closed and you'll hear more of the input signal bleed through. Of course, if you're looking for a brick-wall gating effect, reduce the range to −inf.

The Attack, Hold, and Release settings determine how the Gate is applied. For instance, a sharp/short attack will make the Gate open quickly when the threshold is exceeded, sometimes resulting in harsh audible clicks. A longer attack will sound more relaxed as the Gate takes longer to close on sound crossing the volume threshold. Be aware that having a long attack time may cause the Gate to open after the initial attack of the sound has already passed. Use this setting judiciously.

Similarly, the Hold and Release functions affect how long the Gate remains open. Think of Attack as how quickly the Gate will open and Release and Hold as relating to how quickly the Gate will close. A common Live trick is to tamper with the Hold and Release settings once a Gate is activating most of the time. Here is how to accomplish this:

1 Load a loop into a Clip or Track, then play to create audio.

2 Add a Gate by click-dragging Gate from Live's Effects to the Track/Clip you are working on.

3 Hit Spacebar or launch the loop via the Clip Launch Button.

4 Adjust Gate's Threshold to just above the loop's average volume registered in the vertical signal level section. Leave the floor at −40.0 dB.

5 Turn the Attack down to .04 for a quick acting Gate.

6 Turn the Hold down to 1.00ms.

7 Turn the Release down to 10ms.

8 You should hear a choppy loop. Audio should be cutting in and out. If it is still playing all the way through, raise the threshold. If you are hearing no sound or not enough sound, lower the threshold just a bit.

9 Gradually increase the Hold or Release.

10 Bonus Step: Map the Hold to a MIDI-Control Knob and try adding various amounts of sustain to the Gate.

Delay Effects

Ableton's delay effects group may just be their most creative. Each effect features solid tools for both assembling new rhythmic variations and creating innovative textures with repeated long sounds. While many of the delays have similar Feedback, Lowpass/Highpass filtering, and Dry/Wet controls, each delay is also somewhat of a specialist that features one or two particular kinds of controls. As we explore them one by one, don't be afraid to do lots of experimenting and get lost in your own creativity.

Simple Delay

While you may think we are starting simple, Live's Simple Delay (seen in Figure 9.11) is still a formidable stereo, tempo-synchable delay, with a rhythmic beat division chooser.

Figure 9.11

Live's Simple Delay plug-in.

Looking at the plug-in, we see two separate beat division choosers—one for the left channel and one for the right. If you are in Sync mode—where the small sync box is illuminated in green—each boxed number represents a multiple of the sixteenth-note delay time. For instance, choosing a 4 would mean a four sixteenth-note delay, or a full quarter-note hold before you would hear the delayed note sound. An 8 would be two beats, and 16 would be four beats—typically an entire measure. In either of the beat-division-choosers, you can choose from 1, 2, 3, 4, 5, 6, 8, and 16 times sixteenth-note delay times.

As mentioned, this beat dividing works only if the green Sync button is depressed for that channel (R or L). Sync means that the delay is set to synchronize with the song tempo (beats per minute). If you disengage the Sync, you can manually set up the delay time up to 1/100 of a second by click-dragging (up or down) on the time field box. Note: you may also click-drag the time field box with sync engaged, but note the percentage (%) indicator. This means that you are slowing or speeding up the delay below or above the current project tempo (that you are synchronized to). In other words, you can add a little slop, or even approximate a triplet, if your delays are sounding too strict.

Delay Relay

By setting extremely short delay times (less than 30 milliseconds with the sync off), you can create some wild thickening, phasing, and metallic-sounding results. Try setting both times to 1, 10, and then 30 milliseconds, with the Dry/Wet set 30 percent and Feedback set to 70 percent, to hear what we're talking about. Although these effects may not result in a lingering discernible delay, these flaming, buzzing, and biting sounds can be a creative playground.

The Dry/Wet knob determines how much of the effect versus original sound you hear. *Dry* is the term audio engineers use to refer to the original sound, while *Wet* is the delayed or affected sound. A setting of 12 o'clock (or 50 percent) for Dry/Wet will create a delay signal that is at the same volume as the original. A 100 percent Wet setting means that you will no longer hear the original sound, and will hear only the delay effect.

If Dry/Wet controls the volume of the delay, Feedback controls the intensity. By increasing the percentage of Feedback, you raise the effect's signal output to its own input, in sort of a rerouting to continue the delay's effect. The circular signal created by feedback will radically shape the delay, from flanging disharmonic swells (small percentage of feedback) to a wild echo chamber potentially spiraling out of control (with large amounts of feedback). If your delay does get out of control, reduce the feedback below 80 percent or less. For example, 100 percent feedback will deliver an unbelievable noise—or perhaps a cool effect?

All Wet

When effects plug-ins are located in one of the Return Tracks, it is generally a good idea to set the effect Wet/Dry setting to 100 percent wet. Since the original source sound is likely still being heard through Live's mixer, there is no need to route this signal again through a send.

Figure 9.12

Live's Ping Pong Delay bounces signal from left to right.

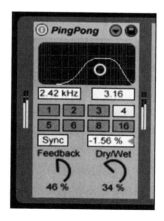

Ping Pong Delay

Like a game of Ping Pong, Ableton's Ping Pong Delay (pictured in Figure 9.12) plays a game of stereo tennis with your sound by serving it up from left to right. In looking at this plug-in, you may notice that many of the controls are similar to the Simple Delay covered earlier. Like Simple Delay, Ping Pong Delay is a stereo delay with built-in tempo synchronizing ability and sports the same delay-time beat-division chooser boxes, as well as the same Dry/Wet and Feedback controls; however, Ping Pong Delay is a little more creative in terms of what frequencies actually get delayed (repeated). You will find a band-pass filter, complete with an adjustable X-Y controller axis to adjust both the cutoff frequency and the width of the frequency band (the Q). You can select between 50Hz and 18kHz and a selectable Q of .5 to 9 dB.

Notice that the same Sync and delay time boxes are also present in Ping Pong Delay. When Sync is activated, Ping Pong Delay will rhythmically synchronize your audio delays—from left to right—according to your beat-division chooser. Once you deactivate the Sync, you can set the delay time manually from 1 to 200 milliseconds.

> ### ❋ Rub-a-Dub
>
> Thanks to the band-pass filter in the Ping Pong Delay, it's possible to simulate old tape-style delays. Every time a sound feeds back through the Ping Pong Delay, it passes through the filter and has part of its sonic character changed.
>
> Set the filter frequency to about 200Hz then set the Q to somewhere around 5. Crank the feedback up all the way then send a single sound, a snare for example, through the effect and listen to it bounce back and forth. As the sound is repeatedly delayed, you'll notice that it gets darker and darker. This is because the filter is removing the high-frequency character of the sound as it repeats. Try automating the band-pass filter as it repeats for more dub-style goodness.

Filter Delay

Last but not least in Live's group of delay effects is the powerful Filter Delay. This effect is actually three delays in one, one stereo delay and two mono delays—one on each stereo channel. Individual delays can be toggled on/off via the L, L+R, and R boxes on the far left, seen in Figure 9.13. Similarly, each high- and low-pass filter can also be switched on/off via the green box labeled on (default setting) in the upper left-hand corner next to the X-Y controllers.

Figure 9.13

Live's Filter Delay.

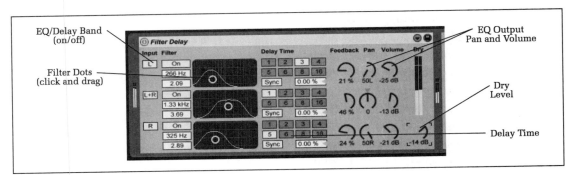

The Filter Delay Device is basically a mating of three Ping Pong Delays. Filter Delay's X-Y controllers work in the exact same way as the Ping Pong Delay described earlier. The Y-axis determines the bandwidth (Q), while the X-axis shifts the frequency. Each delay also features its own beat-division chooser with tempo-synch-able delay times.

On the right-hand side of the plug-in you will see Feedback, Pan, and Volume controls specific to each delay. Each feedback control will reroute the delayed signal back though that delay's input (just like all Live Delays). Interestingly, each delay's panning settings will override their original predisposed location. For instance, if you pan the L delay (top delay) to the right side (with the top panning knob), you will hear it on the right. Volume controls the wet signal or delayed signal for each delay. Finally, a lone Dry control knob is located in the upper right-hand corner. For a 100 percent wet signal, turn the dry setting to zero.

> ### ❄ Super Spacey Echo
>
> To achieve truly cosmic delay dispersion, set the filter on the L delay channel to approximately 7kHz, the L+R channel to 1kHz, and the R channel to 140Hz. Set all Q's to 2.0. Pan the L channel hard-left, the R channel hard-right, and the L+R channel in the center. Choose the same delay value for all three channels but offset the L channel by –1 percent and the R channel by +1 percent. Leave the feedback at zero for all channels at this point.
>
> Now, when a sound is fed into the Filter Delay, the resulting slap-back will happen in stereo. The L channel, which is only high-frequency content, will sound first from the left speaker. The L+R channel will happen next, providing the mid-range component from both speakers. The R channel will follow all of this by giving us the low-frequency content on the right. This makes the delay image in stereo, plus the image moves from left to right as it happens.
>
> Try experimenting with different time offsets to intensify the panning effect. Increasing the feedback on the channels will cause the delay to trail off in three different directions.

Grain Delay

Grain Delay is among Live's more complex, and therefore more creative, plug-ins. The Grain Delay is the same as Live's other delays in that it has many of the same controls—delay time, feedback, dry/wet mix, and beat quantize settings. While the other delays we've seen so far had a filter at the input stage, the Grain Delay has a granular resynthesizer instead. The basic concept is that Grain Delay dissects audio into tiny grains, staggers the delay timing of these grains, and then opens up a toolbox full of pitch, randomized pitch, and spread (called spray) controls for some far out sound design results. While all the common delay controls exist in this Device, the

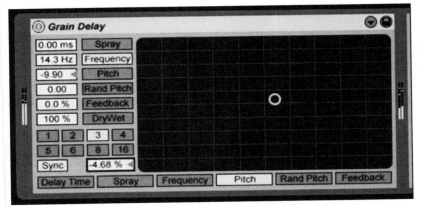

Figure 9.14

Live's Grain Delay takes audio apart, and randomly reassigns the pitch, before replaying the sound.

lion's share of the Grain Delay interface (seen in Figure 9.14) boasts a large parameter-assignable X-Y controller.

With Grain Delay's X-Y interface, you can quickly control two parameters of your choosing (one for X and one for Y), to allow for some wild interaction. Make sure you choose two different modifiers to achieve the maximum tweak factor. Hint: We like to use Feedback on one axis, and then choose either Random P(itch), Pitch, or Frequency on the other.

Frequency
This is the second parameter in the delay interface, but its setting impacts all the others so we'll explain it first. In Ableton's Grain Delay, small grains of sound are quickly dispersed. The frequency setting determines the size and duration of each grain that will be subsequently delayed and can range from 1 to 150Hz. The default setting of 60Hz means that the incoming audio is divided into grains 60 times per second, resulting in 60 grains every second. This means that a low setting creates a large grain while larger frequency settings create smaller grains. High frequency settings (lots of small grains) will help keep sounds with rhythmical timing (such as drum loops) intact through the resynthesis process. Low frequency settings will sound more natural for long sounds like textures and pads. If you are having trouble getting a desirable setting out of the Grain Delay, set the frequency to 150 and work backwards from there.

Spray
The spray parameter roughs up the average delay (like those in Ping Pong and Simple Delay plug-ins) adding noise and garble to the delayed signal. This setting will allow the Grain Delay to choose a random delay offset

amount for each grain. If the frequency setting above is a high value, the effect of spray will be more pronounced as there are more grains to randomize every second. The delay time for spray can range from 0 to 500 milliseconds. Small values tend to create a fuzzy sounding delay effect, while a larger spray setting completely takes apart the original signal. The Live manual jokes that, "this (higher setting) is the recommended setting for anarchists."

Pitch vs. Random Pitch

Like the spray parameter, random pitch tends to throw sound around. The amount of randomness can range from 0 to 161 in terms of intensity (0 being none). The plain old Pitch parameter ranges from 12 to −36 half steps, while allowing for two-decimal point interim values. In other words, fine tuning a delayed signal's pitch to an actual, discernable tone would be best suited for the Pitch control; trying to eliminate, destroy, or add movement to a pitched signal is the strength of high Random Pitch values. You can use both Pitch and Random Pitch in tandem for some robotic and wild pitch modifications. As with the spray control above, the higher the frequency setting, the more pronounced the random pitch effect will be as there are more grains to be resynthesized.

Putting Grain Delay to Use

Now that you get some idea of just what kind of mischief the Grain Delay is up to, let's get familiar with using Grain Delay's X-Y interface.

Along the X (horizontal) interface, lining the bottom portion of the plug-in, you will see the boxes for Delay Time, Spray, Frequency, Pitch, Random Pitch, and Feedback. The vertical Y-axis can be set to control Spray, Frequency, Pitch, Random Pitch, Feedback, and Dry/Wet controls. Each parameter's current value will be displayed in the respective boxes on the left-hand side of the plug-in regardless of which axis is set to adjust them.

Any parameters set to correspond to X or Y can be controlled by moving the yellow circle. Vertical moves affect the Y-axis, while horizontal moves alter the X-axis. Exactly which parameters you control are up to you. To set Feedback to be controlled by the Y-axis, simply click on the vertically aligned box labeled Feedback just above the Dry/Wet setting. To enable the X-axis to control the Delay Time (in terms of beat-division), click on the delay time box while Sync is activated. To control actual delay time, disengage (click on) the Sync button and you can set the delay from 1 to 128 milliseconds.

❋ Shift My Pitch Up

One of the more straightforward applications for the Grain Delay is to provide an echo that is at a different pitch. Leave the spray and random pitch values at zero and choose your delay time normally. If the pitch value is at zero, the Grain Delay will be working like the Simple Delay in that it only delays the incoming signal. Change the pitch setting to cause the echo to be transposed to a new note. For example, choosing a pitch setting of twelve will cause the delayed signal to come back an octave higher than the original. This can be pretty fun on vocal parts.

❋ Chaos Is Good

Another way to use the Grain Delay is to mangle a sound beyond comprehension. This is best achieved when using an impulse sound—something short like a drum or cymbal hit, the last word of a vocal, or a horn stab. Place a bunch of random values into the Grain Delay then feed it your impulse sound. The Grain Delay will spit out something that is a re-arrangement of all the little grains in the impulse sound. Increasing the frequency setting will cause even more randomness to be added to the mix. Try automating some parameters as the Grain Delay runs its course for more movement.

Chorus

When you listen to a group of people singing (commonly called a chorus), each member of the group is singing something slightly different from the others. They may be singing the exact same words with the same melody, but each person will have slightly different timing and intonation. By having all these slightly different voices singing the same thing, the result is a large and lush vocal sound caused by the slight imperfections in all of the voices.

The Chorus effect attempts to recreate this phenomenon by taking the input signal, delaying it varying amounts, adding a touch of random pitch shift, then blending the results with the original. In other words, chorus effects assume that two sounds are better than one. It is common to run synthesizers, guitars, vocals, and strings through a chorus. The doubling, or even tripling, effect of a chorus makes solo voices sound more powerful, take up more space in a mix, and therefore sound more present.

Live's Chorus (Figure 9.15) features two parallel delays that can be set for .01 to 20 millisecond delays or linked by activating a teeny tiny equal sign (=) shown in Figure 9.15.

Delay 1

The effect's first delay will always be active when the Chorus is on. To adjust the delay's timing, slide the fader. The adjustable high-pass filter knob allows you to bypass chorusing low frequencies, which can often become muddier

Figure 9.15

Live's Chorus effect. Note the tiny equal sign (=) between the two delays. This button syncs the two delays.

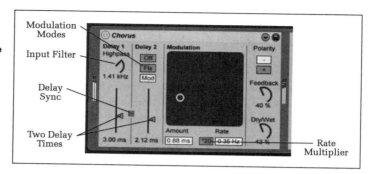

and less defined when doubled. The definable range is 20Hz to 15kHz. Delay 1 can be used on its own or in parallel with Delay 2.

Delay 2

Chorus' Delay 2 can add even more thickness and intensity to your sounds. Delay 2 can run in two separate modes, Fix and Mod, and can be bypassed by selecting the top visible button labeled Off. Fix mode will force Delay 2 to the timing specified by its slider. Mod mode will allow the delay time to be modulated by the effect's mod source.

Modulation

The Chorus' modulation section is where the effect gets its movement. This section controls a sine wave oscillator (an LFO) which can be used to change the timing of the two delays. Whether you are going for completely unrecognizable new sounds or just looking for a little more stereo-spread, you will want to spend some time fiddling (click-dragging) with the Modulation X-Y controller. Horizontal moves change the modulation rate from .03 to 10Hz, while the vertical axis increases the amount of modulation from zero to 6.5 milliseconds. So, if Delay 1 is set to 1ms and you have a modulation amount of 1ms, the LFO will continually change the delay time between 0 and 2ms. The modulation rate changes the speed of the LFO from subtle movements to bubbly vibrations. You also have the option of typing in values by simply clicking on the box, typing a number within the allotted range, and pressing the Enter key.

The LFO will modulate both delays in stereo. This means that the delay times used for the right and left channels will be different, which increases the stereo intensity of the effect. This also means that if both delays are being modulated, there will be four different delay times at any given moment. How's that for fattening up a sound?

If you are looking for radical sonic redesign, the *20 button multiplies the Chorus' LFO rate by 20. While this may not sound great all of the time, the *20 multiplier will push the envelope of the dullest of sounds.

Feedback, Polarity, and Dry/Wet

For increased intensity, the Feedback control will send part of the output signal back through the delays. The more feedback you elect to add, the more robotic and metallic your sounds will become. The positive and negative polarity switch determines whether the signal being fed back to the delays is added to or subtracted from the new input signal. To hear the greatest contrast between the two polarities, you should use short delay times, and increase the Chorus Feedback. The results are often frequency and pitch related; a low frequency sound becomes a high frequency sound, a pitch may shift by as much as an octave, and so forth. Finally, the Dry/Wet control determines the amount of original versus chorused signal going to output.

❄ **Flange and Phase**

If you're accustomed to digital effects, you may have noticed that two "bread-and-butter" effects, flanger and phaser, are not listed among the 17 Live Devices. The good news is that Live does have both a flanger and phaser: the Chorus!

A chorus is built upon the same technology as flangers and phasers, which is the delay. We can use Live's Chorus effect for these other two types of effects by disabling portions of the Chorus. Flanging requires using only Delay 1 (switch Delay 2 to the Off position). Turn down the modulation range to zero and turn up the feedback to about 60 percent. You'll now get that classic flange sound which can be changed either by moving the Delay 1 slider by hand (this keeps the left and right delay times identical) or by applying some modulation (this causes a stereo flange).

The phaser is an even more abbreviated version of the flange in that there's usually no feedback involved (turn it down to zero) and the delay time is only between 0 and 1ms. Set the Delay 1 time to .5ms and increase the modulation range to .5ms. This will cause the delay time to swing back and forth between 0 and 1ms. Set the Dry/Wet mix to 50 percent so the delayed signal can cause the necessary phase interference with the original signal.

Reverb

Reverberation occurs when sound bounces off of a surface, usually many surfaces, several times. In the process of reflecting, the original sound dissipates, becoming diffuse and muddy and eventually disappearing altogether. Depending upon the shape and reflective qualities of the room, various frequencies will be more pronounced than others in the reverberated sound or, *tail*.

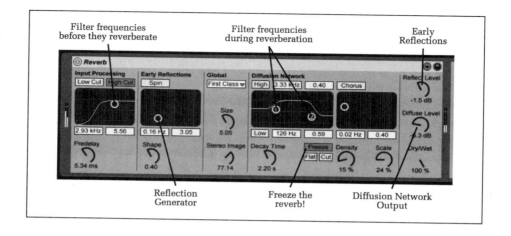

Figure 9.16

Live's feature-laden Reverb plug-in.

While Ableton's Reverb plug-in, added in version 1.5, may not be a full-fledged delay, it is certainly from the same echo-related family. The number of controls may seem daunting, but as we step carefully through the signal path, you will see that each knob and X-Y controller is there only for your benefit. Before we get too deep, take a quick look at Figure 9.16.

Input Processing

The first link in Reverb's signal chain is the Input Processing section. Here you have on/off selectable Low and High Cut filtering as well as a Predelay control. The Low Cut and High Cut X-Y interface allows you to trim your input's frequencies before they are reverberated. Similar to Live's other delays, the horizontal X-axis shifts the frequency of the cut (50Hz to 18kHz), while the vertical Y-axis changes the bandwidth (.50 to 9.0). You can also turn each filter off by deselecting its green illuminated box. I recommend spending some time playing with this filter each time you use this plug-in. Think of these filters as altering the acoustic characteristics of a room. For instance, a concrete room may not reproduce low frequencies as well as an acoustically engineered studio room. Each room will favor completely different frequencies.

Also, check out the Predelay control for adding milliseconds of time before you hear the first *early reflections*, or delayed sound, of the forthcoming reverberation. While the predelay can range from .50 to 250 milliseconds, to simulate a normal sounding room, it is best below 25 milliseconds. For large cannons, go long, baby.

Early Reflections

Early reflections are the first reverberations heard after the initial sound bounces off the walls, floor, or ceiling of the room—yet they arrive ahead of the full reflection, or tail. At times, they sound like slapback delays, or mushy portions of the whole reverberated (diffused) sound. The Reverb plug-in houses two early reflection controls: Shape and Spin. Spin's X-Y interface controls, depth (Y-axis) and frequency (X-axis), apply a subtle modulation to early reflections. Results may range from shimmering highs to whirligig panning flourishes. For quicker decay of early reflections, try increasing the Shape control gradually toward 1.00. Lower values will blend more smoothly with the normal reverb diffusion.

❋ **You Want It Where?**

Because Reverb is Ableton Live 4.0's most robust (processor-intensive) plug-in, we recommend that you use it on one of Live's sends channels instead of inserting it onto individual tracks. This way you can use the same reverb (instance) for other tracks. The added bonus with this strategy is that by using the same reverb, it will sound as if all of the instruments were in fact played in the same room. Of course, this may not be the best idea for every song so use this technique at your discretion.

Global Settings

In Reverb's global settings section, you can select the quality level of the Reverb: Economy (default), Comfort, or First Class. The three settings will demand small, moderate, and large processor power, respectively. You may also determine the apparent volume of the room via the Size (of the imaginary room) control, which ranges from .22 (small/quiet) to 500 (large/loud). A Stereo Image control allows you to select from 0 to 120 degrees of stereo spread in the reverberation. Higher values will be more spread out, while lower ones approach a mono sound.

Diffusion Network

The Diffusion Network is by far the most complex-looking area of the Reverb plug-in. These controls help put the final touches on the actual reverberation that follows closely behind the early reflections. From here you will be able to decorate and control the finer points of the reverberated sound. To begin with, high and low shelving filters can further define your imaginary room's sound. By shaving off the highs, for instance, your room may sound more like a concert hall or large auditorium, while brightening up the diffusion (raising the high shelf) will approximate a "bathroom" reverb. Similar to X-Y interface controlled filters, each filter's X-axis determines frequency, while Y-axis controls bandwidth. Turning these filters off will conserve some system resources.

Beneath the high and low shelving controls, you will find the Reverb's Decay Time settings, which range from an extremely short 200 milliseconds to a cavernous 60-second-long tail. Long reverbs can make audio sound muddy and jumbled, so use with care.

To test the coloring and sonic quality of your reverb, you can use the Freeze control. Any time you press Freeze, Reverb will indefinitely hold and reproduce the diffusion tail. This held reverb can be a handy diagnostic tool for shaping your overall sound or a creative trick to make new sounds from a piece of reverb. Typically I will freeze the reverb when I am first setting it up and then stop all other loops and sounds. After analyzing the reverberated sound for a moment, I often tweak parameters to weed out extreme or obnoxious low or high frequencies, or change the Reverb's modulation.

When Flat is activated, the low- and high-pass shelving filters will be ignored. In other words, your frozen reverb tail will contain all frequencies. An active Cut command prevents further audio from being frozen even if it is passing through the reverb. For instance, you may wish to analyze the tonality of your reverb tail. To do this, you play your audio through the reverb, then press Freeze, and then press Cut (to cut off future audio from snowballing into a wall of useless noise). Even if you stop playback, the frozen reverb sample will continue to play. While frozen, you can make adjustments to the diffusion network settings and more acutely decipher their impact. Try starting and stopping audio a few times to analyze the differences between your project's audio and the reverberating audio. Is the reverb tail adding unwanted mud?

The second X-Y interface in the Diffusion Network, labeled Chorus, can add subtle motion or wobbly effect to the overall reverb tail diffusion. When not in use, deactivate the Chorus button to save system resources and turn the Reverb's Chorus effect off.

The final section in Diffusion Network controls the density (thickness) and scale (coarseness) of the diffusion's echo. The Density control ranges from .1 percent (a lighter sounding reverb), to a 96 percent rich and chewy reverb, while Scale can run from 5 to 100 percent, gradually adding a darker and murkier quality to the diffusion. A high Density setting will diminish the amount of audible change made by Scale controls.

Output

The Output section is the final link in the Reverb signal chain. At this stage, just three knobs: Dry/Wet, Reflect Level, and Diffuse Level, put the finishing touches on your reverb preset masterpiece. Dry/Wet controls the ratio of original unaffected sound to affected reverberated sound that you hear coming from the plug-in's output. When using Reverb in one of Live's Aux Sends, I recommend using a 100 percent wet setting, as opposed to using Reverb on a track, where settings between 10 and 45 percent sound more natural.

The Reflect Level control knob adjusts the amplitude (level) of the early reflections specified in the Early Reflections box from –30 to +6 dB. The louder you make the early reflections, the more you will hear an echo of the true sound (which will sound even more like a slapback delay as opposed to a reverb).

In similar fashion, the Diffuse Level controls the amount of diffusion network level in the final Reverb output. A low diffusion level will diminish the tail of the reverb, while a high amplitude of diffusion network will increase the presence of reverb in your mix.

Resonators

Here's a fun device for techno-heads and sound designers, the Resonators (Figure 9.17). When sound is fed through the Resonators device, it will cause the virtual resonators to start "vibrating" or creating a tone at their set pitches and volumes. This effect is best understood when heard, so drop one on a track and take a listen.

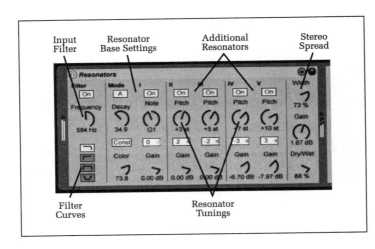

Figure 9.17

The Resonators device will start generating pitches based on an input signal.

To begin with, crank the Dry/Wet mix knob fully clockwise to isolate the sound of the resonators. Turn off the Input Filter so a full-range sound is feeding the device. Adjust the settings for Resonator I first, since the other four resonators base their tones and pitches from number 1. You'll see that you have control of the decay of the resonators (best heard on sparse percussion tracks) as well as the color and pitch. Once the first resonator is set, engage the other resonators and use the pitch knobs to set their frequencies relative to the first. This makes it simple to create chords using multiple resonators, then transpose them all using the first resonator's pitch knob.

Resonators II & III and IV & V can be panned apart from each other by increasing the Width knob. This can help create a lush tonal pad that blends well with a mix. You can also use the input filter to remove frequencies that may be overpowering or saturating the resonator banks. The Gain knobs are used to achieve a blend between the various resonators allowing you to emphasize certain pitches over others.

Tuned Reverb

Try adding a Resonator right after a reverb effect on your vocalist's Return Track. Build a chord with the dials on the effect and set it fully wet. Now the reverb effect will cause the Resonators to ring in tune with the song, adding an ethereal sound to the voice.

Distortions

This brings us to the third and final group of Ableton's effect plug-ins: the distortion effects. While each of these effects can quickly and drastically alter your audio content, taking time to learn the ins and outs of these babies can take your mix to a whole new level.

Figure 9.18

Live's Erosion Plug-in. Erosion's screen is primarily taken up by its unusual X-Y field.

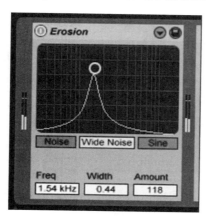

Erosion

Similar to the concepts of subtractive-synthesis and frequency filtering, deconstructing a sound can also be a creative endeavor. Live's Erosion effect is Ableton's most unique plug-in in this regard. Erosion gives you three possible methods for sonic degradation. You can choose from Noise, Wide Noise, and Sine by selecting one of the three buttons beneath the X-Y interface as pictured in Figure 9.18.

Depending upon which mode you currently have active, Erosion will use one of three different sounds (one of two filtered noises or a sine wave) to modulate the sound. Noise, Wide Noise, and Sine all have different characteristics, so you will want to experiment switching between the three.

To control the degree of Erosion's effect on a sound, move the Y-axis (vertically) to change the amount or level of modulation signal. Horizontal moves along the X-axis allow you to control the frequency that you are affecting. To change the Width with the X-Y interface, hold Alt (option) and click on the yellow dot, and move the mouse forward and backward. You can also drag any control vertically, or manually type in a value in Freq, Width, and Amount.

❄ **Ring Tone**

Live's Erosion effect is a ring modulator when in Sine mode. Ring modulation, a very popular decimation technique, is achieved by multiplying the incoming signal with another one, an internally generated sine wave in this case. This makes the incoming signal adapt some of the pitch characteristic of the sine wave. The noise modes multiply the incoming signal with white noise signals which you can tune in the X-Y area of the plug-in. This causes the incoming signal to adapt some of the noises' characteristics.

Redux

While we're digging into new tools for sonic decimation, you will definitely want to check out Live 4.0's Redux plug-in. Redux (Figure 9.19) is a bit-depth and sample-rate reducer that can make even the prettiest of guitars, or anything else for that matter, saw your head off. Of course, results need not be this drastic if you are capable of restraint. In fact, reducing the fidelity of a sample is like a tip of the hat to old Roland, Emu, and Akai 8- and 12-bit samplers—or even old 2- and 4-bit computer-based samplers (Commodore 64, anyone?).

Figure 9.19

Live's Redux plug-in is a talented sample-rate and bit-depth reducer.

The controls for Redux are split into two tidy sections, with a Bit Reduction knob and on/off switch on top, and a Downsample knob and hard/soft switch on the bottom. The default position for Bit reduction is 16 bit (off). As you reduce the bit, you will hear an increasing amount of noisy grit infect the sample. The numerical setting will indicate the bit-depth (i.e., 8=8 bit, 4=4 bit). For extremists, try trimming it down to 1-bit—ouch, that hurts!

When it comes to sample rate reduction, the settings are a little more inexact. In Hard mode, Downsampling will stick with whole integers such as 1, 2, 3, up to 200, while in Soft mode, you can adjust from 1 to 20 to the nearest hundredth of a point (1.00 or 19.99). A setting of 1 means you are not hearing any sample rate reduction—oddly, the higher the number, the lower the rate.

For a quick course, spend a minute perusing the Ableton factory presets such as Old Sampler and Mirage. This will give you a basic template to work from. Also, try toggling back and forth from Hard to Soft Downsampling with different settings (while you are in playback mode) for a cool effect.

> **❄ Reduxion Crescendo**
>
> You can create an ear-ripping build-up by piping your tracks through a Redux and lowering the bit-depth at the build. The Redux chops off the tops of your audio then normalizes it which makes it louder and more distorted at the same time.

Vinyl Distortion

The imperfections of vinyl have actually become quite lovable these days. Whether you are missing the dust pops and crackles of an old record or the warped vinyl sound of a record left out in the sun, vinyl has a certain retro charm. Though CDs and digital recordings are great, they are hopelessly clean and free of these impurities (which is also their strength). Of course, Ableton thought about this too, and as a result: Vinyl Distortion (Figure 9.20).

Figure 9.20

Live's Vinyl Distortion effect hopes to make you miss your turntable just a little bit less.

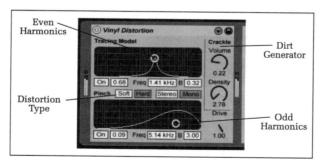

Vinyl Distortion is divided into three separate sections: Tracing Model, Crackle, and Pinch Effect. While the controls for Tracing Model and Pinch Effect look identical, each section generates a totally different sound. Also note the Soft/Hard as well as Stereo/Mono switches are also a part of the Pinch Effect. If Pinch Effect is off, these controls will remain grayed out (inactive).

Tracing Model adds a subtle amount of harmonic distortion to your audio as a means of simulating wear and tear on vinyl or an old stylus. To adjust the intensity of the distortion, increase the drive by moving the yellow circle along the Y-axis (range from 0.00 to 1.00). The frequency of the harmonic can be altered via the X-axis (range of 50Hz to 18kHz), and can also be input manually by typing in the box. To adjust the size of the bandwidth you are affecting, hold down ALT (OPTION) and click-drag forward or backward on the yellow circle.

The Pinch Effect section of Vinyl Distortion is a more drastic and wild-sounding distortion at the input level. The resulting richer stereo image is from Pinch Effect's 180 degrees out of phase harmonic distortions. Like the Tracing Model, you can increase the intensity of the distortion through the Y-axis. The X-axis will configure the Frequency range. You will want to pay special attention to the Soft/Hard boxes to the right of the X-Y interface on the Pinch Effect. Soft mode is engineered to sound like an actual dub plate (acetate), while Hard mode will sound more like a standard vinyl record. Also, the Stereo/Mono switch correlates with Pinch Effect only.

Of course no vinyl simulation plug-in would be complete without a vinyl pop and crackle simulator. Crackle provides two simple controls: Volume and Density. Volume is obviously the level of the hiss and crackle in the mix. Density adds a thicker amount of noise to the output. Note: you will hear the crackle and hiss whether Live is in playback mode or not. If you forget this, you might just take a screwdriver to your audio interface!

Utility

The Utility device (Figure 9.21) gets a section all its own. This device isn't so much an effect that will make your audio sound weird. Instead, it will provide subtle changes to the audio for adding the right touch to a mix.

The first two options may seem redundant: Mute and Gain. You already have a Track Activator and Volume slider on each track, right? Well, the Ableton folks aren't stupid and while you won't use it often, you may find it handy to have this type of control sitting on the Master Track. Have you seen a mute button on there lately? We didn't think so. In fact, this is

Figure 9.21

The simple Utility interface provides easy access to simple tools.

a great device to place on the Master Track for numerous reasons. When doing a mix, especially for TV, it is a good idea to check for mono compatibility. When the sound of the left channel of your mix is blended with the right channel, certain frequencies may start to interfere with one another. In some cases, guitars may not sound as full when heard in mono. Sometimes the vocals will sound too loud. In the most extreme cases, some of the parts may completely disappear from the mix! To hear what your track sounds like in mono, take the Width knob down to 0 percent.

If you do run into phase-cancellation that completely removes a part from the song when in mono, try placing Utility on that track and engage one of the Phase buttons (labeled Phz-L and Phz-R). This will invert the phase of one side of the track, bringing it back into phase with the other side. If you're not worried about mono compatibility, you'll find that kicking one side of a track out of phase from the other will make the resulting audio sound amazingly wide, almost as if the sound was coming from behind your head. This can really make a part jump out of a mix or at least sound separated from the other parts. If you're looking to widen your sound only a little, you can turn the Width control clockwise past 100 percent to a level that suits your taste.

The L and R buttons are for using only one side of the input channel as the output for both sides. For example, if you press the L button, the sound entering on the left side of the channel will be mirrored on both left and right at the output. This in not the same as reducing the Width control to 0 percent. When Width is reduced, both the left and right signals are blended together. When using the L and R buttons, only one side is used while the other is turned off.

10 } Live's MIDI Effects

MIDI Effects, like Audio Effects, allow us to alter data as it's passed from a Clip to the Track output. MIDI Effects can be used by themselves on a MIDI Track whose output is some external MIDI sound device, or they can be used before a plug-in instrument in the Track View. It's important to understand the place of the MIDI effect in the chain of events that occurs on a Track. MIDI data in a Clip is played through the MIDI Effect which alters it in some way. The altered MIDI data is then sent to the MIDI destination, either an external MIDI device or a virtual one loaded in Live, which then reacts accordingly. It is important to understand that MIDI Effects do not change the sound that is produced by an instrument. They change the notes playing on those instruments, resulting in a new part. This is why the Pitch MIDI Effect won't change the pitch of the drums coming from a sampler. More on this as we explore the five MIDI Effects in Live.

Chord

The Chord Effect (Figure 10.1) will generate new MIDI notes at pitch intervals relative to an incoming MIDI note. This will allow one MIDI note to trigger a chord on the receiving instrument.

Figure 10.1

The Chord Effect allows us to build a multi-note (up to six notes) MIDI chord from one input note.

When the Chord Effect is first loaded, it will have no effect on incoming MIDI notes—they will pass straight through. If you move the first Shift knob, it will become active. The knob allows you to set the interval in semitones for the new MIDI note. Setting the Shift 1 knob to +4 and playing a C will cause both a C and E note to be sent from the plug-in. Setting Shift 2 to +7 will create a C major chord when you play just the C note. Playing G will result in a G major chord (G, B, and D). You can define up to six notes to be added to the incoming note using the dials. Just below each dial is a percentage value which determines the velocity of the new note. You can use this if you don't want all of the notes in the chord to be the same volume. If Shift 1 is set to 50%, the E in the resulting chord will only have a velocity of 64 when the incoming C has a velocity of 127. Try slowly changing this value while playing repeated notes to hear how the additional note fades in and out of the chord.

Dance Chords

Chord stabs and pads are a staple of electronic music. Originally, these fixed chords were created by detuning some of the oscillators in a synthesizer so that they sounded at musical intervals (usually +7—a perfect fifth) against the base oscillators.

The Chord Effect can create the same sound on instruments that don't have individual tunings for their oscillators or when using samples by sending the actual chord information to the instrument for you. There are a number of chords already built for your use in the Preset menu.

Pitch

The Pitch Effect can be confusing to someone not familiar with MIDI. It would seem that this Effect would change the pitch of our Track. In a way, it does, but it doesn't do it by shifting the audio from the Track. Instead it transposes the MIDI notes sent to an instrument, resulting in a higher part.

The Pitch Effect (Figure 10.2) is the best way to change the pitch of a MIDI part since no Warping or re-synthesis is involved. We're just telling our instruments to play different notes. The result is that the Track sounds shifted up, but still sounds natural. When dragging in new MIDI parts from the Browser, it's quite possible that they will be in the wrong key. This Effect will allow you to transpose the Track to the appropriate key in the same way you use the Transpose knob to retune an Audio Clip.

There is a situation in which the Pitch Effect will have improper results: when transposing MIDI used to play drum parts. It is a standard convention to

assign drum sounds to individual notes of a scale. By transposing the MIDI notes going to a drum instrument, you are
assigning MIDI notes to new instruments. For example, if a
kick drum sound is loaded into the first cell of the Impulse
Instrument and a snare is loaded into the second pad,
MIDI note C3 will trigger the kick and D3 will trigger the
snare (see the "Impulse" section in the next chapter). So, if
MIDI data is programmed into a MIDI Clip for the kick
drum, the Clip will contain a pattern of MIDI notes, all C3.

Figure 10.2

Twist the Pitch knob to transpose the MIDI data passing
through the Effect. Easy, huh?

If we run this through the Pitch Effect with the Pitch knob set to +2, the MIDI
notes will be transposed up to D3, so the kick program will trigger the snare.
So, instead of pitching up the kick drum, the Pitch Effect transposed the kick
information up to the snare key range.

This situation may also arise when using patches on synthesizers that have
splits. If you try to transpose the MIDI information out of the appropriate
keyzone, the synth will start playing the notes with the patch assigned to the
other zone.

> ❊ **MIDI Range**
>
> The two values at the bottom of the Pitch Device set the range of notes that can be used with the
> Effect. If the bottom value, labeled "lowest," is set to C3, only MIDI notes C3 and higher will be
> allowed to enter the Effect. The "range" value determines, by interval, the highest note that can
> enter the Effect. So, if the range is set to +12, notes C3 through C4 will enter the Effect. Only after
> the incoming notes have passed the range test will they be transposed up or down.

Random

As the name suggests, the Random Device will randomize the incoming MIDI
data. We can determine how liberal Live is with its randomization using the
controls seen in Figure 10.3.

The first control in the Effect is the Chance value. This
knob sets the odds that an incoming MIDI note will be
transposed. At 0%, the Effect is essentially bypassed
because there is no chance a note will be transposed. At
100%, every MIDI note will be subject to randomization.
At 50%, roughly every other note will be randomized.
Once a note is chosen by the Effect to be transposed,
it will be shifted using the rules set up with the three

Figure 10.3

The Random MIDI Device will
shift the pitch of incoming
notes a different amount every
time.

remaining controls. The three parameters make up part of a sort of formula that determines the transposition.

The Choices parameter determines the number of random values that can occur. If the value is set to 3, the Choices parameter will generate values of either 1, 2, or 3. This value is then passed on to the Scale knob. The value of this knob is multiplied by the random value from the Choices knob. The resulting number is the semitones to shift the MIDI note. So, if the Scale knob is set to 2, the resulting random transpositions will be either 2, 4, or 6 semitones. The final variable in the formula are the Sign buttons. If Add is selected, the resulting random value will be added to the MIDI note causing it to move up in pitch. Sub will subtract the random value from the current note. The Bi setting will randomly choose between adding or subtracting the value. The indicator lights on the plug-in panel will show when the note is being transposed up or down.

Let's run some quick examples to make sure we understand the math behind the plug-in:

1 If the Choices knob is set to 1 and the Chance knob is set to 50%, about half the time a transpose value of 1 will be generated by the Choices knob. If the Scale is set to 12 and the Sign mode is set to Add, the incoming notes will be transposed up one octave half of the time.

2 If the Choices knob is set to 4 and the Chance knob is set to 100%, a transpose value between 1 and 4 will be generated for every MIDI note. We then set the Scale knob to 3 and leave the Sign mode on Add. In this situation, every note will be transposed (Chance at 100%) by one of the following semitone amounts: 3, 6, 9, or 12. (1[Choices]×3[Scale]=3, 2×3=6, 3×3=9, and 4×3=12).

3 If the Choices knob is set to 2, the Scale knob is set to 12, and the Sign mode is set to Sub, the resulting transposition will be either 1 or 2 octaves down. (1×12=12 and 2×12=24).

Scale

The first time we played with this effect, the only thought we had was how much fun it would be to sneak this in on an unsuspecting keyboard player. Scale allows an incoming MIDI note to be mapped to another one. We can tell the plug-in that we want every incoming D# transposed up to E. We can also tell it that we want incoming Es to be taken down to Cs. Remapping pitches like this would leave a keyboard player scratching his head wondering what had happened to his keyboard.

While the Scale Effect is perfect for practical jokes, it has practical uses as well. Don't play keyboards well? Don't know your scales? The Scale Device will transpose all the wrong notes you play to the proper pitches for the appropriate key. This mapping is achieved with a 12×13 grid of gray squares. The columns in the grid refer to the input notes while the rows refer to output notes. The Base knob determines the note in the bottom-left corner of the grid. If the Base note is C, then the first column on the left is the input for C notes. The next column over is the input column for C# notes, etc. The row on the very bottom of the grid is the output row for C notes. The next row up from it is the output row for C# notes.

If you look at Figure 10.4, you'll see that the bottom-left grid square is on. This means that when a C note enters the far left column, it runs into the orange indicator in the last row, which is the C output row. So, in this case, all entering C notes will still exit as C notes. The next column over is the input column for C# notes. As we look down the column, we run into the indicator light on the third row from the bottom. If the bottom row is the output row for C notes, then this third row is the output for D notes. This means that when a C# note enters the Scale Effect, it leaves as a D note.

We can use the grid to create musical scales. The pattern of indicators on the grid in Figure 10.4 is that of a major scale. C is chosen as the Base, so we are working with a C major scale. Any attempt to play a black key on the keyboard will result in the MIDI note being transposed up to its nearest neighbor in the scale. Changing the Base control to G will change the scale to a G major. Every key played on the keyboard will now be forced to one of the pitches in the G major scale.

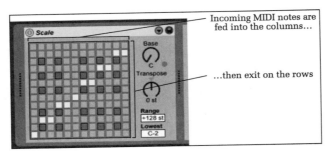

Figure 10.4

The Scale Effect lets us remap MIDI notes using a unique grid interface.

❉ **No Scale?**

So you're just starting out and don't know all your musical scales? No problem. Ableton included the patterns of common scales in the Presets menu of the Effect. You can load one of the patterns then use the Base knob to adapt it to your working key.

The Transpose knob does what the Pitch Effect does. In fact, both the Pitch knob and Range values in the bottom right of the Plug-in are lifted straight from the Pitch Device. Jump back a few sections if you have forgotten what these controls do.

❉ **In Scale**

The Scale Effect can keep you in key, and it can also keep the results of a Random Effect in key, too. If the Random Plug-in is generating too many notes that are out of key, load up a Scale Effect and set it to the appropriate scale. Any stray note from the Random Effect will be knocked into key by the Scale Plug-in.

By combining a Random and Scale plug-in, a random arpeggiator can be made that arpeggiates the pattern of notes entering the chain.

Velocity

The previous four MIDI Effects in Live are concerned with controlling MIDI pitch information. Velocity, on the other hand, deals with (can you guess?) velocity data. It's very much like a compressor or Scale plug-in for velocities. The grid display is like the display used in the Scale Device (see Figure 10.5). Input velocities are mapped across the X-axis (the bottom of the grid) while output velocities are on the Y-axis (the right edge of the grid).

In its default setting, there is a straight line from the bottom-left corner of the grid to the upper-right corner of the grid. This means that every input velocity maps to the same output velocity.

Figure 10.5

The grid of the Velocity Effect shows the effect of adjusting the various parameters in real time.

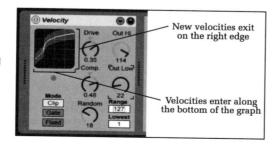

Increasing the Drive knob will cause the line in the grid to begin to curve. This new shape shows that low input velocities (near the left edge of the grid) are mapped to higher output velocities. This will raise the volume of notes played quietly while leaving the loud notes basically unchanged. Decreasing the Drive knob below zero has the opposite effect, causing loud input velocities to be mapped to lower output velocities. Only the loudest input notes will still leave the plug-in with high velocities.

The Comp (compression) knob is like the Drive knob except that it creates two curves instead of one. Turning this knob up past zero makes quiet notes quieter and loud ones louder. Lowering the Comp knob below zero has the opposite effect. Be aware that, like the Pitch Effect, the Velocity Effect is changing the notes fed into an instrument. Because of this, increasing the Comp knob will not make the part sound compressed as it would if a Compressor II was placed after the instrument. It will merely limit the velocities sent to the instrument while the instrument continues to output an uncompressed sound.

The Random knob defines a range of randomness that can be applied to the incoming velocities. As this knob is increased, a gray area will form on the grid showing all the possible velocities that may result from the random factor.

The Out Hi and Out Low knobs determine the highest and lowest velocities that will be output from the Effect. The Range and Lowest values work like their counterparts in the Pitch and Scale Effects. The Clip, Gate, and Fix buttons determine the action taken when an input velocity is outside of the operation range set by the Range and Lowest values. In Clip mode, any velocity outside of the range will be bumped into range. The Gate mode will only allow notes with velocities within range to pass. Fix mode will force every incoming velocity to be set to the value determined by the Out Hi knob.

❋ **Breath of Life**

Velocity randomization can add a human breath of life to a programmed drum part. Humans can't play with the same consistency of a machine, so randomizing the velocities of the drum parts can make the beat sound less repetitive. This is especially effective on high-hats and shakers.

11 } Live's Virtual Instruments

Ableton would have been leaving their customers out to dry if they had added MIDI support to the program but nothing to play it with. Fortunately for us, they have dished up two simple yet powerfully inspiring sound creation devices for our amusement: Impulse and Simpler.

Impulse

What loop-based production system would be complete without a drum machine? Live's Impulse Instrument is a unique take on drum machine design due to its sparse controls but instant usability. Impulse is placed into the Track View of a MIDI track (Figure 11.1) so MIDI Clips can be made to trigger it.

Figure 11.1

The clean and crisp Impulse interface sports eight cells for samples. Clicking the cell displays the editable parameters for the cell.

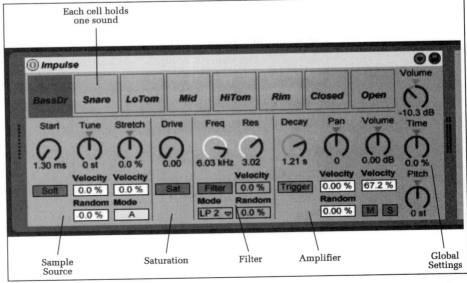

267
❈ ❈ ❈

Overview of the Interface

The upper portion of the Impulse interface is made of eight squares. These can contain one sample each which can be triggered individually—either by MIDI or with the mouse—and edited for customizing the sounds. The editing parameters are divided into five sections: Sample Source, Saturation, Filter, Amplifier, and Global Settings.

The Sample Source controls determine the playback nature of the selected sample. The sample may be re-tuned, stretched or shortened, and can have its front end cut off. Pitch can be randomized and/or modulated by input velocity. The Soft button performs a fade at the beginning of the sample to soften its attack.

The Saturation section is the simplest of the five sections. Engage the Sat (saturation) button and turn up the Drive to achieve overdriven percussion sounds.

The Filter section offers a way to perform some additional sound design on a sample after it's already loaded into a cell. Click the Filter button to engage the section. The menu below the Filter button chooses the filter mode. You'll find the usual suspects here: low-pass, high-pass, band-pass, and notch filters. The Freq knob sets the cutoff frequency of the filter and the Res knob determines the filter resonance. The last two parameters, Velocity and Random, allow you to use incoming velocity or random values to modulate the filter cutoff.

The Amplifier section sets the output volume and position for each sound individually. The pan knob can be used to move the hi-hat to one side of the mix while the volume control pulls it down to the right level. The Decay knob shapes the tail end of a sample. If the associated button is in Trigger mode, the Decay knob will dictate the fade out time from the moment the sample is triggered. In Gate mode, the fade out won't begin until a MIDI note off message is received (when you lift your finger off a key). The Gate mode is fun as it allows you to control the length of your sounds as you play them, such as a long snare sound on beats 2 and 4 with a short snare on beat 4.4. The Vel values determine how much the incoming MIDI velocity affects the output volume and pan position.

The Global section contains a master Volume knob, plus master time and pitch knobs. These knobs are begging for MIDI control as they are wonderful performance parameters. The Time knob can be used to shorten or stretch out all the samples at the same time. The Pitch knob will transpose all the samples together as a group. Try tweaking these values during a drum fill for extra expression.

Importing Sounds

By now, you've probably noticed the consistency in design philosophy behind Live. Because of that, you can probably guess how we get sounds into the Impulse cells: we drag them from our File Browsers! Loading up eight drum sounds is super simple since you can pre-listen to the sounds in the Browser then drag them into the cells.

A more advanced technique involves isolating the portion of the sound you wish to use from the Clip View (Figure 11.2a) and then dragging your sound to any one of the Impulse cells to load it (Figure 11.2b).

Cutting up drum loops for reprogramming has never been easier. If you load a Warped drum loop into the Session View, it is a painless process of isolating portions of the beat since the sample region start and end markers snap to the beats. Isolate the first sound (maybe a kick drum) you want by placing the region markers around it and drag the Clip to an Impulse cell. Then, isolate the next sound (a snare perhaps) in the same Clip and drag it to another Impulse cell. Even though you modified the Clip that was used for the first cell, the cell's sample will not change after it's been added to Impulse. So, we can repeat the process again and again using the same Clip until we populate the Impulse cells with portions of the beat from the drum loop. We can then use a MIDI keyboard to play a new rhythm for the drum sounds.

MIDI Control

The MIDI notes assigned to trigger the eight cells are fixed to the white keys between C3 (middle-C) and C4 (one octave above middle-C). When editing the MIDI data of a Clip driving the Impulse, the normal piano keyboard will be replaced with the names of the samples assigned to each line of the MIDI data.

As always, MIDI assignment of controls is the same as any other control in Live. Press the MIDI assign button in the upper-right corner of the screen. You'll see the telltale blue boxes superimpose themselves over the Impulse controls waiting for your assignments. You can still click the individual cells to display their parameters while in MIDI assignment mode which makes even extensive assignments a piece of cake.

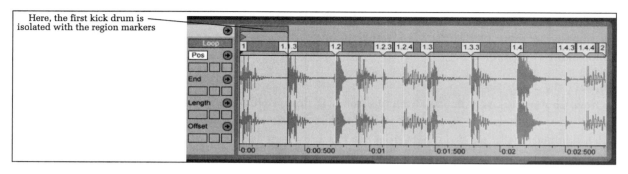

Here, the first kick drum is isolated with the region markers

Figure 11.2a

Isolating a section of the Audio Clip to be loaded into an Impulse cell.

Figure 11.2b

Switch back to the Impulse in Track View then drag the Clip into a cell.

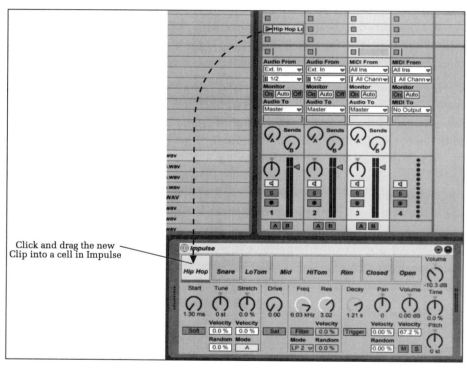

Click and drag the new Clip into a cell in Impulse

Audio Routing

From time to time, you may want to place an effect on one or more of the drum sounds in the Impulse, but you don't want to effect all of the drum sounds. To solve this, each cell of the Impulse has its own dedicated output that can be used as a source for another Audio Track, which can be loaded with any effect you choose.

After you've loaded some sounds into an Impulse, make another Audio Track and set its Audio From to the MIDI channel containing the Impulse

(Figure 11.3). In the channel selector below that, you'll see a list of not only the Track Output, but the individual drum sounds as well.

When one of these channels has been chosen as the input for another Track, that sound will cease to be sent out the normal output of the Impulse Track (this keeps the sound from being doubled). You can now add whatever effect you want to the new track, such as a compressor or reverb, to spice up the sound as you see fit.

Figure 11.3

Routing individual drum sounds to other Tracks is achieved within the Input/Output Routing section.

Simpler

When it comes to quick and imaginative sample playback and manipulation, nothing is simpler than Simpler. What is Simpler? It's a simple sampler, silly. This harmless looking device offers you a way to play a sample with a deeper level of control and flexibility than can be accomplished by just triggering Clips within the Session View. Simpler features the same drag-and-drop simplicity of Impulse and includes many of the parameters found on full-fledged samplers. This instrument is handy for throwing down bass lines, creating synth leads, or lush pads. The possibilities are nearly endless since you are building your sound upon any audio sample you wish.

Overview of the Interface

The Simpler interface (Figure 11.4) looks quite similar to the Impulse, but it has one large sample window instead of eight sample cells. The Simpler only works with one sample at a time and its contents are displayed in the main window. The + and − Zoom buttons will allow you to enlarge part of the waveform for setting accurate start and loop points.

Not one to break with tradition, the Simpler can be loaded with a new sound by either dragging it from the File Browsers or by taking it from the Session and Arrangement Views. Just like the Impulse, the Simpler will use only the portion of the sound that is between the region start and end markers of the imported Clip. Since the Simpler only holds one sample, any new sound dragged into the instrument will replace the previous one.

There are six sections in the Simpler interface: sample source, envelope, filter, LFO, tuning, and volume. The Sample source section is where you'll set all the parameters for the sample playback. The effect of the four knobs can be seen and heard immediately as the changes you make will be shown graphically in the sample display window. The sample play area is shown in dark green while the loop area (when the Loop button is active) is shown is light green (Figure 11.5). As you adjust the knobs, you'll see the green areas change. The first three knobs change the start position, loop length, and end position of the sample. The loop length is based on a percentage from the end of the sample which allows you to loop the tail end of a sound to extend its length. The Fade knob applies a crossfade to the sample loop points to smooth out any pops you may encounter when the sample starts over. The Snap button will help prevent these pops by forcing the start and end points of the loop area to snap to a zero crossing.

The envelope section (just to the right of the sample source section) is where you will shape the volume of the sound as it's played. Every time a MIDI note on message enters the Simpler, it triggers the envelope generator which is used to modulate the volume of the sample. As soon as the MIDI note is received, the envelope enters the attack phase. This is where the output rises from zero to full volume. The amount of time it takes for this increase in volume to happen is set with the Attack knob, which displays its value in milliseconds. After the attack time has passed and the sample has reached full volume, the volume drops to the sustain level. The amount of time it takes to drop is set by the Decay knob. The target level is set with the Sustain knob, which shows a percentage of the full volume. The volume will stay at the sus-

Figure 11.4

The Abletons do it again with another deceptively simple interface.

Figure 11.5

Simpler will only play the sound located in the green area of the sample display window. Playback begins at the far-left edge of the green section and plays all the way through to the end of the green. If the Loop function is activated, Simpler will then begin repeating the section in bright green until a MIDI note off is received.

tain level until Simpler receives a MIDI note off message (i.e., lifting your finger off of the keyboard). Once the MIDI note off is received, the volume will drop off to zero in the amount of time specified by the Release knob.

The filter section (which is engaged with the Filter button) is used to remove certain frequencies in the sample. As usual, you've got your choice of low-pass, high-pass, band-pass, and notch filters. The Freq and Res knobs are used to adjust the base cutoff frequency and the resonance for the filter. The remaining controls are used to modulate the filter cutoff with the envelope, velocity, key position, and LFO (Low-Frequency Oscillator). All of these modulation sources can be used at the same time for complex filter motions. The Env knob scales the amount of envelope signal used to change the filter cutoff. As the envelope value rises, the cutoff will also rise. The Vel value will scale the cutoff based on the incoming MIDI note velocity. If the value is 0%, the velocity will have no effect on the cutoff. The Key value is used to change the cutoff value of the filter based on the pitch of the incoming MIDI note. The higher the pitch, the higher the filter cutoff. This helps emulate real sounds which get brighter as their pitch increases. The LFO knob determines the amount of LFO signal used to modulate the cutoff.

The LFO (engaged with the LFO button) can be used to modulate the filter cutoff and the sample pitch. An LFO can be thought of as an automatic envelope that has a repeating pattern. The shape of the LFO is selected in the small drop-down menu right below the Filter button. The Rate knob changes the speed of the LFO, which can be further modified with the Key value (playing higher notes will speed up the LFO when the key value is

❋ ❋ ❋

increased). The Mod value sets the depth of the pitch modulation. The higher this knob, the more wild the pitch movements.

The last two sections, Pitch and Volume, determine the playback pitch and volume of the sample, respectively. The Pitch knob transposes the playback pitch by semitones while the value below the knob is the fine tune value, which can range from −50 to +50 cents. The Volume knob obviously sets the output volume of the Simpler while the Vel value determines the effect of incoming velocity messages on the output volume. If the value is set to 0%, the sample will play at the same volume no matter how hard a key is played (velocity information will be ignored). The final box determines the *polyphony* of Simpler. Polyphony is the maximum number of simultaneous notes that can be produced by Simpler. If the value is set to 1, the Simpler will be *monophonic*, being able to only play one note at a time. Any time polyphony is exceeded, a previous note will be cut off in favor of playing the new one. This condition is indicated when the indicator next to the polyphony value blinks.

> ### ❄ Analog Presets
>
> Ableton has provided a number of presets (found in the Presets Menu) to get you started. Most are based on small samples which act similar to the waveforms found in analog synthesizers. Indeed, using a saw wave in the Simpler is the same as using a saw wave in an analog synth. These tones will be great for beefy basses and gnarly leads.

MIDI Control

Simpler will respond to any incoming MIDI note to create sound. Just like the other Devices in Live, the Simpler dials and buttons can be assigned to MIDI controls. Press the MIDI Assignment key in the upper-right corner of the screen as usual, click one of the blue boxes superimposed over the Simpler controls and twist a knob. Assigning the Sample source controls to MIDI controllers is an extremely expressive performance technique. Altering the loop length and start positions on the fly can change the timbre and tone of the sample in wild ways as well.

> ### ❄ Saving Grace
>
> You can save your instruments, be they a Simpler patch or an Impulse drum kit, using the Preset controls found in the Title Bar of the Devices. You can save, rename, or delete presets using the same procedure described in Chapter 8.

12 } ReWire

While Live is an amazing audio production environment, you still may wish to use other software tools at your disposal for generating sounds. Virtual instruments and plug-in effects give us access to a plethora of third-party programs. But what do we do if the program we want to use is "bigger" than just a plug-in or effect? What if we want to harness the power of another computer system? Well, we just ReWire them together!

What Is ReWire?

Power users have been synchronizing sequencers and computers for years as it was the only way they could produce the amount of sounds they needed. The limited hardware solutions of yesteryear required that many be used simultaneously to achieve a fully orchestrated sound. Most of the first synthesizers were monophonic (they could only play one note at once) so multiple units were necessary for achieving chords and other simultaneous sounds.

Synchronizing multiple computer systems is common as well. One computer can be playing back audio files through effects while another computer is running virtual instruments. One could be a Mac and the other could be a PC if you wished. The point is that each system doesn't provide the entire solution on its own and has to be augmented by another.

With the wide variety of music-making software, there are bound to be some that have their own unique features, workflow, and sound. But, do we have to run Live on one computer and the other program on another? With the advent of ReWire, the answer is no. ReWire will allow us to run both programs on the same machine simultaneously, but ReWire does much more for us than just allow multiple applications to run. It will keep the applications in sync with each other and allow audio to pass from one to the other.

Masters

In a ReWire setup, there's actually no wiring that we have to be concerned with. ReWire functions transparently between compatible applications allowing operation to be as seamless as possible. In any ReWire setup, there is always one program designated as the *ReWire Master*. The ReWire Master is the program that will be communicating with the computer's audio hardware and will accept audio streams from other ReWire applications. You must open the ReWire Master application before any of the other programs you wish to use.

Slaves

Only one application can be ReWire Master, so all the other programs running will be *ReWire Slaves*. Slaves don't actually communicate with the computer's audio hardware at all. Instead, their audio outputs are routed to the ReWire Master application. This re-routing of audio happens automatically inside the computer once a program is launched as a ReWire Slave. Since the audio is being passed through the Master application, you will not hear the Slave application unless the Master program is set to pass the Slave's audio to the computer's audio hardware.

Using ReWire with Live

Live can act as both a ReWire Master and a ReWire Slave. Not all programs have the ability to function in both modes. For example, Steinberg Cubase SX 2 can only function as a ReWire Master. Propellerhead Reason 2.5 can only be used in Slave mode. So, if you wanted to use Live and Cubase together, Cubase would be the Master and Live would be the Slave. When using Reason, Live would be the Master and Reason would be the Slave. How does the operation of Live differ when running as Master or Slave? Since ReWire was designed to be transparent for the user, little will change in Live's operability either way. There are a few differences, of course, which will be explained next.

Using Live as a ReWire Master

When Live is used as a ReWire Master, it will operate exactly the same as when using Live by itself. Indeed, when Live is the only ReWire application running, it will be in Master Mode. This is true of any ReWire application that is capable of Master mode. Because of this, you'll define your Master application by opening it before any of the others.

When Live is hosting a ReWire Slave application, the Slave's audio outputs will be available as inputs into the Session Mixer (Figure 12.1). In the Input/Output Routing section, you'll be able to choose the ReWire application in the first box and the desired channel(s) from that program in the second box.

Figure 12.1

Here, we are using outputs 3 and 4 from Reason as inputs for channel 4 in the Session Mixer. We can hear the audio output from Reason by switching Monitor to On.

Once we have selected the ReWire source for a channel, it will behave exactly like any other audio channel with an input selected. We can hear the audio from the ReWire source by switching the channel's monitoring to "On" or by arming the Track for recording with monitoring set to "Auto." You can record the audio from the external application as a new Clip in the Track, either by recording a Clip in the Session View or by pressing Record in the Control Bar and recording directly to the Arranger. This is the exact same process for recording any other audio source on an Audio Track, as explained in previous chapters.

If you don't want to record the ReWire Slave as audio, you can still incorporate its audio streams in a Live mixdown when selecting "Render To Disk." If the ReWire Slave applications are running and their channels in the Session Mixer are being monitored, their audio will be mixed in with the rest of your Live Set when rendering. Running the ReWire applications in real-time is often preferred for laptop owners who have fast CPUs. Since laptops generally have slow hard drives, it's easier for the computer to run the ReWire applications as opposed to streaming their audio from disk.

While audio can only flow from the ReWire Slaves to the ReWire Master, it is possible for MIDI to flow in the opposite direction. This allows us to control compatible ReWire Slave applications in the same manner we would control a virtual instrument in Live. Just as you can select a ReWire Slave application as an input to an Audio Track, a Slave can also be selected at the output of a MIDI Track (Figure 12.2). You can select the Slave application with the upper box and the destination channel/device in the lower box.

Figure 12.2

This MIDI Track is being routed to the Subtractor module in Reason. The Subtractor can now be programmed and automated using the power of Clips.

A destination channel will only be listed if there are devices or elements in the Slave application that are active and able to receive MIDI messages. For example, if you load an empty rack into Reason, there will be no output devices listed in the lower box. If you make a few devices, like a Subtractor, Redrum, and NN-XT sampler, these devices will be individually selectable in the lower box of the MIDI Tracks Input/Output section.

Not all ReWire Slave applications are capable of receiving MIDI input from the Master application. If a program is not able to receive MIDI, it will not be listed as an available output device in the MIDI Track.

Remember, in order to hear the results of your MIDI messages sent to the ReWire Slave, you'll need to have an Audio Track set up to monitor the return signal from the Slave. So, instead of the MIDI Track outputting the audio (as would happen when a virtual instrument is loaded onto a MIDI Track), you'll need another Track to hear the results. This means that the MIDI info leaves on one Track and the audio returns on another.

Using Live as a ReWire Slave

Opening Live as a ReWire Slave will depend partly on the ReWire Master application you use. In some cases, you may need to enable ReWire channels before the ReWire Slave program is launched. Be sure to check the ReWire Master's manual on how they recommend to do this. Generally speaking, though, you'll launch the Master first and launch Live second. When launching Live second, it will detect the presence of the Master application and therefore automatically load itself into Slave mode.

When using Live as a ReWire Slave application, you'll notice many subtle differences in available options throughout the program. The first thing to be aware of is that like all ReWire Slave applications, Live will be communicating with the ReWire Master program instead of the computer's audio hardware. Because of this, Live's Audio Preferences will not be available and will instead be replaced with the message seen in Figure 12.3.

Also missing from Live in Slave mode is MIDI Output (Figure 12.4). Only the MIDI inputs will be available as usual for Remote Control and playing virtual instruments.

Another difference will be the available output routings for audio in the Session Mixer. When looking at the Master Track output assignment, you'll find that the list is populated with Mix and Bus names instead of the outputs of your audio interface. These buses are the pathways that lead from Live into the ReWire Master. The ReWire Master will receive the buses individually, allowing you to route one Live Track to a channel of the Master's mixer while routing a different Live Track to another channel of the Master's mixer. You can then process the channels separately in the Master application however you wish.

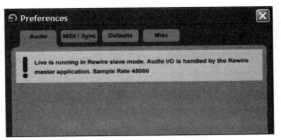

Figure 12.3

Live's Audio Preferences tab is telling us that Live is in ReWire Slave mode and therefore has no audio controls. It does, however, report the current sample rate of the ReWire Master.

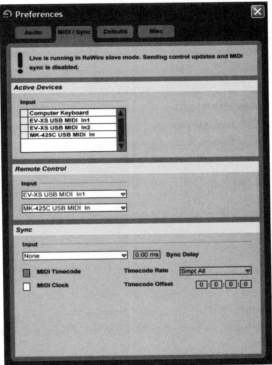

Figure 12.4

The right half of the MIDI Preferences is missing in ReWire Slave mode. Only the MIDI inputs are active.

When we said above that some ReWire Slave applications do not accept MIDI, we were partly referring to Live. You won't be able to send MIDI information to Live from the Master application. Only the computer's MIDI inputs can be fed into Live. Of course, if you really needed to route MIDI back into Live from the Master application, you could route MIDI out of a hardware interface and receive MIDI back into Live through a hardware interface as well. Connect the output to the input with a MIDI cable and you'll have MIDI running back to Live.

ReWire Power

When multiple applications are running together using ReWire, they're basically joined at the hip. What we mean is that the transport controls and locations are kept in perfect sync throughout all of the applications. When you press the Play button on one of the applications, all of the programs will start to play together. If you press Stop in another program, they'll all stop. Furthermore, if you change the start location to bar nine in one application, they'll all begin playing from that time. It doesn't matter if you use the controls of the Master or Slave applications, they'll all respond as if they're one and the same.

Since the transport functions of the programs are synchronized, changes to the tempo in one program will affect all of the others. In the case of Live with its MIDI-assignable tempo control, this real-time feature can be used to change the tempo of programs previously unable to do so on their own. Changing the tempo in Live will cause Cubase and Reason to respond accordingly. In this way, the programs inherit functionality from the others.

Groove by Yourself

While the tempo control in Live will have an effect on all ReWire applications, the Groove setting is solely for the use of Live. Increasing the Groove will cause Live to start swinging while the other applications remain straight.

Since Reason 2.5 doesn't allow the automation of its tempo, running the program in Slave mode with Live as the Master will allow you to automate the tempo in Live. The programmed change of tempo in Live will also change the tempo in Reason, resulting in the desired automation.

Using ReWire Slave applications with Live gives you an expanded list of sound sources to create with. Frequently, you just may wish to create some audio loops in a ReWire Slave application, record them in Live, then close the Slave program. The real-time nature of Live allows you to load ReWire Slaves, use them, then close them, all while Live remains playing—without glitches. This makes ReWire a viable live tool since it can be loaded and unloaded during a performance. Of course, as with all other procedures in Live, be sure to try this out a few times before a show to confirm that your computer can handle the workload of multiple audio applications running at once.

Many users flock to Live because of its ability to operate as a ReWire Slave. Because of this, the unique loop-based and time-compression tools of Live can be used in unison with standard production programs like ProTools. While having Live feeding into ProTools, you can use Live to audition loops at the ProTools tempo. You can quickly add drum loops or MIDI parts that remain under user control. You can add Warp Markers to takes done with ProTools to fix timing problems. Once all the correct parts are made, the results can be rendered as audio into ProTools.

In this chapter, we have looked at the most common ways to use ReWire with Live and other ReWire slave and master applications. ReWire is an incredibly exciting, creative, and fun aspect of Live. Many musicians and producers we have met come to Live because of its ability to ReWire. Rest assured, once you begin linking software applications, you will be hooked. Take time to explore your favorite ways of linking Live. As new applications become ReWire-enabled, and CPUs become increasingly faster, we may soon be linking computers via LAN, or even the Internet in similar ways to ReWire. In the next chapter, we will explore some of our favorite power tips for working with Live.

❋ Who's Using Live?

Pat Mastelotto—Musician

Pat Mastelotto's drumming career spans the Icelandic funk of Bjork's Sugarcubes (percussion) to the definitive 80s pop-crew Mr. Mister (drums) to the artfully Beatlesque XTC (drums). Now retained by art rock luminaries King Crimson, Mastelotto remains ahead of the loop and sample-gadget curve by ReWiring Reason and Live in his Austin, Texas project studio. "(Propellerhead) Reason and (Ableton) Live can be used to write and experiment on the fly and are perfect for an ever-changing band like Crimson," Mastelotto explains. "Live has become my frontline buddy, I'm just lovin' Live," concludes the Crimson drummer. "There's this thing where you can go into the sample and change its Warp settings, kind of like the way you use markers in [Propellerhead] ReCycle to chop up samples. It's awesome, you just move those things randomly, or when you put beats 1, 2, and 3 all within the first 16th note and then spread all the other events between beat 4 and the downbeat of the next bar across the next three beats. Just to move those Warp markers and flags around while it's playing, wow."

Pat Mastelotto. Photo by Bill Munyon.

13 } Playing Live . . . Live

Most books written about music production software would not include a chapter like the one you're about to read. It's not because the writers of this book are deranged or just trying to be different, it's because Live can actually live up to its name in a live performance. As you will discover, it's a true treat to use the same software to create your music *and* perform it. You won't have to worry about converting songs from the type of media used by your composing software into something Live can use. You won't have to worry about transferring effect and instrument settings. The same tools you use to write can be used to play—just like any other instrument. After all, should the two processes really be that different?

Because of its flexible control methods and instant response to user input, Live is the perfect companion for a gigging musician. Live performs wonders in all types of scenarios, ranging from DJ gigs to improvisational Jazz and theater. Regardless of what type of musician you consider yourself to be, we recommend reading all the information presented in this chapter. Any technique relating to the use of Live is pertinent information—innovations can be made by taking ideas from one style of musician and applying it to your own style.

DJ

DJ or not, every one of you reading this book should study this section. Using Live to DJ exploits some of the unique (and potentially confusing) features of the program and extends them to the *n*th degree. You already know that Live can sync loops together using its Warp Engine. DJs use this powerful mechanism to sync *entire songs* together. They'll also use an array of Clips to manufacture new arrangements of the songs, literally creating their own remixes right in front of the dancing masses. By learning the techniques employed here, you'll achieve a firmer grasp on Warp Marking and real-time control.

Assembling Your Audio Files

The process of DJing with Live is twofold: first comes the work of ripping and Warp Marking your songs (prepping the files); this is followed by the joy of putting it all together (performing). As you know, Live reads SDII, AIFF, and WAV files—*only*. This means every song you want to use in your DJ set will have to be in one of those three formats. Of course, you can't buy WAV files of your favorite tracks. You have to get them on CD, vinyl, or off the Internet, none of which are native WAV, AIFF, or SDII formats. You'll therefore have to convert and prep these songs before they can be used in Live.

Ripping

If the song you want to use is on a CD, you will need to copy the music from the CD to your computer using a process known as *ripping*. There are many programs that do this, quite a few of which are free. While you can find a deluge of programs to try by typing "CD Ripper" into a Google search, we recommend Apple's iTunes (www.iTunes.com). It's available for both Mac and PC, it's free, and has a number of features that will prove helpful when building your DJ music collection. We're going to use iTunes in our instructions, but you can use your favorite ripping program instead with the same results.

Take It with You

Before we get too far, we thought it would be appropriate to mention external hard drives. If you're a DJ compiling a collection of audio files for your performances, a big hard drive (maybe two!) is a good thing to have. For starters, they'll typically hold more information than a standard laptop hard drive, a necessity since AIFF and WAV files are uncompressed. Secondly, they have greater access rates, which will allow more tracks to be played simultaneously.

Most importantly, it will keep all of your music in one place. If you have multiple computer systems that you use (a desktop at home and a laptop for gigs), you won't have to store the collection on both systems. The hard drive will become your virtual record case.

Before you start ripping CDs, there are a few setup options for the ripping software to consider. First, you should check the ripping format. Many programs these days default to MP3 or a similar compressed format for ripping so you can transfer the results to a portable player such as an iPod or Nomad Jukebox. As we said before, Live can't use compressed audio files, so set the program to rip in either AIFF or WAV format (iTunes can't rip to SDII format). In the case of iTunes, this setting can be found in the Preferences panel, located in the iTunes menu (Mac users) or in the Edit menu (PC users). Click on the "Importing" tab/button to see the ripping options (Figure 13.1). You'll see that iTunes can rip both AIFF and WAV formats by selecting one of them in the first drop-down menu. You can choose to use whichever you like as both will perform identically with Live on both Windows and Mac systems. Along with specifying the file format, you may also need to check additional parameters such as 44,100 sample rate, 16-bit recording, and stereo-interleaved. While you could rip to any sample rate and bit-depth you'd like, we recommend matching the format of the audio source (in this case, a CD). Using non-CD settings will cause the ripping program to re-sample and dither (change the bit-depth) as it records, which will degrade the quality of your file. iTunes users can simply select "Automatic" in the second menu. For programs other than iTunes, you should be able to access these settings from their preferences or options menus. Check the program's documentation if the location of these parameters is not immediately evident.

Now that we've specified the format to rip our files in, we still need to tell our ripping program where to put them. Some programs will ask you for a location to save the files each time a song is ripped. Others will have you select a destination directory for the audio files. Regardless of the

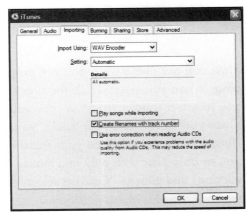

Figure 13.1

The iTunes Importing options allow us to specify WAV as our preferred file type. We're also matching the sample rate and bit-depth settings of the source CD by selecting Automatic.

iTunes Note 1

Really, Apple is not paying us to write this, but this is the first of a number of tips for iTunes users. This tip may not be specific to iTunes (other programs may be able to do it), but we know exactly how to do it in iTunes.

The first tip is checking the "Create file names with track number" option (shown in Figure 13.1 above). This will cause iTunes to place the song's track position on the CD as a two-digit number at the beginning of the file. When you later browse through your music using the Live Browser, the tracks will be shown in the same order as on the CD.

method employed by your software, we do recommend making some sort of logical arrangement of your songs in your collection. For example, you can make a folder called "Breaks" and store all your breakbeat tracks there. You could make another folder called "DnB" and store all your drum 'n bass cuts there. Whatever method you choose, it should be easy for you to navigate during a show. You don't want to be left searching for a song when the currently playing song ends!

❄ **iTunes Note 2**

iTunes can automatically organize your music in folders for you. Click the "Advanced" tab/button in iTunes Preferences. The first window shows the location where iTunes will maintain your library. You can use the "Change..." button to specify a new location, such as your external hard drive. Next, make sure the first two check boxes are checked. This will cause iTunes to maintain the library and also move any imported songs into this location (in case the songs already exist elsewhere on your hard drives).

When you examine your iTunes music folder, you won't see any music files. Instead, you'll find a list of folders with artist names. Inside each of these artist folders are additional folders for albums. Open the album folder and you'll find all the songs you ripped from that album. When accessed through Live's Browser, it makes locating a song a snap.

Now that our audio programs are properly configured, it's time to start ripping. When you insert a CD, the program will identify it and usually allow you to select specific tracks in case you don't want to import the entire CD. Once you've selected your tracks, you can start the ripping process. For iTunes, you'll right-click on your selection to expose the context menu (if you're on a Mac with only one mouse button, hold the [CTRL] key while clicking) and choose "Convert selection to AIFF/WAV." Now sit back and wait . . .

❄ **iTunes Note 3**

When connected to the Internet, iTunes will automatically search for the information on the CD you've inserted. It will usually find any retail CD and load the artist's name, album name, plus all of the track names for the CD and fill them in for you. iTunes is not the only program that can do this, but you may have to enable the feature manually in other applications. If you don't have an Internet connection, it's recommended that you manually type in these names so the program will rip the tracks with the proper file names.

Converting

With the rise in popularity of online music stores, such as Apple's iTunes (really, they're not paying us) or Bleep (www.bleep.com), you may already have the song you want to play as a digital music file on your computer. Perhaps the song is so hard to find that you're only able to buy it as a download. Since these compressed formats aren't usable with Live, you'll need to convert them to AIFF or WAV to use them in your set. iTunes can help us again in this capacity. We can add the song to our music collection by choosing "Add file to Library..." or "Add folder to Library..." from iTunes' File menu. Once the files are imported, select them in and right-click on them. Choose "Convert selection to AIFF/WAV" and iTunes will convert them to uncompressed files.

❊ **iTunes Note 4**

In order to keep the unchecked distribution of music files in control, some companies, such as Apple, have utilized a form of digital copy management into their downloadable files. These files will only play on authorized computers and players. iTunes is unable to convert these protected files into AIFF or WAV files (i.e., formats that can be used in Live). In order to perform this conversion, you'll need to burn an audio CD of the songs you want to use then rip them in just like a standard CD.

Recording

If you don't have your song on CD or as a digital music file, you'll have to import it the hard way. If the track you want is on vinyl, you'll need to connect your turntable to your computer's audio interface. This will probably require that you go through a DJ mixer or home preamp, since most audio interfaces do not allow for a direct connection of turntables. Once you've got your signal entering a channel on Live's Session Mixer, you can record the song as a new Audio Clip (see Chapter 6 if you forgot how to do this). The resulting Audio Clip will then be in a format ready to use with Live (obviously).

❊ **Warp on the Fly**

Did you know you can add Warp Markers to an Audio Clip that is recording? Simply tap along with the song and Live will insert Warp Markers with your tapped beats. This is great when recording tracks that have a varying tempo, such as a song that was recorded without the assistance of computers or metronomes.

Warp Marking Your Songs

Now that you have your songs in AIFF or WAV format, you're ready to begin the second step of prepping a file for DJing. In order to have Live keep the song in time with any others that you may be playing, you'll need to place Warp Markers in the file to indicate the location of beats in the track. Warp Marking an entire song can sound like quite an undertaking, but you'll quickly gain a rhythm that will let you complete a song in only a minute or two (maybe less).

The best way to begin Warp Marking a song is by determining the original tempo of the song. Start by turning off the Warp button in the Clip View. This will make the Clip play at its original speed regardless of the tempo of your Live Set. Launch the Clip and begin tapping along with the song using the Tap Tempo button (we recommend using a key assignment for this instead of clicking with the mouse). After you've tapped some beats, Live's tempo will start to settle around the song's tempo. Since Live's Tempo display is accurate to two decimal places, you'll probably get tempos like 125.82 BPM or 98.14 BPM instead of round numbers like 110.00 BPM or 85.00 BPM. Chances are, however, that the tempo is actually a round number, especially if the song was created by a computer or sequencer. So, if Live says the tapped tempo is 102.15 BPM, it's probably just 102.00 BPM. Go ahead and double-click the Tempo display and type in the rounded tempo then activate the Warp button in the Clip View. Live will place the tempo of the project and in the Clip's Original BPM box (on the rare occasion that this doesn't happen, you can type the tempo into this box by hand).

Now that the tempo has been found, you need to align the grid with the first beat of the song. Zoom in to the waveform display and move Warp Marker 1 into position with the first beat of the file. Don't worry if you don't find the first downbeat until later in the song (perhaps the song has an ambient intro that breaks into the beat further in) since the grid also has negative values (grid lines to the left of Marker 1). You can place the region markers before Marker 1, so starting on bar −16 is starting 16 bars before the beat drops (Figure 13.2). This is especially cool because you can play a song start with a completely nebulous, rhythmless intro, yet drop on the beat perfectly 16 bars later. Try that with a record!

Once the tempo has been determined and Marker 1 has been placed at the first recognizable downbeat of the song, the remaining grid markers to the right should be pretty close, if not dead on the beats. Turn on Live's

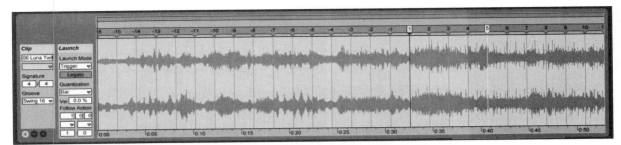

Figure 13.2

Even though we don't hear the first drum beat until bar 17 of our song, we can place Warp Marker 1 at this location and start our song from bar -16.

Metronome and listen to the track against the click. The song should start out perfectly aligned with the click. If the track stays in time all the way through, then the Clip is ready to go; however, chances are that the song will start to drift ahead or behind the click as it plays. This is due to slight differences in BPMs between Live and the song. Perhaps the song is actually running at 101.98 BPM (even computers can be a little off). After a few minutes, the discrepancy will add up to a complete misalignment with the beat, seen in Figures 13.3a and 13.3b.

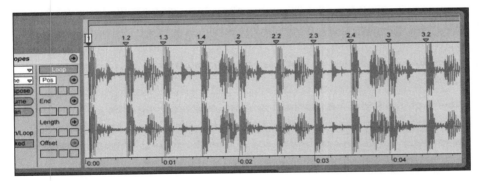

Figure 13.3a

The beginning of the song looks like it's aligned properly . . .

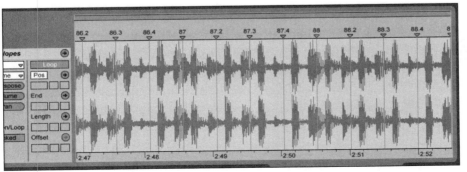

Figure 13.3b

. . . but as we look later in the file, we can see that our grid is no longer aligned.

To compensate for the "drift" you may encounter, you can place Warp Markers to keep the Clip synchronized to Live. Placing a Warp Marker every thirty-two bars is usually sufficient. To make the process as easy as possible, turn on Loop in the Clip View and use the Region/Loop Markers to inspect small sections of the song one at a time. For example, create a two bar loop and place it at the beginning of the Clip. Launch the Clip and listen to the two bars against the click. If the beats are aligned with the click, move the loop region to the right to bar 32. Listen to the loop around these two bars. Here, you may notice that the Clip doesn't line up exactly with the click anymore. Create a Warp Marker in the middle of the loop area (at Bar 33) and move this marker to properly align it with the beats in the Clip (Figure 13.4). You should now hear bars 32 and 33 looping in time with the click. Furthermore, everything between bar 1 and bar 33 should be perfectly aligned as well. You then repeat the process by moving the loop region to the right another thirty-two bars (bar 64). Check this new loop area and adjust if necessary. Repeat the process to the end of the Clip.

Once you've placed your Warp Markers to ensure proper timing, press the Save button in the Clip. This will save the location of the Warp Markers so they'll be recalled the next time you import the Clip from the Browser. You can also check the Warp Mode to make sure that you're using the most effective method for time stretching. Beats Mode is usually the best, but you may want to use Tones or Textures Mode if you stretch the Clip too far from its original tempo.

Now that you know the process for Warp Marking long files, sit back, grab a frosty beverage of your choice, and start clicking away. You'll want to have every file in your collection saved with the correct Warp Markers so that the songs will play in time every time you use them in a set.

Figure 13.4

We're inspecting various sections of the song two bars at a time. When we were listening to this section, we had to create a Warp Marker to align the song to the beat.

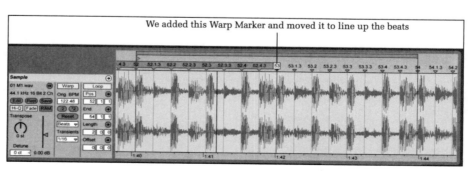

Performance Techniques

Now that you've got your Warp-Marked AIFF and WAV files ready, let's discuss the techniques used for cueing and mixing songs. We will start by looking at traditional DJs, their equipment, and their performance methods. We'll then see how Live can be used to do the same things, plus a few never possible before.

Beat Matching

The whole concept of DJing revolves around blending one great song into another great song, without interrupting the flow or rhythm of music. Quite often, this requires aligning the tempos of the two songs so they play in sync with each other, a technique known as *beat matching*. A DJ using turntables or CD decks will use their pitch adjust sliders to slow down or speed up a new song to match the tempo of one that's already playing. Once the tempos are matched, the DJ will start the new song and begin to fade it in, usually with the crossfader on his/her mixer. Since the tempos are matched and the DJ started the track at the right moment, the beats of the two songs will be playing on top of each other. The beat will remain constant as the old song is replaced by the new one. While performing this mix, the DJ will have to make minute adjustments to the playback speeds of the records or CDs in case they begin to drift out of sync.

The process of beat matching two songs in Live involves nothing more than having files with proper Warp Markers. Once Warp Markers are in the right place, Live will know how to play that file at any tempo. So, any song can be matched in tempo with any other simply by loading the two Clips and launching them. Using Launch Quantization, Live will start the songs in sync so you'll never have to worry about making tiny adjustments to keep the songs from drifting. Just fire and forget. Easy!

The DJ Mixer

The whole DJ setup centers around the DJ mixer, a specialized mixer with controls specific for DJ use. The DJ's audio sources (turntables and CD players) are connected to the mixer and the output is connected to the sound system. The mixer has audio channels with EQ, the ability to pre-listen to tracks (cueing), and a crossfader for mixing between audio sources. Some advanced mixers will also have effect loops, allowing external processing boxes to add beat-synced delays, whooshing flanges, and other tweaks to the mix. To emulate a DJ mixer with Live, you'll use features of the Session Mixer which will be discussed in a moment. But most importantly, you'll want a MIDI control device to offer you the same tactile control DJs are accustomed to.

We briefly mentioned some MIDI controllers in Chapter 3, and a good portion of them can suit a Live DJ quite well. The Evolution's X-Session and the Faderfox's Micromoduls will give you just the right assortment of controls for getting the job done. The most important things are a crossfader control (for assignment to Live's Crossfader), at least two controls to adjust the volumes of the tracks you'll be mixing (these can be faders or knobs), six knobs for using as EQ controls, and some keys or buttons for triggering mutes, EQ kills, and effects. Since Live will allow any MIDI knob or button to be assigned to a control, you could certainly use a different type of MIDI controller from the ones mentioned here for the same tasks. For example, you could use a vertical fader on your device as a crossfader, as long as you can get used to the vertical orientation (you probably won't be pulling off any flares, crab scratches, or cuts with this, but it still works for smoothly blending between tracks). Even though Live displays its volume controls as vertical faders, you could use the knobs of your controller to adjust volumes (there are some DJ mixers that actually use knobs instead of sliders for a vintage feel). If worse comes to worse, you can still achieve a great mix just using your mouse and computer's keyboard; the point is to make sure you have adequate control of your mix so you can shape it at will.

In Figure 13.5, we have set up Live's Session View like a standard 2-channel DJ mixer. There are two Audio Tracks each assigned to different sides of the Crossfader. There are EQ Three's loaded onto each of the Audio Tracks, plus a Compressor II on the Master Track. Two Return Tracks are in use for Ping

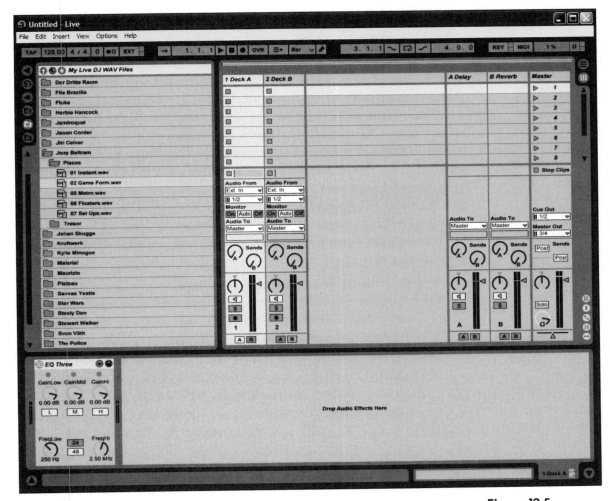

Figure 13.5

A simple Live Set ready for DJing.

Pong Delay and Reverb Devices, but you can load any kind of effects you'd prefer.

In order to cue or preview tracks, you'll need an audio interface with four outputs—two outs for the main mix and the other two to feed your headphones. Some audio interfaces, such as the M-Audio's FireWire series and Echo Audio's Indigo cards, have built-in headphone amps, which are perfect for this application. In the Master Track, choose outs 1/2 for Cue and 3/4 for Master (you may need to enable these outputs in Live's Audio Preferences if they aren't available in the menus). Connect outputs 3/4 to the speakers or sound system and plug a pair of headphones into the audio interface. If your interface doesn't have a built-in headphone amplifier, you can use an external amplifier, such as a home stereo or small mixer, or purchase a small headphone amp box from your local music store.

To make Live's Cue system work, click the Solo button just above the Preview Volume knob (Figure 13.6). The button will change to Cue and you'll see small headphone icons in the buttons where the solos used to be in the Session Mixer. This button will switch only if you've assigned the Cue and Master to different outputs as explained above. Clicking a headphone icon will route that track to the Cue bus, thus allowing you to hear it on your headphones. Please note that enabling Cue on a Track does not remove it from the Master Output. You'll need to turn off the Track Activator button (the speaker icon) so only you may hear it. Once the Track is properly cued, engage the Track Activator to send the track back to the Master mix and out to the dance floor.

To prevent the chance of mistakes caused by forgetting to deactivate the Track Activator, we've made a variation on the setup of the session by adding another Audio Track whose Track Activator is always off (Figure 13.7). By leaving it off and leaving Cue on, any Audio Clip placed in this Track will be heard in the headphones only.

If you've been trying this out while reading this, then you'll know that you can only hear your Cue Track in the headphones. What if you want to hear the main tracks in our headphones, too? We could simply click their Cue buttons, thus adding their signals to our headphones, but we have no control of their volume in relation to the Cue Track. Instead, make another Return Track. In Figure 13.8, you'll see that the new Return Track is number 3 and has been labeled "Cue Mix." Both of the main tracks have their Send 3 knobs fully clockwise, thus feeding their signals into Return Track 3. The trick is in the Input/Output Routing section: the Track Output is set to "Ext.

Figure 13.6

To enable Live's Cue function, click the button above the Preview Volume knob. The solo buttons in each Track will change to headphone icons.

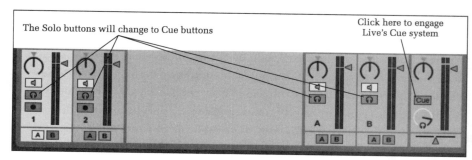

The Solo buttons will change to Cue buttons

Click here to engage Live's Cue system

Out 1/2," the headphone outs! As you turn up the volume slider on this track, the main tracks will blend in with the Cue Track in your cans. You can even pan the main mix over to one side of your phones by panning the "Cue Mix" track.

You're probably starting to see how Live can be "made" into a DJ mixing machine by some thoughtful use of tracks and signal routing. To get your hands on the fun, start assigning controls of your MIDI controller. You can set up your system any way you like, but we have a few recommendations:

❄ **The crossfader**—Even if you don't have a horizontal slider on your MIDI controller to mimic the movement of a real crossfader, assign something—be it

Figure 13.7

This DJ setup features an additional "Cue Track." You can place any Audio Clip you want on this Track for private headphone tweaking before dragging it onto one of the "live" tracks on either side. You don't have to switch any Track Activators or Cue buttons with this method.

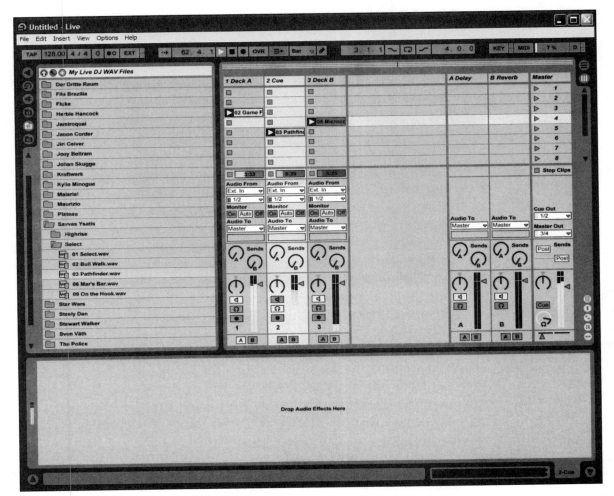

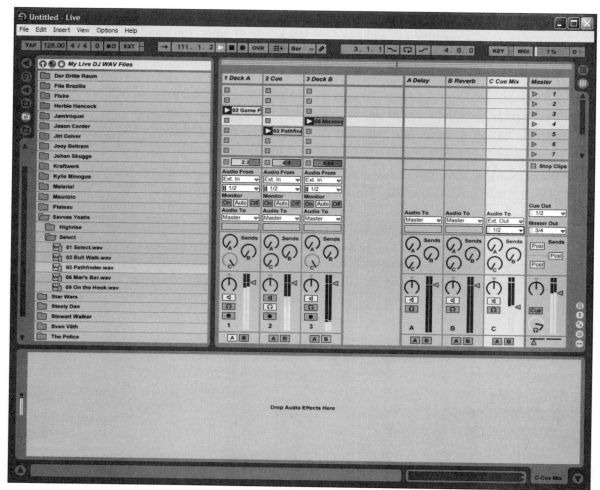

Figure 13.8

By using another Return Track, you can create a mix for your headphones. Isn't the routing flexibility of Live handy?

a vertical slider or a knob—to this control in Live. Even twisting a knob to perform a crossfade can feel smooth and musical, even if not "true to form."

❋ **The track volumes**—While you may think that mixing two tracks should be as simple as setting their volume sliders to the same position and just using the crossfader, you'll find that some songs you play are just louder than others. This could be due to different mastering techniques and sonic content. Regardless of the reason, you'll want to have easy access to the volumes of each track; as you begin crossfading, you may need some extra play in the volumes to keep the mix even.

- ❋ **EQ kills**—As we mentioned above, EQ Three's are loaded onto each of our "live" tracks. Assign MIDI buttons (CTRL [CMND] + M) or keys (CTRL [CMND] + K) on your computer's keyboard to these buttons so you can "cut" frequencies on the fly. When you deactivate the low band of an EQ Three, it will remove almost all the bass and kick drums. The other two buttons, Mid and High, will have the same effect on their own frequency bands. Try taking out the Low from one track while taking out the high from the other. How many 3-band combinations can you make?

- ❋ **Tempo and Groove**—Assign two knobs to these controls—you'll be able to change the speed and feel of your mix at will. Your records have turned into sonic rubber bands!

Impulse

Thanks to the fact that you Warp Marked all of your audio files, you can create MIDI drum parts to augment the beats in your mix. Load Impulse onto a MIDI Track and build a kit of your favorite drum sounds. As your songs are playing, you can record MIDI Clips and overdub rhythms that will be perfectly aligned with the main tracks. Even if you launch a new Track, everything will stay synced together. In Figure 13.9, we've added the Impulse track and have an assortment of MIDI grooves to play stacked in the Session View. We save these Clips as part of our "DJ Setup.als" file so they'll be ready to go at our next gig.

Live Remix

During your set, once you've decided your next song, make a few copies of it in your Cue Track. In your headphones, set a unique start or loop point for each Clip. Set one to start on the song's chorus. Make Clips that start at each of the verses. Loop the breakdown. Be sure to change the Clips' names to indicate what section they are! When you move the Clips into a live track (Figure 13.10), you'll be able to launch the Clips in any order you want, literally remixing the arrangement of the song right in front of your audience. How many Clip variations can you make for your remix?

Band

Many gigging bands are using some form of accompaniment, either prerecorded tracks or beat boxes, to embellish their sound. Many times, the bands feature multi-instrumentalists that write more parts for a song than can be played at once. When you have the multi-tracking capabilities of Live at your disposal, you can easily compile the parts you need for accompaniment

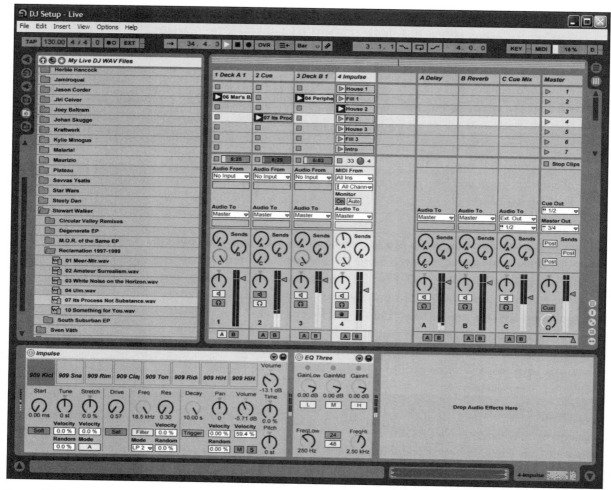

Figure 13.9

There's nothing better than a kick drum part or extra hi-hat pattern for adding emphasis to your mixes. It also helps maintain continuity when fading between tracks—your beats stay solid on top, making the transition sound surprisingly transparent.

and break them into Scenes. As you perform, you can move through the Scenes, or you can record an Arrangement to be played back during a gig.

Click Track

In order to stay synchronized with Live, one or more members of the band may want to listen to a *click track*—which is a metronome sound synchronized with the parts in your song. Usually, this amounts to nothing more than turning on Live's metronome and setting the Cue output to a pair of headphones (like we did in the DJ example above). The drummer will usually be

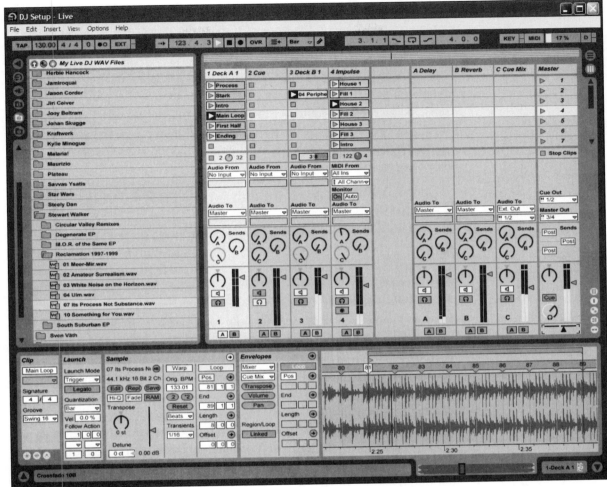

Figure 13.10

The six Clips in the Track 1 are sections from a larger song. You can jump from the intro to the first verse to the second verse, skipping the chorus. You can then come back and play the chorus twice instead of once—whatever you feel.

the one begging for the click. He'll play along with the metronome in the headphones, and the band will play along with him. As a result, you all play together with Live.

Of course, since everything is tempo-synced in Live, you could use a regular drum loop as the click track. Instead of turning on the metronome, load a drum loop onto a Track and send it to the headphones. Many will find it easier to play against a drum loop as opposed to the generic metronome sound.

If needed, don't hesitate to let other members of your band hear the click. A simple earphone run up the back of a shirt will suffice. The more members of the band that are locked in with the click, the tighter the sound.

Tap Tempo

Along with playing to Live's click track, you can make Live play to *your* click track. Assign a MIDI button or key to Live's Tap Tempo button. As your band plays, you can tap in your tempo and Live will follow it. A drummer can assign an electronic trigger to the Tap Tempo, then tap a few beats here and there to keep Live in sync.

> ❋ **Count Off**
>
> Give Live four taps as you count off the beginning of your song. Live will start on the downbeat along with the rest of your band, and it will continue playing at the tempo you tapped.

Live Effects

Besides being a flexible backup player for your band, Live can also act as a sound engineer. To add an echo to your lead singer's vocals, run his or her mic into an input on your computer's audio interface and select it as an input on an Audio Track. Switch the Track's monitoring to On and place a Simple Delay on the Track. Your singer's live vocals will pass through the Delay, which you can control with MIDI or your mouse. You can also record automation for the effect and play it back as part of the Arrangement. You can program Live to turn the delay on and off at specified times, change the feedback, and so on. So you don't completely freak out the sound guy, you can set the output of the vocal processing track to an independent output of your audio interface (Figure 13.11) and run a cable to the engineer so he can still control the overall mix of the show.

Jazz Improvisation

Many jazz musicians shy away from computers, especially in a live situation, because they feel they are too constricting for their type of music, one that is built upon the idea of improvisation. Many jazz pieces have a loose structure; certain sections of the song will be explicitly defined (the entrance, ending, and main musical ideas) while others will be completely nebulous (the solo sections). You can see how a traditional sequence may hamper this free-form approach.

Elastic Arrangement

You've heard us refer to the results of Live's Warp Engine as "elastic audio," allowing you to stretch and pitch audio files any way you'd like. The same thing can be said of a musical arrangement in Live—you can jump around and change the length of any sections of the song on the fly. This is accomplished by arranging your Clips by song section within the Session View (Figure 13.12). You can then launch Scenes as you progress through the song.

As we've said before, it's not necessary to move through the Scenes in a straight top-down order, it's just easier to visualize your song that way when writing. You can set up the Scenes any way you like, just make sure that you have the ability to launch them quickly. Instead of using the mouse to launch the Scenes, we recommend using keyboard keys or assigning MIDI notes to a controller. One of the most intuitive methods involves assigning the Scenes to buttons on your guitarist's pedal board. He can then switch sections of the

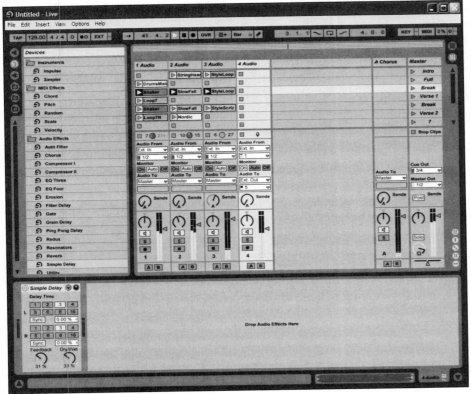

Figure 13.11

Track 4 is processing the live vocals. The effected vocals are being sent to output 5 of the audio interface (outs 3 and 4 are feeding the drummer's headphones).

Figure 13.12

The sections of the song are just waiting to be launched. Launching them live, as opposed to playing to an Arrangement, will let you determine the course and speed of the song as you play it.

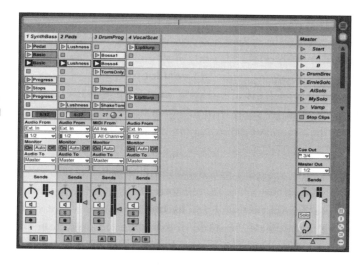

song as easily as he changes guitar tones. Or, your keyboardist can have command of Live. It doesn't matter who controls the arrangement, Live's universal MIDI mapping can allow any MIDI device to control Live. If necessary, you could even trigger Scene changes from an EWI (Electronic Wind Instrument).

The important thing to realize is how easy it is to control Live during a performance. If your sax player is performing the greatest solo of his career, you can extend his solo without doing anything at all. As long as the Clips in the solo section are set to loop, they will repeat indefinitely until he signals to move on to the next section. Once he gives the signal, you can trigger the next Scene. There's no need to do anything to extend a section; it will happen naturally as you allow Live to loop. All you have to do is launch the various sections of the song when you're ready for them.

Real-time Loop Layering

Using Live's recording functions within the Session View, you can easily record new Clips and set them looping on the fly. This is excellent for creating "sound on sound" layers during a show. A guitarist can play a simple bass line and loop it, then layer a rhythm part on top of it. He can then improvise on top of his new loop creations, making a song right before his audience's eyes.

The method for achieving these layers is best accomplished with a MIDI pedal board, like the one explained above. You can control Live with your feet while leaving your hands free to play your instrument. The pedals will each be assigned to the relative MIDI controls in the MIDI Assignment Mode. Tapping a pedal the first time will start recording a part, tapping again will begin looping what you just recorded. If you have eight pedals and eight Audio Tracks, you can grab eight different loops and play them at the same time. For more control, you may want to have a MIDI fader box, like the Doepfer's Pocket Fader or Evolution's UC-33e, for adjusting the mix of your loops.

Live's relative mapping controls are only visible while in MIDI or Key assignment modes. When these modes are active, you'll see another row of play boxes appear above the Input Output Routing Strip (see Figure 13.13). When you assign a MIDI note or Key to these play buttons, they will individually trigger the Clips in the selected scene. In the example, pressing "q" will cause the "Beat2" Clip in the "Bridge" Scene to play. If the Scene highlight is moved to the "Chorus" Scene, pressing the "q" key will launch the "Break7" beat instead.

This relative mapping also works for Tracks that are armed for recording (Figure 13.14). When "q" is pressed now, Live will begin recording a new Clip in the empty slot. When you press "q" again, Live will stop recording and begin playing the looped Clip. By assigning each pedal to one of these relative slots, you can fire off recordings with the push of a pedal. You can

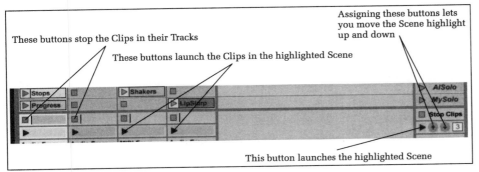

These buttons stop the Clips in their Tracks

These buttons launch the Clips in the highlighted Scene

Assigning these buttons lets you move the Scene highlight up and down

This button launches the highlighted Scene

Figure 13.13

The relative play controls allow you to trigger individual Clips from a selected Scene. These relative controls will disappear when you exit MIDI or Key Assignment mode, but they will still be active.

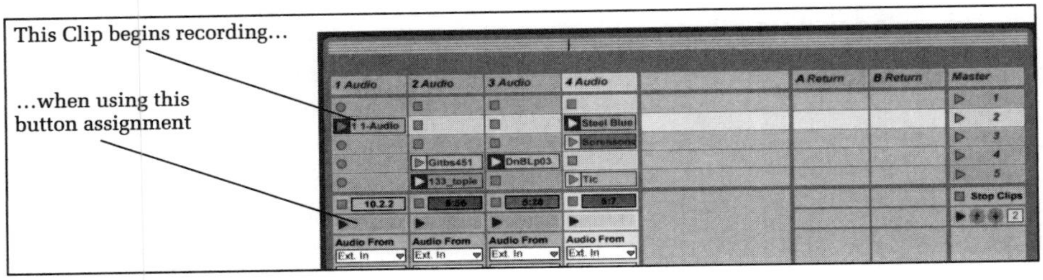

This Clip begins recording...

...when using this button assignment

Figure 13.14

Here, Clips can be recorded using the same relative buttons by arming the Tracks for recording. The stop boxes will stop the playing or recording of any Clip on the Track.

also assign pedals to the stop boxes located right below the relative play controls. You can then stop any playing Clip in a Track by pressing one of these pedals.

Theater

Sound cues are one of the most important elements to adding realism to a stage production. Even though an actor may drop a glass on stage, it is usually accompanied with a breaking-glass sample from the theater's sound system (this ensures everyone in the back hears the glass break). Other sound effects, such as wind, rain, thunder, city traffic, church bells, and crying babies, will also be played through the house system. For small theater companies, musical scores will also need to be played back when there's no room (or budget) for a live orchestra. Live performs wonders in this environment, being able to add all of these elements instantly, all with just the push of a button.

Sound Effects

In order to instantly play a sound when using Live, you'll need to turn off any Launch Quantization that may be on, both in Live's Control Bar and individually in your Clips. You don't want to trigger a sound and have Live wait for the quantize time before playing it. By switching all of these quantize settings off, Live will play the Clip the instant it is triggered. Whenever possible, we also recommend that you switch off Warp so the sample will always play at its original pitch and speed.

One-shot sound effects would include things such as the breaking glass, a gunshot, doorbell, clock chime, or phone ringing. These sounds happen once and do not loop. For these types of sounds, simply turn off the Clip's Loop button. The sound will then play only once every time it's triggered.

For other atmospheric effects, such as rain, traffic, and wind, you will need to loop the sound so it can play for an undetermined amount of time. With the Clip's Loop button engaged, you can launch the Clip then slowly fade it in. The sound will stay there until you turn it down again, usually at the end of a scene. Remember, if you need more than one sound effect playing at a time (perhaps someone gets shot in the streets on a rainy night in Chicago), you'll need to have them all on individual tracks.

❄ **Performance Sounds**

Contemporary theater companies and performance artists are starting to utilize sensors on their actor's bodies to trigger sounds. Each movement they make can generate unique MIDI messages, which Live can use for triggering Clips. A sensor could be used to trigger a gunshot sound when the actor pulls the trigger of his prop gun, thus adding more realism to the performance.

Music Cues

Along with adding sound effects, Live can also be used to play the musical score for the show. Each song, or section of a song, can be made into a Clip, allowing you to trigger it at the right moment. You can vary the speed of the music by adjusting Live's tempo. You can even transpose a musical part to another key if your singer's voice is in a different range.

In essence, each musical piece is treated just like the one-shot sound effects explained above; however, to maintain tempo control, you'll want to have Warp turned on in these Clips. As you fire off the Clips, you can tap a new tempo to keep the music in time with the production. You can even count off the piece with four taps, just like a conductor counting off the beginning of a song. If a piece of music calls for a hold before proceeding to the next section (perhaps there's some dialog between the verses), split the song into two Clips (Figure 13.15). The first Clip will play the song up to the hold and stop. The second Clip will begin right after the hold and continue through the end. You can do this for as many holds as there are in the piece.

Whatever your purpose, either DJing a party, playing at a bar, or performing a stage show, Live can support your endeavors in creative ways that are limited only by your imagination. Since Live is always responding to your input, you will be in control through the entire performance. As you read these sections, we hope you found some interesting applications that you can use in your own performances. To get you started, you'll find a collection of

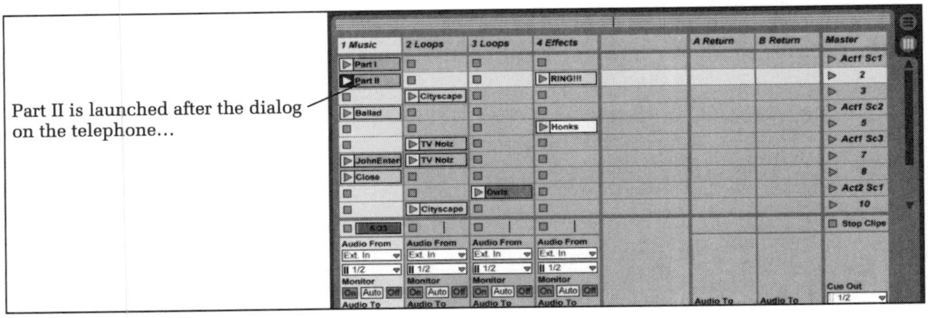

Part II is launched after the dialog on the telephone...

Figure 13.15

The Clips in Track 1 are actually the same song. The first Clip starts at the beginning of the song while the second Clip starts at the beginning of the second verse.

305
❄ ❄ ❄

Live Sets already configured for each of the uses above on the Course Technology Web site, www.courseptr.com, including a beginner and advanced DJ setup, as well as a sound on sound layering template, which will be good launch pads for your own ideas.

❄ Who's Using Live?

Sasha—DJ and Remixer

Dave Hill recently got to hang out with Sasha at New York's Crobar. Sasha is way hot on Live; here are a couple of tips from him:

1. Limits can promote creativity—The temptation with a program like Live is to use lots of Tracks—an unlimited number can be created, after all. However, most pros purposely limit their sets to a specific number of Tracks. Why? This limit actually helps them be more creative. By restricting the boundless options in Live to a maintainable four, or possibly six, Tracks, they are able to focus on the mix as opposed to taming the mayhem. An added bonus when limiting the Track load is that Live will have more CPU cycles at its disposal.

2. Dialing in the mix—One cool trick for controlling the EQ Three is to kill both the High and Low frequencies, then assign MIDI knobs to the LowFreq and HiFreq parameters. This helps to quickly balance multiple tracks with only two knobs per track, using the knobs as high- and low-pass filters.

3. DJ with RePitch Mode—Also interesting is that Sasha uses the RePitch Warp Mode for all songs (though he does use other modes for loops). He then mixes them in like he would records where adjusting the tempo also affects the pitch. This feels more natural to him by mimicking the response of vinyl. Plus, RePitch doesn't time-stretch the audio, thus eliminating any artifacts from the Warp process.

4. Master compression—And for us insiders, he uses a PSP Vintage Warmer plug-in on the Master Track to warm up the mixes and prevent distortion when he pegs a track. Sounds amazing!

14 } Live 4 Power

We've covered a lot of ground since setting Live's Preferences in Chapter 3. You've learned how to record and modify Clips and how to arrange them in the Session and Arrangement Views. You're a master of quantizing and Warp Marking, and you can spiff up your mix with effects.

Everything up to this point has been left-brain oriented, so we're switching gears and will now focus on the creative, right-brained things we can do in Live. We're going to look at how a little "misuse" of some of the tools, such as Warp Markers, can allow us to morph beats into new ones. We'll also show how Follow Actions can make your performing tasks a whole lot easier. You'll even learn how to sync two computers together as well as learn some final optimization techniques. More than anything, you'll see how thinking "outside the box" can help Live continually adapt to your working style.

More Warp Markers

We cannot stress the importance of understanding Warp Markers enough. The amount of groove massaging made possible by Live's Warp Markers is truly limitless. At first, you may be frustrated by how to specifically adjust a beat or loop to make it sound the way you're hearing it in your head, or to get it to align properly within your audio project; but with a little practice, you will develop an intuition for how Warp Markers gradually shift a pattern's events. In the following list, we have outlined a few of our favorite techniques to get you started. After you master our examples, take time to experiment with Ableton's powerful Warp tool. There really are no rules, so go for it!

* **Feel**—The trouble and triumph of loop-based music is that feel often becomes stagnant, unwavering, monotonous, and uninspired. It's why dance music is

often for dancers, and not always for classically trained musicians. To combat the static element in loop-based music, it is important to add a little variety from time to time, even if the results are basically imperceptible to the untrained or unsuspecting ear. There are several methods for doing this, but the easiest we find is to subtly (not randomly!) change the volume of some beats in a few of the repetitions. For instance, you are working in Live's Arrangement View and you have played four measures of a loop. On bar 4, you might try attenuating (reducing) the volume with a Clip Envelope (shown in Figure 14.1). Though a drummer tries to play like a machine, the strength with which he hits the drums will vary slightly throughout his performance. By adjusting the volumes slighty, you can replicate this variability. Remember, it's best to play with the volumes of subdivisions (hi-hats and percussion), not the main beats (such as the kick and snare drums).

❋ **Ahead and behind the beat**—Drummers and bass players have developed a unique relationship through the years. An artist's "feel" is often as important as what is being played. You will often hear musicians or critics say it's not what musicians play, but "how they play it." One musical dialog common to the tradition of drummers and bassists (including organ and synth bass) is that of playing ahead of the beat and behind the beat. The idea is that the bass player (and the rest of the band) plays on the beat, while the drummer plays slightly behind the 2 and 4 snare hits. Generally, you want your kick drum to remain in the same place, meaning squarely on the beat. To play on top or ahead of the beat, the drummer ever so slightly rushes the hit on the snare and even the hi-hats and cymbal parts. This can give the music a rushed or more energetic feel popular in many dance styles. In Figure 14.2a, we have provided a simple drum beat. Notice that the beats line up perfectly with Live's Warp Markers. In Figure 14.2b, we have pushed a few Warp Markers to the left to make the snare hits feel sluggish or behind the beat, while in Figure

Figure 14.1

Altering the volume here and there can add realism to loops.

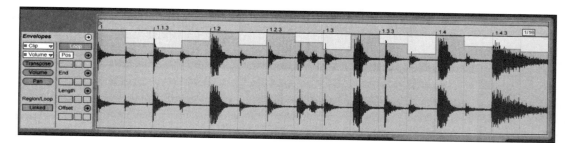

❋ ❋ ❋

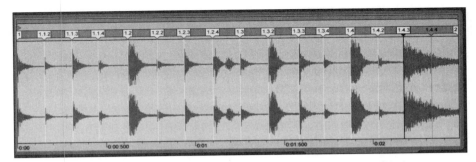

Figure 14.2a

Simple drum groove aligned with Ableton's Warp Markers.

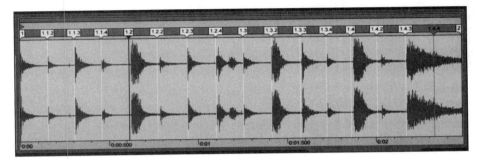

Figure 14.2b

Moving the Warp Markers to the left to make the beat more laid back.

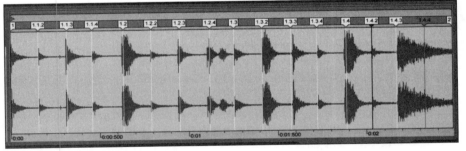

Figure 14.2c

Moving the Warp Markers to the right makes the groove feel "on top."

14.2c, we have pushed the same Warp Markers slightly to the right of the snare for a more rushed feel—ahead of the beat.

❄ **Extending one-shot style loops**—Sometimes a looping sample will play too often. Examples such as a single drum hit firing every eighth-note instead of every quarter, or a horn section blast on every downbeat instead of every measure come to mind. If you wanted the blast (seen in Figure 14.3a) to happen on every measure, you can use a Volume Envelope. By unlinking the length of the envelope and stretching it to a bar in length, you can mute beats 2, 3, and 4, resulting in the blast only being heard on beat 1 (Figure 14.3b).

Figure 14.3a

The one-beat long horn blast. Listening to this loop gets annoying really fast.

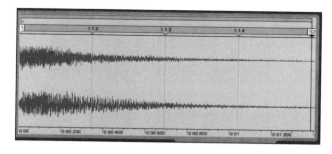

Figure 14.3b

Ah, much better. We've muted the last three beats so we only hear the horns once a measure.

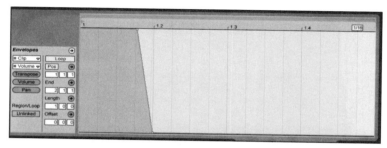

Beat Wreckin' Clinic

Making breakbeats, funky drum patterns, and fills is often best done via trial and error—especially since so much of the music made on computers is programmed in this fashion and not played. That said, here are a few ideas for making your looped drum and percussion grooves freak the beat.

* **Slice 'n' dice**—Take any drum loop in Arrangement View, and use Live's Split command—CTRL (CMND) + E—at common rhythmic subdivisions (1/4, 1/8, and 1/16-note settings), as shown in Figure 14.4a. Then rearrange the order of the newly made clips. We like to do this in the track below the original track as shown in Figure 14.4b. You can copy a slice multiple times if you want and you can leave others out. If you just do this randomly, many a "happy accident" will occur. With practice, you'll work in less random fashion and begin doing edits on purpose. As always, if you are pleased with your results, render the new loop.

* **Double for nothing**—Another quick trick for adding rhythmic variety to stale loops is to use Live's double and halve original tempo buttons (shown in Figure 14.5). Try sectioning off a 1/4 or 1/8-note section of a loop by using Live's Split command, and then double or halve the tempo of the smaller section.

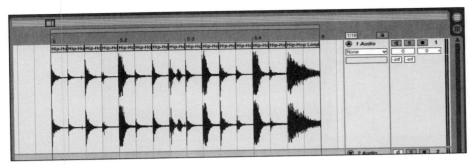

Figure 14.4a

Repeatedly split any clip.

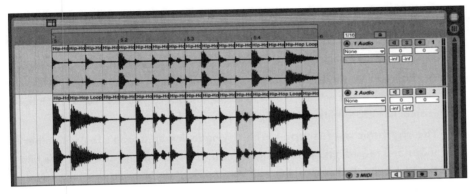

Figure 14.4b

Rearrange and copy the components as you like.

In Figure 14.6, we have halved the last 1/4-note section of the larger loop to give it a slight change in feel. Experiment with other subdivisions and doubling the groove as well for the best results.

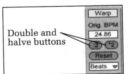

Double and halve buttons

Figure 14.5

Use these buttons to halve or double a small section of a loop.

❄ **From the Offset**—Topping the list of our fave tricks is to take any of the preceding examples and change the Sample Offset for a freshly made loop segment. In Figure 14.7, we have taken the section we halved in Figure 14.6 and moved the start time to 1.2.3. For this particular drum groove, it creates a very realistic and normal-sounding drum fill or groove variation.

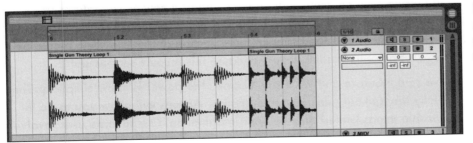

Figure 14.6

Split a loop and then halve the new segment to create a fill.

Figure 14.7

Move Sample Offset to create variety.

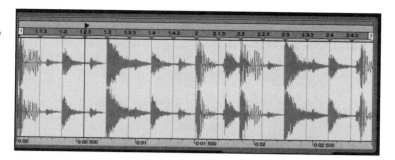

* **Controlling with Clip Envelope**—To take this to an even higher and more complex level, try creating a Clip Envelope to control a loop's Sample Offset. To do this most effectively, make sure you are in Beats Mode, then select the Sample Offset Envelope in the Clip Envelope drop-down menus. Once you see the flat red line, use Live's Pencil tool to scramble the beat as you like. With some practice you will learn how to reshape loops as you like. Note: Each horizontal line represents a single 1/16 note offset from the now time.

* **The rhythmic microscope**—When trying to line up a loop's feel with other loops and recordings, try working with smaller sections one at a time. We find this trick helpful when working with varying degrees of swing or unusual syncopations. In other words, we will work with the first half of the loop until it feels like it complements the feel of the song, and then move to the second half.

* **Programmable slices**—While cutting a beat into tiny slices that you can rearrange is a great way to create micro-edited beats, you can also load these individual slices into the pads of the Impulse instrument by dragging them from the Session or Arrangement Views into the cells of the Impulse. You can then use the slick precision of the MIDI editor to program patterns of these slices which you can launch at will.

Harnessing Follow Actions

It may sound silly, but even with all the wonderful new MIDI features of Live 4.0, the thing we like the most are the new Follow Actions. Can anybody say hidden genius? Really, the Follow Actions section of the Clip View should be in huge, obnoxious flashing letters because this is some serious stuff.

We've said it before and we'll say it again: the power is in the simplicity. The carefully thought-out rules governing Follow Actions will allow you to do innumerable things limited only by your imagination. Our favorite uses revolve

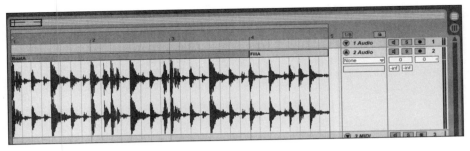

Figure 14.8

This four bar arrangement gives us three bars of the "BeatA" Clip followed with a bar of "FillA."

around enhancing our live perfor-mances with them.

Figure 14.9

By setting the top Clip as shown on the left and the bottom Clip as shown on the right, the same arrangement will be played as that in Figure 14.8.

- ❄ **Mini song structures**—If you want to play one Clip for three bars followed by another Clip for one bar, you could copy the two Clips to the Arrangement, stretch the first to be three bars, then tack the second Clip on the end (Figure 14.8). You could then consolidate the Clips into a new one which could be dragged back to the Session.

  With Follow Actions, we can create the same arrangement in the Session View without rendering a new Clip. By stacking the two Clips on a Track, we can set the Follow Actions as shown in Figure 14.9. The top Clip will play for three bars, then trigger the Clip below it. The bottom Clip will then play for a bar and trigger the top Clip, starting the cycle over again.

- ❄ **Loop variations**—We've tried to suggest ways to spice up your loops to keep them from getting too stale, and here's another one. This involves a col-lection of parts that are subtly different from one another. One example is two drum Clips that are the same, but where one has an extra snare hit in it. Set the Follow Action of the first Clip to randomly trigger the second one from time to time. You'll set the second Clip to re-trigger the first. The result is that you get a constant beat which has an additional snare hit thrown in from time to time, mimicking the way a real drummer will modify his beat on the fly. When you set up your Follow Actions, make sure one of the options triggers another Clip while the other option is set to "Play Again." Play Again ensures that the Follow Action will be performed again in the case Live chooses not to trigger the other Clip (check out the Follow Action section in Chapter 5 in case you forgot this little stipulation).

❄ ❄ ❄

Figure 14.10

The Clip needs to play all the silence at the beginning in order to come in at the right place.

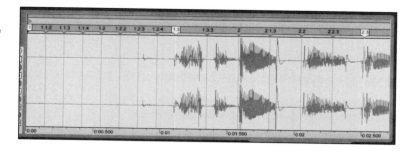

* **Pickup notes**—You know, not every musical phrase starts on the downbeat of a bar. Some start just a few notes before. Take the song "Happy Birthday to You," for example. The two syllables in "hap-py" take place before the downbeat—the word "birthday" happens on the downbeat. Normally we would have to trigger this Clip a bar before we wanted it to start. The Clip would play silence until it reached the first word (Figure 14.10). While this does work, it doesn't always "feel" right to trigger a Clip that early before you want to hear it. The second way is to start the Clip right on "happy" and change its Launch Quantize setting to 1/4 so you can launch it on the right beat. The downside is that you no longer have the "comfort zone" of the Bar Quantization.

With Follow Actions, we get the best of both worlds: we can Launch the Clip with the accuracy of a low Quantize setting, while being assured that the part will continue on the beat. To see what we mean, take a look at how "Happy Birthday" is now set up using two Clips (Figures 14.11a and 14.11b). The first Clip is "happy" while the second Clip is "birthday to you, happy birthday..." and so on. The second Clip has a Launch Quantization of "Bar." No matter what, this Clip will play in time. The first Clip, however, has a quantize setting of 1/16. Its Follow Action will trigger the next Clip after only 1 sixteenth-note (its Follow Action Time is set to 0.0.1). So, a sixteenth after the "happy" Clip is triggered, the main Clip is triggered; however, the next Clip will not start immediately since it has to wait for its Quantize setting. This means that if the pickup ("happy" Clip) is played a little early or late, the rest of the song will still play in time. This can be a neat tool if your pickup phrase is a whole bar in length. You can trigger it at a bar, half bar, one beat, or any amount and still have the rest of the phrase in time. You'll just hear more or less of the first Clip depending on when you launch it.

* **Start before loop**—Since the early days of Live, many sample heads have wondered why they can't start a Clip before its loop region. Live always keeps the start marker within the loop. This can be frustrating when dealing with a

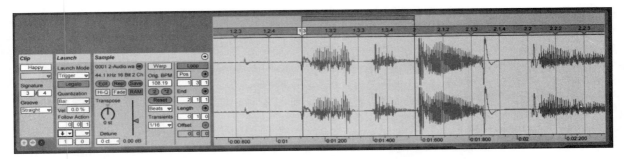

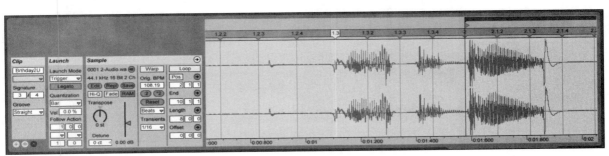

two bar loop where a sound in the first bar should only be heard once. For example, a two bar drum beat has a crash cymbal right at the beginning. You want to trigger the Clip, have it play the first bar with the crash, but then loop just the second bar so the beat keeps going without additional crashes. Follow actions allow you to do this by making two Clips, one with the first bar of the drums and the other with the second bar. The first Clips is set to trigger the next one after a bar. The second loop has no follow action so it repeats indefinitely.

❋ **Drum fills**—This is my (Chad's) favorite of them all. Triggering drum loops during a live show is so fun, but I don't like having to re-trigger the main beat once I'm done with my fills. Follow Actions allow me to play all sorts of beats while Live makes sure to restart the main beat when I'm done. Figure 14.12 shows a stack of drum parts, which happen to be MIDI Clips playing an Impulse. The top Clip is the main beat. Every Clip below it is a variation or drum fill. Each of these variations has Follow Actions settings matching the ones shown in the figure. By having each of the fill Clips trigger the main beat right after they start, I'm guaranteed that the main beat will start on the next bar (the main beat Clip is set to Bar Quantization). In fact, since each of the fill Clips has a launch Quantization of only 1/16, I can launch multiple Clips one after the other, literally piecing my fill together in real time. I always make sure

Figure 14.11a

This is the "happy" Clip. It is set to trigger the next Clip, the "birthday" Clip, only one sixteenth-note after it is triggered. Since Live won't let you type in a value of 0.0.1 into the boxes, click and drag down on the time value to reduce it to 0.0.1.

Figure 14.11b

The Clip on the right, however, will not play until the downbeat because its Quantize is set to an entire bar.

315
❋ ❋ ❋

Figure 14.12

The top Clip is set to Bar Quantization while the others are set to a sixteenth. Each fill Clip will launch the first, so the beat always kicks in after the fills.

to have a Clip with straight sixteenth notes on the snare and another with sixteenths on the kick. These are really effective when dropped in the fill.

Don't just try this with beats, try it with musical parts, too. Create multiple Clips and treat them with different effects and parameter tweaks. Set them to Legato mode so that the playback position is traded off as you switch Clips. It will sound like you're performing crazy processing on the part as you switch between the Clips. Most importantly: assign these fill Clips to MIDI notes for playability!

* **Drum wreck**—Take the concept above and make dozens (hundreds?) of variant Clips. Set them all to Legato with an "Any" Follow Action. Set the Follow Action Times to something pretty short (1/8 or 1/16) and let it rip. Live will start randomly jumping between all your variations at light speed. Render the results so you can grab a great part when it happens.

Clip View Creativity

Improvising with a Clip's settings while you are in Arrangement Record Mode can be a great way of making new samples, beats, and effects. Here is how to do this:

1 Load a drum or rhythmic synth/guitar loop into a Clip Slot in Session View.

2 Put Live in Arrangement Record Mode, by clicking the Arrangment Record button in the Control Bar.

3 Begin recording and play (Launch) the Clip.

4 While recording and the Clip is playing, grab the Clip's Loop Offset arrow and drag it back and forth. You'll find that gradually jogging it back and forth from left to right around the middle of the loop works best.

5 Then, try messing with the sample's Transpose setting. You can use this to make melodies or just for re-pitch effects. Either way, it can be extremely powerful.

6 Stop recording and go to Live's Arrangement window. You will now see a separate Clip for each tweak made during the recording process (Figure 14.13).

7 Listen to your performance and make a mental note of sections that sound particularly good. You can usually clean up and then render these subsections into a larger performance.

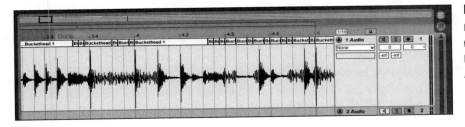

Figure 14.13

Each Clip adjustment during the recording process becomes a new Clip in Arrangement View.

❄ Again with the Pops?

After all of this beat wreckin', sample manglin', and creative re-pitchin', you may end up with a few digital pops. You can clean these up in Arrangement View by creating a super-quick volume dip using Live's volume automation. We have created an example (Figure 14.11) by cleaning up a small glitch occurring in the mess made in Figure 14.14.

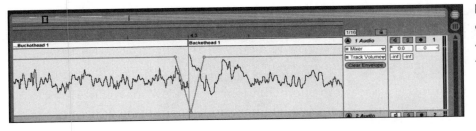

Figure 14.14

Cleaning up digital pops in Arrangement View by using Automation.

❄ ❄ ❄

Minimizing Performance Strain

Effects guzzle plenty of valuable CPU juice. To combat the ill effects of, well, too many effects, we frequently rely on the following tips and workarounds (listed in order of preference).

❅ **Streamline effects**—Many of Live's included effects contain sections or modules that can be turned off. We've mentioned that by deactivating unnecessary bands of Live's EQ Four, you can shave a couple of points from your CPU meter. Live's Reverb functions in three separate "quality" modes—economy, comfort, and first class modes can be chosen under the Global tab. Other sections of the effects that will save processing power when omitted (if you don't need them) are Reverb's Filtering, Spin, Diffusion, and Chorus Activation buttons, Chorus's Delay 2 Portion, Filter Delay's L, L+R, or R delays or filters, Vinyl Distortion's tracking model or pinch effect, and/or Redux's bit reduction. In Figure 14.15, we have turned off Reverb's Spin and Diffusion options and we're using Reverb's Economy setting. The difference is about five percent less CPU drain.

❅ **Sends and Returns**—In Chapter 8, we recommended taking advantage of Live's Return channels. Simply take any effect that you have created on more than one track and, instead, "share" it on a Return Track. For example, if you are using several instances of Live's Reverb on several different tracks, try consolidating by placing one Reverb on a Return, and then turn up the Send knobs on each of the tracks to be effected. You can then delete the multiple Reverb plug-ins for each Track and save a virtual ton of processing power. If the sound changes too dramatically for you, try using the Sends Only output on the channels (as seen in Figure 14.16). You can have up to twelve Sends and Returns in a given ALS (Ableton Live Set).

❅ **Render audio with effects**—Sometimes using the Returns or streamlining the effects just doesn't do the trick. If this is the case, you may ask yourself if all the effects are absolutely necessary (often the answer is no); however, sometimes you do need all of the effects to achieve the sound you're going for. In this instance, you can render the effect-laden loop(s) (or Scene(s) in

Figure 14.15

Turn off modules of an effect plug-in to save power.

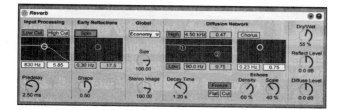

Session View) into individual Clips. In other words, you'll make a permanent copy of the loop/sample and use this file in place of the CPU-intensive effects and original dry loop(s). After doing so, you can delete the original files and effects from your Live Arrangement and save the set with a new name to ensure that you can always view the originals. In Figure 14.17a, we have selected a Scene with several loops running through multiple audio effects plug-ins. In Figure 14.17b, we have rendered that Scene, imported the Clip, and can now play the rendered Scene from a single Clip with dramatically improved CPU efficiency. You could do this for each Scene in a song if you are concerned about crashes or dropouts. Remember that once you have rendered a Scene, you will no longer be able to adjust levels of its individual components—they've all been mixed together in the new Clip. Make a habit of saving the original mix so you can always return to the original in case you change your mind.

Markers

Some of you may have noticed a strange omission from the Arrangement View: user-configurable markers. The only marker's you get are the beat and bar markers. When arranging a song, it's usually helpful to have markers indicating the beginning of the verses, choruses, or other sections, especially once your arrangement gets extremely complicated.

The good news is that you can, in fact, create a form of markers in the Arrangement View using empty MIDI Clips on a MIDI Track. Make the MIDI Track and place it at the top or bottom of the Arrangement View. You can then create empty MIDI Clips and name them the sections of your song. By placing these Clip on the MIDI Track, you can show where song sections begin (Figure 14.18). Additionally, as you make changes to the Arrangement, such as inserting or removing time, the Markers will adjust themselves, too.

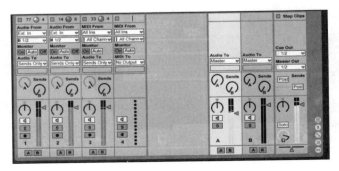

Figure 14.16

Route a Track's output to Sends Only to simulate the effect at the channel level, like an insert.

Figure 14.17a

Several heavily affected Clips playing in Live.

Figure 14.17b

Rendered as a single loop, you will no longer need original effects and loops.

Figure 14.18

The Clips in the top MIDI Track are acting as Markers for the Arrangement. The Clips contain no MIDI data and the MIDI Track has no instruments or effects loaded.

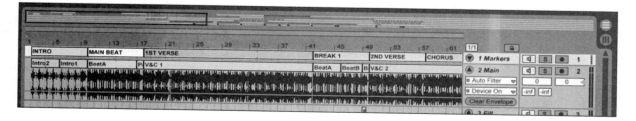

Templates

Live lets you save only one template, and it is loaded every time you launch the program; however, with all the different uses for Live, chances are that you won't be able to create a "one-size-fits-all" template to handle every situation. You can, however, create a collection of templates by saving empty Live Sets. Load up Live, set the Track count, effects, instruments, tempo, MIDI and Key assignments, etc., then save the Set. When you need to use the template, load the empty set and start working. We recommend making a directory or folder on your computer for saving these various setups. Examples of some templates may be "Basic DJ Setup," "DJ Setup with Impulse," "Multi-Track Recorder," "Fav MIDI Instruments," etc. The DJ templates may resemble those shown in Chapter 13. The Multi-Track template may have eight Audio Tracks already set to individual outputs. The Metronome may also be on and pre-routed to the Cue output. The Fav MIDI Instruments template may load virtual instruments that you always use, such as Linplug Albino, NI Pro-53, and GMedia Music impOSCar. Any time you start a new song, you can load the template that will get you going quickly.

Rename Me!

When loading an empty Live Set as a template, immediately save it under its own name. This will prevent you from accidentally overwriting the template with your current project, such as when pressing CTRL (CMND) + S.

Sample Editing

Now that you have a good basic working knowledge of Live, you may discover that your audio content (samples and loops) could use a little extra cleaning up, examination, and/or processing. This kind of detail work requires additional software, such as a specific audio waveform/sample editing application (see the next section, "Which Audio Editor to Use?"). Whether or not you decide to purchase specific audio editing software, we're going to teach you a few more tricks and tips for getting the most out of your sounds—the fuel for your Live songs. In our experience, these techniques and concepts are some of the least talked about, yet fundamentally the most important and relevant concepts for any computer-based musician or producer to understand. Specifically, we are talking about professionalizing your sound and fixing the digital audio challenges that every producer faces.

Earlier in the book, we pointed out the Launch Sample Editor button located in Live's Clip View (seen in Figure 14.19). If you have not already designated a sample editor in Live's Preferences, pressing the Launch Sample Editor (Edit) button will bring up the message: "No sample editor application has been selected. Would you like to select one now?" Press OK to call up the folder browser and then locate the application (or application's shortcut). Once you have done so, you can quickly open any Clip in your audio editor by pressing Edit. If your wave editing application isn't already open, the Edit button will launch it and open the AIFF or WAV file. Once you are done working with the file, save and close it. Live will automatically reopen the new file (with any changes) once you revisit your Live session.

> ❋ **Wave of Warning**
>
> Be especially careful when saving audio files from an audio editing application. Any edits done will be destructive, or permanent, once they are saved. Live, on the other hand, invariably saves all Live Set files (ALS) as non-destructive, or changeable, and therefore keeps all of your original samples intact. This is especially important if you plan to use an edited audio file in another project. To protect yourself, always save your song as self-contained before doing any wave editing.

Which Audio Editor to Use?

At the time of this writing, there are several exceptional, versatile, and professional audio editor applications (also called wave or sample editors) on the market. Most pro-level audio editors are also fairly expensive (roughly $250 to $500 US), or as much as twice the cost of Live. With this in mind, we put together a list so you can choose your audio editor quickly and confidently. Be aware that most companies make several versions at various prices and in various configurations, ranging from limited to full feature sets. For example, make sure your audio editor can handle 24-bit audio—Peak DV, a limited version of Peak, cannot. The following list compares the professional versions of each application.

Figure 14.19

The Launch Sample Editor button found in Clip View.

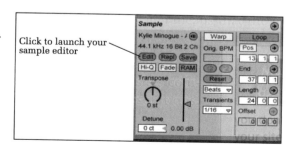

- ❀ **Adobe Audition (www.adobe.com)**—A good deal cheaper than the competition and an excellent value, but is, unfortunately, PC only. Adobe Audition is also a multi-track recorder that hosts a variety of fun and inspiring features.

- ❀ **DSP-Quattro by DSP-Quattro (www.dsp-quattro.com)**—Originally available as a shareware application called D-Sound Pro, DSP-Quattro is an inexpensive yet fully featured audio editor for both Mac OS 9 and OS X. This audio editor appears to be an excellent value and has a downloadable demo.

- ❀ **Goldwave by Goldwave (www.goldwave.com)**—Inexpensive (around $45), and a little bit ugly, Goldwave will get you up and running (on a PC only) if you are saving your pennies for a more robust application.

- ❀ **Peak by Bias (www.bias-inc.com)**—Peak users are a loyal crew, and for good reason. The interface is slick, the features are deep, and the sound is amazing; however, if you are composing your music on a PC, you will be left wondering—Peak is for Macs only. Also, Peak's pro version is as expensive as Sound Forge or Wavelab (see next).

- ❀ **Sony Sound Forge (www.sonypictures.com)**—Sound Forge is an expensive, comprehensive, and widely used PC-based audio editor. You can attain a "lite" version of this product, but keep in mind that these versions don't support higher and more professional sample rates and bit depths.

- ❀ **Spark XL by TC Works (www.tcelectronic.dcom)**—Comparable with Peak, Spark XL is a professional grade audio editor for Mac OS 9 and OS X. Spark includes many powerful effects and features.

- ❀ **Wavelab by Steinberg (www.steinberg.net)**—Steinberg's Wavelab is a favorite among DJs who choose to digitize their vinyl and is priced around the $500 mark.

❀ **Sound Investment**

While we are only touching on some basics in this chapter, each of the aforementioned wave editing applications is outfitted with hundreds of features for editing any sound (music, voice, or effect), audio mastering, and CD burning/ripping. You can think of a wave editor as sort of a Swiss Army knife of multimedia. If you are a professional musician, engineer, or producer, you should consider investing in a professional-grade wave/sample editor.

Wave Editor Tips

Like sampling, editing audio waveforms has become both a craft and an art form. Though you will not master it in a day, we find that a basic understanding helps a great deal when working within Live. After some initial practice, working with visual audio, a.k.a. waveform (see Figure 14.20), can be a whole new way of developing, working with, and designing new sounds. If this sounds vaguely familiar, it is because we touched on the concept of visual audio back in Chapter 2, "Back to School." Now would be a good time for a review if you need it.

Sprucing Up Your Loops

Wave editors are great for diving deeper into your loops and samples. Like looking under the hood of a car to check out a mysterious noise, you may be surprised to pop open an audio file and discover volume inconsistencies, clicks/pops, and other digital maladies. And similar to a car, you may not be entirely sure what you are looking at.

In this section, we will look at a couple of gain-maximizing tricks (including normalizing), how to de-click your digital audio, and a couple of musical ideas related to audio editing. Since these tips will only be a taste of what any decent wave editor is capable of, you might need to spend some extra time with that application's manual (or relevant tips/tricks book) to take your digital noise to the next level.

Normalizing

Remember, nothing exposes the lack of audio engineering professionalism quite like quirky volume levels. Too much gain during the recording process, or excessively boosting audio with a filter or EQ can cause level peaking,

Figure 14.20

A basic waveform.

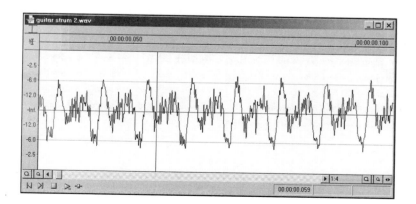

which in the realm of digital audio is just plain ugly. Conversely, a signal level that's too low often sounds wimpy and feeble, and can weaken an otherwise perfect mix. Other times, audio will develop a combination of the two problems, with great peaks and deep valleys providing an ultimately unsettling experience for the listener. For these reasons, audio engineers rely on a process called normalization. Live musicians (or artists using other loop-based applications), should also take great care to normalize loops and samples.

Normalization is the process of raising the level of an entire audio file so that its loudest parts are as close as possible to the maximum level possible, without peaking. In other words, the entire file is made to behave as a "normal" file should. This is great for extended tracks, where the volume may fluctuate a great deal; however, keep in mind that when you normalize, you increase the bad along with the good, and that normalization is not the same as audio compression or limiting (discussed in the "Volume Maximizing" section of this Chapter).

> ✳ **No Wave Editor? No Problem.**
> Even if you haven't yet made the leap and purchased a wave editor, you can still normalize like all the cool kids. Normalizing is actually a built-in feature of Live's rendering options. So, if you are having trouble making levels match up, turn back to Chapter 5, "Making Music in Live," and reread the section called "Rendering Techniques."

In Figure 14.21, we have opened the Normalize dialog box in our audio editor (Sonic Foundry's Sound Forge 6.0). Like many audio editors, you can normalize in terms of percent of maximum dB, where 100 percent means that the highest peak in your waveform will be brought to the brink of the digital maximum. You can also determine more advanced settings, such as how the application looks for the highest gain values, and how peaks are handled. We typically normalize only problem loops/samples (too quiet) and all of our finished mixes, but some musicians normalize every single sample. The latter technique will provide more consistency, but may also be less urgent if your original recording levels are closely monitored. For loops to be used in Live, we usually normalize at 95 percent and up, while for finished mixes, closer to 100 percent (depending upon the dynamic nature of the material)—it is important for the more dance- and radio-oriented pieces to be maximized in terms of volume.

Figure 14.21

Sound Forge's Normalize dialog box

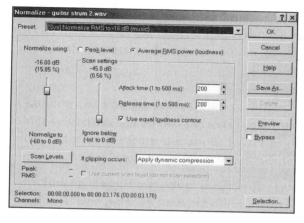

Volume Maximizing

To further support your volume consistency efforts, most audio editors feature at least one compressor, one or two limiting options, and often one volume maximizing (mastering) tool. Each of these effects can help volume peaks and valleys appear less dramatic, but can also remove some of the dynamic (loud to soft) musicality of your sample's performance. You may also want to maximize your small one-shot audio samples (as well as loops). For instance, a single drum hit such as a kick or snare might sound good compressed, but a jazz drum set or guitar rhythm might become more sterile sounding with an even dynamic range.

Compression

As we discussed when learning about Live's Compressor in Chapter 9, "Live's Audio Effects," a compressor minimizes audio's peaks at a given threshold. This is usually done for two reasons, first to alleviate the shock of a volume spike, and second, to allow for the overall mix volume to be increased. Compression can help even out the dynamic range of an erratic loop, as well as add presence to a lifeless performance.

❄ Creative Compression

Compressing audio can be either a sonic Band-Aid—such as microphone-level enhancement—or a creative endeavor—as when over-compressing a drum loop. Sometimes, severe compression can lead to entirely new sounds, or strange yet musical effects. While experimenting, listen carefully to each compressor's (hardware or software) personality. We find Live's compressor adequate for slight adjustments, but prefer our wave editor or compression plug-ins for bass, guitar, and vocals, as well as drum and percussion loops.

While each compressor or compressor plug-in will have a different interface, the basic ratio, threshold, attack, release, input/output level controls will remain the same. Some compressors also include other kinds of effects such as EQs or even distortion to make for some powerful and creative combo plug-ins.

Limiters

Similar to a compressor, a limiter is able to squeeze a mix (in part by reducing spikes in volume). A limiter can also add gain to quieter sounds, and therefore elevate the overall mix's presence to just shy of peaking (more standardized) gain levels. The results can sound less severe than a compressor, depending upon the dynamic nature of the music. For instance, music with a wide dynamic range will sound the most affected by compressors, and slightly less so by a limiter. Most mastering engineers will use limiting instead of normalization because of its compression-like qualities.

De-Clicking

Clicks and pops are an unfortunate occurrence in digital audio. They occur for a variety of reasons, including cutting off a sample midway through the wave cycle, system strain (CPU, RAM, or hard drive), or inadequate audio interfaces/drivers. Manually removing these annoying little guys can range from simple to next-to-impossible; however, there are several existing click-removal applications for both PC and Mac—although most that we have tried tend to dampen, or diminish, audio clarity for the rest of the audio as well as take out the clicks. So, try the demo before you buy the plug-in/application.

Often times, manual removal is your best and only option. Let's take a look at how to do this.

1 First, you must locate the offending click. To do this, open the sample in your audio editor and loop a small section of audio to see if you can zero in on exactly where the pop is sitting inside the waveform. Occasionally, we will make a marker where we hear the pop occurring during playback (which in Sound Forge can be done by pressing the shortcut key M).

2 Zoom in on the waveform to a magnification that makes sense with the audio you are working on. See Figure 14.22 as an example of a pop we found and zoomed in on in the waveform.

3 Activate your audio editor's Draw tool and carefully round out the harsh angle or jag that is most likely giving you the pop. If you accidentally draw too much

Figure 14.22

By zooming in on the click/
pop, you can prepare to fix it.

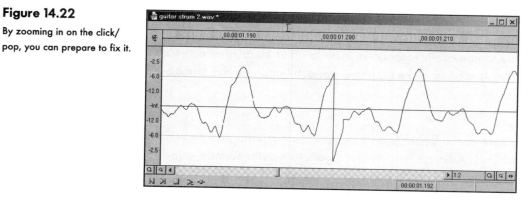

or make some other mistake, Undo your last action. The shortcut for Undo is almost invariably CTRL (CMND) + Z.

4 Check your work. Play the same looped section in step 1 to hear if the click is partially or completely gone. Listen for any other ill effects such as a muffled sound, additional clicks, or other sonic problems. Sometimes you can make things worse in a hurry by drawing on the waveform. If it does get worse, consider starting over and drawing a less severe curve or fix.

❋ Fade In and Out

The most common clicks in digital audio occur when slicing a sample at a point other than where the waveform crosses the middle horizontal line (often called the zero crossover). If you hear a click at the beginning or end of your sample, you will know that this is your culprit. To rid yourself of these kind of glitches, create a very small (less than 5 millisecond) fade-in at the beginning, and a fade-out at the end of your sample.

Streamlining Loops for Live

Laptops are often limited versions of their desktop brethren. They may be a little short of RAM, extra hard drive space, or processor speed, but they are designed as a sleeker, more portable stand-in for your desktop (as opposed to the fully featured multi-processor computers that are common in most recording studios). Since many Live musicians will be porting their music from rehearsal to club to recording session on a laptop, here are a few tips for streamlining audio loops and samples for maximum musicality and minimum system drain in these situations.

Stereo or Mono?

In a typical club, a true stereo field will be experienced by only a small percentage of listeners. Some clubs or performance halls will not even support stereo (right and left) channels. Mono files require roughly half the processing and system resources as stereo files. Also, mono audio files will tend to sound more "present" and deliver a bit more punch (particularly in a dance music environment). To convert your files to mono, you can either render each file in Live (using the render as mono option) or in a wave editor. The following steps detail how we create a mono file from a stereo file using Sonic Foundry's Sound Forge 6.0—most other wave editors will contain similar features.

1   Open the loop by clicking on Edit in Clip View.

2   Once the wave editor is open (Sound Forge in this case), select File > Save As and choose Mono in your Save options (see Figure 14.23). Most wave editors allow you to grab one side of the audio waveform (to make a mono loop stereo), but be warned that this is not the true stereo image made mono. For example, if you have a stereo drum track with several different pan settings, grabbing one side only will disproportionately represent your original recording.

3   Since you have created a new file, you need to take advantage of Live's replace (Repl in Live) command, conveniently located in Live's Clip View next to the Edit button (seen in Figure 14.24).

4   Save your newly configured set as self-contained.

Once you have made your stereo loops mono, your set should demand significantly less CPU power. You will also likely need to readjust your volume, panning, and some effect settings since the new loops/samples will have changed.

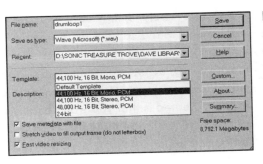

Figure 14.23

Select mono in your wave editor's Save options—note the highlighted bar in the Description drop-down menu in Sound Forge's Save As options.

Figure 14.24

The Replace/File Locator button calls up the Chooser (Explorer on the PC) so you can swap the files.

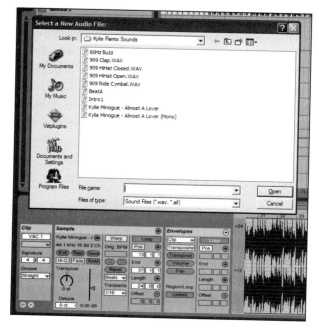

Effects

When running effects within Live, you will continually put pressure on your CPU. Some Live musicians have found it helpful to apply effects from a wave editor, particularly if they are looking for a single effect applied consistently on a single loop. For example, say you want to add a bit of compression to a drum loop, but don't really need a continuous instance of a compressor plug-in loaded in Live. Simply import the drum loop into your wave editor (press Edit in Clip View), and then call up the desired compression plug-in (seen in Figure 14.25). After you apply the effect, save the file and switch back over to Live. Live will update itself with the modified (compressed) file. Warning, this sort of modification is destructive and permanent, so, as they say, choose wisely. Simply save your Set as Self-Contained to be sure you are working with a copy of the original loop—then be as destructive as you want to be. Also, you should take special care when using any delay-based effect (reverb, echo, chorus, or delay). These effects will carry on after the initial loop has stopped playing to create a tail (see the Rocktail note). The problem created is that you won't hear a tail until the first several notes have sounded. When looped, the first couple of dry notes of the loop can sound stark or cut off.

Figure 14.25

Digilogue's Blue Compressor plug-in in WaveLab.

If you are wondering what other kinds of effects are possible in an audio editor, you will be impressed. Most wave editors include a large and varied section of VST (Mac or PC), Direct X (PC only), as well as included mastering, audio restoration, and signal maximizing helpers. Figure 14.26 shows just a few of the effects offered in Sonic Foundry's Sound Forge 6.0.

If you have yet to purchase a wave editor you may be salivating after reading this chapter (don't say we didn't warn you). An audio editor is a powerful

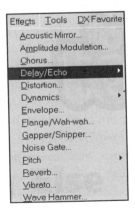

Figure 14.26

Sound Forge 6.0's included effects.

tool and ally in the digital recording world. Still, by knowing what is possible, and what sort of pitfalls to avoid, you will fare far better as a Live musician, producer, or DJ.

Linking Two Computers

In earlier chapters, we explored several ways to synchronize Live with your software applications (using ReWire) and with your hardware (using MIDI). For our last tip, we will combine the two sync concepts by inviting your friends over to jam. Simply decide whose computer will be the master, establish a MIDI link (master computer's MIDI output to slave computer's MIDI input), set up the master to send Time Code and the slave to receive it, and go. Inexpensive MIDI splitters and multiple outputs can make the number of players limitless, though some musical orchestration (organization) is recommended. You might assign one musician to cover the drum and percussion loops, another the synths, and another sound effects. Or, you might have two Live musicians playing within the same band, or add a singer for a futuristic improv trio. The future of Live may just include two, three, or more musicians getting together, patching their laptop into the MIDI chain, firing up a ReWire application or two, and then jamming the night away. For added fun, try recording the output to some kind of multi-track recorder.

As you can imagine, there are many more tricks and tips still waiting to be discovered in Live 4.0. As you spend time experimenting with new ways of working, you will certainly discover what works for you. Also, check out Ableton's user forum that now features a section called Tips & Tricks. We encourage you to share your ideas and interact with other Live users. It's a great community to be a part of. We learn something nearly every time we drop by.

In closing, Dave and I would like to sincerely thank you for reading our book. While *Ableton Live 2 Power!* was Dave's first book, this update is my first project as well. Both Dave and I spent months learning, inventing, and testing the procedures outlined in this book. Should you stumble onto a tip, trick, or scrap of info that doesn't quite do what we said it is supposed to do, there is most likely an update waiting for you at www.Ableton.com (click on downloads), or a note at this book's web page at www.courseptr.com. This book was based on version 4.0.3, and was tested on both an Apple Macintosh Powerbook G4 1 GHz with 1 GB of RAM, and a Dell Inspiron 5150 3.06 GHz (with 512 MB of RAM) running Windows XP.

We can attest that Ableton Live 4.0 is a stable, elegant, musical, forward thinking, dynamic, and inspirational software application. We hope you find it to be the same, and enjoy many hours of making your own musical vision a reality.

Appendix

A Shortcut Keys

Shortcut keys streamline standard operations and common tasks in Live. You certainly have access to every function in Live if you relegate yourself to the mouse, but you'll be moving back and forth, making multiple clicks to access the same options from the menu over and over. This can be a real pain in the wrist. By assigning menu commands to the keyboard, you can "fire them off," just like assigning keys to the Clips in the Session View.

If you own the packaged copy of Live 4, you already have a handy Shortcut Key reference card in the back of the manual. If you opted for the downloaded version (you're environmentally conscious), make a copy of these pages and keep them by your computer.

Even though we've mentioned numerous shortcut keys throughout the book, take a moment to read through this list. You'll see many familiar commands (you may already be accustomed to them if you've been playing along), but you may see a few that catch you by surprise. To make these commands second nature, we recommend that you practice each command several times in the context of working on a song. Like practicing an instrument, repetitive short-cutting can be a great way to memorize and truly integrate these time (and wrist) savers into your workflow.

 Handy Hint

At the risk of sounding obvious, right-handed users should get used to using their left hand for all keyboard shortcuts—since their right hand is guiding the mouse. This way you can double your efforts by both mousing and keying simultaneously. Left-handed people (who are set up with the mouse to the left of the keyboard) should use their right hand for shortcuts.

General Shortcuts

Some shortcuts are universal—we'll call these *general shortcuts* because these can be used in any Live view. They also happen to be the most common shortcuts you'll use.

- ❋ **Tab**—This command will always toggle Session and Arrangement Views.
- ❋ **Spacebar**—Start and stop audio playback (or recording if it is armed).
- ❋ **SHIFT + Spacebar**—Continues playback from where you stopped it instead of returning to the Start Marker.
- ❋ **CTRL (CMND) + Spacebar**—Starts playback from the insert point in the Arrangement.
- ❋ **CTRL (CMND) + C**—Copies any selected clip or selection of audio.
- ❋ **CTRL (CMND) + V**—Pastes from the clipboard the last clip copied or cut.
- ❋ **CTRL (CMND) + X**—Cuts any clip or selection of audio and places it on the clipboard.
- ❋ **CTRL (CMND) + T**—Inserts an Audio Track into your Ableton Live Song.
- ❋ **CTRL (CMND) + SHIFT + T**—Inserts a new MIDI Track.
- ❋ **CTRL (CMND) + ALT + T**—Inserts a Return Track into your Ableton Live Song.
- ❋ **CTRL (CMND) + B**—Turns the Pencil tool on and off.
- ❋ **F1–F8 keys**—Toggle mute and un-mute for tracks 1 through 8; an excellent live performance tool.
- ❋ **F9**—Arms the Automation Record Button. While the track is armed and Live is playing, use this shortcut to begin recording.
- ❋ **F11**—Toggles Live back and forth from Full Screen mode to windowed view.
- ❋ **F12**—Toggles from Clip View and Track (Effects on selected Track) View.
- ❋ **SHIFT + F12**—Hides or shows the Clip or Track View.
- ❋ **"+" and "–"**—Zooms in and out of your current view.
- ❋ **"?"**—Toggles Live's Info view. For this command, press **SHIFT + ?** with your right hand.

❋ **Select Tip**

When selecting multiple Clips, hold down CTRL (CMND) and then mouse-click on each Clip. You can then cut, copy, or duplicate the selected audio files. For selecting a range of Clips or time within an Arrangement, hold down the SHIFT key while mouse-clicking over the desired selection. If you want to select all Clips in Session View, or your entire arrangement in Arrangement View, use CTRL (CMND) + A.

> **❉ Function Keys on the Mac Powerbook**
>
> Mac laptops use the function keys to control various settings by default, such as screen brightness and speaker volume. If you wish to use the Live functions assigned to these keys, press and hold the "fn" key on your laptop's keyboard while pressing the function key combinations explained above.

Session View Shortcuts

When working in Session View, we have found several shortcuts to be invaluable during both live performance and recording sessions.

- ❉ **Return**—Launches selected Clip or Scene.
- ❉ **Arrow keys**—Move throughout Clip Slot Grid.
- ❉ **CTRL (CMND) + D**—Duplicates the current Clip to the Scene below.
- ❉ **CTRL (CMND) + SHIFT + D**—Copies (inserts and duplicates) an entire Scene below the currently highlighted Scene.
- ❉ **CTRL (CMND) + I**—Inserts a new blank Scene below the currently highlighted Scene or Clip Slot.
- ❉ **CTRL (CMND) + SHIFT + I**—Captures the currently playing Clips as a new Scene.
- ❉ **CTRL (CMND) + M**—Toggles MIDI Map Mode on or off. This can be done while playing.
- ❉ **CTRL (CMND) + K**—Toggles the Key Map Mode on or off. This can also be done while Live is playing.
- ❉ **CTRL (CMND) + E**—A multi-function shortcut. If you select a Clip Slot, this will toggle the Clip Stop Button on and off. If you click on the name of a Track or Scene, this key combo will allow you to rename it.

Arrangement View Shortcuts

Arrangement View requires a different group of tasks than Session View, though many of the same shortcuts apply. Take a few moments to practice these commands. Repeat each one several times to see if you can't form a good habit or two.

- ❉ **CTRL (CMND) + D**—Copies and pastes (duplicates) the current selection immediately after itself. This is a great command for extended repeating of a complexly edited section or group of Clips.
- ❉ **CTRL (CMND) + SHIFT + D**—Inserts a copy (duplicate) of all Tracks occurring at the same time as your selection at the end of your selection. This is a great command for quickly building an Arrangement.

❋ **CTRL (CMND) + I**—Inserts the amount of silence corresponding with your selection. If you select four measures and then use this command, you will insert four new measures of silence.

❋ **CTRL (CMND) + DELETE**—Deletes all breakpoint envelope automation for all parameters in the selected portion of the Arrangement.

❋ **CTRL (CMND) + E**—Splits any selected Clip at the Insert Mark. This is a great tool if you want to segment your Clips so that changes can be made to smaller portions of the original Clip.

❋ **CTRL (CMND) + L**—Loops your current selection.

❋ **CTRL (CMND) + J**—Consolidates your current selection into a new Clip.

❋ **CTRL (CMND) + F**—Instructs Live to scroll through the Arrangement as it plays. This way you can watch the events as they happen.

❋ **Grid Settings**

You can change the resolution of Live's grid in both Clip and Arrangement Views using the following key commands:

CTRL (CMND) + 1 makes the grid resolution smaller

CTRL (CMND) + 2 makes the grid resolution larger

CTRL (CMND) + 3 toggles triplet mode on and off

CTRL (CMND) + 4 toggles the entire grid on and off

Other Handy Strokes

These last few keystrokes may not revolutionize your workflow, but they are still handy to know when working in Live for extended periods of time.

❋ **CTRL (CMND) + S**—Saves your current Set. Get in the habit of doing this from time to time.

❋ **CMND + ,** (the comma key)—Opens Live's Preferences on the Mac. **Esc** closes it again (saving any changes).

❋ **CTRL (CMND) + U**—Quantizes the notes in a MIDI Clip.

❋ **CTRL (CMND) + R**—Brings up the Render to Disk dialog.

❋ **CTRL (CMND) + ALT (OPTION) + O**—Toggles Overview in Session View.

❋ **CTRL (CMND) + ALT (OPTION) + I**—Toggles Input/Output view in the Session View.

- **CTRL (CMND) + ALT (OPTION) + S**—Toggles Sends and Returns in and out of view in both Session and Arrangement views.
- **CTRL (CMND) + ALT (OPTION) + M**—Toggles Live's Mixer controls in and out of view in both Session and Arrangement views.

Appendix

B

Web Resources

Ableton Live 4 Power! Web Site

Earlier in this book, we mentioned that a Web site has been created so that you can download some starter loops and a few helpful Ableton Live (ALS file) templates. We will also use this site to post any notable *Ableton Live 4 Power!* updates and corrections, as well as other relevant Live 4.0 news and notes. What follows are some helpful hints and general information about the Web site.

- ❉ The site will be hosted at www.courseptr.com.

- ❉ You will find Live templates, loops, *Ableton Live 4 Power!* news, and perhaps even a trick or two.

- ❉ The templates are yours to use and abuse, and can be downloaded as often as you need. Do with them what you will.

- ❉ Loop and sample content is treated a bit differently. Any sample or loop down-loaded from the site is intended strictly for personal use. These loops are for your own individual learning and experimentation. If you want to use the material in a song, performance, or commercial application, you must contact the original vendor or sample/loop creator and pay them for their creation.

- ❉ From the site, you will be able to contact us, the authors. Have a suggestion? Something to say? Ideas about how to use Live? Please send us a note and let us know what you are doing with Live.

❉ **The Horse's Mouth**

When it comes to getting the skinny on Ableton Live-related products (including both software plug-ins, helper applications, and studio/stage hardware), make sure that you visit www.ableton.com, and then click on links—located under the support tab. From there you will find a healthy assort-ment of links subcategorized into music software, hardware, magazines, research, and more.

Live Templates

We mentioned in Chapter 14 that templates can increase your productivity by providing a familiar setup for various projects. On our Web site, you'll find a collection of starter files for this very purpose. Thanks to Live's new Lessons View, you'll be able to read about the setup, its MIDI and Key mappings, as well as any other special tricks employed in its design right within the Live window. DJ templates, loop capturing setups, and multi-track layouts are all available. If you've got a handy template of your own, you can upload it and share it with others.

Example Sets

Throughout the book, we've been showing examples of principles through explanation and screenshots. Some concepts are better heard than read; therefore, on the Web site you'll find some additional Live Sets for these tricky examples. The examples are sorted by chapter, making them easier to cross reference with explanations in the book.

Where To Get Plug-ins

While Live includes an extensive collection of fine effects and versatile instruments, you can grow your collection by obtaining additional plug-ins—both effects and instruments—from third-party developers. The Web offers access to many of these exciting companies, some of which offer downloadable demos or free versions of their plug-ins. Here's a list of places to investigate when you're looking for some new toys:

Commercial Plug-in Developers

* **www.cycling74.com**—With over 100 plug-ins for $199, Cycling 74's Pluggo effect pack is the perfect example of "bang for the buck." Uh, sorry PC people—Mac only!

* **www.pspaudioware.com**—Poland's first software company, but one of the world's finest audio developers. For cool "tube" simulation, check out Vintage Warmer, or for crazy delay effects (quite unlike Ableton's own brand) try out the Lexicon PSP 42 (or 84).

* **www.steinberg.net**—The inventors of VST technology offer several effects plug-ins and instruments.

* **www.native-instruments.com**—Amazing instruments and effects with a refined look and feel. Expensive, but you get a lot for your money.

- ❊ **www.tcworks.com**—Excellent, professional, and typically work well in Live.
- ❊ **www.waves.com**—Recognized the world over for premium quality (and priced) plug-ins. Their mastering and restoration plug-ins are amazing. Quite possibly overkill for rocking a club with Live.
- ❊ **www.ohmforce.com**—If aesthetics alone determined the quality of their plug-ins, Ohmforce would be the kings of cool. Maybe not for everybody, but some wildly interesting effects can be found here.

Free Plug-in Developers

Though the saying "you get what you pay for" certainly holds merit, the Internet was built on freeware, shareware, and try-before-you-buy business models. If you are pinching pennies or just looking for a quick batch of new sounds, the following list should keep you busy for a while.

- ❊ **www.db-audioware.com**—Dave Brown is the self-proclaimed first third-party developer to post VST effect freeware plug-ins on the Internet. He still provides the original four.
- ❊ **www.mda-vst.com**—MDA generously provides 23 (at the time of this writing) plug-ins, which, I might add, aren't too shabby. Let's see, 23 times zero is still zero! What a bargain.
- ❊ **www.funk-station.co.uk/effect.htm**—A funky, and a little clunky, filter effect.
- ❊ **www.smartelectronix.com**—DestroyFX, Magnus, and other plug-in makers live here. You'll find some stable, interesting, and experimental effects. Check out the Supa Trigga remixing plug-in—this is one of our favorites.

Staying Informed

Since the Internet changes every second, staying current can be a full-time job. Here are a couple of pit stops that we have found helpful over the last couple of years for keeping up to date on the latest happenings.

- ❊ **www.ableton.com**—For any serious Live user, the Ableton Forum is not to be missed.
- ❊ **www.kvr-vst.com**—This site is updated daily with new instrument and effect plug-in information. Just follow the links.
- ❊ **www.osxaudio.com**—This is a great site for Mac OS X users looking for the latest plug-ins and general compatibility talk.
- ❊ **www.hitsquad.com**—Hit Squad can be difficult to surf, but is informative.

* **www.harmonycentral.com**—This site is packed with music news of all shapes and sizes. Still, we recommend it for VST and software development news.

Don't forget to check your favorite search engines as well. We found some way-out-there plug-ins by searching for "freeware vst plugin" on Google!

Where To Get Loops

The following list is but a sampling (pun intended) of our favorite loop purveyors. Nearly all of their Web sites feature downloadable demos or even free content for you to play with. If you happen upon a collection of samples that really work for your project or sound, most sites will also recommend other titles, similar to the way Amazon.com recommends books—if you liked this, then try that.

* **AMG** (www.amguk.uk.co)
* **Bigfish Audio** (www.bigfishaudio.com)
* **East West** (www.soundsonline.com)
* **Electronisounds** (www.electronisounds.com)
* **Ilio** (www.ilio.com)
* **M-Audio** (www.m-audio.com)
* **Q-UP Arts** (www.quparts.com)
* **Sonic Foundry** (www.sonicfoundry.com)
* **Sample Craze** (www.samplecraze.com)
* **Peace Love Productions** (www.peaceloveproductions)
* **PowerFX** (www.powerfx.com)
* **Wizoo** (www.wizoo.com)
* **Zero-G** (www.zero-g.uk.co)

Internet Resources

If you just can't wait for a sample CD, or if you prefer to shop via the Internet, there are several established and professional sample houses that offer downloadable wares. You can preview the files first and download the ones you like (for approximately two or three bucks per loop). This can be a convenient and inexpensive way to shop, considering that some sample CDs will only provide you with a few loops that give you what you are looking for.

- ※ **Sonomic** (www.sonomic.com)—One of the most respected pure online sample retailers on the net, Sonomic will even store your sounds for you on a secure drive in case you need to access your sounds from the road.
- ※ **Sound Dogs** (www.sounddogs.com)—While Sound Dogs specializes in movie and television sound effects, their online database will turn up several quality loops of virtually every musical style. Also, you might be amazed what a little "space ship rumble" might do for your next ambient dub jam.
- ※ **PowerFX** (www.powerfx.com)—PowerFX sells both CDs and loop download packs from their Web site. Download packs, usually in the $10 range, provide a solid batch in a given style (for example Hip Hop, Techno, etc.).
- ※ **Platinum Loops** (www.platinumloops.com)—Platinum Loops offers 9000 original loops and samples for download, or in DVD and CD formats.

By doing a couple of Google searches, you will stumble across many other pros, hobbyists, and startup sample making companies. The next two caught my eye.

- ※ **Loop Kit Pro** (www.loopkit.com)
- ※ **Acid Fanatic** (www.acidfanatic.com)

※ Zipping Along

Oftentimes loops and samples are zipped or stuffed in order to save you download time. Zipping and stuffing files is a form of compression, and, upon download, the files will need to be opened (uncompressed). To do this, you will need to download a free helper application called WinZip (for PC), which can be found at www.winzip.com, or Stuffit (for Mac), located at www.stuffit.com. Once you have downloaded and installed the helper application, any zipped or stuffed file can be opened and its contents extracted to your hard drive.

} Index

Note: italicized page locators indicate figures.